From PROPHECY
to TESTAMENT

From PROPHECY to TESTAMENT

The Function of the
Old Testament in the New

CRAIG A. EVANS, EDITOR

Hendrickson Publishers, Inc.
P. O. Box 3473
Peabody, Massachusetts 01961-3473

ISBN 1-56563-765-8

Printed in the United States of America

First Printing — March 2004

Library of Congress Cataloging-in-Publication Data

From prophecy to testament : the function of the Old Testament in the New /
    edited by Craig A. Evans.
        p. cm.
    Includes bibliographical references and indexes.
    ISBN 1-56563-765-8 (hardcover : alk. paper)
    1. Bible. N.T.—Relation to the Old Testament. I. Evans, Craig A.
    BS2387.F76 2004
    230'.041—dc22
                                                    2003027733

Contents

Preface

Interest in the origins of sacred literature and in how early communities of faith interpreted this literature remains high. Investigation into the hermeneutics of late antiquity and how it was shaped by theology and in turn shaped theology itself is vital for a better understanding of the origins of Judaism and Christianity. The papers that make up the present volume probe significant dimensions of this topic in important ways. The role of language, differing versions, writings inside and outside the "canon," festivals, customs, worship, and strategies of persuasion are explored.

The book is designed to serve as an introduction and reader in the subject of the function of the Old Testament in the New. The introduction, written primarily with the student in mind, not the veteran scholar, orients readers to the larger issues, surveys the principal primary and secondary literature, and comments on the scholarly contributions found in this book. Since the chapters of this collection represent technical work that advances the discussion and sets forth new ideas, veteran scholars and students alike will find much of interest.

The editor wishes to express his gratitude to the contributors, who waited longer than usual to see their work appear in published form, and to Shirley Decker-Lucke of Hendrickson Publishers, who rescued our work and guided it through the press in an efficient and timely manner. Thanks also go to Scott Kohler and Adam MacGregor, who are pursuing graduate studies at Acadia Divinity College, for assisting in the preparation of the indexes.

All translations of the Bible not marked as RSV or NRSV are those of the author of each chapter.

Craig A. Evans

Contributors

Gary A. Anderson
University of Notre Dame, South Bend, Indiana

Bruce Chilton
Bard College, Annandale-on-Hudson, New York

A. J. Droge
University of California at San Diego

Craig A. Evans
Acadia Divinity College, Wolfville, Nova Scotia

Simon J. Gathercole
University of Aberdeen, Scotland

Brigitte Kahl
Union Theological Seminary, New York, New York

James L. Kugel
Bar Ilan University, Ramat Gan, Israel

Michael Labahn
Martin Luther University, Wendeburg, Germany

James A. Sanders
Ancient Biblical Manuscript Center and Claremont Graduate University, Claremont, California

Robert F. Shedinger
Luther College, Decorah, Iowa

James C. VanderKam
University of Notre Dame, Notre Dame, Indiana

Rikk E. Watts
Regent College, Vancouver, British Columbia

Abbreviations

Miscellaneous

b.	born
ca.	circa
cf.	*confer*, compare
ch(s).	chapter(s)
col(s).	column(s)
d.	died
diss.	dissertation
DSS	Dead Sea Scrolls
e.g.	*exempli gratia*, for example
ed(s).	editor(s), edited by
Eng.	English
esp.	especially
et al.	*et alii*, and others
ET	English translation
fl.	*floruit*, flourished
frg(s).	fragment(s)
FS	Festschrift
HB	Hebrew Bible
Heb.	Hebrew
i.e.	*id est*, that is
ibid.	*ibidem*, in the same place
lit.	literally
LXX	Septuagint (the Greek OT)
MS(S)	manuscript(s)
MT	Masoretic Text (of the OT)
NF	Neue Folge (new series)
NRSV	New Revised Standard Version
NT	New Testament
OL	Old Latin
OT	Old Testament
P.Oxy.	Oxyrhynchus Papyri
par.	parallel (to indicate textual parallels)
pl(s).	plural, plate(s)
RSV	Revised Standard Version

sg.   singular
trans.   translator, translated by
v(v).   verse(s)
viz.   *videlicet*, namely

Old Testament Pseudepigrapha

Apoc. Ab.	*Apocalypse of Abraham*
2 Bar.	*2 Baruch (Syriac Apocalypse)*
1 En.	*1 Enoch (Ethiopic Apocalypse)*
Jub.	*Jubilees*
L.A.B.	*Liber antiquitatum biblicarum* (Pseudo-Philo)
L.A.E.	*Life of Adam and Eve*
Let. Aris.	*Letter of Aristeas*
Mart. Ascen. Isa.	*Martyrdom and Ascension of Isaiah*
Mart. Isa.	*Mart. Ascen. Isa.* 1–5
Pss. Sol.	*Psalms of Solomon*
T. Ab.	*Testament of Abraham*
T. Ash.	*Testament of Asher*
T. Benj.	*Testament of Benjamin*
T. Dan	*Testament of Dan*
T. Gad	*Testament of Gad*
T. Iss.	*Testament of Issachar*
T. Jud.	*Testament of Judah*
T. Levi	*Testament of Levi*
T. Naph.	*Testament of Naphtali*
T. Reu.	*Testament of Reuben*
T. Sim.	*Testament of Simeon*
T. Sol.	*Testament of Solomon*

Dead Sea Scrolls and Related Texts

1QpHab	*Pesher Habakkuk*	
1QS	*Serek Hayaḥad* or *Rule of the Community*	
1Q28a	1Qsa	*Rule of the Congregation* (Appendix a to 1QS)
4Q156	4QtgLev	
4Q157	4QtgJob	
4Q266	4QD^a	*Damascus Document*^a
4Q285	*Sefer Hamilḥamah*	
4Q320	4QCalDoc A	*Calendrical Document A*, formerly *Mishmarot A*
4Q418	4QInstruction^a	*Instruction*^a, formerly *Sapiental Work A*^a

4Q510	4QShir^a	*Shirot* ^a or *Songs of the Sage* ^a
4Q521	4QMessAp	*Messianic Apocalypse*
11Q5	11QPs^a	*Psalms Scroll* ^a
11Q10	11QtgJob	
11Q13	11QMelch	*Melchizedek*
CD	Cairo Genizah copy of the *Damascus Document*	

Philo

Abraham	*On the Life of Abraham*
Alleg. Interp. 1, 2, 3	*Allegorical Interpretation* 1, 2, 3
Contempl. Life	*On the Contemplative Life*
Decalogue	*On the Decalogue*
Embassy	*On the Embassy to Gaius*
Migration	*On the Migration of Abraham*
Moses 1, 2	*On the Life of Moses* 1, 2
Names	*On the Change of Names*
Prelim. Studies	*On the Preliminary Studies*
Sacrifices	*On the Sacrifices of Cain and Abel*
Spec. Laws	*On the Special Laws*

Josephus

Ag. Ap.	*Against Apion*
Ant.	*Jewish Antiquities*
J.W.	*Jewish War*
Life	*The Life*

Mishnah, Talmud, and Related Literature

b.	Babylonian
m.	Mishnah
t.	Tosefta
y.	Jerusalem
ᶜ*Abod. Zar.*	ᶜ*Abodah Zarah*
ʾ*Abot*	ʾ*Abot*
B. Bat.	*Baba Batra*
Ber.	*Berakot*
ᶜ*Ed.*	ᶜ*Eduyyot*
ᶜ*Erub.*	ᶜ*Erubin*
Giṭ.	*Giṭṭin*
Ḥag.	*Ḥagigah*
Hor.	*Horayot*

Ker.	Kerithot
Ketub.	Ketubbot
Mak.	Makkot
Meg.	Megillah
Menaḥ.	Menaḥot
Ned.	Nedarim
Nid.	Niddah
Pesaḥ	Pesaḥim
Qidd.	Qiddušin
Sanh.	Sanhedrin
Šabb.	Šabbat
Šeb.	Šebiᶜit
Taᶜan.	Taᶜanit
Yebam.	Yebamot
Yoma	Yoma (=Kippurim)

Targumic Texts

Frg. Tg.	Fragmentary Targum
Tg. 1 Chron.	Targum 1 Chronicles
Tg. Esth. I, II	First or Second Targum of Esther
Tg. Ezek.	Targum Ezekiel
Tg. Hab.	Targum Habakkuk
Tg. Hos.	Targum Hosea
Tg. Isa.	Targum Isaiah
Tg. Jer.	Targum Jeremiah
Tg. Job	Targum Job
Tg. Jon.	Targum Jonathan
Tg. Lam.	Targum Lamentations
Tg. Mal.	Targum Malachi
Tg. Nah.	Targum Nahum
Tg. Neof.	Targum Neofiti
Tg. Obad.	Targum Obadiah
Tg. Onq.	Targum Onqelos
Tg. Prov.	Targum Proverbs
Tg. Ps.	Targum Psalms
Tg. Ps.-J.	Targum Pseudo-Jonathan
Tg. Qoh.	Targum Qohelet
Tg. Ruth	Targum Ruth
Tg. 1 Sam.	Targum 1 Samuel
Tg. 2 Sam.	Targum 2 Samuel
Tg. Song	Targum Song of Songs
Tg. Zech.	Targum Zechariah
Tg. Zeph.	Targum Zephaniah

Other Rabbinic Works

ʾAbot R. Nat.   ʾAbot de Rabbi Nathan
Mek.   Mekilta de Rabbi Ishmael
Midr.   Midrash I (+ biblical book)
Pirqe R. El.   Pirqe de Rabbi Eliezer
Rab.   Rabbah

Apostolic Fathers, Ancient Christian and Non-Christian Writers

Aristotle
    Metaph.   Metaphysica
Barnabas
    Barn.   Barnabas
Dio Chrysostom
    Or.   Orationes
Epiphanius
    Pan.   Panarion (Adversus haereses)
Eusebius
    Praep. ev.   Praeparatio evangelica
Jerome
    Comm. Isa.   Commentariorum in Isaiam libri XVIII
Justin
    Dial.   Dialogus cum Tryphone
Novatian
    Trin.   De trinitate
Origen
    Ep. Afr.   Epistula ad Africanum
Pliny the Elder
    Nat.   Naturalis historia
Ptolemy
    Flor.   Letter to Flora
Tertullian
    Marc.   Adversus Marcionem

Secondary Abbreviations

ABD   Anchor Bible Dictionary. Edited by D. N. Freedman. 6 vols.
          New York: Doubleday, 1992
ABRL   Anchor Bible Reference Library
Aev   Aevum: Rassegna de scienze, storiche, linguistiche, e filologiche
ALGHJ   Arbeiten zur Literatur und Geschichte des hellenistischen
          Judentums

AnBib	Analecta biblica
ANRW	*Aufstieg und Niedergang der römischen Welt: Geschichte und Kultur Roms im Spiegel der neueren Forschung.* Edited by H. Temporini and W. Haase. New York: de Gruyter, 1972–
AOS	American Oriental Series
APOT	*The Apocrypha and Pseudepigrapha of the Old Testament.* Edited by R. H. Charles. 2 vols. Oxford: Clarendon, 1913
ArBib	The Aramaic Bible
ArOr	*Archiv Orientální*
ASTI	*Annual of the Swedish Theological Institute*
ATDan	Acta theologica danica
BAG	Bauer, W., W. F. Arndt, and F. W. Gingrich. *Greek-English Lexicon of the New Testament and Other Early Christian Literature.* Chicago: University of Chicago Press, 1957
BAGD	Bauer, W., W. F. Arndt, F. W. Gingrich, and F. W. Danker. *Greek-English Lexicon of the New Testament and Other Early Christian Literature.* 2d ed. Chicago: University of Chicago Press, 1979
BETL	Bibliotheca ephemeridum theologicarum lovaniensium
BEvT	Beiträge zur evangelischen Theologie
BFT	Biblical Foundations in Theology
BHT	Beiträge zur historischen Theologie
Bib	*Biblica*
BibInt	*Biblical Interpretation*
BibOr	Biblica et orientalia
BibS(N)	Biblische Studien (Neukirchen, 1951–)
BIS	Biblical Interpretation Series
BJRL	*Bulletin of the John Rylands University Library of Manchester*
BJS	Brown Judaic Studies
BN	*Biblische Notizen*
BNTC	Black's New Testament Commentaries
BRev	*Bible Review*
BSL	Biblical Studies Library
BST	Basel Studies of Theology
BTS	*Bible et terre sainte*
BWA(N)T	Beiträge zur Wissenschaft vom Alten (und Neuen) Testament
BZ	*Biblische Zeitschrift*
BZAW	Beihefte zur Zeitschrift für die alttestamentliche Wissenschaft
BZNW	Beihefte zur Zeitschrift für die neutestamentliche Wissenschaft
CBET	Contributions to Biblical Exegesis and Theology
CBQ	*Catholic Biblical Quarterly*
CBQMS	Catholic Biblical Quarterly Monograph Series

CBS	Catalogue of Babylonian Section in the University of Pennsylvania
CC	Continental Commentaries
CJAS	Christianity and Judaism in Antiquity Series
CNS	*Cristianesimo nella storia*
ConBNT	Coniectanea neotestamentica or Coniectanea biblica: New Testament Series
ConBOT	Coniectanea biblica: Old Testament Series
CRAI	Comptes rendus de l'Académie des inscriptions et belles-lettres
CRINT	Compendia rerum iudaicarum ad Novum Testamentum
CSCO	Corpus scriptorum christianorum orientalium. Edited by I. B. Chabot et al. Paris, 1903–
CSEL	Corpus scriptorum ecclesiasticorum latinorum
DJD	Discoveries in the Judaean Desert
DJG	*Dictionary of Jesus and the Gospels.* Edited by J. B. Green and S. McKnight. Downers Grove, Ill.: InterVarsity, 1992
DNTB	*Dictionary of New Testament Background.* Edited by C. A. Evans and S. E. Porter. Downers Grove, Ill.: InterVarsity, 2000
DSD	*Dead Sea Discoveries*
EKKNT	Evangelisch-katholischer Kommentar zum Neuen Testament
EncJud	*Encyclopaedia Judaica.* 16 vols. Jerusalem: Keter, 1972
ErIsr	*Eretz-Israel*
EstBib	*Estudios bíblicos*
ETL	*Ephemerides theologicae lovanienses*
ExpTim	*Expository Times*
FAT	Forschungen zum Alten Testament
FB	Forschung zur Bibel
FC	Fathers of the Church
FF	Foundations and Facets
FOTL	Forms of the Old Testament Literature
FRLANT	Forschungen zur Religion und Literatur des Alten und Neuen Testaments
GKC	*Gesenius' Hebrew Grammar.* Edited by E. Kautzsch. Translated by A. E. Cowley. 2d ed. Oxford: Oxford University Press, 1910
GNS	Good News Studies
HKAT	Handkommentar zum Alten Testament
HR	*History of Religions*
HSM	Harvard Semitic Monographs
HTKNT	Herders theologischer Kommentar zum Neuen Testament
HTR	*Harvard Theological Review*
HUCA	*Hebrew Union College Annual*

HUCM	Monographs of the Hebrew Union College
ICC	International Critical Commentary
ILS	*Inscriptiones Latinae Selectae.* Edited by H. Dessau. Berlin: Weidmann, 1892–1916
Int	*Interpretation*
IOSCS	International Organization for Septuagint and Cognate Studies
JBL	*Journal of Biblical Literature*
JETS	*Journal of the Evangelical Theological Society*
JJS	*Journal of Jewish Studies*
JNES	*Journal of Near Eastern Studies*
JPOS	*Journal of the Palestinian Oriental Society*
JQR	*Jewish Quarterly Review*
JSJ	*Journal for the Study of Judaism in the Persian, Hellenistic, and Roman Periods*
JSNT	*Journal for the Study of the New Testament*
JSNTSup	Journal for the Study of the New Testament: Supplement Series
JSOT	*Journal for the Study of the Old Testament*
JSOTSup	Journal for the Study of the Old Testament: Supplement Series
JSP	*Journal for the Study of the Pseudepigrapha*
JSPSup	Journal for the Study of the Pseudepigrapha: Supplement Series
JSSSup	Journal of Semitic Studies: Supplement
JTS	*Journal of Theological Studies*
KAT	Kommentar zum Alten Testament
KBANT	Kommentare und Beiträge zum Alten und Neuen Testament
KEK	Kritisch-exegetischer Kommentar über das Neue Testament (Meyer-Kommentar)
LBS	Library of Biblical Studies
LD	Lectio divina
LSJ	Liddell, H. G., R. Scott, H. S. Jones, *A Greek-English Lexicon.* 9th ed. with revised supplement. Oxford: Clarendon, 1996
Mils	*Milltown Studies*
MNTC	Moffatt New Testament Commentary
NCB	New Century Bible
NETS	New English Translation of the Septuagint
NIGTC	New International Greek Testament Commentary
NovT	*Novum Testamentum*
NovTSup	Supplements to Novum Testamentum
NTA	*New Testament Abstracts*
NTAbh	Neutestamentliche Abhandlungen
NTS	*New Testament Studies*
NTTS	New Testament Tools and Studies

OBO	Orbis biblicus et orientalis
Or	*Orientalia*
OrChr	*Oriens christianus*
OTL	Old Testament Library
OTP	*Old Testament Pseudepigrapha.* Edited by J. H. Charlesworth. 2 vols. Garden City, N.Y.: Doubleday, 1983
PAAJR	*Proceedings of the American Academy for Jewish Research*
PGM	*Papyri graecae magicae: Die griechischen Zauberpapyri.* Edited by K. Preisendanz. 2 vols. Leipzig: B. G. Teubner, 1928–1931
RB	*Revue biblique*
ResQ	*Restoration Quarterly*
RevExp	*Review and Expositor*
RevQ	*Revue de Qumran*
RTP	*Revue de théologie et de philosophie*
SAC	Studies in Antiquity and Christianity
SBLDS	Society of Biblical Literature Dissertation Series
SBLEJL	Society of Biblical Literature Early Judaism and Its Literature
SBLMS	Society of Biblical Literature Monograph Series
SBLSCS	Society of Biblical Literature Septuagint and Cognate Studies
SBLSP	Society of Biblical Literature Seminar Papers
SBS	Stuttgarter Bibelstudien
SBT	Studies in Biblical Theology
Scr	*Scripture*
SD	Studies and Documents
SJLA	Studies in Judaism in Late Antiquity
SJT	*Scottish Journal of Theology*
SNT	Studien zum Neuen Testament
SNTSMS	Society for New Testament Studies Monograph Series
SP	Sacra pagina
SPhilo	*Studia philonica*
SSEJC	Studies in Scripture in Early Judaism and Christianity
ST	*Studia Theologica*
STDJ	Studies on the Texts of the Desert of Judah
StPatr	*Studia patristica*
Str-B	Strack, H. L., and P. Billerbeck. *Kommentar zum Neuen Testament aus Talmud und Midrasch.* 6 vols. in 7. Munich: Beck, 1922–1961
SUNT	Studien zur Umwelt des Neuen Testaments
SVTP	Studia in Veteris Testamenti pseudepigraphica
TDNT	*Theological Dictionary of the New Testament.* Edited by G. Kittel and G. Friedrich. Translated by G. W. Bromiley. 10 vols. Grand Rapids: Eerdmans, 1964–1976

Text	*Textus*
TJT	*Toronto Journal of Theology*
TS	*Theological Studies*
TSAJ	Texte und Studien zum antiken Judentum
TynBul	*Tyndale Bulletin*
USQR	*Union Seminary Quarterly Review*
VCSup	Supplements to Vigiliae christianae
VT	*Vetus Testamentum*
VTSup	Supplements to Vetus Testamentum
WBC	Word Biblical Commentary
WMANT	Wissenschaftliche Monographien zum Alten und Neuen Testament
WUNT	Wissenschaftliche Untersuchungen zum Neuen Testament
YJS	Yale Judaica Studies
ZAW	*Zeitschrift für die alttestamentliche Wissenschaft*
ZBK	Zürcher Bibelkommentare
ZKG	*Zeitschrift für Kirchengeschichte*
ZTK	*Zeitschrift für Theologie und Kirche*

From Prophecy to Testament:
An Introduction

Craig A. Evans

Half a century ago the great Cambridge scholar C. H. Dodd published a small but very influential book on the function of Old Testament (OT) Scripture in the New Testament (NT).[1] The subtitle of the book reflected an important thesis of his work: *The Substructure of New Testament Theology*. About a decade later Barnabas Lindars published a book on the same subject, in which he too underscored the significance of the contribution that the OT made to the theology of the NT writers.[2] Most of the numerous books and studies that have appeared in the last forty years have driven home this point: The theology of the NT is fundamentally indebted to, and a reflection of, major OT themes, images, and language.[3] There is simply no significant element in NT theology that is not in some way a development of a tradition or theology expressed in the sacred writings that eventually

---

[1] C. H. Dodd, *According to the Scriptures: The Substructure of New Testament Theology* (London: Nisbet, 1952).

[2] B. Lindars, *New Testament Apologetic: The Doctrinal Significance of the Old Testament Quotations* (Philadelphia: Westminster, 1961).

[3] Many studies could be mentioned, e.g., F. F. Bruce, *New Testament Development of Old Testament Themes* (Grand Rapids: Eerdmans, 1968); idem, *The Time Is Fulfilled: Five Aspects of Fulfillment of the Old Testament in the New* (Grand Rapids: Eerdmans, 1995); H. M. Shires, *Finding the Old Testament in the New* (Philadelphia: Westminster, 1974); D.-A. Koch, *Die Schrift als Zeuge des Evangeliums: Untersuchungen zur Verwendung und zum Verständnis der Schrift bei Paulus* (BHT 69; Tübingen: Mohr [Siebeck], 1986); J. A. Sanders, *From Sacred Story to Sacred Text* (Philadelphia: Fortress, 1987); D. A. Carson and H. G. M. Williamson, eds., *It Is Written—Scripture Citing Scripture: Essays in Honour of Barnabas Lindars* (Cambridge: Cambridge University Press, 1988); R. B. Hays, *Echoes of Scripture in the Letters of Paul* (New Haven: Yale University Press, 1989); R. Liebers, *"Wie geschrieben steht": Studien zu einer besonderen Art frühchristlichen Schriftbezuges* (New York: de Gruyter, 1993); D. Marguerate and A. Curtis, eds., *Intertextualités: La Bible en échos* (Le monde de la Bible 40; Paris: Labor et Fides, 2000); S. Moyise, ed., *The Old Testament in the New Testament: Essays in Honour of J. L. North* (JSNTSup 189; Sheffield, England: Sheffield Academic Press, 2000).

came to be what Christians call the Old Testament (OT), Jews call the Tanakh, and scholars call the Hebrew Bible (HB).[4]

Not surprisingly, in recent years scholars have investigated the approaches and methods of biblical exegesis in late antiquity. The hermeneutical principles of Philo, Josephus, the authors of the Dead Sea Scrolls, the OT Apocrypha and Pseudepigrapha, NT writers, the various recensions and translations of Scripture, and early rabbinic and ecclesiastical literature have been investigated and continue to be studied.[5] Building upon this work, several detailed studies have appeared that investigate specific scriptural passages or themes.[6]

The function of the OT in the NT often revolves around the theme of fulfillment, a theme driven by the conviction of early Christians that the prophecies of the First Testament have been fulfilled in the events described in the Second Testament. Hence the title of the present collection of studies: *From Prophecy to Testament*. We do not mean to imply that prophecy was the only impulse that led to interpretation and resignification of the older revelation, but it was a major impulse. Nor do we mean to imply that prophecy has as its primary refer-

---

[4]It is important to remark also that much of the Scripture that makes up the Old, or First, Testament is itself a product of interpretation of older sacred tradition. In other words, it was not *after* the completion of the OT that interpretation began; it was *during*. See J. A. Sanders, *Torah and Canon* (Philadelphia: Fortress, 1972); idem, *From Sacred Story*.

[5]For representative studies, see J. W. Doeve, *Jewish Hermeneutics in the Synoptic Gospels and Acts* (Assen: Van Gorcum, 1954); J. Barr, *Old and New in Interpretation: A Study of the Two Testaments* (London: SCM Press, 1966); R. N. Longenecker, *Biblical Exegesis in the Apostolic Period* (Grand Rapids: Eerdmans, 1975); D. Patte, *Early Jewish Hermeneutic in Palestine* (SBLDS 22; Missoula, Mont.: Scholars Press, 1975); E. E. Ellis, *Prophecy and Hermeneutic in Early Christianity* (Grand Rapids: Eerdmans, 1978); L. Goppelt, *Typos, The Typological Interpretation of the Old Testament in the New* (Grand Rapids: Eerdmans, 1982); M. Fishbane, *Biblical Interpretation in Ancient Israel* (Oxford: Oxford University Press, 1985); J. L. Kugel and R. Greer, *Early Biblical Interpretation* (Philadelphia: Westminster, 1986); D. Instone Brewer, *Techniques and Assumptions in Jewish Exegesis before 70 C.E.* (TSAJ 30; Tübingen: Mohr [Siebeck], 1992); J. H. Charlesworth and C. A. Evans, eds., *The Pseudepigrapha and Early Biblical Interpretation* (JSPSup 14; SSEJC 2; Sheffield, England: JSOT Press, 1993). For an excellent bibliographical summary of the most important older work, see M. P. Miller, "Targum, Midrash, and the Use of the Old Testament in the New Testament," *JSJ* 2 (1971): 29–82.

[6]For representative studies, see D. M. Hay, *Glory at the Right Hand: Psalm 110 in Early Christianity* (SBLMS 18; Nashville: Abingdon, 1973); M. C. Callaway, *Sing, O Barren One: A Study in Comparative Midrash* (SBLDS 91; Atlanta: Scholars Press, 1986); D. H. Juel, *Messianic Exegesis: Christological Interpretation of the Old Testament in Early Christianity* (Philadelphia: Fortress, 1988); C. A. Evans, *To See and Not Perceive: Isaiah 6.9–10 in Early Jewish and Christian Interpretation* (JSOTSup 64; Sheffield, England: JSOT Press, 1989); C. R. Koester, *The Dwelling of God: The Tabernacle in the Old Testament, Intertestamental Jewish Literature, and the New Testament* (CBQMS 22; Washington, D.C.: Catholic Biblical Association, 1989); K. E. Pomykala, *The Davidic Dynasty Tradition in Early Judaism: Its History and Significance for Messianism* (SBLEJL 7; Atlanta: Scholars Press, 1995); P. E. Enns, *Exodus Retold: Ancient Exegesis of the Departure from Egypt in Wis 15–21 and 19:1–9* (HSM 57; Atlanta: Scholars Press, 1997).

ence *prediction* or *foretelling* this event or that. Rather, we understand it in its classical sense of *making known* the word of God. The older revelation is probed and pondered, and out of it comes forth new meaning and new application. The word of God speaks afresh. The primary goal of the interpreter, translator, and paraphraser in late antiquity was to allow the sacred text to speak to the new situation, to address the new problems, to answer the new questions.

The Task

Study of the function of the OT in the NT requires consideration of many versions, texts, and traditions and of the contexts and communities of faith from which they emerged. These traditions functioned, more or less, as the raw materials out of which new texts could be fashioned, texts that gave expression to the faith and beliefs of the new community that sprang from Jewish roots. Surveying these materials and citing some of the most important bibliography will be helpful for beginning students.

The Contents of Scripture

When most students consider the question of how the OT functions in the NT, they usually assume a particular set of writings. But when the NT authors were at work (not knowing, by the way, that what they were writing would ever become a "New Testament"), there was no finalized canon of Scripture. Consequently, it was not always clear what could be quoted and interpreted as authoritative and what could not be. Was *Enoch* Scripture? Was Sirach? Evidently in the first century some Jews did recognize these writings as authoritative; so did many in the early church (and in the church today).

It is sometimes assumed that the three divisions of the HB were established and recognized in the first century, when most of the books of the NT were written. But this is far from evident. The Torah, or Law of Moses, was recognized several centuries before the NT era. The Prophets were also recognized, though the place of Daniel was uncertain.[7] The Writings, however, were far from settled. That there were authoritative writings outside the Law and the Prophets seems clear enough. But how many and which ones were questions that would not be settled until well into the Christian era itself (cf. *m. Yad.* 3:5).[8]

---

[7] Christians eventually recognized the book of Daniel as part of the prophetic corpus. But in the Jewish Bible Daniel is placed with the Writings.

[8] The most pertinent texts from late antiquity include the prologue to the Wisdom of Sirach; Sir 39:1; 4Q397 14–21 ii 10–12; 2 Macc 2:13; and Philo, *Contempl. Life* 25. In the gospel tradition, Jesus regularly refers to "the Law and the Prophets" (e.g., Matt 5:17; 7:12; 11:13; Luke 16:29, 31). Some scholars point to the words of the risen Jesus in Luke 24:44 as evidence of a recognized tripartite canon of Scripture in the first century. For example, the RSV translates (with numbers inserted in square brackets): "in [1] the Law of Moses and [2] the Prophets and [3] the Psalms." But in the Greek the definite article occurs only

Consequently, when speaking of the function of the "Old Testament" in the New, we must not assume that everything quoted was necessarily viewed as authoritative Scripture. One of the factors that guided early Christians in deciding which writings were authoritative, and which ones were not, was inspiration. That is, did a given writing speak with a prophetic voice, conveying the will and mind of God? Writings believed to reveal the mind of God were studied in hopes of finding new inspiration and insight. Writings widely believed to reveal the mind of God eventually were recognized as authoritative Scripture. Writings believed by relatively few to be inspired did not gain such recognition but eventually found themselves classified as part of the Apocrypha, Pseudepigrapha, or Apostolic Fathers (see pp. 11–20, "Cognate Literatures," below). Some of these writings survive only in brief quotations in later writings (e.g., *Eldad and Modad*) or are lost altogether.

Versions of Scripture

Appreciation of the function of the OT in the NT must also take into account the text type and language of the former. The writings that make up the OT were originally composed and handed down in Hebrew and Aramaic.[9] But in NT times portions of the OT circulated in Greek, Latin, and Aramaic. The NT writers quote the Greek more than any other version, though sometimes they appear to have been acquainted with the Hebrew and the Aramaic.

But the picture is even more complicated, for there were several versions of the Hebrew, Greek, Aramaic, and Latin texts of Scripture. Qumran attests at least four versions of Hebrew Scripture (viz., proto-Masoretic, Samaritan, Septuagintal, and a fourth, previously unknown).[10] The Dead Sea region has also given us the *Greek Minor Prophets Scroll* of Naḥal Ḥever, which at many points differs

---

twice, not three times; this suggests that we translate the text this way: "in [1] the Law of Moses and [2] the Prophets and Psalms." The syntax suggests that the Psalms are in some sense part of the Prophets. Thus, the words of the risen Jesus imply that the Psalms are prophetic. The eschatological commentaries found at Qumran (i.e., the pesharim), which interpret the Prophets and the Psalms, support this understanding of Luke 24:44. For further discussion of the development of canon, see L. M. McDonald, *The Formation of the Christian Biblical Canon: Revised and Expanded Edition* (Peabody, Mass.: Hendrickson, 1995); L. M. McDonald and J. A. Sanders, eds., *The Canon Debate* (Peabody, Mass.: Hendrickson, 2002).

[9] Most of the OT was originally composed in Hebrew. Aramaic is limited to Gen 31:47 (two words), Jer 10:11 (one sentence), Dan 2:4–7:28 (five stories and a vision), and Ezra 4:8–6:18 and 7:12–26 (mostly concerning the rebuilding of the Jewish temple).

[10] See the helpful synthesis in E. Ulrich, "Pluriformity in the Biblical Text, Text Groups, and Questions of Canon," in *The Madrid Qumran Congress: Proceedings of the International Congress on the Dead Sea Scrolls, Madrid, 18–21 March 1991* (ed. J. Trebolle Barrera and L. Vegas Montaner; STDJ 11; New York: E. J. Brill, 1991), 23–41; and E. Tov, "Scriptures: Texts," in *Encyclopedia of the Dead Sea Scrolls* (ed. L. H. Schiffman and J. C. VanderKam; 2 vols.; Oxford: Oxford University Press, 2000), 2:832–36.

from the LXX, the better-known Greek translation.[11] Qumran has also yielded two small fragments of Targumim to Leviticus and Job, and a large fragmentary scroll of Aramaic Job.[12] These texts differ significantly from the fully preserved Targumim of the later rabbinic period. Even the Old Latin (which predates the late-fourth-century Vulgate) probably circulated in more than one version.[13]

The multiformity of the biblical text must be taken into account when studying OT quotations and allusions in the NT and in other writings of late antiquity. What at first may appear to be an inaccurate quotation, or a quotation of the LXX, itself thought to be an inaccurate translation of the underlying Hebrew, may in fact be a quotation of a different textual tradition.[14]

Let us briefly review the principal versions of Scripture, along with basic bibliography:

Hebrew. Prior to the discovery of the Dead Sea Scrolls in 1947–1956, the oldest copies of the HB dated to the tenth century and the beginning of the eleventh century (viz., the Aleppo Codex, ca. tenth century; and the Leningrad Codex, 1008 C.E.). The region of the Dead Sea has yielded more than two hundred scrolls (mostly fragmentary) of Hebrew Scripture. Only the book of Esther is unattested. The best-preserved scroll is the Great Isaiah Scroll (1QIsaᵃ), found in the first cave, which may date to the second century B.C.E. Amazingly, the Dead Sea Bible scrolls push back the date of the extant Hebrew text more than one thousand years. The official Hebrew Bible of Judaism and the Christian OT is the Masoretic Text (MT; named after the sixth- to ninth-century Jewish scholars who vocalized and annotated the text). The Hebrew scrolls of Qumran antedate the MT by several centuries.

Bibliography. For the text of the (Masoretic) Hebrew Bible, see K. Elliger and W. Rudolph, eds., *Biblia Hebraica Stuttgartensia* (Stuttgart: Deutsche Bibelgesellschaft, 1983). For discussion, see L. Goldschmidt, *The Earliest Editions of the Hebrew Bible* (New York: Aldus, 1950); and E. Tov, *Textual Criticism of the Hebrew Bible* (Minneapolis: Fortress, 1992). Eugene Ulrich and others are preparing a Hebrew Bible based on the Dead Sea Scrolls. For an English translation of the Bible as preserved at Qumran and at other locations in the Dead Sea region, see M. G. Abegg, P. W. Flint, and E. Ulrich, *The Dead Sea Scrolls Bible: The Oldest Known Bible Translated for the First Time into English* (San Francisco: HarperCollins, 1999).

---

[11] See E. Tov, *The Greek Minor Prophets Scroll from Nahal Hever (8HevXIIgr)* (Seiyâl Collection 1; DJD 8; New York: Oxford University Press, 1990).

[12] M. Sokoloff, *The Targum to Job from Qumran Cave XI* (Ramat-Gan, Israel: Bar-Ilan, 1974).

[13] E. Würthwein, *The Text of the Old Testament* (Grand Rapids: Eerdmans, 1979), 87–95.

[14] Recognition of the multiformity of the biblical text in late antiquity, especially before 70 C.E., renders obsolete the older notions of accuracy in quotation, as seen in studies such as C. Goodwin, "How Did John Treat His Sources?" *JBL* 73 (1954): 61–75; and S. V. McCasland, "Matthew Twists the Scriptures," *JBL* 80 (1961): 143–48.

Aramaic. The Aramaic paraphrases of the Hebrew Scriptures developed in the synagogue. How old this practice was and how far back the Aramaic tradition can be dated are complicated questions. Fragments of Targumim to Leviticus and Job found at Qumran make it clear that the practice antedates Jesus and the early church, but how much of the later, fully extant targumic tradition reaches back to this early period is uncertain and disputed. Several studies show convincingly that at least some elements of this tradition were, in one form or another, in circulation in the first century.

Bibliography. For texts of the Targumim, see A. Sperber, *The Bible in Aramaic: Based on Old Manuscripts and Printed Texts* (4 vols. in 5; Leiden: E. J. Brill, 1959–1973); A. Díez Macho, *Neophyti 1: Targum palestinense Ms de la Biblioteca Vaticana* (5 vols.; Madrid: Consejo Superior de Investigaciones Científicas, 1968–1978); and E. G. Clarke, *Targum Pseudo-Jonathan of the Pentateuch: Text and Concordance* (Hoboken, N.J.: Ktav, 1984). For introductory studies and studies that explore the relevance of the targumic tradition for NT interpretation, see J. Bowker, *The Targums and Rabbinic Literature* (Cambridge: Cambridge University Press, 1969); P. Grelot, *What Are the Targums? Selected Texts* (Collegeville, Minn.: Liturgical Press, 1992); M. McNamara, *The New Testament and the Palestinian Targum to the Pentateuch* (2d ed.; AnBib 27A; Rome: Pontifical Biblical Institute, 1978); idem, *Targum and Testament: Aramaic Paraphrases of the Hebrew Bible: A Light on the New Testament* (Grand Rapids: Eerdmans, 1972); and B. D. Chilton, *A Galilean Rabbi and His Bible: Jesus' Use of the Interpreted Scripture of His Time* (GNS 8; Wilmington, Del.: Glazier, 1984). For an English translation of the Targum, see the multivolume series *The Aramaic Bible,* launched by Michael Glazier and continued by Liturgical Press. This series is nearly complete.

Syriac. Another Semitic version of Scripture is the Syriac; it is known as the Peshitta ("simple"). Like the Targumim, the antiquity of this version as well as its provenance are disputed. The Syriac gives evidence of being influenced by both the Aramaic and the Greek. Both Testaments of the Syriac version, the Old and the New, may potentially make important contributions to questions of textual development.

Bibliography. For the Syriac text, see *Ktabe Qadishe* [Holy Bible] (London: United Bible Societies, 1979), and *Ktabe Qadishe* (Beirut: Bible Society in Lebanon, 1995). E. J. Brill is publishing a critical edition of the Syriac text (the OT in Syriac according to the Peshitta version), sponsored by the Peshitta Institute of the University of Leiden. See also A. Kiraz, ed., *Comparative Edition of the Syriac Gospels* (4 vols.; New York: E. J. Brill, 1996). For a critical study, see M. Weitzman, *The Syriac Version of the Old Testament: An Introduction* (Cambridge: Cambridge University Press, 1999). For an English translation, see G. Lamsa, *The Holy Bible from Ancient Eastern Manuscripts* (Nashville: Holman, 1933).

Greek. Beginning in the third century B.C.E. and probably beginning with the books of Moses, the Hebrew and Aramaic Scriptures were translated into Greek. Much of this translation was probably done in Egypt, especially Alexandria, but some of it may have taken place in other locations, including Israel itself. By the first century C.E. the Law and the Prophets were probably widely circulated in Greek. The NT writers quoted the Greek version more often than any other version. Not surprisingly, the Greek version of the Bible became the standard text in the Christian church (though Jewish Christians, or Ebionites, continued to make use of the Hebrew version).

Bibliography. The standard text has been A. Rahlfs, ed., *Septuaginta* (2 vols.; Stuttgart: Württembergische Bibelanstalt, 1935; repr., 1971). This edition, with its limited critical apparatus, is being replaced, however, by the Göttingen Septuagint, which for many years was edited by the late Joseph Ziegler. For critical studies and an introduction, see H. M. Orlinsky, *The Septuagint: The Oldest Translation of the Bible* (Cincinnati: Union of American Hebrew Congregations, 1949); K. Hanhart, "Die Bedeutung der Septuaginta in neutestamentlicher Zeit," ZTK 81 (1984) 395–416; S. Olofsson, *The LXX Version: A Guide to the Translation Technique of the Septuagint* (ConBOT 30; Stockholm: Almqvist, 1990); E. Tov, *The Text-Critical Use of the Septuagint in Biblical Research* (2d ed.; Jerusalem Biblical Studies 8; Jerusalem: Simor, 1997); K. H. Jobes and M. Silva, *Invitation to the Septuagint* (Grand Rapids: Baker, 2000); R. T. McLay, *The Use of the Septuagint in New Testament Research* (Grand Rapids: Eerdmans, 2003).

The Göttingen Septuagint project is not yet complete, but a great many volumes have been published. See R. Hanhart and J. W. Wevers, eds., *Das Göttinger Septuaginta-Unternehmen: Joseph Ziegler zum 75. Geburtstag, 15. 3. 1977* (Göttingen: Vandenhoeck & Ruprecht, 1977). Mention also should be made of A. E. Brooke, N. McLean, and H. St. J. Thackeray, eds., *The Old Testament in Greek* (Cambridge: Cambridge University Press, 1906–1940). The textual notes of these editions are rich. There are two English translations of the LXX: Charles Thomson, *The Holy Bible, Containing the Old and the New Covenant, Commonly Called the Old and the New Testament* (4 vols.; Philadelphia: Jane Aitken, 1808); and Lancelot C. L. Brenton, *The Septuagint Version of the Old Testament, according to the Vatican Text* (2 vols.; London: S. Bagster & Sons, 1844; repr., Peabody, Mass.: Hendrickson, 1986). A New English translation of the LXX (NETS) has been launched by the International Organization for Septuagint and Cognate Studies (IOSCS). The first fascicle to appear is by Albert Pietersma, *The Psalms: A New English Translation of the Septuagint* (Oxford: Oxford University Press, 2000). Members of the IOSCS are also preparing a commentary on the LXX. Their work will take into account the manner in which the Greek translators rendered the underlying Hebrew. Taking a different approach, a team of scholars assembled by Stanley Porter is preparing a commentary on the LXX that emphasizes the LXX as Greek literature read by Greek speakers.

Latin. When Pompey entered Jerusalem in 63 B.C.E., Israel became part of the Roman Empire. It was inevitable that the sacred scriptures of Israel would eventually be translated into Latin, though exactly when and where this took place are not known. North Africa is a good candidate. This Latin version of Scripture, usually called the Old Latin version (OL), is attested by Latin-speaking church fathers, such as Tertullian (b. ca. 160) and Cyprian (d. ca. 258). In the latter part of the fourth century, Pope Damascus I (366–384) commissioned Jerome to prepare a Latin translation of the Christian Bible. Eventually this version became known as the Vulgate (i.e., "common"). Although influential persons such as the great church father Augustine urged Jerome to translate the Greek OT, Jerome based his translation on the Hebrew.

Bibliography. For the Latin text, see R. Weber, *Biblia Sacra iuxta Vulgatam Versionem* (2 vols.; 3d ed.; Stuttgart: Deutsche Bibelgesellschaft, 1985). For critical studies, see F. Stummer, *Einführung in die lateinische Bibel* (Paderborn: F. Schöningh, 1928); H. J. Vogels, *Vulgatastudien: Die Evangelien der Vulgata untersucht auf ihre lateinische und griechische Vorlage* (Münster: Aschendorff, 1928); J. Barr, "St. Jerome's Appreciation of Hebrew," *BJRL* 49 (1966/1967): 281–302; B. Kedar-Kopfstein, "The Vulgate as a Translation: Some Semantic and Syntactical Aspects" (PhD diss., Hebrew University, 1968).

General Bibliography. For comprehensive studies pertinent to all of the versions of Scripture that have been mentioned, see M. J. Mulder, ed., *Mikra: Text, Translation, Reading, and Interpretation of the Hebrew Bible in Ancient Judaism and Early Christianity* (CRINT 2.1; Philadelphia: Fortress, 1988); and especially D. Barthélemy et al., *Critique textuelle de l'Ancien Testament* (3 vols.; OBO 50; Fribourg: Presses Universitaires, 1982–).

Interpretive Approaches

The interpretation of Scripture in late antiquity took many forms. One such form—translation and paraphrase—was implicit and often unconscious. But other forms were explicit. These include midrash, pesher, allegory, and typology. These interpretive approaches were not always consciously recognized or distinguished. In fact, elements of allegory and typology often appear in midrash and pesher, and the latter often overlap. Nevertheless, there are distinctive features, the recognition of which will aid the modern interpreter.

Midrash. Midrashic exegesis is usually associated with rabbinic Judaism, though it has roots that reach back into the intertestamental period and into biblical literature itself.[15] Midrash is religious, literary, academic, and collegial, often taking

---

[15] See S. Sandmel, "The Haggada within Scripture," *JBL* 80 (1961): 105–22. For other studies on midrash, see S. Zeitlin, "Midrash: A Historical Study," *JQR* 44 (1953):

form in didactic settings and collegial debate. The principal objective of midrash (from Heb. *darash,* "to search") is, as its name implies, the searching of Scripture for clarification and further teaching. The Johannine Jesus alludes to this approach when he says, "You search the scriptures, because you think that in them you have eternal life" (John 5:39; cf. 7:52: "Search and you will see that no prophet is to rise from Galilee" RSV). Searching the Scriptures for life (cf. Luke 10:28, "Do this and you will live" RSV; *Tg. Onq.* Lev 18:5, "which if a man does, he will live by them in eternal life") is the whole point of biblical interpretation.

Scripture had to be searched, for it was believed that it contained all that really mattered (cf. *m. ʾAbot* 5:22: "for everything is in it . . . you cannot have a better guide than it"). Tradition holds that the great sage Hillel formulated seven rules, or *middoth,* for searching the Scripture (*ʾAbot R. Nat.* 37; *t. Sanh.* 7.11). Whether he in fact did so is not known and does not matter. What is significant is that we find evidence of several of these rules in practice in many of the NT writings themselves.

Pesher. At Qumran, Scripture was viewed as containing mysteries that needed explanation (or the covenanters of Qumran needed scriptural clarification of their own bewildering and painful experience). The pesher was the explanation of the mystery: "the pesher of this [passage of Scripture] concerns the Teacher of Righteousness, to whom God made known all the mysteries of the words of His servants the prophets" (1QpHab 7:4–5).

It was assumed that the text spoke of and to the Qumran community and of eschatological events about to unfold. As in NT exegesis (cf. Mark 12:10–11 [citing Ps 118:22–23]; 14:27 [citing Zech 13:7]; Acts 2:17–21 [citing Joel 2:28–32]; 15:16–17 [citing Amos 9:11–12]), pesher exegesis understands specific biblical passages as fulfilled in specific historical events and experiences.[16]

Allegory. Allegorical interpretation entails extracting a symbolic meaning from the text. It assumes that a deeper, more sophisticated interpretation is to be found beneath the obvious letter of the passage. The allegorist does not, however, necessarily assume that the text is unhistorical or without literal meaning. His exegesis

---

21–36; A. G. Wright, *The Literary Genre Midrash* (Staten Island, N.Y.: Alba, 1967); G. G. Porton, "Midrash: Palestinian Jews and the Hebrew Bible in the Greco-Roman Period," *ANRW* 2.19.1:103–38; idem, "Defining Midrash," in *Study of Ancient Judaism* (ed. J. Neusner; New York: Ktav, 1981), 55–94; J. Neusner, *What Is Midrash?* (Philadelphia: Fortress, 1987); G. G. Porton, "Rabbinic Literature: Midrashim," *DNTB* 889–93.

[16] See J. A. Fitzmyer, "The Use of Explicit Old Testament Quotations in Qumran Literature and in the New Testament," *NTS* 7 (1961): 297–333; M. P. Horgan, *Pesharim: Qumran Interpretation of Biblical Books* (CBQMS 8; Washington, D.C.: Catholic Biblical Association, 1979); G. J. Brooke, *Exegesis at Qumran: 4QFlorilegium in Its Jewish Context* (JSOTSup 29; Sheffield, England: JSOT Press, 1985); D. Dimant, "Pesharim, Qumran," *ABD* 5:244–51; M. Bernstein, "Introductory Formulas for Citation and Re-citation of Biblical Verses in the Qumran Pesharim," *DSD* 1 (1994): 30–70; G. J. Brooke, "Pesharim," *DNTB* 778–82.

is simply not concerned with this aspect of the biblical passage. The best-known first-century allegorist was Philo of Alexandria, whose many books afford a wealth of examples of the allegorical interpretation of Scripture, primarily the books of Moses.[17] There is some allegory in the NT—in a few places in Paul, in Hebrews, and in some of Jesus' parables.[18] (See more on Philo below.)

Typology. Typology is not so much a method of exegesis as a presupposition underlying the Jewish and Christian understanding of Scripture, particularly its historical portions. Typology is based upon the belief that the biblical story of the past has some bearing on the present or, to turn it around, that the present is foreshadowed in the biblical story. Unlike allegory, typology is closely tied to history, for the events of history exemplify the very patterns of divine activity and, accordingly, adumbrate the plans of God yet to unfold. Typology therefore enables interpreters to weld the past together with the present and the future, thus providing a reassuring continuity between sacred story and present experience.[19]

---

[17] See J. Z. Lauterbach, "The Ancient Jewish Allegorists," *JQR* 1 (1911): 291–333; G. L. Bruns, "Midrash and Allegory: The Beginnings of Scriptural Interpretation," in *The Literary Guide to the Bible* (ed. R. Alter and F. Kermode; Cambridge: Harvard University Press, 1994), 625–46; R. Boer, "National Allegory in the Hebrew Bible," *JSOT* 74 (1997): 95–116; R. Kasher, "Metaphor and Allegory in the Aramaic Translation of the Bible," *Journal of the Aramaic Bible* 1 (1999): 53–77; E. M. Menn, "Targum of the Song of Songs and the Dynamics of Historical Allegory," in *The Interpretation of Scripture in Early Judaism and Christianity: Studies in Language and Tradition* (ed. C. A. Evans; JSPSup 33; SSEJC 7; Sheffield, England: Sheffield Academic Press, 2000), 423–45.

[18] S. G. Sowers, *The Hermeneutics of Philo and Hebrews: A Comparison of the Interpretation of the Old Testament in Philo Judaeus and the Epistle to the Hebrews* (BST 1; Richmond: John Knox, 1965); C. K. Barrett, "The Allegory of Abraham, Sarah, and Hagar in the Argument of Galatians," in *Rechtfertigung: Festschrift für Ernst Käsemann* (ed. J. Friedrich; Tübingen: Mohr [Siebeck], 1976), 1–16; repr. in *Essays on Paul* (London: SPCK, 1982), 154–70; C. E. Carlston, "Parable and Allegory Revisited: An Interpretative Review," *CBQ* 43 (1981): 228–42; S. Fowl, "Who Can Read Abraham's Story? Allegory and Interpretive Power in Galatians," *JSNT* 55 (1994): 77–95; T. Löfstedt, "The Allegory of Hagar and Sarah: Gal 4.21–31," *EstBib* 58 (2000): 475–94.

[19] See J. Daniélou, *Sacramentum Futuri* (Paris: Beauchesne, 1950); G. W. H. Lamp and K. J. Woollcombe, *Essays on Typology* (SBT 22; London: SCM Press, 1957); G. von Rad, "Typological Interpretation of the Old Testament," in *Essays on Old Testament Hermeneutics* (ed. C. Westermann; Richmond: John Knox, 1963), 17–39; M. D. Goulder, *Type and History in Acts* (London: SPCK, 1964); P. J. Cahill, "Hermeneutical Implications of Typology," *CBQ* 44 (1982): 266–81; L. Goppelt, *Typos, The Typological Interpretation of the Old Testament in the New* (Grand Rapids: Eerdmans, 1982); C. K. Barrett, "The Significance of the Adam-Christ Typology for the Resurrection of the Dead: 1 Co 15, 20–22, 45–49," in *Résurrection du Christ et des chrétiens* (1 Co 15) (ed. L. de Lorenzi; Série monographique de "Benedictina": Section biblico-oecuménique 8; Rome: Abbaye de S. Paul, 1985), 99–126; repr. in *Jesus and the Word and Other Essays* (Edinburgh: T&T Clark, 1995), 163–84; F. Foulkes, "The Acts of God: A Study of the Basis of Typology in the Old Testament," in *The Right Doctrine from the Wrong Texts? Essays on the Use of the Old Testament in the New* (ed. G. K. Beale; Grand Rapids, Mich.: Baker Books, 1994), 342–71; F. Young, "Typology," in *Crossing the Boundaries: Essays in Biblical Interpretation in Honour of Michael D. Goulder* (ed. S. E. Porter et al.; BIS 8; New York: E. J. Brill, 1994), 29–48; J. W.

Cognate Literatures

One of the most challenging aspects of serious biblical exegesis for the beginning student is the myriad of cognate literatures. Identifying the pertinent materials, rightly assessing their relevance and potential contributions, and gaining critical control of the materials are daunting tasks. These literatures are diverse, spanning centuries and emanating from various geographical and cultural settings, and, of course, they are extant in several languages. Moreover, their origins are sometimes obscure, often because they represent (exegetically) reworked traditions, usually moving from Jewish to Christian circles (*4 Ezra / 2 Esdras* an illustrative case in point).[20]

What is listed and briefly summarized below represents only the minimum of the literatures that exegetes must take into account. Other materials, including papyri, inscriptions, coins, and artifacts must also be considered but are not discussed here. Once again basic bibliography is provided.[21]

Apocrypha. The most important intertestamental corpus is the OT Apocrypha, or deuterocanonical books (called such because they are viewed as a second group of books to be recognized as canonical). Fifteen books make up this corpus if we count the Epistle of Jeremiah separately and do not include 3–4 Maccabees, and Psalm 151. The latter are usually included with the OT Pseudepigrapha.

The Apocrypha include several types of writings. Among them, some are historical (1 Esdras, 1–2 Maccabees), some are romantic (Tobit, Judith, Susanna), some are moralistic (Baruch, Epistle of Jeremiah, Bel and the Dragon, Sirach [or Ecclesiasticus]), and some devotional (Prayer of Azariah, Song of the Three Young Men, Prayer of Manasseh). One is apocalyptic (2 Esdras). Most of the books of the OT Apocrypha were written in Greek.

Aageson, "Typology, Correspondence, and the Application of Scripture in Romans 9–11," *JSNT* 31 (1987): 51–72; repr. in *The Pauline Writings: A Sheffield Reader* (ed. S. E. Porter and C. A. Evans; Biblical Seminar 34; Sheffield, England: Sheffield Academic Press, 1995), 76–97; G. M. Stevenson, "Communal Imagery and the Individual Lament: Exodus Typology in Psalm 77," *ResQ* 39 (1997): 215–29.

[20] *Fourth Ezra* is extant as 2 Esdras 3–14. *Fourth Ezra* was composed, in either Aramaic or Hebrew, by a Palestinian Jew near the end of the first century C.E. A generation later a Christian added two chapters at the beginning of the composition (i.e., 2 Esdras 1–2 = 5 Ezra), and a century later another Christian added two more chapters at the end of the composition (i.e., 2 Esdras 15–16 = 6 Ezra). These additions were originally in Greek, but only fragments are extant. The document as a whole survives in Latin, and large portions survive in other languages. See T. A. Bergren, *Fifth Ezra: The Text, Origin, and Early History* (SBLSCS 25; Atlanta: Scholars Press, 1990), idem, *Sixth Ezra: The Text and Origin* (Oxford: Oxford University Press, 1998); and M. E. Stone, *Fourth Ezra: A Commentary on the Book of Fourth Ezra* (Hermeneia; Minneapolis: Fortress, 1990).

[21] For a general introductory survey, see C. A. Evans, *Noncanonical Writings and New Testament Interpretation* (Peabody, Mass.: Hendrickson, 1992).

Bibliography. The text of the Greek Apocrypha is found in the LXX (see above). For an English translation, see E. J. Goodspeed, *The Apocrypha: An American Translation* (Chicago: University of Chicago Press, 1938); and for the RSV, B. M. Metzger, *The Apocrypha of the Old Testament* (New York: Oxford University Press, 1977 [for the NRSV, New York: Oxford University Press, 1989]). For a concordance of the Apocrypha in English, see B. M. Metzger, ed., *A Concordance to the Apocryphal/Deuterocanonical Books of the Revised Standard Version* (Grand Rapids: Eerdmans, 1983). For introductions and surveys, see W. O. E. Oesterley, *An Introduction to the Books of the Apocrypha* (London: SPCK, 1953); B. M. Metzger, *An Introduction to the Apocrypha* (New York: Oxford University Press, 1957); D. J. Harrington, *Invitation to the Apocrypha* (Grand Rapids: Eerdmans, 1999); D. A. DeSilva, *Introducing the Apocrypha: Message, Context, and Significance* (Grand Rapids: Baker, 2002). For commentaries on the individual books of the Apocrypha, see the Anchor Bible series (Doubleday).

Pseudepigrapha. The writings of the OT Pseudepigrapha are numerous and diverse. Several literary genres are represented in this amorphous collection. Their dates of composition also cover a broad period of time, with *Ahiqar* the oldest, at about the seventh or sixth century B.C.E., and *Apocalypse of Daniel* the most recent, at about the ninth century C.E. Many of these books were among those to which *4 Ezra* refers: "Ninety-four books were written. And . . . the Most High spoke to me, saying, 'Make public the twenty-four books that you wrote first and let the worthy and unworthy read them; but keep the seventy that were written last, in order to give them to the wise among your people. For in them is the spring of understanding, the fountain of wisdom, and the river of knowledge'" (14:44–47).[22] The "twenty-four" books are the books that make up the Jewish Bible, or what Christians call the Old Testament. The "seventy" books are the books of the OT Apocrypha and Pseudepigrapha. The author of *4 Ezra* was probably very close to the truth.

The word *pseudepigrapha* is a Greek word meaning "falsely superscribed," or what we moderns might call writing under a pen name. The classification "Old Testament Pseudepigrapha" is a label that scholars have given to these writings. Although some of the writings have been grouped together or associated in one way or another, most never had any connection to one another. Most of the writings are Jewish or Christian, most are attributed to an OT worthy (e.g., Adam, Enoch, Abraham, Moses, Elijah, Ezra), and most build on OT stories or themes. Many of them were written before the Christian era or at least contain traditions that antedate the NT writings. Accordingly, these writings often shed light on ideas found in the NT.

Bibliography. For an introduction and English translation, see R. H. Charles, ed., *The Apocrypha and Pseudepigrapha of the Old Testament* (2 vols.; Oxford: Claren-

---

[22] Bruce M. Metzger, "The Fourth Book of Ezra," in *Old Testament Pseudepigrapha* (ed. J. H. Charlesworth; 2 vols., N.Y.: Doubleday, 1983), 516–59.

don, 1913); J. H. Charlesworth, ed., *The Old Testament Pseudepigrapha* (2 vols.; ABRL; New York: Doubleday, 1983–1985). For a bibliography, see J. H. Charlesworth, *The Pseudepigrapha and Modern Research, with a Supplement* (2d ed.; SBLSCS 7; Chico, Calif.: Scholars Press, 1981); and L. DiTommaso, *A Bibliography of Pseudepigrapha Research, 1850–1999* (JSPSup 39; Sheffield, England: Sheffield Academic Press, 2001). The latter work is massive, comprising more than 1000 pages, and invaluable for research in the OT Pseudepigrapha. For an assessment of the value of the Pseudepigrapha for NT study, see J. H. Charlesworth, *The Old Testament Pseudepigrapha and the New Testament* (SNTSMS 54; Cambridge: Cambridge University Press, 1985); repr. as *The Old Testament Pseudepigrapha and the New Testament: Prolegomena for the Study of Christian Origins* (Harrisburg, Pa.: Trinity Press International, 1998).

Dead Sea Scrolls. The Dead Sea Scrolls probably constitute the single most important biblically related literary discovery of the twentieth century. The Scrolls have made important contributions to biblical scholarship in several fields: (1) the study of the ancient writing and making of books/scrolls; (2) textual criticism of the OT; (3) linguistic studies in Hebrew and Aramaic; (4) apocryphal and pseudepigraphal studies; (5) the study of sects and groups, particularly the Essenes, within Palestinian Jewry; (6) ancient methods of biblical interpretation; (7) intertestamental history; (8) first-century doctrines and religious ideas; and (9) NT background studies.

Bibliography. The official editions of the Scrolls, which are now nearly complete, have appeared in the Discoveries in the Judaean Desert series (Oxford University Press). More than sixty scholars have participated in publishing these texts. There is also a convenient edition, with Hebrew- and Aramaic-English facing pages, by F. García Martínez and E. J. C. Tigchelaar, *The Dead Sea Scrolls Study Edition* (2 vols.; vol. 1, New York: Brill, 1997; vol. 2, Boston: Brill, 1998). A multivolume series, the Princeton Theological Seminary Dead Sea Scrolls Project, edited by James Charlesworth (Mohr [Siebeck] and Westminster John Knox), is about half complete. For an introduction to the Scrolls, see J. C. VanderKam, *The Dead Sea Scrolls Today* (Grand Rapids: Eerdmans, 1994). See also L. H. Schiffman and J. C. VanderKam, eds., *Encyclopedia of the Dead Sea Scrolls* (2 vols.; Oxford: Oxford University Press, 2000).

There are also English editions by G. Vermes, *The Dead Sea Scrolls in English* (4th ed.; New York: Penguin, 1995); and M. O. Wise, M. G. Abegg Jr., and E. M. Cook, *The Dead Sea Scrolls: A New Translation* (San Francisco: HarperCollins, 1996). Perhaps the most important scholarly assessments are those by L. H. Schiffman, E. Tov, and J. C. VanderKam, eds., *The Dead Sea Scrolls: Fifty Years after Their Discovery: Proceedings of the Jerusalem Congress, July 20–25, 1997* (Jerusalem: Israel Exploration Society and Israel Antiquities Authority, 2000); and P. W. Flint and J. C. VanderKam, eds., *The Dead Sea Scrolls after Fifty Years: A*

Comprehensive Assessment (2 vols.; Boston: Brill, 1998–1999).[23] For a recent assessment of the value of the Scrolls for NT interpretation, see J. C. VanderKam and P. W. Flint, *The Meaning of the Dead Sea Scrolls: Their Significance for Understanding the Bible, Judaism, Jesus, and Christianity* (San Francisco: Harper-Collins, 2002).

Philo. Philo Judaeus of Alexandria (ca. 20 B.C.E.–50 C.E.) was a prolific writer. Although he was Jewish, his language was Greek, the principal language of his city. Most of his writings are extant, but scholars dispute whether they represent exegesis, philosophy, apologetics, or even psychology. Philo's writings probably reflect all of these interests. But his principal purpose, in my judgment, was to show that Judaism, particularly as seen in the scriptures of Judaism, constitutes a superior worldview. His allegorical exegesis should be understood in this light. Philo was not interested in what actually happened but in how the biblical story could speak to thinking persons of the Greco-Roman world. Philo carried out this purpose by interpreting the biblical stories (mostly those of the Pentateuch) in terms of neoplatonism (i.e., the view that what the physical senses perceive on earth below is but an imperfect reflection of the true and perfect reality of heaven above). Like Stoic philosophers who allegorized Homer's epics, Philo read allegorical meanings into the biblical narratives. For example, Cain is to be understood as "foolish opinion," which is to be replaced by Abel, to be understood as "good conviction" (*Sacrifices* 2 §5). Or again, when Abram was commanded to depart from his home country, the patriarch was thereby commanded to escape the prison house of his physical body and turn his thoughts God-ward (*Migration* 1–2 §1–12).

Of special interest is the relationship of Philo's exegesis to the targumic traditions of the synagogue and to the midrashic traditions of the rabbinic academies. Some scholars have attempted to relate Philo's legal interpretations (halakah) to those of the rabbis, concluding that Philo's halakic interpretation is distinctive to Alexandria.[24] Others disagree, thinking that it is in basic continuity

---

[23] A few other learned collections should be mentioned: D. Dimant and U. Rappaport, eds., *The Dead Sea Scrolls: Forty Years of Research* (STDJ 10; New York: E. J. Brill, 1992); E. Ulrich and J. C. VanderKam, eds., *The Community of the Renewed Covenant: The Notre Dame Symposium on the Dead Sea Scrolls* (CJAS 10; Notre Dame: University of Notre Dame Press, 1994); M. O. Wise, N. Golb, J. J. Collins, and D. G. Pardee, eds., *Methods of Investigation of the Dead Sea Scrolls and the Khirbet Qumran Site: Present Realities and Future Prospects* (Annals of the New York Academy of Sciences 722; New York: New York Academy of Sciences, 1994); S. E. Porter and C. A. Evans, eds., *The Scrolls and the Scriptures: Qumran Fifty Years After* (JSPSup 26; Roehampton Institute London Papers 3; Sheffield, England: Sheffield Academic Press, 1997); D. W. Parry and E. Ulrich, eds., *The Provo International Conference on the Dead Sea Scrolls: Technological Innovations, New Texts, and Reformulated Issues* (STDJ 30; Leiden: Brill, 1998).

[24] See E. R. Goodenough, *The Jurisprudence of the Jewish Courts of Egypt* (New Haven: Yale University Press, 1929; repr., Amsterdam: Philo, 1968); Isaak Heinemann, *Philons griechische und jüdische Bildung* (Breslau: M. & H. Marcus, 1932; repr., Hildesheim: Olms, 1962).

with Palestinian halakah.[25] Yet others think Philo and early Palestinian rabbis had very different interpretive intentions;[26] this may be so, but the similarities nevertheless call for explanation.

Philo's allegorical interpretation of Scripture has shed some light on the NT. Peder Borgen has shown that the use of manna tradition in John 6 coheres at many points with Philonic and early rabbinic interpretation.[27] Wayne Meeks found additional points of coherence between John and Philo (and other early Jewish materials) in their respective interpretations of Moses.[28] Hebrews is another NT writing that has often been compared to Philonic principles of interpretation.[29] Its writer's comparisons between the earthly priesthood and the heavenly, the earthly tabernacle and the heavenly, and the earthly sacrifice and the eternal are very much in step with the neoplatonic approach taken by Philo.

Bibliography. The standard critical edition of Philo's works is L. Cohn and P. Wendland, *Philonis Alexandrini opera quae supersunt* (7 vols.; Berlin: G. Reimer, 1896–1930; repr. 1962). For the Greek text and English facing pages, see F. H. Colson et al., *Philo* (12 vols.; LCL; Cambridge: Harvard University Press, 1929–1953). For a concordance, see P. Borgen, K. Fuglseth, and R. Skarsten, *The Philo Index: A Complete Greek Word Index to the Writings of Philo of Alexandria* (Boston: Brill, 2000). For critical studies, see T. H. Tobin, *The Creation of Man: Philo and the History of Interpretation* (CBQMS 14; Washington, D.C.: Catholic Biblical Association, 1983); D. T. Runia, *Philo in Early Christian Literature* (CRINT 3.3; Minneapolis: Fortress, 1993); D. M. Hay, "Defining Allegory in Philo's Exegetical World," in *SBL Seminar Papers, 1994* (ed. E. H. Lovering;

---

[25] See E. Stein, *Philo und Midrasch* (BZAW 57; Giessen: Töpelmann, 1931); Samuel Belkin, *Philo and the Oral Law* (Cambridge: Harvard University Press, 1940).

[26] S. Sandmel, *Philo's Place in Judaism: A Study of Conceptions of Abraham in Jewish Literature* (New York: Ktav, 1971). For an assessment, see the studies by R. D. Hecht, "The Exegetical Contexts of Philo's Interpretation of Circumcision," in *Nourished with Peace: Studies in Hellenistic Judaism in Memory of Samuel Sandmel* (ed. F. E. Greenspahn et al.; Scholars Press Homage Series 9; Chico, Calif.: Scholars Press, 1984) 51–79; idem, "Preliminary Issues in the Analysis of Philo's *De specialibus legibus*," *SPhilo* 5 (1979): 1–56.

[27] P. Borgen, *Bread from Heaven: An Exegetical Study of the Concept of Manna in the Gospel of John and the Writings of Philo* (NovTSup 10; Leiden: E. J. Brill, 1965; repr., 1981).

[28] W. A. Meeks, *The Prophet-King, Moses Traditions, and the Johannine Christology* (NovTSup 14; Leiden: Brill, 1967). See also A. W. Argyle, "Philo and the Fourth Gospel," *ExpTim* 63 (1951–52): 385–86; R. McL. Wilson, "Philo and the Fourth Gospel," *ExpTim* 65 (1953–54): 47–49; H. Chadwick, "St. Paul and Philo of Alexandria," *BJRL* 48 (1966): 286–307; P. Borgen, "Observations on the Targumic Character of the Prologue of John," *NTS* 16 (1970): 288–95; D. A. Hagner, "The Vision of God in Philo and John: A Comparative Study," *JETS* 14 (1971): 81–93; T. H. Tobin, "The Prologue of John and Hellenistic Jewish Speculation," *CBQ* 52 (1999): 252–69.

[29] See L. K. K. Dey, *The Intermediary World and Patterns of Perfection in Philo and Hebrews* (SBLDS 25; Missoula, Mont.: Scholars, 1975); S. Sowers, *The Hermeneutics of Philo and Hebrews: A Comparison of the Interpretation of the Old Testament in Philo Judaeus and the Epistle to the Hebrews* (Zürich: EVZ-Verlag, 1965); R. Williamson, *Philo and the Epistle to the Hebrews* (ALGHJ 4; Leiden: Brill, 1970).

SBLSP 33; Atlanta: Scholars Press, 1994), 55–68; A. A. Long, "Allegory in Philo and Etymology in Stoicism: A Plea for Drawing Distinctions," *SPhilo* 9 (1997): 198–210.

Josephus. The writings of Josephus provide us with invaluable information touching history, politics, religious ideas, Jewish sects, and biblical interpretation. Born in the year of Gaius Caligula's accession (37/38 C.E.), young Joseph ben Matthias studied Jewish law, contemplated which sect he would join (Pharisees, Sadducees, or Essenes), and visited the Roman capital. When the first war with Rome broke out (66 C.E.), Josephus (as he later calls himself) assumed command of part (or all) of Galilee. Besieged at Jotapata for forty-seven days, he surrendered to the Romans and prophesied that Vespasian, the commander of the Roman forces in Israel, would someday become the Roman emperor. When his prophecy came to pass in 69 C.E., Josephus was released from custody and was made part of the advisory council of Vespasian's son Titus. Shortly after the war ended in 70, Josephus went to Rome, where he was granted Roman citizenship. He took the name Flavius from the family name of Vespasian and Titus. In the late 70s he wrote the *Jewish War* (seven books). (An earlier version of this work, written in Aramaic, was sent to Jews of Mesopotamia to discourage them from revolt.) In the mid-90s he completed the *Jewish Antiquities* (twenty books). Shortly after 100 C.E. he published his *Life* (an appendix to the *Antiquities*) and *Against Apion* (two books). (From *Ant.* 20.12.1 §267 one may infer that much of the *Life* had been written by 93–94 C.E., although it would not be published for about another seven years.) Josephus died in the early years of the second century. All of his writings, with the exception of the earlier draft of the *Jewish War*, were originally published in Greek. Greek was not Josephus's mother tongue, but he had studied it and could with some difficulty write and speak it. He had assistance with the Greek in composing his books, as he himself explains (*Ag. Ap.* 1.9 §50).

Several topics treated in the writings of Josephus are especially relevant to NT study. His description of the religious/political sects (Pharisees, Sadducees, Essenes, and the so-called Fourth Philosophy) is of great importance (cf. *Life* 2 §10–12; *J.W.* 2.8.2–14 §§119–166; *Ant.* 18.1.2–6 §§11–23). His account of the Samaritan-Jewish hostility (*J.W.* 2.12.3 §§232–244; *Ant.* 18.2.2 §30; 20.6.1–3 §§118–136) helps us understand what the NT presupposes (Matt 10:5; Luke 9:52; 10:30–39; John 4:9; 8:48). His portrait of Pontius Pilate as insensitive and brutal is illuminating, if not somewhat gratuitous (*Ant.* 18.3.1–3 §§55–62; *J.W.* 2.9.2–4 §§169–177; cf. Philo, *Embassy* 38 §§299–305), and coheres with the NT (Luke 13:1–2; Acts 4:27). Josephus's portrait of the high priesthood reveals corruption, avarice, collaboration with Rome, and, on occasion, violence (*Ant.* 20.8.8 §181; 20.9.2 §§206–207)—details that certainly cohere with the portrait found in the Gospels and Acts (Mark 14:1, 43, 53–65; 15:1–15, 31–32; Acts 4:1–3; 5:17–18; 7:1; 8:1; 9:1–2; 23:2; 24:1). Jesus' critical stance toward the ruling priests is thus clarified (Mark 11:15–17, 27–33; 12:1–12, 38–40, 41–44). Josephus's personal prophecies (*J.W.* 3.8.3 §§351–352; 6.2.1 §109; 6.4.5 §250; 6.5.4 §311) and the prophecies of others (*J.W.* 6.5.3 §§301–309) that he records regarding the destruction of Jerusalem and the temple are instructive for comparison with Jesus' similar prophecies (Mark 13:1–2; Luke 19:41–44; 23:27–31). Finally, his description of would-be kings and prophets, his retelling of the biblical narratives, and his references to John the Baptist and Jesus provide us with useful data.

Bibliography. There are two critical editions of the writings of Josephus, one by S. A. Naber, *Flavii Josephi Opera omnia* (6 vols.; Leipzig: Teubner, 1888–1896), and another by B. Niese, *Flavii Josephi Opera* (7 vols.; Berlin: Weidmann, 1885–1895). The Greek text and an English translation are presented in H. St. J. Thackeray, R. Marcus, A. Wikgren, and L. H. Feldman, trans., *Josephus* (9 vols., LCL; Cambridge: Harvard University Press, 1926–1965). The standard concordance is K. H. Rengstorf, ed., *A Complete Concordance to Flavius Josephus* (4 vols.; Leiden: Brill, 1973–1983). For critical studies, see H. St. J. Thackeray, *Josephus: The Man and the Historian* (Hilda Stich Stroock Lectures 1; New York: Jewish Institute of Religion, 1929); S. Schwartz, *Josephus and Judaean Politics* (Columbia Studies in the Classical Tradition 18; New York: E. J. Brill, 1990); L. H. Feldman and G. Hata, eds., *Josephus, Judaism, and Christianity* (Detroit: Wayne State University Press, 1987); L. H. Feldman and G. Hata, eds., *Josephus, the Bible, and History* (Detroit: Wayne State University Press, 1989); R. Gray, *Prophetic Figures in Late Second Temple Jewish Palestine: The Evidence from Josephus* (Oxford: Oxford University Press, 1993); L. H. Feldman, *Josephus' Interpretation of the Bible* (Berkeley: University of California Press, 1998); idem, *Studies in Josephus' Rewritten Bible* (New York: Brill, 1998). For recent introductory works, see T. Rajak, *Josephus: The Historian and His Society* (Philadelphia: Fortress, 1984); P. Bilde, *Flavius Josephus between Jerusalem and Rome: His Life, His Works, and Their Importance* (JSPSup 2; Sheffield, England: JSOT Press, 1988); S. Mason, *Josephus and the New Testament* (2d ed.; Peabody, Mass.: Hendrickson, 2003). Mason is giving editorial direction to a new translation and commentary on Josephus (E. J. Brill).

Rabbinic Writings. Rabbinic writings that have relevance for the study of early Christianity fall into three categories: Targum, Talmud, and midrash. The first category was mentioned under "Aramaic," above. The writings that fall into the category of Talmud constitute the Mishnah, the Tosefta, the Jerusalem (or Palestinian) Talmud (Heb. Talmud Yerushalmi), and the Babylonian Talmud (Heb. Talmud Babli) along with its several minor tractates. The remaining writings, from *Mekilta* to *'Aggadat Esther,* fall into the category of midrash.

These rabbinic writings also fall into two broad periods of time: Tannaitic (or Tannaic) and Amoraic. The Tannaitic period was roughly from 50 B.C.E. to 200 C.E., that is, from the establishment of the early academies, Bet Shammai ("House of Shammai") and Bet Hillel ("House of Hillel"), to the compiling and editing of the Mishnah under Rabbi Judah ha-Nasi ("the Prince" or "the Patriarch"; 135–217 C.E.) in about the first decade of the third century C.E. The teachers or sages of this period are called the Tannaim ("teachers," from the Aramaic word *tana,* which literally means "to repeat"). Midway through this period, probably following Yavneh (or Jamnia; late first century C.E.), ordained sages were given the title "rabbi," which literally means "my master." Informal use of "rabbi," of course, was earlier, as seen in the NT gospels. Babylonian scholars were called "Rab." The achievement of the Tannaitic period was the production of the Mishnah. Tannaitic sayings found in later writings outside the Mishnah are called *baraitoth* (an Aramaic word literally meaning "standing outside"; sg. *baraita*). The Amoraic period was from 220 C.E. to 500 C.E. Its rabbis are called the Amoraim ("expounders" or "spokesmen," from the Aramaic word *amar*, "to say"). The achievement of the Amoraic period was the production of the two Talmuds and several of the midrashim.

The principal dangers in making use of rabbinic literature are anachronism and misleading generalization. Scholars and students must critically assess the traditions relating to events and customs said to have taken place or to have been observed during Second Temple times. At least partial corroboration is required before accepting these traditions as historically sound. Moreover, one must exercise caution regarding the attributions of sayings and teachings to various rabbinic authorities. The work of Jacob Neusner and others has made important contributions to recognizing and dealing with this problem.

Bibliography. For texts and translations of the Mishnah, see P. Blackman, *Mishnayot* (6 vols.; New York: Judaica, 1977); J. Rabbinowitz, *Mishnah Megillah* (Oxford: Oxford University Press, 1931); H. Danby, *The Mishnah* (Oxford: Clarendon, 1933); and J. Neusner, *The Mishnah: A New Translation* (New Haven: Yale University Press, 1988). For texts and translations of the Tosefta, see S. Lieberman, *Tosefot Rishonim* (4 vols.; Jerusalem: Bamberger & Wahrmann, 1936–1939); M. S. Zuckermandel, *Tosephta: Based on the Erfurt and Vienna Codices* (2d ed.; Jerusalem: Bamberger & Wahrmann, 1937); and J. Neusner, ed., *The Tosefta: Translated from the Hebrew* (6 vols.; New York: Ktav, 1977–1986; repr. 2 vols.; Peabody, Mass.: Hendrickson, 2002). For the text and a translation of the Babylonian Talmud, in the format of English-Hebrew facing pages, see I. Epstein, ed., *Hebrew-English Edition of the Babylonian Talmud* (30 vols.; London: Soncino, 1960; repr., 1990). For introductions to the rabbinic literature, see S. Safrai, ed., *The Literature of the Sages* (CRINT 2.3/1; Philadelphia: Fortress, 1987); H. L. Strack and G. Stemberger, *Introduction to the Talmud and Midrash* (Minneapolis: Fortress, 1992); and J. Neusner, *Introduction to Rabbinic Literature* (ABRL; New York: Doubleday, 1994). For liturgy and the synagogue, see I. Elbogen, *Jewish Liturgy: A Comprehensive History* (Philadelphia: Jewish Publication Society; New York: Jewish Theological Seminary of America, 1993).

New Testament Apocrypha and Early Patristic Writings. The so-called NT Apocrypha and Pseudepigrapha is a misnomer, seeming to imply that these are writings of the NT itself. In reality these are post-NT Christian apocryphal and pseudepigraphal writings, some of them dating from the Middle Ages. The earliest patristic writings are mostly found in the collection of so-called Apostolic Fathers; some are genuinely ascribed (e.g., the letters of Ignatius and *1 Clement*), whereas others are either anonymous or pseudonymous (e.g., *Barnabas*). *First Clement* may date to the end of the first century, but the others range across the second century.

The most important writings of the NT Apocrypha are the gospels, such as the Jewish gospels (esp. the *Gospel of the Nazarenes* and the *Gospel of the Ebionites*) and gospels whose fragments have been discovered in more recent times (e.g., the Egerton Papyrus, the *Gospel of Peter,* and the *Gospel of Thomas*). Scholars hotly dispute the antiquity, independence, and value of these writings. If they are early and perhaps even independent of the NT gospels (and this is highly doubtful), they could make important contributions to our understanding of the meaning and development of the canonical gospels.

The dangers of making use of early patristic and extracanonical writings are analogous to those in the case of the rabbinic literature. Some of the earliest material may contain traditions that reach back to the NT and that may be independent from the writings of the NT themselves. Accordingly, they may clarify the meaning of certain passages and themes and therefore should be taken into account.

Bibliography. For Greek texts and translations of the Apostolic Fathers, see K. Lake, *The Apostolic Fathers* (2 vols.; LCL 24–25; Cambridge: Harvard University Press, 1912–1913); also see J. B. Lightfoot, *The Apostolic Fathers: Clement, Ignatius, and Polycarp* (5 vols.; 1889–1890; repr., Peabody, Mass.: Hendrickson, 1989); J. B. Lightfoot, *The Apostolic Fathers* (ed. J. R. Harmer; New York: Macmillan, 1891). There is also an English translation, with some commentary, edited by R. M. Grant, *The Apostolic Fathers* (6 vols.; New York and Camden, N.J.: Thomas Nelson, 1964–1968); and a new edition of Lightfoot's English translation, *The Apostolic Fathers* (ed. M. W. Holmes; rev. ed.; Grand Rapids: Baker, 1989). The Hermeneia commentary series (Fortress) is producing critical commentaries on these writings. See W. R. Schoedel, *Ignatius of Antioch: A Commentary on the Letters of Ignatius of Antioch* (Hermeneia; Philadelphia: Fortress, 1985); K. Niederwimmer, *The Didache* (Hermeneia; Minneapolis: Fortress, 1998); C. Osiek, *The Shepherd of Hermas: A Commentary* (Hermeneia; Minneapolis: Fortress, 1999).

For collections, introductions, notes, and bibliography of the NT Apocrypha, see W. Wright, *Contributions to the Apocryphal Literature of the New Testament: Collected and Edited from Syriac Manuscripts in the British Museum, with an English Translation and Notes* (London: Williams & Norgate, 1865); M. R. James, *The Apocryphal New Testament* (Oxford: Clarendon, 1924; corrected ed., 1953); W. Schneemelcher, ed., *New Testament Apocrypha* (2 vols.; rev. ed.; Louisville: Westminster John Knox, 1991–1992); J. K. Elliott, *The Apocryphal New Testament: A Collection of Apocryphal Christian Literature in an English Translation Based on M. R. James* (Oxford: Clarendon, 1993). For works that tend to accept the antiquity and independence of one or more of the extracanonical gospels (esp. the *Gospel of Thomas,* the *Gospel of Peter,* the *Secret Gospel of Mark,* and the *Egerton Papyrus*), see R. Cameron, ed., *The Other Gospels: Non-canonical Gospel Texts* (Philadelphia: Westminster, 1982); J. D. Crossan, *Four Other Gospels: Shadows on the Contours of Canon* (New York: Harper & Row, 1985; repr.,

Sonoma, Calif.: Polebridge, 1992); H. Koester, *Ancient Christian Gospels: Their History and Development* (Philadelphia: Trinity Press International, 1990); R. J. Miller, ed., *The Complete Gospels* (Sonoma, Calif.: Polebridge, 1992).

The Present Work

The essays that have been collected in this volume illustrate the principles and tasks that have been outlined above. They illustrate in various ways the nature of the work that is required, the texts that must be taken into account, and the problems that must be addressed.

The first two studies explore the ways in which the Aramaic version of Scripture assists in NT interpretation. Bruce Chilton examines how the paraphrasing and interpretive tendencies in the Aramaic (i.e., the Targumim) clarify similar tendencies in the NT. Chilton defines "Targum" and then cites several examples of dictional and thematic coherence between various NT passages and the Aramaic version of the Bible. Chilton rightly argues that these examples are not instances of dependence upon the Targum (or of the Targum upon the NT) but evidence of common interpretive traditions and locutions that appear in two independent streams of literature.

Craig Evans also treats the Targum but narrows the discussion to the Aramaic Psalter and its relevance for NT interpretation. Consistent with the observations and conclusions of Chilton, Evans finds interpretive tradition common to the Aramaic and the major components of the NT, including the Gospels and the Pauline Letters. In several instances it is the Aramaic version of Scripture that clarifies the point being made in the NT, especially as it concerns the messianism of Jesus himself and the subsequent Christology articulated by others, not least the Apostle Paul.

The next two studies probe the function of OT Scripture in the infancy narratives. Rikk Watts takes into account the wider Isaianic context of Isa 7:14, the Immanuel passage, which is cited by the Matthean evangelist. He concludes that this passage, fulfilled in the birth of Jesus, conveys a warning of judgment as much as it offers a promise of salvation. Israel must repent and receive its anointed deliverer lest, as in the days of the feckless and faithless king of Judah, the nation be divided and buffeted by a series of judgments.

Robert Shedinger examines the quotation and interpretation of Mic 5:1 in Matt 2:6. The focus, however, is primarily textual and linguistic. His study turns an old issue on its head. It used to be assumed that discrepancies between NT quotations of the OT were indications of either misquotation (accidental or deliberate) or use of a faulty Greek translation of the Hebrew. But now, thanks to the Dead Sea Scrolls and other old versions, Shedinger rightly wonders if the discrepant quotations of the OT in the NT might not be witnesses to early, pre-Christian textual variants. He finds that the NT itself, in its various versions, including Tatian's *Diatessaron,* may in fact aid the task of OT textual criticism.

The next two studies probe the function of the OT in the Gospel of Luke. Simon Gathercole investigates the use and interpretation of Lev 18:5 in early Judaism and clarifies its importance for understanding the allusions to it in several NT passages. He concludes that Lev 18:5 in late antiquity was a text of major significance, informing significant beliefs about righteousness and salvation, beliefs at issue in NT passages such as Luke 10, Romans 10, and Galatians 3. Gathercole makes creative use of Philo, the Dead Sea Scrolls, the Pseudepigrapha, and rabbinic literature.

Michael Labahn explores the meaning of Isaiah 61 for Luke 7, especially in the light of the *Messianic Apocalypse* (4Q521). He calls into question the oft-heard notion that in Q there was little interest in eschatology and apocalyptic. Labahn rightly concludes that Jesus points to what is happening in his ministry as evidence of the arrival of the kingdom of God and that Jesus is saying that he is himself the tool through which God is bringing about this eschatological reality. The remarkable parallels found in the *Messianic Apocalypse,* drawn from the same Isaianic passages to which Jesus himself alludes, clarify the meaning of Jesus' reply to the imprisoned John the Baptist, pointing unmistakably to the eschatological significance of his ministry. Whereas the eschatological drama foreseen in the *Messianic Apocalypse* (and in other Qumran scrolls) is still awaited, in Jesus' ministry the drama has begun to unfold in the present time.

A. J. Droge provides our only study of the Fourth Gospel. Making interesting comparisons with Philo, he probes the link between the tradition of the unseen and unseeable God and the Fourth Evangelist's presentation of the eternal Word of God. Despite OT traditions that speak of a host of individuals who are said to have seen God (patriarchs, prophets, and others), the Fourth Evangelist declares that "no one has seen God." Droge wonders if this apparent contradiction may tell us something about the evangelist's view of Scripture—of what is authoritative Scripture and what is not or, put in another way, tells us something about the difference between the living word versus the written word. Thus, Droge's provocative study is not limited to a specific text but plunges into the larger and more complicated picture of Johannine hermeneutics and understanding of canon. If his conclusions are valid, our views of the Fourth Evangelist's assumptions about Scripture will have to be revised.

James VanderKam and James Kugel explore aspects of the OT in the book of Acts. VanderKam unpacks the OT background of the Festival of Weeks and its relevance for understanding the context and meaning of Peter's Pentecost sermon. He finds several points of agreement between Jewish traditions of the giving of the Law at Sinai and details in Acts 2. Kugel probes the exegetical context of Stephen's speech in Acts 7, in which the history of Israel is midrashically presented. He observes several points at which the summary of Israel's history is at variance with the history as recorded in either the Hebrew Bible or the Greek Bible. These departures, which at times cohere with Samaritan traditions, are often part of a midrash on Israel's sacred story.

The final two studies focus on the Pauline tradition. Brigitte Kahl offers an intriguing study of Paul's understanding of the Hagar story and its implications for membership in the Christian church, a membership composed of Jews and Gentiles. She concludes that Paul's command in Galatians to "drive out the slave" means ending the hierarchical division of humanity into superior and inferior, an idea sharply at variance with the political philosophy regnant in the Roman Empire (as is so well illustrated in Josephus's version of a speech by Agrippa).

Gary Anderson tackles the difficult passage in 1 Timothy that assigns culpability to Eve. On what grounds does the Pauline author develop this charge? The reasoning of the author cannot be understood apart from careful consideration of the Jewish traditions presupposed, especially in the pseudepigraphal *Life of Adam and Eve*. Anderson believes that the key to the argument in 1 Timothy 2 lies in this pseudepigraphon, in which Eve's culpability is emphasized.

The collection of essays is brought to a close in an epilogue by veteran scholar James Sanders, who ponders why the theme of the present book and the approaches taken by the several authors matter. Sanders reminds us that early Judaism was an expression of faith in God, in which the revelation of God, the Scriptures, were "searched" (the root meaning of *midrash*) out of the conviction that everything of importance was in them. Sanders rightly points out that, by its very authoritative nature, sacred scripture was understood to speak to the end time in a dynamic, adaptable way, all the time declaring the unity and integrity of God. In this sense it is right to say that all of Scripture is prophetic and that both Testaments, in their own ways, attempt to affirm that God is truly One.

The essays that make up this volume illuminate important aspects of NT theology and the ways in which its authors appropriated and interpreted older Scripture. May the essays also serve a heuristic purpose, suggesting approaches and methods for further fruitful study.

1

From Aramaic Paraphrase to Greek Testament

Bruce Chilton

Well-Known Cases of Similarity and the Problem of Chronology

The significance of the Targumim for appreciating Jesus and the Gospels follows naturally from an assessment of their purposes, origins, and dates. The Targumim present evidence of first importance for the way in which the Hebrew Scriptures were understood not simply among rabbis but more commonly, by the congregations for whom the Targumim were intended and by whom they were, to some extent, actually used. Insofar as what is reflected in a Targum is representative of the reception of Scripture in the first century, that targumic material is of crucial importance for any student of the NT. But care must also be taken lest the perspective of later materials be accepted uncritically as representative of an earlier period: this would result in anachronistic exegeses. In the Targumim there are clearly readings that presuppose events long after the death of Jesus. One example, from one of the earlier Targumim, is *Tg. Isa.* 53:5, in its reference to "*the sanctuary which was profaned* for our *sins, handed over* for our iniquities."[1] The Targum clearly supposes that those who hear or read its interpretation know all too well that the temple was burned and destroyed by the Romans (in 70 C.E. and 135 C.E.).

---

[1] The italics here and in other quotations are mine. The figure of the Messiah, in his association with the law, the rebuilding of the temple, and prayer in view of Israel's sin, is throughly rabbinic; see J. Ådna, "Der Gottesknecht als triumphierender und interzessorischer Messias: Die Rezeption von Jes 53 im Targum Jonathan untersucht mit besonderer Berücksichtigung des Messiasbildes," in *Die leidende Gottesknecht: Jesaja 53 und sien Wirkungsgeschichte* (ed. B. Janowski and P. Stuhlmacher; FAT 14; Tübingen: Mohr [Siebeck], 1996), 129–58. Ådna correctly agrees, however, that the Messiah in Isa 53:12 is characterized as risking his life, and to that extent an earlier interpretation may be shining through; see B. Chilton, *The Isaiah Targum: Introduction, Translation, Apparatus, and Notes* (ArBib 11; Wilmington, Del.: Glazier, 1987), 105.

A particular problem for current study is the persistent notion that a "Palestinian Targum" that substantially represents the understanding of the Hebrew Bible (HB) in the time of Jesus is somewhere extant today. At one time this was a comprehensible position because it was taken that "Palestinian Aramaic" was more ancient than "Babylonian Aramaic."[2] Today, however, the discoveries at Qumran have cast a dazzling new light on *Targum Onqelos* and *Targum Jonathan* that makes them appear more ancient in linguistic terms than was supposed sixty years ago and more similar to Aramaic as spoken in Palestine. *Targum Pseudo-Jonathan*, once taken to be the best example of "the Palestinian Targum," appears to represent a more recent tendency, not only in its language but also in its historical allusions and its form. Moreover, the present understanding of the variety of early Judaism—and particularly of the emergence of the institution of the synagogue—does not suggest that a single, authoritative tradition of rendering, such as "the Palestinian Targum," could have emerged while the temple still stood.

The difficulty of assessing the precise form of targumic tradition(s) within the first century should also make us wary of any claim that we know the dialect(s) of Aramaic current in that period. The literary remains of the language are sporadic, dialect variation was great, and there sometimes appears to have been a significant difference between the language as spoken and the language as written. For all these reasons, attempts to "retranslate" the Greek gospels into Jesus' own language are extremely speculative; when the Targumim are appealed to as antecedent (as if they could actually be dated within the period of the NT in their present form), speculation is piled upon speculation. In purely linguistic terms, it is evident that the Aramaic of Qumran, not of the Targumim or of other later sources, is the appropriate point of departure in any project of retroversion into Aramaic.

The composite nature of the Targumim is nonetheless such that, upon occasion, one may discern in them the survival of materials that did circulate in the time of Jesus and that therefore influenced his teaching and/or the memory of that teaching among the disciples who were familiar with such traditions. Leviticus 22:28 in *Pseudo-Jonathan* is an example of such a survival: "My people, children of Israel, since our father is merciful in heaven, so should you be merciful upon the earth." The expansion in the Targum is unquestionably innovative as compared with what may be read in the MT, and there is a possible echo with Luke 6:36, within the address known conventionally as the Sermon on the Plain: "Become merciful, just as your Father is also merciful." Since this compares closely with the Targum, and no other source has so far been identified, the

[2] For a classic exposition of the hypothesis, see M. McNamara, *The New Testament and the Palestinian Targum to the Pentateuch* (AnBib 27; Rome: Pontifical Biblical Institute, 1966), and *Targum and Testament: Aramaic Paraphrases of the Bible—A Light on the New Testament* (Grand Rapids: Eerdmans, 1972). The linguistic foundation of the hypothesis, which has long since eroded, was laid by P. Kahle, *The Cairo Geniza* (Oxford: Blackwell, 1959), and M. Black, *An Aramaic Approach to the Gospels and Acts* (Oxford: Blackwell, 1967; repr. Peabody, Mass.: Hendrickson, 1998).

possibility should logically be entertained that the targumic tradition was current during the first century and that it influenced Jesus. It is, of course, theoretically possible that the saying originated with Jesus and was then anonymously taken up within the Targum. Yet the statement is rhetorically more at home within Luke than in *Pseudo-Jonathan*, where it appears unmotivated. But it seems inherently unlikely that *Pseudo-Jonathan*, which of all the pentateuchal Targumim is perhaps the most influenced by a concern to guard and articulate Judaic integrity, would inadvertently convey a saying of Jesus.[3] More probably, both *Pseudo-Jonathan* and Luke's Jesus are here independently passing on wisdom of a proverbial nature: both sources convey material from the stock of folk culture. After all, the same Targum twice explains love of another person (whether an Israelite or a stranger) with the maxim "that which is hateful to you, do not do" (*Tg. Ps.-J.* Lev 19:18, 34; cf. Luke 6:31; Matt 7:12).[4] Luke shows that this stock goes back to the first century, and *Pseudo-Jonathan* shows that it continued to be replenished until the seventh century. The targumic echo is therefore most certainly not immediately the source of Jesus' statement, but it may help us to describe the nature, general type, and origin of Jesus' statement.[5]

Examples such as Lev 22:28 in *Pseudo-Jonathan* demonstrate that the Targumim might have a heuristic value in illustrating the sort of Judaism that Jesus and his followers took for granted. (The value of a source is called "heuristic" from the Greek verb εὑρίσκω, which means "to find"; the point of the designation is that one can find useful material in a document without claiming that it predates Jesus and his movement.) The example cited is a case in which a Targum just happens to be the best resource for understanding Judaism in the first century. Targumim may therefore enable us to find materials that are useful in comparison with the Gospels and the rest of the NT. Recent study has greatly increased the catalog of such instances. Later in this discussion, I will present the best-substantiated instances from that catalog.

But there are also cases in which Jesus appears to have cited a form of Scripture that is closer to the Targum than to any other extant source. In such cases, an awareness of the fact helps us to understand better his preaching in a much more specific way than the general similarity between Luke and *Pseudo-Jonathan*

---

[3] At a stage later than the willingness to use this paraphrase, the Jerusalem Talmud discourages the usage, perhaps with an awareness that it had been co-opted within Christianity. See *y. Ber.* 5.3 (9c); *y. Meg.* 4.9 (75c); and the discussion in M. McNamara, *Palestinian Judaism and the New Testament* (GNS 4; Wilmington, Del.: Glazier, 1983), 218–19.

[4] There is also a well-established connection with *b. Šabb.* 31a. For a discussion of the question, see B. Chilton and J. I. H. McDonald, *Jesus and the Ethics of the Kingdom* (BFT; Grand Rapids: Eerdmans, 1988), 8; for further texts, see A. Díez Macho, *Neophyti 1: Targum palestinense Ms de la Biblioteca Vaticana* (5 vols.; Madrid: Consejo Superior de Investigaciones Científicas, 1968–1978), 3:502–3.

[5] A similar claim can be made for the use of the phrase "high priests" in *Pseudo-Jonathan* (e.g., Lev 16:1), which shows that the plural usage in the NT is no error. See M. Maher, *Targum Pseudo-Jonathan—Leviticus: Translated, with Notes* (ArBib 3; Collegeville, Minn.: Liturgical Press, 1994), 165.

illustrates. *Targum Isaiah* 6:9–10 is an especially famous example, and it helps to explain Mark 4:11–12. The statement in Mark could be taken to mean that Jesus told parables with the purpose that (ἵνα) people might see and not perceive, hear and not understand, lest they turn and be forgiven:

> And he was saying to them, "To you the mystery has been given of the kingdom of God, but to those outside, everything comes in parables, so that [ἵνα] while seeing they see and do not perceive, and while hearing they hear and do not understand, lest they repent and it be forgiven them."

The Targum also (unlike the MT and the LXX) refers to people not being "forgiven" (rather than not being "healed"), and this suggests that the Targum may give the key to the meaning supposed in Mark. The relevant clause in the Targum refers to people who behave *in such a way*—"so that" (*d* in Aramaic)— they see and do not perceive, hear and do not understand, lest they repent and they be forgiven. It appears that Jesus was characterizing people in the targumic manner, as he characterizes his own fate similarly in Mark with a clause employing ἵνα (cf. 9:12), not acting in order to be misunderstood.

In this famous case from Mark,[6] then, the underlying Aramaism of using the clause with Aramaic *d* caused the saying of Jesus to use the term ἵνα in Greek, which may mean "in order that" or "so that." If the former meaning obtains, Mark's Jesus speaks so as not to be understood and in order deliberately to preclude the forgiveness of those who do not understand. If the latter meaning obtains, then Jesus referred to Isaiah in its targumic form in order to characterize the kind of people who do not respond to his message, and what happens to them. The fact of the similarity in wording with the Targum shows us that the second meaning is preferable, as does the fact that Jesus elsewhere in Mark refers to *his own followers* as being hard-hearted, with unseeing eyes and unseeing ears (Mark 8:17–18). His point in alluding once again to Isaiah 6 is given at the end of the rebuke: "Do you not yet understand?" (Mark 8:21). Jesus' citation of Isaiah 6 in its targumic form was intended to rouse hearers to understanding, not to make their misunderstanding into his own program.

The two examples given above, taken from *Targum Pseudo-Jonathan* and *Targum Isaiah,* instance cases in which the similarity between the NT and the Targumim is a matter of shared wording and meaning, and even a common exegesis of Scripture with that shared wording and meaning. But there is another type of similarity that is much broader than wording or meaning, involving a

---

6 See T. W. Manson, *The Teaching of Jesus* (Cambridge: Cambridge University Press, 1955), 76–80; B. Chilton, *A Galilean Rabbi and His Bible: Jesus' Own Interpretation of Isaiah* (London: SPCK, 1984), 90–98; C. A. Evans, *To See and Not Perceive: Isaiah 6.9–10 in Early Jewish and Christian Interpretation* (JSOTSup 64; Sheffield, England: JSOT Press, 1989). A recent attempt by Michael Goulder to deny the similarity between Jesus' saying and *Targum Isaiah* is refuted in B. Chilton and C. A. Evans, "Jesus and Israel's Scriptures," in *Studying the Historical Jesus: Evaluations of the State of Current Research* (ed. B. Chilton and C. A. Evans; NTTS 19; New York: E. J. Brill, 1995), 281–335, 300–304. Cf. M. D. Goulder, "Those Outside (Mk. 4:10–12)," *NovT* 33 (1991): 289–302.

common presentation. Time and again, the Targumim present a synoptic relationship among their materials.

At Gen 4:8, an argument breaks out—in the Cairo Genizah fragments, *Targum Pseudo-Jonathan, Targum Neofiti,* and the *Fragmentary Targum*—between Cain and Abel before the primal murder by Cain. In all these Targumim from the rabbinic center in Tiberias, the two brothers dispute whether God was just in preferring the offering of Abel to that of Cain. The wording of the dispute is comparable in the four versions, but there is also complex diversity among them. And what is most striking, in comparison with the synoptic relationship among the first three Gospels, is that the order of the dispute differs from Targum to Targum.

In the "Poem of the Four Nights," a liturgical hymn associated with keeping Passover, the Tiberian Targumim present the night of the exodus (Exod 12:32) as the third in the sequence of four great divine acts: the creation, the call of Abraham, the exodus, and the redemption that is to come. This order, and the scriptural references associated with it, remains rather constant, but the radical abbreviation—or expansion, from the opposite point of view—in comparison with material in the Synoptic Gospels is notable.

The Aqedah (Genesis 22 in the Palestinian Targumim and Isa 33:7 in the margin of Codex Reuchlinianus) also presents features comparable to synopticity in the Gospels.[7] Because the synopticity of the Targumim is evinced among four documents, not three (as in the Gospels), it is even more complicated to trace a purely documentary, rigidly literary relationship among the texts. The study of the synoptic aspect of the Targumim remains in its infancy, but it appears possible that once it is better understood, we will conceive of the literary relationship among the Gospels in a different way.

The Targumim are a rich source of that form of early Judaism and rabbinic Judaism where the folk and the expert aspects of the religion met. For this reason, serious students of the NT might well read them so as to comprehend the context within which Jesus taught and his movement first developed, before the transition to a Hellenistic compass and the Greek language. In particular cases, the Targumim uniquely present material that helps to illuminate Jesus' teaching. (In other instances, they may support what we know from other sources.) It might be that a Targum just happens to preserve proverbial material that Jesus cites or alludes to. But there are also cases in which Jesus seems to have been influenced by a specifically targumic understanding of the Bible. Finally, quite apart from what they may tell us of particular passages in the Gospels, the Targumim give us an example of how composite documents evolved within Judaism and to that extent they may provide an analogy for understanding the Gospels themselves.

---

[7] For the study of such cases, see B. Chilton, *Profiles of a Rabbi: Synoptic Opportunities in Reading about Jesus* (BJS 177; Atlanta: Scholars Press, 1989); *Targumic Approaches to the Gospels: Essays in the Mutual Definition of Judaism and Christianity* (Studies in Judaism; Lanham and London: University Press of America, 1986); and *Judaic Approaches to the Gospels* (International Studies in Formative Judaism and Christianity 2; Atlanta: Scholars Press, 1994).

Four Types of Comparison between the Targumim and the New Testament, and the Assessment of Analogies

The examples cited above, with a bit of supplementation, provide us with illustrations of the four main types of affinity between the NT and the Targumim that are cataloged in this chapter. Once I have explained the types and the principles for distinguishing among them, we can then proceed, in the third section of this discussion, to a catalog of texts.

The first type is of the most stringent sort of affinity. Here there must be evidence of comparable material with cognate wording, associated with the same text of Scripture. The comparison between Isaiah 6 in the Targum and its citation in Mark 4:12, discussed above, provides an instance of the first type. A weaker instance of the first type of comparison is when the NT and a Targum share wording but there is no particular reason to assume that the wording arose as an interpretation of a biblical passage. The example of Lev 22:28 in its relationship to Luke 6:36 (see above) instances a weaker case of an analogy of this first type.

The second type of affinity does not include the sharing of explicit wording, but it does presuppose a comparable understanding of the same biblical passage in the Targumim and the NT. An example is Jesus' parable of the Vineyard in Matt 21:33–46; Mark 12:1–12; and Luke 20:9–19. After he has told his story of the abuse suffered by those the owner sends to acquire his share of the vintage, the Synoptic Gospels agree that the opposition to Jesus among the Jewish authorities hardened to the point that they wanted to seize him. When the symbolism of the vineyard in *Tg. Isa.* 5:1–7 is considered, the opposition to Jesus becomes easily explicable. There the vine is a primary symbol of the temple, so that the tenants of Jesus' parable are readily identified with the leadership of the temple. They knew he was telling the parable against them.[8]

It is apparent that the second type of affinity is not as strong as the first. Because wording is not shared, the connection between the Targumim and the NT is not as demonstrable. Moreover, an image such as the vineyard is so resonant that several biblical passages may be used to illustrate and/or understand it. Nonetheless, when a given passage in a Targum permits us to appreciate more clearly the text of the NT, this is an affinity that should not be ignored.

In the third type of affinity, characteristically targumic phrases appear within the NT. The best example is the central category of Jesus' theology: the kingdom of God, which also appears in the form "kingdom of the Lord" in the Targumim (see *Tg. Onq.* Exod 15:18; *Tg. Isa.* 24:23; 31:4; 40:9; 52:7; *Tg. Ezek.* 7:7;

---

[8] See Chilton, *Galilean Rabbi*, 111–14; "Jesus and Israel's Scriptures," 304–6. The importance of the targumic contribution is missed in J. S. Kloppenborg Verbin, "Egyptian Viticultural Practices and the Citation of Isa 5:1–7 in Mark 12:1–9," *NovT* 44 (2002): 134–59. See the reply by C. A. Evans, "How Septuagintal Is Isa 5:1–7 in Mark 12:1–9?" *NovT* 45 (2003): 105–10.

Tg. Obad. 21; *Tg. Zech.* 14:9).[9] The first usage in *Targum Isaiah* (24:23) associates the theologoumenon of the kingdom of God with God's self-revelation on Mount Zion, where his appearance is to occasion a feast for all nations (see 25:6–8). The association of the kingdom with a festal image is comparable to Jesus' promise in Matt 8:11 and Luke 13:28–29 that many will come from the ends of the earth to feast with Abraham, Isaac, and Jacob in the kingdom of God.

In the fourth type of affinity, the NT and the Targumim share a thematic emphasis. Just as the second type of affinity is less substantial than the first, so the fourth is less demonstrable than the third, and for much the same reason. Comparability of wording is not at issue; rather, the less obvious question of themes is in play. Jesus, for example, lamented the persistent refusal to listen to the prophets (Matt 5:12; Luke 6:23); the *meturgeman* (Aramaic, "interpreter, translator") of Isaiah also lamented that "with *odd speech* and *mocking* tongue this people *were scoffing at the prophets who prophesied to them*" (*Tg. Isa.* 28:11). Although the relationship with the targumic interpretation may be helpful in understanding Jesus' perspective, since the Targum at Isaiah 28 is pointed in its condemnation of cultic abuses (as Jesus famously was), it must be born in mind that abuse by the prophets is a topos within the Judaism of the period.[10]

Comparisons of the First Type

"Lest It Be Forgiven Them"

In the case of *Targum Isaiah,* the relationship between Isa 6:9–10 and Mark 4:11–12 has already been discussed above. There it became apparent that Jesus' usage was designed to characterize the attitude of those who were so dense when it came to seeing and hearing that forgiveness was not theirs. Characteristically, Jesus directed such warnings to people who were trying to listen to him, such as his own disciples (cf. Mark 8:17–18).

Unquestionably, however, the present setting of Mark 4:11–12 gives Jesus' statement a fresh, rather elitist meaning. The initial setting is revealed in the claim that Jesus directs to "those around him with the Twelve": that the mystery of the kingdom has been given to them whereas "to those outside everything happens in parables" (Mark 4:10–11). Here the understanding of Jesus' teaching is restricted, so that what was originally a rebuke of dense hearers (including disciples) becomes the warrant for the exclusive possession of the "mystery" by a select few. The term "mystery" appears only here in the Gospels, but it is found rather frequently in the Pauline corpus (taking this designation in its broad

---

[9] For the comparable phrasing, "of the Lord is the kingship," see Exod 15:18 in *Neofiti,* an evident analogy of the statement in *Targum Onqelos.* McNamara has argued for a particular relationship with Rev 4:2–11 in *The New Testament,* 204–8.

[10] See O. H. Steck, *Israel und das gewaltsame Geschick der Propheten: Untersuchungen zur Überlieferung des deuteronomistischen Geschichtsbildes im Alten Testament, Spätjudentum, und Urchristentum* (WMANT 23; Neukirchen-Vluyn: Neukirchener Verlag, 1967).

sense), and in the Revelation of John. This fact comports with another: the reference to people who do not belong to the movement as "those outside" fits with the usage of later Christianity (see 1 Cor 5:11–13; 1 Thess 4:12; Col 4:5).

The probable source of Jesus' saying in its present context is the circle around James, Jesus' brother, in Jerusalem. This would account for several factors: (1) the Aramaism with its targumic source, (2) the reference to "those around Jesus" *before* the Twelve, and (3) the exclusive claim to interpret and apply the teaching of Jesus. The last trait is expressly attributed to James in the Acts of the Apostles (15:13–29) when he adjudicates the dispute over whether circumcision was necessary, along with baptism, for salvation (see Acts 15:1). His decision, which is presented as his own judgment, is that the uncircumcised must observe certain basic rules of purity out of loyalty to the Law of Moses. The meeting of the leaders who are present endorses this judgment and demands by letter that uncircumcised Christians in Antioch follow the policy. In Mark 4:10–12 also, the claim exclusively to interpret is deployed.

The Sword

"All those who grasp a sword will perish by a sword" (Matt 26:52): the sword, like the measure (see below), seems to have been a proverbial figure. In *Tg. Isa.* 50:11, it is applied quite graphically:[11] "Behold, all you who kindle a fire, *who grasp a sword!* Go, *fall in the* fire *which you kindled* and on the *sword which you grasped!*" A link to the passage in Isaiah (or any passage of Scripture) cannot be demonstrated in Jesus' saying, so the correspondence seems to be of the proverbial type, like the saying about the measure. Nonetheless, the close agreement in wording and imagery makes this a comparison of the first type.

Gehenna

The final verse of *Targum Isaiah* clearly identifies who will suffer where at the end of time: "*the wicked* shall be *judged in gehenna until the righteous will say concerning them, 'We have seen enough'*" (66:24). Gehenna is what Jesus associates with the phrase "their worm will not die and their fire will not be quenched" (Mark 9:48; see vv. 44, 46 in many MSS), which is taken from the same verse of Isaiah.[12] The term "gehenna" refers, in a literal sense, to the valley of Hinnom in the Kidron Valley, just across from the temple in Jerusalem. But because idolatrous human sacrifice by fire had occurred there (see 2 Kgs 16:3; 21:6), King Josiah deliberately destroyed and desecrated the site as part of his cultic reform during the seventh century B.C.E. (see 2 Kgs 23:10). As a result, gehenna came to be known as the place of the definitive punishment of the wicked.

---

[11] The similarity has been recognized for some time; for a discussion, see Chilton, *Galilean Rabbi*, 98–101.

[12] In the Targum, the first part of the phrase reads, "their *breaths* will not die." For a discussion of the passage, see ibid., 101–7.

Apart from Jas 3:6, the term appears only in sayings of Jesus in the NT. Otherwise only the Pseudepigrapha (especially *Enoch*) and rabbinic literature provide us with examples of the usage from the NT period so that we can see what the usage means. Gehenna is the place of fiery torment for the wicked. But it is not known as such in the LXX, Josephus, or even Philo;[13] evidently, the usage is at home in an Aramaic environment. Rabbi Akiba also is said to have associated gehenna with the end of the book of Isaiah (see *m. ʿEd.* 2:10): "The judgment of the wicked in gehinnom lasts twelve months, as it is said (Isa 66:23), 'And it shall be from new moon to new moon.'" Akiba, however, refers to punishment in gehenna having a limit of twelve months;[14] for Jesus, as in *Targum Isaiah*, part of the threat of gehenna was that its limit could not be determined in advance. "The correspondence between the Targumic Gehinnam, both the term and the concept, and the New Testament Gehinna is particularly close."[15]

Jannes and Jambres

Martin McNamara has pointed out that the names Jannes and Jambres are given to the sorcerers who opposed Moses in *Pseudo-Jonathan* at Exod 7:11–12, just as we might expect to find on the basis of the reference to them in 2 Tim 3:8–9.[16] In a searching criticism, Lester Grabbe has objected that the Greek form of the names in the Targum shows that "the form known to us is at least as late as the 7th century."[17] To his mind, this refutes McNamara's two principal contentions, (1) that there was a "Palestinian Targum" extant during the first century and (2) that the names given in 2 Timothy correspond only to that Targum. On this basis, Grabbe goes on to conclude, "*Ergo,* McNamara's arguments, according to his own criteria, are totally irrelevant in this particular case." Grabbe grants that his argument may appear "facetious," although its harshness seems little to do with humor.

The reason for the heat of his finding is that Grabbe wishes to join the criticism of the assumption of "the Palestinian Targum" in the first century.

---

[13] See D. F. Watson, "Gehenna," *ABD* 2:926–28.

[14] Why twelve months, and not one month? Akiba seems to be thinking of the new moon of Passover in particular.

[15] K. J. Cathcart and R. P. Gordon, *The Targum of the Minor Prophets* (ArBib 14; Wilmington, Del.: Glazier, 1989), 133, citing *Tg. Nah.* 1:8, *Tg. Ps.* 88:13, and the many uses in the Gospels. They are particularly struck by the emphasis on gehenna as a place of darkness, as in *Tg. Ps.* 88:13 and Matt 8:12. C. Mangan, *The Targum of Job* (ArBib 15; Collegeville, Minn.: Liturgical Press, 1991), 27 n. 15, notes the frequent usage of the term in *Targum Job,* the most striking case perhaps being "fire *of gehenna*" in 20:26 (cf. Matt 5:22); see also M. Maher, *Targum Pseudo-Jonathan—Genesis: Translated, with Introduction and Notes* (ArBib 1B; Collegeville, Minn.: Liturgical Press, 1992), 30. But gehenna can also be cold in *Targum Job* (e.g., 28:5; 38:23) and can refer to how one feels (17:6) at the point of death (5:4; 38:17); these are quite evolved images.

[16] See McNamara, *The New Testament,* 83–85.

[17] L. L. Grabbe, "The Jannes/Jambres Tradition in Targum Pseudo-Jonathan and Its Date," *JBL* 98 (1979): 400.

That is why the Greek form of the names (for Yochanan and Mamre in Hebrew or Aramaic) strikes him as so telling. But once it is granted that the sharing of the names does not prove the existence of any such thing as "the Palestinian Targum," the simple fact of the similarity remains. And although the first name in the pair appears in the *Damascus Document* from Qumran (CD 5:17–19) and Pliny the Elder (*Nat.* 30.2.11), both extant in the first century, the two names together prove more elusive. Eusebius, the church historian of the fourth century, in *Praep. ev.* 9.8.1 quotes Numenius, a second-century Greek writer, as referring to them, and the Babylonian Talmud includes a reference (*b. Menah.* 85a), but in neither case is there a close fit with the passage in Exodus or 2 Timothy. Unless one were to argue that 2 Timothy has influenced *Pseudo-Jonathan,* the similarity would incline one to the view that the naming of the two sorcerers is not the invention of 2 Timothy but is grounded in a contemporary tradition in Greek and perhaps in Aramaic. At the same time, it is evident that the further tradition in *Pseudo-Jonathan,* according to which Jannes and Jambres successfully interpreted Pharaoh's dream as referring to Moses' birth (*Tg. Ps.-J.* Exod 1:15), is a later development.[18]

Comparisons of the Second Type

The similarity between the synoptic parable of the Vineyard and the song of the vineyard in *Tg. Isa.* 5 has already been discussed. It is worth noting in addition, however, that both Matthew (21:33) and Mark (12:1) allude to Isa 5:2 when they refer to a hedge set around the vineyard. Their allusion is to the LXX version of Isa 5:2, so that any conscious awareness of the Targum at the time of the composition of these Gospels cannot be claimed. The point is rather that the memory of allusion to Isaiah 5 is preserved; what the targumic version of Isaiah explains, while other versions do not, is why the priestly opposition to Jesus would feel particularly engaged by his parable.

In his Letter to the Galatians, Paul uses the phrase "hanging upon a tree" in order to describe Jesus' execution. The wording itself comes from Deut 21:23, and Paul applies it to argue that, in being crucified, Jesus was subject to the curse of "everyone who hangs upon a tree" (Gal 3:13, which follows the LXX in its wording). The argument assumes that crucifixion carries with it some sanction of Judaic law. This is just what we find in *Targum Ruth* when Naomi says, *"We have four kinds of death for the guilty: stoning with stones, burning with fire, execution by the sword, and hanging upon a tree"* (1:17). Derek Beattie observes the contradiction of the Mishnah (cf. *Sanh.* 7:1) in equating crucifixion with the punishment envisaged in Deuteronomy. This is

---

[18] And here the general agreement with the positive evaluation in Numenius is perhaps telling. The relevant texts are set out by McNamara and in a summary form by Grabbe.

a principal support for his suggestion of "an ancient origin, at least for that part of the Targum."[19]

The argument is vitiated by the severe criticism recently leveled at any form of the assertion that a statement appearing to be anti-mishnaic in content must be pre-mishnaic in origin. After all, the logic of midrash may explore almost any exegetical and historical possibility, precisely because it is not identified with halakic authority. And *Targum Ruth* is midrashic in nature. But Beattie's insight can be supported by reference to what Paul says. After all, here is an indisputably first-century usage in which the midrashic connection between crucifixion and Deut 21:23 is explicitly made. Taken together, Galatians and *Targum Ruth* show us that this connection is indeed as ancient as Beattie suggests and that Paul was making an argument that was within the idiom of midrashic possibility.[20]

Comparisons of the Third Type

Mention has already been made of *Targum Isaiah*'s usage of the phrase "kingdom of God." Influence of such a usage on Jesus would help to account for one of the most striking features of Jesus' theology: his insistence that the kingdom is a dynamic, even violent intervention in human affairs.[21] *Targum Isaiah* provides a theological precedent for the usage that Jesus developed further.

The MT develops a picture of the Lord descending upon Mount Zion as a lion that is not afraid of the shepherds who attempt to protect the prey. *Targum Isaiah* (31:4) explicitly applies this arresting image to the kingdom:

> As *a* lion, *a* young lion *roars* over its prey, and, when a band of shepherds *are appointed* against it, it is not *broken up* at their shouting or *checked* at their *tumult*, so *the kingdom of* the Lord of hosts will *be revealed to settle* upon *the* Mount *of* Zion and upon its hill.

This passage simply refutes the outworn generalization that the kingdom within Judaic usage was static in nature and that the dynamic aspect was Jesus' innovation. The kingdom's dynamism was not original with Jesus; his particular contribution was his portrayal of how the kingdom comes.

Targum Job speaks of God making the righteous sit "upon the throne *of his kingdom with established* kings" (36:7), in a way that invites comparison with Luke 22:28–30 and Matt 19:28. Here the motif of entry into the kingdom and joint reign with the just is clearly articulated. Stress upon the ethical conditions that make entry into the kingdom possible was characteristic of Jesus' message (see Matt 19:16–30 as a whole, with its parallels).

---

[19] See D. R. G. Beattie, *The Targum of Ruth: Translated, with Introduction, Apparatus, and Notes* (ArBib 19; Collegeville, Minn.: Liturgical Press, 1994).

[20] In the same letter, Paul alludes to the idea that the Torah was mediated by angels (Gal 3:19; cf. Acts 5:53 and, e.g., *Tg. 1 Chron.* 29:11), although he then uses that well-known motif to suggest that the Law is derivative in its authority (Gal 3:20–29).

[21] For a full discussion, see Chilton, *Pure Kingdom: Jesus' Vision of God* (Studies in the Historical Jesus 1; Grand Rapids: Eerdmans, 1996).

"With *the* measure you *were measuring with they will measure you*" appears in *Tg. Isa.* 27:8; a saying of Jesus' is strikingly similar: "In the measure you measure it shall be measured you" (Matt 7:2; Mark 4:24). The measure in *Targum Isaiah,* however, is applied to a single figure, the oppressor of Jacob, rather than to a general group, as in Jesus' saying. A similar aphorism, crafted in the third person, was common in rabbinic literature (see, e.g., *b. Soṭah* 8b and *Tg. Ps.-J.* Gen 38:25),[22] so we have here a proverb in Aramaic that Jesus and a *meturgeman* of Isaiah both happened to use.[23] This is a case in which, despite close verbal agreement, no case for dependence can be made one way or the other.

Other usages from *Targum Isaiah* may be mentioned under the category of comparisons of the third type. The phrase "mammon of deceit" in *Targum Isaiah* (cf. 5:23; 33:15) is certainly not unique within rabbinic or Judaic usage,[24] but *Tg. 1 Sam.* 8:3; 12:3; *Tg. 2 Sam.* 14:14; and *Tg. Isa.* 5:23; 33:15 provide an analogy with Jesus' usage in the parable of the Unjust Steward (cf. Luke 16:9), because in all those cases bribery is at issue. In any case, "mammon" is a shared usage between Jesus and the Targumim.[25] "*The people inquire of their idols, the living from the dead*" is a turn of phrase that is an obvious rebuke in the Targum (8:19), and it may be echoed in the pointed question to the women at the tomb of Jesus (Luke 24:5).

Also in Luke, Jesus cites in a synagogue (4:18–19) what appears to be a passage from Isaiah 61, but it turns out to be a mixture of several passages or themes from the book of Isaiah. Among them is Isaiah 42, which in the Targum (42:3, 7) especially refers to the poor, the blind, and prisoners, who are pointedly mentioned in Jesus' "citation." At the time of Jesus' baptism, a voice is said to attest that God "is well pleased" with him (so Matt 3:17; Mark 1:11; Luke 3:22). In *Targum Isaiah,* God is said to be well pleased with Israel or Jacob (41:8–9; see also 43:20; 44:1) and the Messiah (43:10), whereas the MT speaks only of God's choice of such figures. Similarly, the idiom that there is (or is not) "pleasure before" God is shared by the Gospels (Matt 18:14) and the Targumim (for example, *Tg. Zeph.* 1:12).[26] Paul portrays "the scribe" in particular as led astray by the wisdom of God (1 Cor 1:20–21), and in this portrayal he agrees with *Targum Isaiah* (3:1–3) as well as with *Targum Jonathan* more generally.

Céline Mangan has helpfully observed that it is specifically "*new* wine" that splits wineskins in *Tg. Job* 32:19, and this invites comparison with Jesus' saying in

---

[22] For a discussion, see Maher, *Targum Pseudo-Jonathan—Genesis,* 130.

[23] For other instances and further discussion, see Chilton, *Galilean Rabbi,* 123–25.

[24] See ibid., 117–23.

[25] See Cathcart and Gordon, *Minor Prophets,* 40, 152, also citing *Tg. Hab.* 2:9, *Tg. Jer.* 6:13, and Matt 6:24; Luke 16:9, 11, 13; Mangan, *Targum of Job,* 6, citing *Tg. Job* 22:3; 27:8.

[26] See Cathcart and Gordon, *Minor Prophets,* 167. On p. 190 they come to the conclusion that the usage is so ubiquitous that "it is very unlikely . . . that there is theological significance in *Tg.*'s less than literal rendering." The present point is not theological but regards the turn of phrase in itself.

Matt 9:17, Mark 2:22, and Luke 5:37. The underlying image is already similar to the MT, and Mangan herself comments that the wine is also "new" in Symmachus (the Judaic rendering of the second century).[27] But the agreement between the Targum and the Gospels is nonetheless well worth noting. Similarly, the phrase *"flesh and blood"* is used innovatively in *Targum Job* (in MS 110 of the Bibliothèque Nationale) to refer to human beings and their limited knowledge (37:20, within the speech of Elihu). Mangan notes this and the similar usage in Matt 16:17 and *1 Enoch* 15:4.[28] But she does not mention that the following chapter (*Tg. Job* 38:17, the LORD's reply to Job) poses the question, *"Is it possible* that the gates of death have been revealed to you, or have you seen the gates of *the shadow of death of Gehenna?"* When Peter is told in Matt 16:17–18 that "flesh and blood" has not revealed the identity of Jesus to him and that "Hades' gates" will not prevail against the church of which he is the rock (*kefa'* in Aramaic), this may be taken to be a comparable usage of imagery. Similarly, these echoes join the resonance of the passage with *Tg. Isa.* 22:22, where shutting and opening are made into specifically priestly functions.[29]

It is interesting that some of the later Targumim contain phrases that echo usages of the NT. Other examples include the statement that Jacob kept the dreaming of Joseph *"in his heart"* (*Tg. Ps.-J.* Gen 37:11), which is reminiscent of Luke 2:51,[30] and the use of the verbs "releasing" and "forgiving" as synonyms (see *Tg. Neof.* Gen 4:7, 13 and Matt 16:19; 18:18; John 20:23).[31] Although no direct connection, one way or the other, with the NT can be claimed, it is striking that in *Tg. Ps.-J.* Exod 10:28 Pharaoh tells Moses, *"I will deliver you into the hands of those who were seeking your life"*—phrasing that Michael Maher compares with the prediction of Jesus' death in Mark 9:31.[32] Maher also observes that the phrase *"high priests"* (in the plural) appears in *Pseudo-Jonathan* (at Lev 16:1), as it does in the NT.[33] Such cases are reminders that the Targumim, like rabbinic literature as a

---

[27] Mangan, *Targum of Job*, 73.

[28] Ibid., 83.

[29] See B. Chilton, "Shebna, Eliakim, and the Promise to Peter," in *Targumic Approaches to the Gospels*, 63–80; repr., in *The Social World of Formative Christianity and Judaism* (ed. J. Neusner, P. Borgen, E. S. Frerichs, and R. Horsley; Philadelphia: Fortress, 1989), 311–26.

[30] See Maher, *Targum Pseudo-Jonathan*, 125. He also points out (p. 39) that the positive reference to Noah's *"good works"* at Gen 6:9 in both *Targum Neofiti* and *Targum Pseudo-Jonathan* is reminiscent of Eph 2:10 and Titus 2:14.

[31] See M. McNamara, *Targum Neofiti 1—Genesis: Translated, with Apparatus and Notes* (ArBib 1A; Collegeville, Minn.: Liturgical Press, 1992), 66. See also Lev 4:20, 31; 5:10, 13, 16, 18, 26; 19:22, cited in M. McNamara and R. Hayward, *Targum Neofiti 1—Leviticus: Translated with Apparatus, Introduction, and Notes* (ArBib 3; Collegeville, Minn.: Liturgical Press, 1994), 10.

[32] See M. Maher, *Targum Pseudo-Jonathan—Exodus: Translated, with Notes* (ArBib 2; Collegeville, Minn.: Liturgical Press, 1994), 188.

[33] Maher, *Targum Pseudo-Jonathan—Leviticus*, 165 (citing Matt 2:4; 16:21; 21:15). It should be noted, however, that Josephus also reflects the usage; see B. Chilton, "Judaism," *DJG* 398–405.

whole, may illuminate the language and imagery of the NT, even at the remove of several centuries. As we have already seen, Lev 19:18 includes the negative form of the golden rule in *Pseudo-Jonathan,* which is attributed to Hillel in *b. Šabb.* 31a and is frequently compared to the teaching of Jesus, and *Tg. Neof.* Num 24:3 says of Balaam that *"what has been hidden from all the prophets has been revealed to him"* (see Matt 13:17; Luke 10:24).[34]

The Gospel according to John has not featured prominently in discussion of possible affinity with the Targumim, but McNamara has called attention to a notable convergence. The phrasing of Jesus' promise in John 14:2, that he goes "to prepare a place" for his followers, is similar to the general theme expressed in the pentateuchal Targumim that God or his Shekinah prepares for Israel a place of encampment or rest. As McNamara points out, the usage renders a variety of Hebrew terms in the MT and should therefore be seen as characteristically targumic.[35] The usage in John is not sufficiently specific to make the targumic connection more than possible, but the convergence remains notable.

Comparisons of the Fourth Type

Jesus shared with the Judaic tradition, including *Targum Isaiah,* the theme of the consequences of not attending to the voice of the prophets, but Jesus also formulated a demand based on the unique experience of his followers (Matt 13:17; cf. Luke 10:24): "Amen I say to you that many prophets and just people wished to see what you see and did not see, and hear what you hear and did not hear." *Targum Isaiah* (48:6a) also reflects this conviction that a fresh experience of God demands a new response: "You have heard: *has what is revealed to you been revealed to* any *other people;* and will you not declare it?" Obviously, no case for dependence can be made here, but the thematic coherence is nonetheless worthy of note.[36]

Similarly, *Targum Isaiah* speaks of *"the righteous, who desire teaching as a* hungry *person desires bread,* and *the words of the law, which they desire as a* thirsty *person desires water"* (32:6). This interpretation of hunger and thirst is reminiscent of the Matthean Jesus, who blesses those who hunger and thirst after righteousness (see Matt 5:6). The comparison does not extend to the Lukan Jesus (cf. Luke 6:21), and this raises the possibility that the present wording in Matthew was shaped during the course of transmission along the lines of targumic interpretation. Similarly,

---

34 So M. McNamara, *Targum Neofiti 1—Numbers: Translated, with Apparatus and Notes* (ArBib 4; Collegeville, Minn.: Liturgical Press, 1995), 136. But might this be a case of anti-Christian polemic?

35 He first called attention to the usage in *Targum Neofiti* Exodus in McNamara, *Targum and Testament,* 88–89, but then observed that it is also characteristic of *Onqelos, Pseudo-Jonathan,* the *Fragmentary Targum,* and even the Peshitta; see M. McNamara, " 'To Prepare a Resting-Place for You': A Targumic Expression and John 14:2f.," *Mils* 3 (1979): 100–108. He especially cites their renderings of Num 10:33 (regarding the ark) and Deut 1:33.

36 As already mentioned, the similar phrasing associated with Balaam in *Targum Neofiti* may or may not be relevant.

Craig A. Evans has suggested that the Targum's association of the lame with sinners and exiles might illuminate Matt 21:14–15 (see 2 Sam 5:8; Zeph 3:19; Isa 35:6; Mic 4:6–8, all in *Targum Jonathan*).[37] The statement "Blessed are you, the righteous" in *Tg. 2 Sam.* 23:4 might also be mentioned. Robert Hayward has observed a similar comparison, citing *Tg. Jer.* 23:28b: *"Behold, just as one separates* the straw *from the* grain, *so one separates the wicked from the righteous,* says the LORD." The image appears both in the preaching of John the Baptist (Matt 3:12) and in a parable of Jesus (Matt 13:30).[38] But the statement by John also appears in Luke 3:17, so a purely Matthean usage cannot be claimed; still, a compositional pattern manifested more clearly in Matthew than in any other gospel is evident. Perhaps even more striking is the phrase *"doers of* the truth," which appears in *Tg. Jer.* 2:2 and in Johannine literature (John 3:32; 1 John 1:6).[39] A more general, but less exact, analogy exists between Jesus' complaint about the "adulterous and sinful generation" he found himself in (see Matt 12:39; 16:4; Mark 8:38) and the cognate characterization in *Tg. Isa.* 57:3. Jesus' reference to sin as "debt" (see Matt 6:12; 18:23–35) appears to be an idiom shared with the Targumim.[40]

Targum Proverbs presents several usages of imagery that may help to cast light on the Gospels. The ant is said to have no *"harvest,"* rather than no "chief" in Prov 6:7, and John Healy has compared this to the characterization of animals in Matt 6:26 and Luke 12:24.[41] But because the point of Proverbs is to promote industry whereas the Gospels commend carelessness, the similarity should not be pressed; in any case, Proverbs is in line with the LXX. A stronger case may be made for the statement, "It is a snare for a man *that he vows to the sanctuary* and afterwards *his soul rejoices"* (*Tg. Prov.* 20:25). The basic situation is as envisaged in Matt 15:4–6 and Mark 7:10–13: the practice of dedicating property to the temple while continuing to enjoy its use.[42] But since the LXX renders the verse similarly, there is no question of a particular comparison with the Targum.

---

[37] C. A. Evans, "A Note on Targum 2 Samuel 5:8 and Jesus' Ministry to the 'Maimed, Halt, and Blind,'" *JSP* 15 (1997): 79–82.

[38] See R. Hayward, *The Targum of Jeremiah* (ArBib 12; Wilmington, Del.: Glazier, 1987), 27, 75, 113. As he mentions, the usage is associated with the well-established connection between the image of harvest and judgment at the end of time. For the related motif of the handling of chaff (see Matt 3:12; 13:30; Luke 3:17), see *Tg. Hos.* 13:3; *Tg. Zeph.* 2:2.

[39] See Hayward, *Jeremiah*, 53, for further references. Hayward also (pp. 27, 187) sees a comparison between 1 Pet 2:1–10 and *Tg. Isa.* 28:6; *Tg. Jer.* 51:26. That connection (and several others mentioned by Hayward) strikes us as too tenuous to mention, but there may be some merit in the exegeses he proposes. It is more plausible to take the image of the stone messianically; cf. Cathcart and Gordon, *Minor Prophets,* 194 (commenting on *Tg. Zech.* 4:7).

[40] The general point is made in Cathcart and Gordon, *Minor Prophets,* 139.

[41] J. F. Healy, *The Targum of Proverbs* (ArBib 15; Collegeville, Minn.: Liturgical Press, 1991), 21.

[42] So ibid., 45; for further discussion, see B. Chilton, *The Temple of Jesus: His Sacrificial Program within a Cultural History of Sacrifice* (University Park: Pennsylvania State University Press, 1992), 127–28.

The Targumim participate in a particular cosmology of how eschatological reward or punishment is to be worked out. It is unlikely that that the targumic scheme is original; more probably it reflects widespread expectations. But sometimes the Targumim illuminate otherwise esoteric statements within the NT. *Targum Isaiah* 63:6 specifies the *"lower* earth" as the place to which God will cast the *"mighty men"* of his enemies. A similar phrase is used in Eph 4:9 in order to refer to Christ's descent to the dead.[43] Divine anger is specified in *Tg. Isa.* 3:16–24 against women who adorn themselves—especially their hair—in an exaggerated fashion, and this invites comparison with 1 Tim 2:9 and 1 Pet 3:3. God's anger is understood to whiten (*Tg. Mal.* 3:2), in a way that may illuminate passages such as Mark 9:3 and Rev 7:14.[44] The definitive punishment of the wicked is that they are to suffer the "second death"; that is the threat of both *Tg. Jon.* Isa 22:14; 65:6, 15; Jer 51:39, 57 and Rev 2:11; 20:6, 14; 21:8.[45] Any extension of time is to allow for the possibility of repentance (see *Tg. Isa.* 26:10; 42:14; *Tg. Hab.* 1:13; 3:1–2; 2 Pet 3:9; Rev 2:21).[46] When the God who judges in this fashion takes notice now of people, a "memorial" or "remembrance" may be said to come before him; this is a generally targumic expression—amply attested in *Targum Jonathan*[47]—that also appears in the NT (see Acts 10:4; Matt 26:13; Mark 14:9). It is a foretaste of the *"consolation(s)"* they are to enjoy as a consequence of divine judgment (see *Tg. 2 Sam.* 23:1; *Tg. Isa.* 8:2; 18:4; 40:1–2; *Tg. Jer.* 12:5; 31:6, 26; *Tg. Hos.* 6:2, with Luke 2:24–25; 6:24; Acts 4:36; Rom 15:5; 2 Cor 1:7; 1 Thess 2:3–4).[48] Favorable judgment may be attributed to an angelic advocate, designated by the Greek term *paraklētos* (so *Tg. Job* 33:23 and John 14:16–17, 26; 15:26; 16:7; 1 John 2:1–2). In all this, God acts as sovereign, the king of the ages (cf. *Tg. Isa.* 6:5; 30:33; *Tg. Jer.* 10:10; *Tg. Zech.* 14:16; 1 Tim 1:17; [Rev 15:3]), who is able to raise the dead with the sound of a trumpet (see 1 Cor 15:52; 1 Thess 4:16; Exod 20:18).[49]

In contrast, Hayward suggests that the statement in *Tg. Jer.* 33:25 contradicts Christian belief that God would cause the present heaven and earth to pass away.[50] Similar cases include the rendering of *Tg. Hos.* 11:1, "Out of Egypt I have called *them* sons," which corrects the passage away from the singular application of "Out of Egypt I have called to my son," long used as a Christian *testimonium*

---

[43] Indeed, the similarity should settle the question in favor of that reading, instead of seeing it as a reference to the incarnation: cf. E. F. Scott, *The Epistles of Paul to the Colossians, to Philemon, and to the Ephesians* (MNTC; New York: Harper, 1930), 208–209.

[44] See Cathcart and Gordon, *Minor Prophets*, 235.

[45] This threat is elegantly explained in L. Smolar and M. Aberbach, *Studies in Targum Jonathan to the Prophets* (LBS; New York: Ktav, 1983), 183.

[46] See Cathcart and Gordon, *Minor Prophets*, 155.

[47] See Hayward, *Jeremiah*, 93 n. 13.

[48] See ibid., 131. For further discussion, and citation of *Tg. Neof.* Num 23:23, see McNamara, *Targum Neofiti 1—Numbers*, 133.

[49] See Maher, *Targum Pseudo-Jonathan—Exodus*, 219.

[50] Hayward, *Jeremiah*, 34, 143; he cites 2 Pet 3:10–13; Rev 20:11; 21:1 by way of comparison, as well as *1 Enoch* 91:16 and the Stoic teaching that the world would be destroyed by fire. As Cathcart and Gordon point out (*Minor Prophets*, 158), elsewhere the Targumim would seem to agree with such a teaching.

(see Matt 2:15). For much the same reason, *Targum Zechariah* omits the references to "thirty pieces of silver" at 11:12, to "the potter" at 11:13 (cf. Matt 27:3–10), and to "him whom they have pierced" at 12:10 (cf. John 19:37; Rev 1:7).[51] It has also been suggested that the surprising rendering of Malachi 2:16, "But *if you* hate *her, divorce her,*" which contradicts the straightforward meaning of the Hebrew ("But he hates *divorce*"), is designed to militate against the stricter Christian teaching (see Matt 5:31–32; 19:3–9; Mark 10:2–12; Luke 16:18; Rom 7:2–3; 1 Cor 7:10–11).[52]

On the other hand, *Tg. Zech* 14:21 refers to the time when there will be no "trader," rather than no Canaanite, in the temple; this may be an antecedent of Jesus' complaint in John 2:16.[53] The idea that an animal that has been strangled is offensive to God (because its blood has not been drained away) is shared by Acts 15:20 and *Tg. Mal.* 1:13.[54] These connections are too slight to warrant the conclusion of direct contact; similarly, passages such as Matt 26:64, Mark 14:62, and Luke 22:69 represent a convergence with the well-known Judaic tendency to refer to divine "power" rather than to God himself.[55] The interpretation of incense offered to God as prayer is perhaps a somewhat more specific connection

---

[51] Cathcart and Gordon (*Minor Prophets,* 54) cite the support of Matt 2:15 for the MT, but they do not speculate on the reasons for the departure of the Targum from the other versions. Along the same lines, they have little to say about the targumic treatment of Zechariah 11 in comparison to the NT (pp. 412–15). They do, however, make a connection between *Tg. Zeph.* 2:1 and Matt 7:3–5; Luke 6:41–42 that is based on the speculation that a reading of the term "straw" (Heb. *qash*) was applied verbally. The idea is that a pun such as "Be 'strawed' and then 'straw'" is behind Jesus' usage (letter of Robert P. Gordon to author). Their treatment of *Tg. Zech.* 12:10 in respect to the NT (pp. 218–19) is far more balanced and develops the insight of Smolar and Aberbach, *Studies,* 165.

[52] See Smolar and Aberbach, *Studies,* 3, where the interpretation is assigned to the school of Akiba on the basis of *m. Giṭ.* 9:10 and *b. Giṭ.* 90b; see also Cathcart and Gordon, *Minor Prophets,* 235. Smolar and Aberbach cite another alleged contradiction of Christian halakah (pp. 1–3) that strikes me as less convincing. Similarly, it is perhaps a bit of a strain to conceive of interpreters imputing seduction to Hezron simply because he is mentioned in the genealogy of Jesus. So J. S. McIvor, *The Targum of Chronicles: Translated, with Introduction, Apparatus, and Notes* (ArBib 19; Collegeville, Minn.: Liturgical Press, 1994), 50, citing *Tg. 1 Chron.* 2:21 and Matt 1:3; Luke 3:33. After all, the name of the resulting son is not the same in the Targum as in the NT. McIvor also suggests (p. 41) that naming Shem as *"the great priest"* in *Tg. 1 Chron.* 1:24 is a response to claims about Melchizedek and Jesus in Hebrews 7. It seems more plausible that the association with Shem shows the kind of force and affiliation the image of Melchizedek exercised; see B. Grossfeld, *The Targum Onqelos to Genesis: Translated, with a Critical Introduction, Apparatus, and Notes* (ArBib 6; Wilmington, Del.: Glazier, 1988), 69, citing *Tg. Onq.* Gen 14:18. It is nonetheless of interest that Grossfeld, 58, accepts the anti-Christian reading of Melchizedek in *Pseudo-Jonathan.* But this is because he sees the verb "to minister" as denying priestly function when in fact this term is quite consistent with a priestly understanding of Melchizedek.

[53] So Cathcart and Gordon, *Minor Prophets,* 226.

[54] So ibid., 231.

[55] See S. H. Levey, *The Targum of Ezekiel* (ArBib 13; Wilmington, Del.: Glazier, 1987), 63 n. 8, citing *Tg. Ezek.* 20:22; Hayward (*Jeremiah,* 67) notes the frequency of "power" in the Targumim, although he cites the wrong passage in Mark.

(see *Tg. Mal.* 1:11 and Rev 5:8; 8:3–4), as is the image of water as a multitude of people (*Tg. 2 Sam.* 22:17; *Tg. Hab.* 3:8; Rev 17:15).[56]

Conclusion

Our initial finding must be categorical and negative. The comparison of the second type, where the NT and the Targumim share a common, literary understanding of the same biblical passage, resulted in the smallest number of cases of all the categories of comparison we have considered. This strongly underlines what has emerged as a theme in this discussion as a whole: in their literary form, the Targumim had not fully emerged by the first century. Had that been the case, the literary category of comparison would have been much more strongly represented.

It may seem paradoxical, but the fact is that comparison of the first type, where wording is involved (in the interpretation of the same scriptural passage or in a more general assertion), represents a stronger relationship between the NT and the Targumim. Why should this be the case? Each instance included a saying of Jesus, and a saying of Jesus in regard to a key concept within his teaching (forgiveness, violence, and gehenna). Evidently, the Targumim represent traditions that were a formative influence on the tradition of the Gospels at an early stage. Once the Gospels emerged in their Greek form, however, targumic influence all but disappeared (which is why the second, literary type of comparison yielded so few results).

This complex relationship, in which the Targumim represent traditions from the earliest period of formative Judaism in texts that are relatively late in their literary forms, is best attested in the third type of comparison. Here many of Jesus' most famous sayings find their echoes: the kingdom of God, the measure by which one is measured, mammon, the citation of Isaiah 61, new wine, the promise to Peter, being merciful as God is merciful, and the golden rule. But this comparison (unlike the comparison of the first type) is not limited to sayings of Jesus. Characteristic expressions of God being well pleased, of seeking the living among the dead, of keeping things in one's heart, of being delivered to death, and of a plurality of high priests also find their place here. This raises interesting questions regarding contacts that may be posited between the Targumim and the NT; these will be pursued in the second part of this conclusion.

Finally, the fourth type of comparison includes more passages than may be mentioned here, but it is instructive in its range. It offers Jesus' statement about the revelation to Jesus' own followers of what was hidden from the prophets and about those who hunger and thirst after righteousness, divine judgment as the separation of straw and grain, the present generation as adulterous and sinful, and the danger of vows concerning the temple. Although we should remember that comparisons of the fourth type do not concern typically targumic

---

[56] Cathcart and Gordon, *Minor Prophets*, 231, 158.

expressions, the very fact of this overlap means they are of value in an understanding of the NT. For all the variety of the dates, with different degrees of distance from the first century, the Targumim include material that is resonant with some of the most primitive materials in the NT. Here again (as in the third category) this resonance involves more than sayings of Jesus. Expressions such as "doing truth" (as in 1 John 1:6), "the lower earth" (Eph 4:9), and "the second death" (Rev 20:14; 21:8) find their place here, as does the particular concern about women decorating their hair (1 Tim 2:9; 1 Pet 3:3).

Literary Comparison and Historical Analogy

The study of the Targumim in their relationship to the NT is complex, and it has been hampered by the binary opposition between two equally untenable points of view. The hypothesis of "the Palestinian Targum" has been raised to a nearly dogmatic status among some scholars, so that it is routinely argued that the Targumim are earlier than the evidence indicates and they are effectively treated as being pre-Christian. (The passages, cited in the fourth type of comparison, that reflect responses to Christian claims eloquently falsify this treatment.) But it is the mirror image of such dogmatism to assert that just because the Targumim emerged relatively late as documents, their traditions can teach us nothing about the emergence of the NT.[57]

Our approach has been more critical. This is why I have insisted upon knowing what kind of comparison we have been pursuing in each case, and why we have not assumed either the priority or the irrelevance of targumic material in any case. Even so, we need to close on a note of caution. As has been pointed out, similarity to targumic materials is no guarantee of what is commonly called the "authenticity" of a given passage in the NT. Simply put: a targumic analogy is no proof in itself that Jesus said what the Gospels claim he said. As a matter of fact, in the first case of the first type of comparison we have observed (in the teaching about those who fail to see and hear), the formative influence of the circle around James was emphasized.[58] The types of comparison I have offered are of two bodies of traditional literature and should not be confused with historical findings.

Historical relationship is somewhat different from verbal and literary comparison. Once a verbal or literary comparison has been developed, it opens the historical question: why should the two kinds of literature be related as they are? In global terms, we have provided an answer to this question: the Targumim were in the process of formation during the period in which the NT emerged. But is it

---

[57] This kind of dismissal is characteristic of the attitude of some scholars of the NT toward rabbinic literature as a whole. Even the basic requirements of comparison (competence in Aramaic and Hebrew as well as in Greek) are not built into the normal graduate programs in many cases.

[58] As in Chilton, *Galilean Rabbi*, 94–97.

possible to go further and specify in given cases how the NT's resonance with the Targumim is to be accounted for?

First of all, resonance of the sort we have seen does not by itself demonstrate contact or priority between the two literatures. As a matter of inference, Jesus' citation of Isaiah 6 in a targumic form and the subsequent development of this citation in the circle of James are consistent with the evidence, but they are by no means proven by this evidence. In historical terms, resonance only suggests that there might be an analogy between the two literatures being compared.

Historical analogies between the NT and the Targumim might be of three types. The first type involves common reference. Mark 9:47–48 and *Tg. Isa.* 66:24 both relate the wording at the close of the book of Isaiah to gehenna, understood as the place of ultimate judgment. No causal relation between Mark and the Targum can be argued on this basis alone, but the commonality of reference is an immediate inference. By secondary inference, the question of contact may be addressed, and it seems in this case that targumic tradition has influenced the NT. The second type of analogy involves shared context. The understanding that the vineyard is a symbol for Israel is manifest in Jesus' parable of the Vineyard (Matt 21:33–43//Mark 12:1–12//Luke 20:9–19) and also in the fifth chapter of *Targum Isaiah.* Here no commonality of wording or direct reference is at stake, but it is evident that all the documents speak from a common context of the association of Israel and the vineyard. (As we have seen, the literary history of the Targumim makes this a rather rare analogy with the NT.) Finally, the third type of analogy is systemic. The kingdom of God, it turns out, is not a phrase uniquely attributed to Jesus (as is still widely asserted). The precise wording also appears in the Targumim, where the issue is not, in the least, of the legalistic sort that many scholars still attribute to Judaism. Rather, it is an explicitly eschatological concept, comparable to Jesus' and presented without any indication of a reaction against Christian thinking.

The reference to Jesus (inevitably within the study of the NT) raises an issue within scholarly discussion that mirrors the debate regarding the dating of the Targumim. Because familiarity with Judaism is so rudimentary among scholars of the NT, the argument is sometimes stated or implied that any similarity with a rabbinic institution must be attributed to Jesus rather than his followers (who— it is supposed—were non-Judaic Hellenists). Such a presupposition ignores the findings in which Jesus seems to be better understood by contrasting him with his contemporaries, whether they happen to have been associated with his movement or not. Whether the analogies at issue are of common reference, of shared context, or of systemic expression, no assumption for or against what is usually called the historicity of the Gospels can be assumed.

The Gospels refer back to Jesus as their source, but there is no "historical Jesus" in the sense of a person whose deeds and character are accessible by means of verifiable public evidence. The literarily historical Jesus, on the other hand, is a fact of reading. We cannot understand the documents unless we identify the Jesus they believe they are referring to. This Jesus, of course, is an object of their belief. He becomes historical for us in the literary sense when we discover that we must suppose facts about Jesus (e.g., his teaching of the kingdom with an eschatological meaning) in order to explain the generation of a given text. Jesus is a figure of critical history to the extent, and only to the extent, that he permits us to explain how certain texts arose in their mutual relations and in their literary milieu. Literary comparison of the NT with the Targumim by itself does not solve "the problem of the historical Jesus," but it can proceed in a way that does not exacerbate it and that may be productive for further analysis. Finally, the "historical Jesus" is a variable in the overall equation of how the NT arose; for this reason, comparative study with the Targumim may be expected to provide that variable with more specific value than is usual in today's general assertions about Jesus. That next stage of comparison, historical rather than literary, is not our present purpose; the work of volumes such as this may be regarded as part of the foundation of that enterprise.

The Aramaic Psalter and the New Testament: Praising the Lord in History and Prophecy

Craig A. Evans

Study of the Aramaic Psalter is a relatively undeveloped field. There is no critical edition of the text, and the long-awaited English translation for the Michael Glazier Aramaic Bible series is yet to appear. Bruce Chilton's essay (the previous chapter in the present book) has provided us with a masterful overview of the potential contribution that the Aramaic tradition can make to our understanding of the NT. The present essay focuses on the distinctive contribution that the Aramaic Psalter can make.

Before we can investigate the relevance of *Targum Psalms* for the NT, it will be necessary to consider the Targum itself. Unlike most of the other Targumim, *Targum Psalms* has not been studied extensively, nor has any study investigated at length what contribution, if any, it may make to NT interpretation. The present essay consists of four parts: (1) a review of previous research on the Aramaic Psalter, (2) an assessment of the character of the Aramaic Psalter, (3) consideration of the date of *Targum Psalms,* and (4) the Aramaic Psalter and the NT.

The reader will observe the alternation between "Aramaic Psalter" and "*Targum Psalms.*" By "Aramaic Psalter" is meant the Aramaic tradition as a whole, from oral to written, in all of its diversity of expression (i.e., different MSS and the added notes often called *targum aher,* "another translation") and development (i.e., in synagogue, academy, and private study). By "*Targum Psalms*" is meant the surviving Targum, extant in several MSS, a critical edition of which does not yet exist. I understand "Aramaic Psalter" in a more inclusive sense, in which "*Targum Psalms*" would be understood as a narrower, more limited expression of the Aramaic Psalter. This is an important distinction to bear in mind, especially regarding comparison with the NT. At no point is it assumed that Jesus and NT writers were acquainted with *Targum Psalms.* Such a notion is anachronistic. It will be argued, however, that Jesus and some NT writers were familiar with the Aramaic Psalter, out of which eventually *Targum Psalms* would grow.

Previous Research in the Aramaic Psalter

Given the importance of the Psalter in the life of the Jewish people and the Christian church and given its scholarly attention in the modern period, the relative neglect of the Aramaic version is somewhat surprising. But perhaps it is not. No critical version of its text appears in Alexander Sperber's *Bible in Aramaic*.[1] And no single MS or printed version has enjoyed wide acceptance.[2] The point of departure is usually Paul Lagarde's printed text.[3] Luis Díez Merino has prepared an edition of the Zamora MS,[4] and Alter Wein has published a commentary with limited notes.[5] And as mentioned, the English edition in the Aramaic Bible series, published by Liturgical Press, has not yet appeared.[6] The ensuing dearth of scholarly attention is regrettable, for this part of the Aramaic Bible has much to offer students of the NT and early Judaism. [7]

Let us briefly survey, in more or less chronological order, the scholarship that has occurred concerning the Aramaic Psalter.[8] Our point of departure is the long-lived and prolific Leopold Zunz (1794–1886), who from his lectures on Jewish worship published one of the first scholarly studies on the place of

---

[1] A. Sperber, *The Bible in Aramaic Based on Old Manuscripts and Printed Texts* (5 vols.; Leiden: Brill, 1959–1973).

[2] An important step in this direction has been taken by Emanuel White, "A Critical Edition of the Targum of Psalms: A Computer Generated Text of Books I and II" (PhD diss., McGill University, 1988).

[3] P. Lagarde, ed., *Hagiographa Chaldaice* (Leipzig: B. G. Teubner, 1873; repr., Osnabrück: O. Zeller, 1967), 2–85.

[4] L. Díez Merino, *Targum de Salmos: Edición príncipe del ms. Villa-Amil n. 5 de Alfonso de Zamora* (Bibliotheca hispana biblica 6; Madrid: Consejo Superior de Investigaciones Cientificos, 1982). For a helpful overview of the Aramaic MSS and critical editions, see idem, "Targum Manuscripts and Critical Editions," in *The Aramaic Bible: Targums in Their Historical Context* (ed. D. R. G. Beattie and M. J. McNamara; JSOTSup 166; Sheffield, England: JSOT Press, 1994), 51–91.

[5] A. T. Wein, תהלים :התרגומים על הטוב יין (The good wine on the Targumim: Psalms) (Rehovot, Israel: Mekhon Yerushalayim, 1985). Wein translates the Targum into modern Hebrew; the notes mostly point out parallels with rabbinic literature.

[6] E. M. Cook has produced an English translation, which he has made available at http://www.tulane.edu/~ntcs/pss/tg_ps_index.htm.

[7] M. Bernstein ("Torah and Its Study in the Targum of Psalms," in *Hazon Nahum: Studies in Jewish Law, Thought, and History Presented to Dr. Norman Lamm on the Occasion of His Seventieth Birthday* [ed. Y. Elman and J. S. Gurock; New York: Yeshiva University Press, 1997], 39–67) plausibly speculates that the size of the Psalter, the assumption that it is quite late, and its nonusage in the Jewish liturgy are probable factors in the scholarly neglect of the Aramaic Psalter.

[8] The bibliographies assembled by Bernard Grossfeld are indispensable. See B. Grossfeld, *A Bibliography of Targum Literature* (3 vols.; vols. 1 and 2, Bibliographica judaica 3, 8; New York: Ktav, 1972–1977; vol. 3, New York: Sepher-Hermon, 1990). A few of the items that will be noted are scarcely more than homiletical treatments of this or that passage. The recently launched *Journal for the Aramaic Bible* (continuing under the new title *Aramaic* Studies) very helpfully provides ongoing bibliographical updates.

Targum Psalms in Jewish faith and learning.[9] A generation later Wilhelm Bacher's study of the Aramaic Psalter appeared, representing one of the first critical studies of this part of the Targum.[10] His approach is thematic, systematic, and remarkably critical. In the first part of his study, he reviews the exegetical approach of the *meturgeman* (Aramaic, "interpreter, translator"), including his vocabulary, syntax, interpretive additions, and understanding of the Psalter itself. In the second part, Bacher focuses on the departures from the Hebrew of the MT, some of which are due to haggadic interests, others to probable variants in the Hebrew *Vorlage* itself. Bacher's studies have become foundational for subsequent work in the Aramaic Psalter.

Making use of the Aramaic text of *Targum Psalms* edited by Lagarde, which appeared in 1873, Friedrich Baethgen investigated the value of the Targum, as well as other translations, for textual criticism of the HB.[11] Baethgen not only examined readings in the LXX, Peshitta, Latin, and Aramaic but also took into account OT quotations in the NT.[12] His lengthy studies are a veritable gold mine of data, though one must exercise caution because the texts he used are now badly dated. Three years later Berthold Oppenheim published a study on the Syriac text of the fifth book of the Psalter; in it he makes comparison with the Hebrew, Greek, and Aramaic versions.[13]

At the turn of the century, L. Techen published two small volumes in which he attempts a collation of the major Aramaic variants, using Lagarde's work as his

---

[9] L. Zunz, *Gottesdienstliche Vorträge der Juden, historisch entwickelt: Ein Beitrag zur Alterthumskunde und biblischen Kritik zur Literatur- und Religionsgeschichte* (Berlin: A. Asher, 1832).

[10] W. Bacher, "Das Targum zu den Psalmen," *MGWJ* 21 (1872): 408–16, 463–73. We have another early, but quite brief, study in L. Eisler, "מכתב," *Kokheve Yitshaq* 34 (1867): 27–30. Eisler treats *Targum Job* as well as *Targum Psalms*. See also the tiny study by E. Plessner, "Eine kritische Targumstelle," *Magazin für jüdische Geschichte und Literatur* 2 (1875): 12; Plessner discusses *Tg. Ps.* 81:5, which reads, "he made a covenant for Israel" instead of "it is a statute for Israel." See also the series of exegetical notes on *Targum Psalms* by D. Oppenheim, "הערות והארות על תרגום של תהלים," *HaMagîd* 20 (1876): 114, 122, 132–33, 140, 148.

[11] F. Baethgen, "Der textkritische Werth der alten Übersetzungen zu den Psalmen," *Jahrbuch für protestantische Theologie* 8 (1882): 405–59, 593–677. The same year a brief study appeared by J. Reifmann, "מחקרים שונים של תרגום תהלים," *Beth Talmud* 2 (1882): 152–57; Reifmann compares several passages where the Aramaic and the Hebrew texts read differently and then shows parallels in rabbinic literature.

[12] R. F. Shedinger, "The Gospels and the Text of the Hebrew Bible: Mic 5:1 (Matt 2:6) in Tatian's *Diatessaron*," in the present book, furthers this interesting line of inquiry.

[13] B. Oppenheim, *Die syrische Übersetzung des fünften Buches der Psalmen (Psalm 107–150) und ihr Verhältnis zu dem massoretischen Texte und den älteren Übersetzungen, namentlich den LXX, Targum* (Leipzig: W. Drugulin, 1891). The following year a semischolarly journal printed a series of brief studies by J. Reiss, "Erläuternde Bemerkungen zu einigen Stellen im Targum zu den Psalmen und Sprüchen," *Jüdisches Litteratur-Blatt* 21 (1892): 127, 131, 134–35, 139; Reiss tries to show that some readings of the Targum may clear up textual problems in the Psalms and Proverbs.

base text.[14] The first volume lists variants for all 150 psalms. The second volume analyzes tendencies in the respective Aramaic manuscripts, cataloguing a host of examples. His work underscores the broad range of variants and discrepancies among the MSS. Three decades later Moshe Ginsburg published a brief work that selectively treats passages from the Prophets and Writings, particularly the Five Scrolls.[15] A few years later Pinkhos Churgin published an analysis of the Targum to the Hagiographa, including *Targum Psalms*.[16] He provides a great number of rabbinic parallels, many drawn from the *Midrash Tehillim*.[17]

In 1955 Harold Eugene Hill completed a study of the messianism of *Targum Psalms*. He finds the expectation of a nonsupernatural Davidic Messiah who in the coming age will rule Israel as king, though completely subordinate to God, Israel's true King.[18] The Targum says almost nothing, however, about the Messiah's expected activities, apart from his fidelity to the Law. Samson Levey's subsequent study of the messianic content in the Targum is consistent with Hill's findings.[19]

Studies of other aspects of the theology of *Targum Psalms* appeared in the 1960s and 1970s. Yehudah Komlosh and Jonathan Shunary published important studies of halakic and haggadic traditions in the Aramaic Psalter.[20] Komlosh investigates the *meturgeman's* distinctive techniques and emphases. Shunary, who probes the *meturgeman's* attitude toward anthropomorphisms encountered in the biblical text, finds that the Aramaic Psalter is not as sensitive to anthropomorphisms as are other Targumim.[21] Several other minor studies appeared during this period.[22]

---

[14] L. Techen, *Das Targum zu den Psalmen* (2 vols.; Wismar, Germany: Die Groszen Stadtschule zu Wismar, 1896–1907).

[15] M. Ginsburg, תרגום דהתרגום: ביאור התרגום מנביאים וכתובים וגם חמש מגלות (Lodz, Poland: Liebskind, 1936; repr., Tel Aviv: Zion, 1971). That same year a brief note on *Tg. Ps.* 18:44 was published by B. Schmerler, "תרגום תהלים יח מד:," *Otsar HaHayim* 12 (1936): 29.

[16] P. Churgin, *The Targum to Hagiographa* (New York: Horeb, 1945), esp. 17–62, for study of *Targum Psalms*.

[17] Ibid., 31–44.

[18] H. E. Hill, *Messianic Expectations in the Targum to the Psalms* (PhD diss., Yale University, 1955).

[19] S. H. Levey, *The Messiah—an Aramaic Interpretation: The Messianic Exegesis of the Targum* (HUCM 2; Cincinnati: Hebrew Union College–Jewish Institute of Religion, 1974), 105–24. Levey remarks on the relatively modest messianic interest on the part of *Targum Psalms*.

[20] Y. Komlosh, "אופיניים תרגום תהלים," in *Sefer Segal: Studies in the Bible Presented to M. H. Segal* (ed. J. M. Grintz and J. Liver; Jerusalem: Israel Society for Biblical Research, 1964), 265–70; J. Shunary, "Avoidance of Anthropomorphism in the Targum of Psalms," *Text* 5 (1966): 133–44.

[21] Shunary ("Avoidance of Anthropomorphism," 143) concludes that in general *Targum Psalms* "saw no theological difficulty in literal anthropomorphic translation." Circumlocutions in this Targum are small in number. This topic is pursued further and in much greater detail by S. Shacknai, "Studies in the Targum of the Book of Psalms: Anthropomorphisms, Anthropopathisms, Shekinta and Memra, Mythology, and the Like" (PhD diss., Hebrew Union College–Jewish Institute of Religion, 1969).

[22] S. Speier, "Sieben Stellen des Psalmentargums in Handschriften und Druckausgaben: 3,7 44,17 45,6 49,11 68,15.20 125,1," *Bib* 48 (1967): 491–508; and a critical note on

In recent years interest in *Targum Psalms* seems to be growing. Luis Díez Merino, Max Wilcox, and especially Moshe Bernstein have published important studies that, along with the eventual appearance of the Psalms volume in the Aramaic Bible series, should stimulate further research and give this important textual tradition its due. Díez Merino investigates the haggadic elements in the Targum, assigning them to a series of categories[23] that the next part of the present study will take into account. Wilcox wrestles with the problem of the textual diversity of the MS tradition of the Aramaic Psalter.[24] He concludes that *Targum Psalms* seems to be an eclectic combination of a number of Aramaic traditions.[25] His study has implications for the date of this Targum, which will be considered shortly.

Moshe Bernstein has published several studies on *Targum Psalms* and other Targumim as part of an interest reaching back to his graduate work. Two studies call for special notice. In the first, Bernstein analyzes the *meturgeman's* technique in translating the Hebrew.[26] Bernstein calls for greater precision in our description of targumizing, noting that it is insufficient merely to speak of "literal" and "paraphrastic," as though these categories explain the chief characteristics of the Targumim. Regarding the Aramaic Psalter, he finds that the *meturgeman's* goal was to clarify the text, even at the expense of the original shape of the Hebrew, in that the poetry of the Psalter is transformed into prose. This is seen in Psalm 137, whose lament for the loss of Zion (in the Hebrew version) becomes in the

---

Tg. Ps. 10:8 in *Leshonenu* 35 (1970/1971): 80 (in Hebrew). As his point of departure, Speier quotes the rabbinic tradition that understands the activity described in Neh 8:8 ("And they read from the book, from the law of God, clearly; and they gave the sense, so that the people understood the reading") as referring to the Targum (cf. *b. Meg.* 3a; *b. Ned.* 37b, *y. Meg.* 4.1; *Gen. Rab.* 36.8 [on Gen 9:26–27]), and he goes on to try to identify early elements of interpretive tradition in the Aramaic Psalter. In a brief study in *Beth Miqra* 18 (1973): 533–39 (in Hebrew), A. J. Brawer compares *Tg. Ps.* 68 with rabbinic interpretation from the East; R. Kasher, in a study in *Sinai* 79 (1976): 14–25 (in Hebrew), probes the Aramaic interpretation of Ps 42:7b ("I remember thee from the land of Jordan and of Hermon, from Mount Mizar"), which in the Targum is rendered, "I will remember you [among] those who dwell yonder in the land of Jordan, and those who dwell on the mountains of Hermoni, and the people who accepted the Torah on mount Sinai, which is lowly and small." The ambiguous "Mount Mizar" in the Targum is understood as a "small mountain," which because of smallness and humility is chosen as the site of revelation.

[23] L. Díez Merino, "Haggadic Elements in the Targum of Psalms," in *Proceedings of the Eighth World Congress of Jewish Studies, Division A: The Period of the Bible* (ed. D. Krone; Jerusalem: World Union of Jewish Studies, 1982), 131–37.

[24] M. Wilcox, "The Aramaic Targum to Psalms," in *Proceedings of the Ninth World Congress of Jewish Studies, Division A: The Period of the Bible* (ed. D. Assaf; Jerusalem: World Union of Jewish Studies, 1986), 143–50.

[25] Here Wilcox (ibid., 150 n. 3) cites B. L. Roberts, *The Old Testament Text and Versions: The Hebrew Text in Transmission and the History of Ancient Versions* (Cardiff: University of Wales Press, 1951), 209

[26] M. J. Bernstein, "Translation Technique in the Targum to Psalms: Two Test Cases: Psalms 2 and 137," in *SBL Seminar Papers, 1994* (ed. E. H. Lovering; SBLSP 33; Atlanta: Scholars Press, 1994), 326–45.

Targum a drama, complete with characters and speaking parts. We observe this very tendency at work in Psalm 118, which will be considered below.

Bernstein's second study focuses on the role of Torah in *Targum Psalms*.[27] He observes that the *meturgeman* greatly emphasizes the Law, adding a reference to it dozens of times (also observed by Díez Merino and others), possibly reflecting rabbinical interests. Perhaps the most fascinating feature of Bernstein's study is his observation that a significant portion of the Torah material that has been added to the text is without parallel in the extant rabbinic literature. This could suggest that only a fraction of the rabbinic corpus has survived. Although Bernstein says nothing about the date of *Targum Psalms* in this context, one may wonder if attestation of lost rabbinic tradition argues for the antiquity, not lateness, of elements in this Targum. After all, the loss of ancient (i.e., Tannaitic) material seems more likely than the loss of later (i.e., Amoraic or medieval) material.

Character of the Aramaic Psalter

The same year that Díez Merino's study appeared, Bruce Chilton published a major study on *Targum Isaiah*.[28] Chilton identified fifteen characteristic terms or phrases in this Targum, whose identification facilitated the recognition of an interpretive framework that emerged in the period between the two major wars (i.e., 70–135 C.E.). Chilton's fifteen terms or phrases, which function for the *meturgeman* and his heirs as theologoumena, are (1) Law, (2) sanctuary, (3) Jerusalem, (4) exile, (5) house of Israel, (6) repentance, (7) Abraham, (8) Holy Spirit, (9) prophet(s), (10) my Memra, (11) my Shekinah, (12) glory, (13) kingdom of God, (14) the righteous, and (15) Messiah. Díez Merino calls attention to sixteen themes in *Targum Psalms*, some of which overlap with the terms and phrases studied by Chilton: (1) love for the Torah, (2) son of man, (3) angels, (4) Messiah, (5) exile, (6) patriarchs, (7) community of Israel, (8) concepts of Memra, Shekinah, Yeqar (glory), (9) mountains, (10) temple, (11) judgment, (12) death, (13) hell, (14) heavens (future life, eternity, world to come), (15) Zion, and (16) spirit of prophecy.[29] To Díez Merino's list we may add Bernstein's observation of the tendency on the part of the Aramaic Psalter to historicize passages where allusions to Israel's history are present in the Hebrew and sometimes where no specific allusion is present.

Chilton, Díez Merino, and Bernstein together have pointed out about eighteen terms, clusters, or phrases in the Aramaic Psalter. A few of these are distinctive to *Targum Psalms;* most are common to other Targumim, though the high degree of overlap with *Targum Isaiah* is suggestive and will call for comment shortly.

---

[27] M. J. Bernstein, "Torah and Its Study."

[28] B. D. Chilton, *The Glory of Israel: The Theology and Provenience of the Isaiah Targum* (JSOTSup 23; Sheffield, England: JSOT Press, 1982 [title page wrongly states 1983]); Díez Merino, "Haggadic Elements." Because the studies of Chilton and Díez Merino appeared the same year, neither refers to the other. The coincidence of their respective observations is all the more striking.

[29] Díez Merino, "Haggadic Elements," 132–33.

Law

Díez Merino and Bernstein have called attention to the prominence of Law, or Torah, in *Targum Psalms.* Chilton also noted and discussed the importance of Law in *Targum Isaiah.* Bernstein has observed that the term תורה (Torah or Law) occurs thirty-six times in the Hebrew Psalter. If the occurrences in Psalm 119, which is a lengthy psalm devoted to the Law, are excluded, we are left with eleven occurrences. Eleven occurrences of Torah in 149 psalms indicate that the Law was not a major emphasis in the Hebrew Psalter. This is not the case in *Targum Psalms,* however, where there are about a hundred occurrences of the Aramaic equivalent אוריתא.[30] The majority of these occurrences have no analogue to Law in the Hebrew Psalter, but they are often suggested by words and references that are sometimes associated with the Law. For example, the psalmist petitions,

> Consider and answer me, O LORD my God; lighten my eyes, lest I sleep the sleep of death. (Heb. 13:4 [Eng. 13:3 RSV])

> Pay heed and receive my prayer, O LORD my God; illumine my eyes by your Torah, lest I sin and sleep with those who deserve death. (Targ.)

The Psalmist declares,

> This God—his way is perfect; the promise of the LORD proves true. (Heb. 18:31 [Eng. 18:30 RSV])

> God, whose ways are true, the Torah of the LORD is tested. (Targ.)

The first paraphrase may have been suggested by the Psalter itself (e.g., Ps 119:105: "Thy word is a lamp to my feet and a light to my path" RSV), though a much closer parallel is found in Isa 51:4: "Listen to me, my people, and give ear to me, my nation; for a law will go forth from me, and my justice for a light to the peoples" (RSV). The second paraphrase may well reflect a general understanding of the promises made to the patriarchs and the promises that accompany the Sinai covenant. Thus, the mention of promise in the Hebrew text prompts in the Aramaic thoughts of the Torah.[31] Elsewhere in the Aramaic, "Law" is introduced as the dynamic equivalent of "staff" (23:4), "works" (28:5), "strength" (29:11), and "command" (68:11) and often is added to complete a thought, as in 51:15, where the Hebrew "open my lips" becomes the Aramaic "open my lips with the Torah."[32] Moses himself is sometimes introduced in contexts that speak of the Law (cf. 62:12; 68:12, 19).

---

[30] My tallies of the occurrences of terms and phrases in *Targum Psalms* will often be qualified by the adjective "about." This is because there is no standardized Aramaic text and because I sometimes take into account variant readings (including examples of the *targum aher*).

[31] One should also note Paul's repeated linkage of law and promise in reference to Abraham (cf. Rom 4:13, 14, 16; Gal 3:17, 18, 19).

[32] On the modus operandi of the Psalms *meturgeman,* see Bernstein, "Torah and Its Study," 43–55.

It appears to be important to the *meturgeman* to teach that restoration and forgiveness come to those who turn to the Torah and obey it faithfully:

> For thou, O LORD, art good and forgiving, abounding in steadfast love to all who call on thee. (86:5 RSV)

> > For you are the LORD, good to the righteous and forgiving to those who turn to his Torah, and multiplying favor to all who pray in your presence. (Targ.)

> Restore to me the joy of thy salvation, and uphold me with a willing spirit. (51:14 [Eng. 51:12 RSV])

> > Return your Torah to me, to exult in your redemption; and may the spirit of prophecy support me. (Targ.)

> For not by their own sword did they win the land, nor did their own arm give them victory; but thy right hand, and thy arm, and the light of thy countenance; for thou didst delight in them. (44:4 [Eng. 44:3 RSV])

> > For they did not inherit the land by the strength of their swords, and the might of their arms did not redeem them, for [it was] your right hand, and your strong arm and the light of your glorious splendor; for whenever they occupied themselves with the Torah, you were pleased with them. (Targ.)

> But God will ransom my soul from the power of Sheol, for he will receive me. (49:16 [Eng. 49:15 RSV])

> > David said in the spirit of prophecy, "Truly God will ransom my soul from the judgment of Gehenna, for he will teach me his Torah forever." (Targ.)

> As they go through the valley of Baca they make it a place of springs; the early rain also covers it with pools. (84:7 [Eng. 84:6 RSV])

> > The wicked who cross over the valleys of Gehenna, weeping—he will make their weeping like a fountain; also those who return to the teaching of his Torah he will cover with blessings. (Targ.)

Consistent with this expectation is the depiction of David, the template for his messianic son, as a scholar of Torah. In addition to *Tg. Ps.* 49:16 (cited above) is this passage:

> The LORD spoke by his decree to give me the dominion in exchange for sitting in study of Torah. "Wait at my right hand until I make your enemies a support for your feet." (*Tg. Ps.* 110:1, apud *targum aher*)

The association of Torah with redemption (see further discussion below) coheres with ideas and hopes expressed in some circles in the aftermath of the destruction of the Jewish temple in 70 C.E.[33] Writing near the end of the first century C.E., the author of *2 Baruch* says, "When you endure and persevere in his fear

---

[33] See Chilton, *Glory of Israel,* 17–18.

and do not forget his Law, the time again will take a turn for the better for you" (44:7; cf. 46:5–6; 85:3: "Zion has been taken away from us, and we have nothing now apart from the Mighty One and his Law"; *4 Ezra* 7:133: "he is gracious towards those who return to his Law"; *L.A.E. [Vita]* 29:7).[34] Elements in *Targum Psalms* may reflect these hopes, which were nurtured in the years leading up to the Bar Kokhba revolt.

Sanctuary/Temple

References to the sanctuary (usually "sanctuary house") occur about fifty-eight times in the Aramaic, which is about three times the number in the Hebrew. Often the Hebrew invites reference to the sanctuary, as in Ps 2:6 ("I have set my king on Zion, my holy hill" RSV), which in the Aramaic becomes "I have anointed my king, and appointed him over my Sanctuary." The "holy hill" primarily refers to the city of Jerusalem itself,[35] made holy by God's presence (for more examples of glossing "holy hill" as "Sanctuary," see *Tg. Ps.* 3:5; 15:1; 24:3 ["hill" only]; 43:3). The equation of the "hill" with the sanctuary is also seen in *Tg. Isa.* 5:1–2: "I gave them a heritage on a high hill in fertile land . . . I built my Sanctuary in their midst." This interpretation is attested at Qumran in a small, fragmentary text dating to the middle of the first century B.C.E.: ". . . your winepress, built of stone . . . at the gate of the holy height [לשער מרום הקודש] . . . your planting and glorious channels . . . your vine[yard] . . ." (4Q500).

The palace of Israel's king (Ps 45:12–15 [Eng. 45:13–16]) is transformed into the "Temple of the King of Worlds" (*Tg. Ps.* 45:16). In Ps 47:4 [Eng. 47:5] the "pride of Jacob" becomes in Aramaic the "Sanctuary of Jacob." The simple reference to "house" is often upgraded to "Sanctuary" (e.g., Ps 26:8; 27:4; 52:8 [Eng. 52:9]; 92:13 [Eng. 92:14]; 93:5), while God's "courts" can become "courtyard of your Sanctuary" (Ps 84:10 [Eng. 84:11]). One of the more innovative glosses is seen in Ps 122:5, which in Hebrew reads, "There thrones for judgment were set, the thrones of the house of David" (RSV), but in Aramaic reads, "For there thrones were set; in Jerusalem thrones are in the Sanctuary for the kings of the house of David."

The destruction of the temple is an important part of the temple theme that runs throughout the Aramaic Psalter. The post-70 reality is starkly attested in the following passages:

> I will accept no bull from your house, nor he-goat from your folds. (50:9 RSV)

> From the day that my sanctuary was laid waste, I have not accepted a bull from your hands, or rams from your flock. (Targ.)

---

34 See P. Volz, *Die Eschatologie der jüdische Gemeinde im neutestamentlicher Zeitalter* (Tübingen: Mohr, 1934; repr., Hildesheim: Georg Olm, 1966), 43.

35 C. A. Briggs and E. G. Briggs, *A Critical and Exegetical Commentary on the Book of Psalms* (2 vols.; ICC; Edinburgh: T&T Clark, 1906–1907), 2:15; P. C. Craigie, *Psalms 1–50* (WBC 19; Dallas: Word, 1983), 66.

Do I eat the flesh of bulls, or drink the blood of goats? (50:13 RSV)

> From the day my sanctuary was laid waste, I have not accepted the flesh of the sacrifice of fatlings, and the priests have not sprinkled the blood of rams before me. (Targ.)

O God, the heathen have come into thy inheritance; they have defiled thy holy temple; they have laid Jerusalem in ruins. (79:1 RSV)

> A psalm composed by Asaph about the destruction of the temple. He said in the spirit of prophecy: O God, the Gentiles are entering your inheritance; they have defiled your holy temple, they have made Jerusalem a desolation. (Targ.)

For they have devoured Jacob, and laid waste his habitation. (79:7 RSV)

> For they have destroyed the house of Jacob, and made desolate his sanctuary. (Targ.)

We should also consider the following passage even though there is no explicit mention of the destruction of the temple:

> Remember, O LORD, against the Edomites the day of Jerusalem, how they said, "Rase it, rase it! Down to its foundations!" (137:7 RSV)

> Said Michael, prince of Jerusalem, "Remember, O LORD, the people of Edom, who laid waste Jerusalem, who say, 'Destroy, destroy, to the foundations of it.'" (Targ.)

In the Hebrew Bible, at least before 70 C.E., Psalm 79 was concerned with the destruction of the first temple. But it is probable that after 70 this psalm came to be understood as referring to the destruction of the second temple (though not exclusively). The same probably applies in the case of Psalm 137, though the primary reference remains the destruction at the hands of the Babylonians. We see in *2 Baruch* how the destruction of the first temple served as a foil for understanding and lamenting the destruction of the second temple.

Hopes of restoration of the sanctuary may be attested in *Targum Psalms:*

> in many-colored robes she is led to the king, with her virgin companions, her escort, in her train. (45:15 [Eng. 45:14 RSV])

> In their decorated garments they will offer their sacrifices before the king of the world, and the rest of their fellows who are scattered among the Gentiles will be brought in joy to you to Jerusalem. (Targ.)

Thou hast a mighty arm; strong is thy hand, high thy right hand (89:15 [Eng. 89:14 RSV])

> Yours is the arm with strength; your hand will be strong to redeem your people; your right hand will be raised to perfect your Sanctuary. (Targ.)

There may also be a reference to the hope of rebuilding the temple in Psalm 132. The original meaning was historical, in reference to the building of the first temple. But again, the passage may have taken on a typological significance after the destruction of the second temple:

> until I find a place for the LORD, a dwelling place for the Mighty One of Jacob. (132:5 RSV)

> Until I find a place to build the Sanctuary of the LORD, tents for the mighty one of Jacob. (Targ.)

Elsewhere in the targumic tradition hopes for rebuilding the temple are expressed (e.g., *Tg. Isa.* 53:5; *Tg. Zech.* 6:13). These hopes probably reflect the period between the destruction in 70 C.E. and the outbreak of war under the leadership of Simeon bar Koziba (Bar Kokhba) in 132 C.E.[36] In *Barn.* 16 we have Christian commentary that is highly critical of these Jewish hopes: "Finally, I will also speak to you about the temple, and how those wretched men went astray and set their hope on the building, as though it were God's house, and not on their God who created them. . . . This is happening now. For because they went to war, it was torn down by their enemies, and now the very servants of their enemies will rebuild it" (16:1, 4).

Patristic scholars believe that the pseudepigraphal *Barnabas* was composed after the destruction of the temple but before Hadrian's building of the temple in honor of Jupiter. J. B. Lightfoot narrowed the date to the reign of Vespasian, whose style of rule, with its involvement of his sons Titus and Domitian, may be in view in *Barn.* 4:4, which reads (according to Lightfoot), "Ten reigns shall reign upon the earth, after them shall arise a little king, who shall bring low three of the kings under one." Lightfoot and others think the "ten reigns" (or ten kingdoms) are the Roman Caesars, with Vespasian the tenth. The three kings destined to be brought low are the Flavians—Vespasian and his two sons. The "little king" is Nero, whose return was continually rumored during Vespasian's reign. If this interpretation is correct (and not all accept it), then a date of 70–79 seems probable.[37] In any case, the author of this pseudepigraphon is clearly reacting to Jewish hopes of rebuilding the temple, hopes that were alive in the aftermath of 70 but less so after 135.

Accordingly, we may again have in the Aramaic Psalter evidence of the presence of interpretive tradition that reaches back to the first century. This is not

---

[36] So Chilton, *Glory of Israel*, 95–96.

[37] J. B. Lightfoot, *The Apostolic Fathers* (ed. J. R. Harmer; New York: Macmillan, 1891), 240–41 (interpretation), 271 (translation). K. Lake (*The Apostolic Fathers* [2 vols.; LCL; Cambridge: Harvard University Press, 1912–1913], 1:338) does not commit himself to Lightfoot's interpretation, saying instead, "The document no doubt belongs to the end of the first or beginning of the second century." See also R. A. Kraft, *The Didache and Barnabas* (vol. 3 of *The Apostolic Fathers: A Translation and Commentary*; New York: Thomas Nelson, 1965), 42–43 (on date), 88–89 (commentary on *Barn.* 4), 130–33 (commentary on *Barn.* 16). J. A. T. Robinson (*Redating the New Testament* [Philadelphia: Westminster, 1976], 313–19) agrees with Lightfoot's date; other scholars opt for later dates, usually closer to the Bar Kokhba revolt.

to say that traditions about the sanctuary did not develop further in later times; it is only to say that some of the interpretive orientation toward the sanctuary has early roots.

Jerusalem

The name of the famous city occurs seventeen times in the Hebrew Psalter. But in the Aramaic it occurs about thirty times. Again we have coherence with *Targum Isaiah* at some points but not at others.

Sometimes Jerusalem appears in order to qualify the text. In Ps 42:5 we hear of the "procession to the house of God, with glad shouts and songs of thanksgiving, a multitude keeping festival" (RSV). But in the Targum we hear of those who are going "to the Sanctuary of the LORD with a voice of petition and praise, a tumult of peoples coming to keep festival in Jerusalem." Not only does "house of God" become the familiar "Sanctuary of the LORD"; Jerusalem as the destination is made explicit (see also 45:15 [Eng. 45:14]; 48:2 [Eng. 48:1]; 76:3 [Eng. 76:2]; 101:8; 122:5). Sometimes the city appears where one would not expect it (as in 72:16). Other appearances are not surprising (as in 80:11 [Eng. 80:10]; 107:7; 127:1; 133:1). Psalm 120:6, "Too long have I had my dwelling among those who hate peace" (RSV), in the Targum is rendered, "More than these, my soul abides with Edom, the hater of peace," and may allude to Rome. We have no clear examples of the exaltation of Jerusalem, in contrast to the destruction or humiliation of Rome (as we have in *Targum Isaiah*).

Targum Psalms's perspective of the city of Jerusalem seems to reflect, at least at points, the period between 70 and 135. The *meturgeman* is mindful of the destruction of the second temple, as seen in his expansion of 79:1:

> A psalm composed by Asaph about the destruction of the Temple. He said in the spirit of prophecy: O God, the Gentiles are entering your inheritance; they have defiled your holy temple, they have made Jerusalem a desolation. (Targ.)

Asaph's psalm "about the destruction of the Temple" and the desolation of Jerusalem is spoken "in the spirit of prophecy." On one level, of course, the historical Asaph has foretold the destruction of the first temple. But on another level, one deeply felt by the synagogue in the aftermath of 70, Asaph's prophecy also anticipates the second destruction.

At the same time, however, there is no clear indication that *Targum Psalms* has reacted to the fearful post-135 realities, in which Jerusalem loses its name, the Jewish people and the teaching of Torah are banned from it, and a Roman temple in honor of Jupiter is erected on the very place where the holy temple once stood. For example, according to 68:30, "From your temple you will accept sacrifices; your presence abides on Jerusalem" (Targ.). The Targum has added "your presence abides on Jerusalem." With or without the temple, Jerusalem remains. Not only does God still abide in Jerusalem; God's people still inhabit Jerusalem. It is not easy to explain this addition if the original perspective was post-135.

Moreover, Ps 107:7 ("he led them by a straight way, till they reached a city to dwell in" RSV) in the Targum is expanded to read, "And he guided them on a straight way, to come to Jerusalem, the inhabited city." Targumic additions such as these are more easily understood as reflections of the two generations that lay between the two great rebellions in the land of Israel rather than as reflections of the aftermath of the defeat in 135 and Rome's attempt to end once and for all the presence of the Jewish cultus in Jerusalem.[38]

House of Israel

The epithet "house of Israel" occurs about twenty-six times in the Aramaic Psalter but only three times in the Hebrew. The house of Israel constitutes God's covenant people, whether faithful and obedient or foolish and sinful. Some of the references are part of a historicizing paraphrase of the Psalter (e.g., 68:7; 74:14; 76:4; 78:5; 90:1; 107:33).

Consistent with the emphasis already seen regarding the Torah, the primary duty of the house of Israel is to devote itself to the Torah, which sustains and prepares the people for better days that lie ahead. The interpretive expansion in 110:3 is especially instructive:

> Your people will offer themselves freely on the day you lead your host upon the holy mountains. From the womb of the morning like dew your youth will come to you. (RSV)

> > Your people are those of the house of Israel who devote themselves to the Torah; you will be helped in the day of your making battle with them; in the glories of holiness the mercies of God will hasten to you like the descent of dew; your offspring dwell securely. (Targ.)

The context of this paraphrase is very illuminating. According to one Aramaic version, David is promised the kingdom "in exchange for sitting in study of Torah" (*Tg. Ps.* 110:1, apud *targum aher*). When David prepares for battle, he will be assisted by his people, the house of Israel, who have devoted themselves to Torah. The messianic orientation becomes clear in v. 4, where reference to the mysterious Melchizedek is transformed to read, "The LORD has sworn and will not turn aside, that you are appointed leader in the age to come, because of the merit that you were a righteous king." It is the Davidic Messiah who will be "appointed leader in the age to come"[39] because David had been a "righteous king" (from the meaning of the name Melchizedek, which means "My king is

---

[38] Regarding *Targum Isaiah*'s perspective on Jerusalem, Chilton (*Glory of Israel*, 28) reaches a similar conclusion.

[39] Levey (*Messiah*, 122, esp. 141: Psalm 110 is "not rendered messianically") does not cite Psalm 110 as messianic, probably because the epithet "Messiah" does not appear. But taken as a whole, this psalm is clearly eschatological and messianic. The linkage elsewhere in *Targum Psalms* of Messiah with "age to come" (cf. 61:7) confirms the messianic interpretation of Psalm 110.

righteous"). Kings will be struck down, the Gentiles will be judged, the earth will be filled with slain wicked (vv. 5–7), and the avenging Messiah "will receive instruction from the mouth of the prophet on the way." This portrait of a vindicated, Torah-observant house of Israel fits without difficulty the years between the two great rebellions.

Exile

Consistent with other Targumim, especially *Targum Isaiah*, *Targum Psalms* is confident that Israel's exiles will return to the land. The language of the Hebrew Psalter facilitates the development and expression of this hope:

> When the LORD restores the fortunes of his people, Jacob shall rejoice, Israel shall be glad. (Heb. 14:7 [Eng. 14:6 RSV])

> > When the LORD brings back the exile of his people, Jacob will rejoice, Israel will be glad. (Targ.)

> For thou dost deliver a humble people. (Heb. 18:28 [Eng. 18:27 RSV])

> > Because you are going to redeem the people, the house of Israel, who are esteemed among the peoples in exile. (Targ.)

Calls for restoration are interpreted as pleas to end the exile. This interpretive orientation is plainly evident in Psalm 80, where redemption and end of exile are equated:

> Restore us, O God; let thy face shine, that we may be saved! (Heb. 80:4 [Eng. 80:3 RSV])

> > O God, bring us back from our exile, and shine the splendor of your countenance upon us, and we will be redeemed. (Targ.)

> Restore us, O God of hosts; let thy face shine, that we may be saved! (Heb. 80:8 [Eng. 80:7 RSV])

> > O God of hosts, bring us back from our exile, and shine the splendor of your countenance upon us, and we will be redeemed. (Targ.)

> Restore us, O LORD God of hosts! let thy face shine, that we may be saved! (Heb. 80:20 [Eng. 80:19 RSV])

> > O LORD God of hosts, bring us back from exile; shine the splendor of your countenance upon us and we will be redeemed. (Targ.)

The *meturgeman* clings to the hope that Israel will be returned to the land, for one day in Jerusalem is better than one thousand days in exile (Ps 84:11 [Eng. 84:10]; see also 88:7 [Eng. 88:6]; 102:24 [Eng. 102:23]; 106:27).

Patriarchs

The patriarchs and heroes of Israel's sacred story make frequent appearances in the Aramaic Psalter. Chilton has observed the important role played by Abraham in *Targum Isaiah,* where the great patriarch is the supreme example for Israel and his righteousness and fidelity assure the continuance of God's covenant relationship with a people that is all too often wayward.[40] The portrait in *Targum Psalms* is similar, but it is applied more broadly, regarding several patriarchs. Abraham himself occurs twelve times in the Aramaic (only four times in the Hebrew), and Isaac four times in the Aramaic (only once in the Hebrew). Jacob is harder to calculate, for reference to his name is often in terms of the people of Israel and not of the patriarch himself (his name occurs thirty-nine times in the Aramaic, thirty-four times in the Hebrew). Others include Moses (eighteen times in the Aramaic, eight times in the Hebrew), Aaron (eleven times in the Aramaic, nine times in the Hebrew), Joseph (six times in the Aramaic, five times in the Hebrew), Samuel (three times in the Aramaic, once in the Hebrew), Jesse (five times in the Aramaic, once in the Hebrew), and David (105 times in the Aramaic, 85 in the Hebrew). Some of these occurrences will be taken up below.

Abraham receives pride of place and sometimes even encroaches on the honors accorded the Davidic king:

> I have made a covenant with my chosen one, I have sworn to David my servant. (Heb. 89:4 [Eng. 89:3 RSV])

> I have made a covenant with Abraham my chosen; I have confirmed it with my servant David. (Targ.)

The insertion of Abraham at this point is bold and breaks up the parallelism, in which David is understood as God's "chosen one."

God helps Israel because of the merit of Abraham:

> God is in the midst of her, she shall not be moved; God will help her right early. (Heb. 46:6 [Eng. 46:5 RSV])

> The presence of the LORD is within it; it will not be shaken; the LORD will help her for the merit of Abraham who prayed on it at the morning hours. (Targ.)

Of course, it is not the merit of Abraham alone but the merit of the three great patriarchs that benefits Israel:

> Thou hast set up a banner for those who fear thee, to rally to it from the bow. That thy beloved may be delivered, give victory by thy right hand and answer us! (Heb. 60:6–7 [Eng. 60:4–5 RSV])

> You have given those who fear you a sign by which to be lifted up, because of the honesty of Abraham forever. Because of the merit of Isaac, those who love

---

[40] Chilton, *Glory of Israel,* 46–48.

you will be delivered; redeem your right hand because of the piety of Jacob, and accept my prayer. (Targ.)

In the sight of their fathers he wrought marvels in the land of Egypt, in the fields of Zoan. (78:12 RSV)

In front of Abraham, Isaac, and Jacob, and the tribes of their ancestors, he performed wonders in the land of Egypt, the field of Tanis. (Targ.)

The Amoraic doctrine of the Aqedah is not present in *Targum Psalms*[41] (nor is it in *Targum Isaiah*), which supports the view that the patriarchal themes, at least in part, are Tannaitic.[42]

Repentance

The verbal and nominal forms of repent and repentance occur about a dozen times in the Aramaic and three times in the Hebrew (cf. Ps 7:13 [Eng. 7:12], "If a man does not repent [יְשׁוּב] . . . ; 22:28 [Eng. 22:27], "All the ends of the earth shall remember and turn [וְיָשֻׁבוּ] to the LORD"; and 85:9 [Eng. 85:8], "he will speak peace to his people, to his saints, to those who turn [יָשׁוּבוּ] to him in their hearts").

The wicked are defined as those who have not repented (cf. *Tg. Ps.* 50:16; no such qualification in the Hebrew). Repentance makes it possible to avoid gehenna (68:15 [Eng. 68:14], apud *targum aher*). Moses gave gifts only to the repentant (68:19 [Eng. 68:18]; more on this passage below). God shows mercy to his people when they repent (76:11 [Eng. 76:10], apud *targum aher*). God all along knew that repentance was necessary, for Israel was prone to sin:

Before the mountains were brought forth, or ever thou hadst formed the earth and the world, from everlasting to everlasting thou art God. (90:2 RSV)

When it was manifest in your presence that your people were going to sin, you established repentance; before ever the mountains were lifted up and the earth and the world's inhabitants created, and from this age to the age to come, you are God. (Targ.)

---

[41] Unless one finds it in the expanded paraphrase seen in 18:26: "With Abraham, who was found pious in your presence, you showed much mercy; with his seed, Isaac, who was complete in fear of you, you completed your favorable word." Do we have here an allusion to the binding of Isaac (cf. Genesis 22)? Later Amoraic interpreters think so, as seen in *Midr. Pss.* 18.22 (on Ps 18:26–27). The Aramaic paraphrase of *Tg. Ps.* 18:26 probably represents an early step in a line of interpretation that would later understand this passage as an allusion to the Aqedah. One must also consider *Tg. Ps.* 118:27, where Samuel the priest orders, "Bind the טליא for a festal sacrifice." טליא can mean either "lamb" or "lad." If the latter is intended, then we may have an allusion to the Aqedah.

[42] Chilton draws the same conclusion regarding *Targum Isaiah*. See Chilton, *Glory of Israel*, 48; idem, "Isaac and the Second Night: A Consideration," *Bib* 61 [1980]: 78–88.

Thou dost sweep men away; they are like a dream, like grass which is renewed in the morning . . . (90:5 RSV)

> And if they do not repent, death will come upon them, they will be as those who are sleeping; and in the age to come, they will disappear like crumbling grass. (Targ.)

In *Targum Isaiah* repentance is sometimes linked to the idea of the remnant. This association is not present in *Targum Psalms*. The explanation for this lies in the fact of Isaiah's preoccupation with this theme, which the Isaianic *meturgeman* interpreted. There will be a remnant of Israel because they will repent. In *Targum Psalms*, however, the emphasis falls on the need for repentance to avoid God's wrath and judgment.

Holy Spirit

The Hebrew Psalter contains two references to God's Spirit without qualification (104:30, "When thou sendest forth thy Spirit, they are created"; 139:7, "Whither shall I go from thy Spirit?" RSV), one mention of God's "good Spirit" (143:10), and one mention of "Holy Spirit" (51:13 [Eng. 51:11]). The Aramaic Psalter has about twenty-eight occurrences of "Spirit," of which six are qualified with the adjective "holy" (51:13; 78:1; 104:30; 106:33; 137:5; 143:10). The first example simply repeats the Hebrew, and two other examples (104:30; 143:10) simply add the adjective. Two of three remaining passages, where the Hebrew text itself provides no prompt for mention of the Holy Spirit, link the Spirit with speech:

> Give ear, O my people, to my teaching; incline your ears to the words of my mouth! (78:1 RSV)

> A teaching of the Holy Spirit, composed by Asaph. Hear, O my people, my Torah; incline your ears to the utterances of my mouth. (Targ.)

> If I forget you, O Jerusalem, let my right hand wither! (137:5 RSV)

> The voice of the Holy Spirit replies and says, "If I forget you, O Jerusalem, I will forget my right hand." (Targ.)

The association of Spirit and speech or Spirit and prophecy (see below), is also attested in *Targum Isaiah*, where Isa 40:13 ([Heb.] "Who has directed the Spirit of the LORD, or as his counselor has instructed him?" RSV) in the Targum becomes "Who has directed the Holy Spirit in the mouth of all the prophets, is it not the LORD?"; and Isa 59:21 ([Heb.] "And as for me, this is my covenant with them, says the LORD: my spirit which is upon you, and my words which I have put in your mouth" RSV) in the Targum becomes "And as for me, this is my covenant with them, says the LORD, my Spirit which is upon you, and my words, which I shall put in your mouth."

It is fascinating to observe a similar association between the Spirit (often in reference to "filling") and speech in the book of Acts (cf. Acts 2:4, "they were all filled with the Holy Spirit and began to speak" RSV; 4:8, "Peter, filled with Holy Spirit, said" RSV; 4:31, "they were all filled with the Holy Spirit and spoke the word of God" RSV; 7:55–56, Stephen, "full of the Holy Spirit . . . said" RSV; 13:9–10, "But Saul, who is also called Paul, filled with the Holy Spirit, looked intently at him and said" RSV; 28:25, "The Holy Spirit was right in saying to your fathers through Isaiah the prophet" RSV). In all of these cases the adjective "holy" is employed, which in the intertestamental period had become commonplace (e.g., in the Dead Sea Scrolls there are more than thirty occurrences of "Holy Spirit"; for other examples, see *Jub.* 1:21, 23 [alluding to Ps 51:12]; *Mart. Isa.* 5:14, where speaking and the Holy Spirit are linked; *4 Ezra* 14:22, where the Holy Spirit will enable the prophet to write; *Pss. Sol.* 17:37, where the Holy Spirit provides strength and wisdom). These examples lead one to think that the similar diction in *Targum Psalms* points to an early date.

Prophets and Prophecy

The word "prophecy" occurs fifteen times in the Aramaic text, not once in the Hebrew. Thirteen times the Aramaic mentions prophets or prophecy, in contrast to only three occurrences in the Hebrew. The premiere prophet is David, whose words and praise are often given by the "spirit of prophecy," a phrase that occurs in the Aramaic about ten times (e.g., 14:1; 18:1; 18:16 [Eng. 18:17]; 49:15 [Eng. 49:16]) and is found in the intertestamental writing *Jubilees* (31:12, "and the spirit of prophecy came down into his [Jacob's] mouth"; cf. 8:18, which says of Noah that "he had spoken with his mouth in prophecy"). The identification of David as one who speaks through the Holy Spirit is attested in the book of Acts:

> "Brethren, the scripture had to be fulfilled, which the Holy Spirit spoke beforehand by the mouth of David, concerning Judas who was guide to those who arrested Jesus." (1:16)

> "who by the mouth of our father David, thy servant, didst say by the Holy Spirit, 'Why did the Gentiles rage, and the peoples imagine vain things?'" (4:25)

But the closest parallel is found in the large *Psalms Scroll*[a] from Qumran, which says, "And David, the son of Jesse, was wise, and a light like the light of the sun, and literate, and discerning and perfect in all his ways before God and men. And the Lord gave him a discerning and enlightened spirit . . . All these things he spoke through prophecy, which was given to him from the Most High" (11QPs[a] 27:2–4, 11).[43] It should also be noted that in Ps. 45:2 [Eng. 45:3], the spirit of prophecy is said to have been placed on the lips of the Messiah.

---

[43] The translation is based on J. A. Sanders, *The Psalms Scroll of Qumran Cave 11 (11QPs^a)* (DJD 4; Oxford: Clarendon, 1965), 92.

Again, the dictional and thematic parallels encourage us to date the language of prophecy in *Targum Psalms* to the Tannaitic period rather than the Amoraic.

Memra

This word (for "word") is ubiquitous in the Aramaic Psalter, occurring about 174 times. This circumlocution (and that is its primary function) plays a variety of roles, not unlike what is found in the other Targumim, including *Targum Isaiah.* For example, it is the "Memra of the Lord," not the Lord himself, that mocks the wicked (2:4); the faithful do not take refuge in God, they trust in his Memra (Ps. 5:12 [Eng. 5:11]; 7:2 [Eng. 7:1]); and it is the Memra of the Lord that judges the wicked (7:9 [Eng. 7:8]).

Shekinah

This word (for the dwelling of God among humankind) is also commonplace in *Targum Psalms,* though occurring only about fifty-eight times. Its primary function is to denote the presence of God and as such sometimes functions similarly to the Memra. For example, reference to God's "seat on high" (Ps 7:8 [Eng. 7:7 RSV]) becomes in the Aramaic "the place of your Shekinah"; or the Hebrew's "Sing praises to the LORD, who dwells in Zion!" (9:12 [Eng. 9:11 RSV]) in the Aramaic becomes "Sing praise before the LORD who made his Shekinah rest in Zion"; or, finally, the Hebrew's "Keep me as the apple of the eye; hide me in the shadow of thy wings" (17:8) in the Aramaic becomes "Guard me like the circle that is in the middle of the eye; in the shadow of your Shekinah you will hide me."

Glory

This word is similar in function to "Memra" and "Shekinah," occurring about ninety times in the Aramaic, though often merely translating the corresponding word in the Hebrew text. When added to the text, it is usually in reference to God's glory. For example, the Hebrew's "As for me, I shall behold thy face in righteousness; when I awake, I shall be satisfied with beholding thy form" (17:15) in Aramaic becomes "I in truth will see your countenance, I will be satisfied at the time that I awake, from the glory of your face." See also 18:13 (Eng. 18:12).

Judgment/the Wicked/Gehenna

Targum Psalms emphasizes the theme of judgment and shifts it from the temporal perspective of the Hebrew to the eternal. The picturesque language of the Hebrew, where there is mention of fire and smoke or of being consumed, often prompts the *meturgeman* to speak of gehenna, a locution in the NT Gospels and in at least one place corresponding with a specific passage from *Targum Isaiah* (compare Mark 9:48 with *Tg. Isa.* 66:24; both passages speak of gehenna). The word "gehenna" (or "gehinnom") appears about fifteen times in the Targum.

Angels/Demons

Angelology and demonology in *Targum Psalms* is accentuated. It is not absent in the Hebrew Psalter, but it is enhanced and modernized in the Aramaic. The angels sometimes reflect the sensitivities that lie behind the use of circumlocutions such as "Memra" or "Shekinah." In Ps 8:5 (Eng. 8:6) the *meturgeman* is uncomfortable with the comparison between human and God:

> Yet thou hast made him little less than God, and dost crown him with glory and honor. (RSV)

> And you have made him a little less than the angels, and you will crown him with glory and brightness. (Targ.)

In two passages angels take the place of the Heb. *elim* ("heavenly beings" or "gods") to avoid any suggestion of two or more gods of heaven:

> Ascribe to the LORD, O heavenly beings, ascribe to the LORD glory and strength (29:1 RSV).

> A psalm of David. Give praise in the presence of the LORD, O bands of angels; give glory and might in the LORD's presence. (Targ.)

> For who in the skies can be compared to the LORD? Who among the heavenly beings is like the LORD? (Heb. 89:7 [Eng. 89:6 RSV])

> For who in the clouds can be set beside the LORD? Who resembles the LORD in the multitudes of angels? (Targ.)

The "angel of death" also appears in the Aramaic Psalter:

> What man can live and never see death? Who can deliver his soul from the power of Sheol? (Heb. 89:48 [Eng. 89:49 RSV])

> Who is the man *who* will live and not see *the angel of* death, who will deliver his soul from *his* hand, *and not go down to his grave* forever? (Targ.)

> You will not fear the terror of the night, nor the arrow that flies by day. (91:5 RSV)

> Be not afraid of the terror of demons who walk at night, of the arrow of the angel of death that he looses during the day. (Targ.)

Let not the slanderer be established in the land; let evil hunt down the violent man
speedily! (140:11 RSV)

> The man who speaks with deceitful tongue—they cannot dwell in the land of
> life; the angel of death will hunt down the men of evil rapacity, he will smite
> them in Gehenna. (Targ.)

The association of the angel of death with gehenna is to be noted. Linked
also to the angel of death are the demons. Demons appear to be referred to in the
Hebrew Psalter at 106:37: "They sacrificed their sons and their daughters to the
demons." The Targum translates this verse literally. In *Tg. Ps.* 89:32 [Eng. 89:33]
the wicked are plagued by demons. In *Tg. Ps.* 91:5–6, part of which has already
been cited, demons walk at night and attack at noon while the angel of death lets
fly his deadly arrows. Moreover, the faithful need to know that they are protected
from morning demons and the Liliths, who attack at night (cf. *Tg. Ps.* 121:6). The
addition of Solomon to Psalm 91—the psalm devoted to dangers and terrors in
the night—is especially interesting:

> Because you have made the LORD your refuge, the Most High your habitation, no
> evil shall befall you, no scourge come near your tent. (91:9–10 RSV)

>> Solomon answered and said, "For you are my confidence, O LORD; in the high-
>> est dwelling place you have placed the house of your presence." The lord of the
>> world responded and thus he *said:* "No harm shall happen to you; and no
>> plague or demon shall come near to your tents." (Targ.)

In the first century there is abundant evidence of interest in Solomon, son
of David, as exorcist par excellence. This evidence will be reviewed below. For
early references to Lilith, usually thought of as a female demon, see 4Q510 frg. 1,
line 5 ("all the spirits of the destroying angels, spirits of the bastards, Lilith, howlers and desert dwellers"); the same in 4Q511 frg. 10, line 1, and *2 Bar.* 10:8 ("I
shall call the Sirens from the sea, and you Lilin [or Lilith], come from the desert,
and you, demons and dragons from the woods").[44] Indeed, Qumran's 4Q184,
which has been called the "Wiles of the Wicked Woman," is probably not in reference to a mortal woman but to Lilith herself.[45]

Righteous(ness)

The epithet "the righteous" occurs about ninety-two times in the Aramaic,
about twice as often as in the Hebrew Psalter. The word "righteousness" occurs
about fifty times in the Aramaic, only slightly more often than in the Hebrew.
The primary purpose of the *meturgeman's* interpretive work is to enhance the

---

[44] The name Lilith also appears on Aramaic incantation bowls; cf. C. H. Gordon,
"Two Magic Bowls in Teheran," *Or* 20 (1951): 306–15, esp. 310; J. A. Montgomery, *Aramaic Incantation Texts from Nippur* (Philadelphia: University Museum, 1913), 190.

[45] As is argued by J. M. Baumgarten, "On the Nature of the Seductress in 4Q184,"
RevQ 15 (1991): 133–43, here 140.

description of the faithful and at the same time to widen the gulf between them and the wicked. One might say that there is no gray area in the Targum's ethical categories. A few examples should suffice:

> Offer right sacrifices, and put your trust in the LORD. (Heb. 4:6 [Eng. 4:5 RSV])

>> Subdue your impulses and it will be reckoned to you as a righteous sacrifice; and hope in the LORD. (Targ.)

> He has prepared his deadly weapons, making his arrows fiery shafts. (Heb. 7:14 [Eng. 7:13 RSV])

>> On his account, he has prepared the weapons of death; he will make his arrows for those who pursue the righteous. (Targ.)

> The LORD has made himself known, he has executed judgment; the wicked are snared in the work of their own hands. (Heb. 9:17 [Eng. 9:16 RSV])

>> Manifest before the LORD is the judgement he executed: through the works of his hands, the wicked man stumbled, the righteous will rejoice forever. (Targ.)

> Thou dost see; yea, thou dost note trouble and vexation, that thou mayst take it into thy hands; the hapless commits himself to thee; thou hast been the helper of the fatherless. (10:14 RSV)

>> It is manifest in your presence, because you will inflict misery and wrath upon the wicked man; look carefully to pay a good reward to the righteous by your hand; the poor will place their hope on you; you have been a helper to the orphan. (Targ.)

The contrast between the righteous and the wicked is commonplace in the Hebrew Psalter (e.g., 1:5–6 [Eng. 1:6–7]; 7:10 [Eng. 7:9]) and in all parts of the HB (e.g., Gen 18:23, 25; Exod 23:7; Prov 3:33; and many others, including examples in the prophets) as well as the literature of late antiquity (e.g., *1 En.* 1:1; 50:2; *2 Bar.* 48:48). *Targum Psalms* has intensified what was already in the text and has made it complement other themes.

Redemption/Redeem/Redeemer

Words for "redemption," "redeem," and "redeemer" occur more than 140 times in the Aramaic, about ten times the number found in the Hebrew text. Calls for help or deliverance are often translated in the Aramaic with calls for redemption, sometimes explicitly in reference to exile. There is semantic overlap, granted, but one gains the impression that the *meturgeman* has deliberately reoriented the perspective of the Psalter to reflect the post-70 conditions of the people of Israel, many of whom were living outside the land. Their need was not so much for help (from any given danger or distress) but for redemption with all of its eschatological implications. Here are a few examples:

"Because the poor are despoiled, because the needy groan, I will now arise,"
says the LORD; "I will place him in the safety for which he longs." (Heb. 12:6 [Eng.
12:5 RSV])

> "Because of the oppression of the poor, because of the cry of the needy, now I
> will arise," says the LORD; "I will give redemption to my people, but against the
> wicked I will give testimony of evil." (Targ.)

But I have trusted in thy steadfast love; my heart shall rejoice in thy salvation. (13:6
[Eng. 13:5 RSV])

> But I have placed my trust in your goodness, my heart will rejoice in your re-
> demption; I will give praise in the LORD's presence because he rewards me with
> good things. (Targ.)

For thou dost deliver a humble people; but the haughty eyes thou dost bring down.
(Heb. 18:28 [Eng. 18:27 RSV])

> Because you are going to redeem the people, the house of Israel, who are es-
> teemed among the peoples in exile; and by your word you will abase the mighty
> nations who prevail over them. (Targ.)

Messiah

The late Samson Levey assessed the messianism of the Aramaic Psalter. Although his nonmessianic interpretation of Psalm 110 has not been followed by
most scholars, his overall description of messianism in *Targum Psalms* seems fair.
He finds the Targum conservative in its approach, in that it does not attribute too
much messianism to the text. The "Targum utilizes only a choice few [psalms] to
interpret with reference to the Messiah."[46] A few examples should be noted.

The rhetorical questions of Ps 18:32 (Eng. 18:31), "For who is God, but the
LORD? And who is a rock, except our God?" occasion qualification and explanation by the *meturgeman:*

> For because of the miracle and deliverance that you will perform for your Messiah,
> and for the remnants of your people who will remain, all the peoples, nations, and
> tongues will confess and say, "There is no God but the LORD, for there is none be-
> sides you"; and your people will say, "There is none mighty except our God."

For the Psalms *meturgeman,* almost always "miracles" refers to God's
mighty acts of salvation in Israel's history (e.g., 9:2; 18:1 [in reference to David];
40:6; 48:6; 105:5; 116:14, 14). In one case, "miracles" may have a revelatory meaning, perhaps eschatological as well: "Let the works of your miracles appear to
your servants, and let your splendor be upon their sons" (*Tg. Ps.* 90:16). The very
next verse petitions, "And may the pleasantness of the Garden of Eden be upon
us." It is perhaps in this sense that we should understand the reference to "the

---

[46] Levey, *Messiah,* 141.

miracle and deliverance" that God "will perform for" his "Messiah, and for the remnants of" his "people who remain." The day will come when the Gentiles will confess, "There is no God but the LORD, for there is none besides you," which is an unmistakable allusion to Isa 45:21 and/or 46:9.

About seven times in *Targum Psalms* the Messiah is called "King Messiah" (and a few times "Messiah," without qualification, e.g., at 89:52 [Eng. 89:51] and 132:17, which simply follow the Hebrew). This epithet is common in the Pentateuch Targumim (e.g., *Tg. Ps.-J.* Gen 3:15; 35:21; 49:1; *Frg. Tg.* Gen 49:10–12; *Frg. Tg.* Exod 12:42; *Frg. Tg.* Num 11:26; and many more) and in some of the other Targumim of the Writings (e.g., *Tg. Song* 1:8, 17; 7:14; 8:1, 2, 4; *Tg. Ruth* 1:1; 3:15; *Tg. Lam.* 2:22; 4:22; *Tg. Qoh,* 1:11; 7:24), but it is rare in the Targumim of the Prophets. The epithet does not occur in the Babylonian Talmud (*b. Sanh.* 99a is the only passage that comes close: "Now, who is the one king? The Messiah, of course"). It occurs a few times in the Jerusalem Talmud (e.g., *y. Ber.* 2:3, 4; *y. Taʿan.* 4.5, the last in reference to Simeon bar Koziba) and about two dozen times in *Midrash Rabbah* (but not in the earlier midrashim).[47]

One might infer from these data that the epithet "King Messiah" is of late, rabbinic coinage. Perhaps, but the appearance of similar language in *Psalms of Solomon,* a pseudepigraphon that dates to the first century B.C.E., cautions against making this inference too quickly. The pertinent passages read,

> See, Lord, and raise up for them their king, the son of David, to rule over your servant Israel in the time known to you, O God. (*Pss. Sol.* 17:21)

> He will be a righteous king over them, taught by God . . . and their king shall be the Lord Messiah. (17:32)

The messianic figure envisioned here is not called "King Messiah" exactly, but both elements are applied; he is Israel's king and he shall be the Messiah. The NT itself may shed some light on this question. The crucified Jesus is taunted in Mark, "Let the Messiah, the King of Israel, come down now from the cross" (Mark 15:32 RSV). In Luke's account of the hearing before Pilate, Jesus is accused, "We found this man perverting our nation, and forbidding us to give tribute to Caesar, and saying that he himself is Christ a king" (Luke 23:2). In both passages we have the words "king" and "Messiah" ("Christ") juxtaposed. Luke's λέγοντα ἑαυτὸν χριστὸν βασιλέα εἶναι could, however, be translated, "saying that he is King Messiah." Even Mark's ὁ χριστὸς ὁ βασιλεὺς Ἰσραήλ could be translated "the King Messiah of Israel."

Another common rabbinic epithet for the Messiah is "son of David" (e.g., *y. Sukkah* 5.1; *y. Taʿan.* 1.1; *b. ʿErub.* 43a; *b. Yoma* 10a; *b. Sukkah* 52a, 52b; *b. Meg.* 17b; *b. Ḥag.* 16a; *b. Yebam.* 62a, 63b; *b. Soṭah* 48b; *b. Ketub.* 112b; *b. Sanh.* 38a, 97a, 97b, 98a, 98b; *b. ʿAbod. Zar.* 5a; *b. Nid.* 13b; *Gen. Rab.* 97 [on Gen 49:10]; *Exod. Rab.* 25:12 [on 16:29]; *Tg. Jer.* 30:9; *Tg. Esth II* 1:1). It occurs once in

---

[47] For an assessment of messianism in rabbinic literature, see J. Neusner, *Messiah in Context: Israel's History and Destiny in Formative Judaism* (Philadelphia: Fortress, 1984).

Targum Psalms, though augmented with the title "King": "Composed by Solomon, uttered in prophecy. O God, give your just rulings to the King Messiah, and your righteousness to the son of King David" (72:1).

This epithet also reaches back to the NT period and even earlier. *Psalms of Solomon* 17:21 has already been cited ("raise up for them their king, the son of David, to rule over your servant Israel"). Jesus calls into question the scribal practice of calling the Messiah the "son of David" (cf. Mark 12:35–37) although he himself had been addressed this way by blind Bartimaeus (cf. Mark 10:47, 48: "Son of David, have mercy on me!"; cf. also *T. Sol.* 20:1, "King Solomon, son of David, have mercy on me!" and the Aramaic incantation found in CBS 9012, where protection from sickness is petitioned "by the seal of King Solomon, son of David"; see below).

The messianic terminology of *Targum Psalms* reflects the diversity found in the literature of late antiquity and beyond. It is accordingly very difficult to date. We may suspect that some elements are early, reflecting the period between the great rebellions, and other elements are late, probably reflecting the Amoraic tendency to use the epithet "King Messiah." The lack of coherence with rabbinic midrash is another sign of the diversity of the origins of the Psalm Targum's messianism. If we take the passages where the Messiah is called "King Messiah," the epithet that is found most frequently in Amoraic (and later) sources, there is, surprisingly, almost no correlation with *Midrash Psalms.* Only Ps 21:2 [Eng. 21:1], 21:8 [Eng. 21:7], and (partially) 72:17 are treated messianically in the *Midrash Psalms;* Ps 18:32 [Eng. 18:31], 45:3 [Eng. 45:2], 45:5 [Eng. 45:4], 61:7–9 [Eng. 61:6–8], 72:1, 80:16 [Eng. 80:15], and, surprisingly, 89:52 [Eng. 89:51] (though it is messianic in *m. Soṭah* 9:15, an early midrashic tradition) are not treated messianically in the *Midrash Psalms.* The failure to exploit these passages messianically is not for lack of interest in messianism on the part of the compilers of this midrash; far from it: many passages are interpreted messianically (cf. 2:3, 9, 10 [on Ps 2:2, 7, 8]; 16:4 [on Ps 16:4]; 18:5 [on Ps 18:1]; 21:1, 2, 4 [on Ps 21:1–2, 4]; 42/43:5 [on Ps 42:6]; 60:3 [on Ps 60:6]; 72:5, 6 [on Ps 72:6, 16]; 87:6 [on Ps 87:4]; 90:12, 17 [on Ps 90:3, 15]; 92:10 [on Ps 92:5]; 93:3 [on Ps 93:2]; 110:4 [on Ps 110:1]; 119:16 [on Ps 119:33]).

An early, less developed form of messianism in the Psalter, shown below, supports the suggestion here that some elements of messianism in *Targum Psalms* probably do reach back to early Tannaitic times.

Historicizing Tendencies

One of the already mentioned features of the Aramaic Psalter is its tendency to historicize the text, transforming hymnic and liturgical materials into historical narrative,[48] with speaking parts assigned to various OT worthies.

---

[48] Bacher ("Targum zu den Psalmen," 414) describes this phenomenon as a tendency "to dramatize." It will be shown below that aspects of the *meturgeman's* historicizing is indeed dramatization.

Bernstein rightly speaks of the transformation of the text, but one should not infer that the hymnic character is necessarily eliminated. In my judgment, the text remains as hymnic and liturgical as ever, with characters singing to one another antiphonally. This feature will be considered shortly.

The historicizing tendency of the Aramaic Psalter is readily seen in the insertion of biblical names. Among the better-known figures, Pharaoh occurs twice in the Hebrew Psalter but seven times in the Aramaic; Moses, eight times in the Hebrew but eighteen times in the Aramaic; Aaron, nine times in the Hebrew but eleven times in the Aramaic; Joseph, five times in the Hebrew but six times in the Aramaic; David, about eighty-five times in the Hebrew but 105 times in the Aramaic; Saul, five times in the Hebrew but eight times in the Aramaic; Samuel, one time in the Hebrew but three times in the Aramaic; Jesse, once in the Hebrew but five times in the Aramaic; Elijah does not appear in the Hebrew, but he appears once in the Aramaic (at least in some of the MSS); Adam does not appear in the Hebrew, but he appears four times in the Aramaic; Sennacherib does not appear in the Hebrew, but he appears once in the Aramaic; Noah does not appear in the Hebrew, but he too appears once in the Aramaic; Goliath does not appear in the Hebrew, but he appears twice in the Aramaic; and the Philistines, who do not appear in the Hebrew, appear seven times in the Aramaic. Other kings (e.g., Hezekiah, Zedekiah) and prophets (e.g., Jonah, Joel) appear once or twice.[49]

Typically, the *meturgeman* finds a parallel between an event in Israel's history and a theme in the Psalter. Accordingly, the Hebrew's "Some sat in darkness and in gloom, prisoners in affliction and in irons" (107:10 RSV) becomes in the Targum a reference to the tragic fate of king Zedekiah and his contemporaries, who "were exiled to Babylon." In the same psalm the Hebrew's "Some went down to the sea in ships" (107:23 RSV) becomes in the Aramaic a word "concerning Jonah," who prophesied concerning the seamen who went down in the sea. In Psalm 78 we hear of the priests who "fell by the sword" (v. 64 RSV). The context suggests an event from the history of 1 Samuel—which one or ones is not easy to say. The *meturgeman*, however, tells us that it was "the time when the Philistines captured the ark of the LORD, and the priests of Shiloh, Hophni and Phineas, fell by the sword."

Other times the *meturgeman* is guided by the Hebrew Psalter itself, by the superscriptions, or by clues in the psalm's contents. We see this when the Hebrew's "thou with thy own hand didst drive out the nations" (44:3 [Eng. 44:2]) becomes in the Aramaic "you drove out the Canaanite Gentiles with your mighty hand," or the Hebrew's "he turned the sea into dry land; men passed through the river on foot" (66:6) becomes in the Aramaic "he turned the Red Sea to dry land; the sons of Israel crossed the River Jordan on their feet; he conveyed them to his holy mountain" (see also Psalm 74, which in the Aramaic introduces many details from the exodus and the crossing of the sea, and Psalm 81, which in the Aramaic adds details from the story of Joseph).

---

[49] All of the numbers just given are somewhat tentative, given variant readings.

Other themes have been suggested as characteristic of *Targum Psalms*. Díez Merino lists the epithet "son of man" as a "theme" in the Targum.[50] I agree with him that the data themselves do need to be studied and that they may in fact contribute to efforts to understand better Jesus' application of the epithet to himself, but I do not think we should speak of a *theme*. Rather, the numerous occurrences of "son of man" or "sons of men" in this Targum appear to be consistent with Aramaic usage in general.

One might also suppose that "wisdom" functions thematically in *Targum Psalms*. The noun "wisdom" and the adjective "wise" are added to several passages (e.g., 14:2; 41:2 [Eng. 41:1]; 50:17; 53:3 [Eng. 53:2]; 68:12 [Eng. 68:11]; 101:2; 105:17; 119:100), often as a complement to obedience to, or study of, Torah. But this theme is already present in the Hebrew Psalter. The Targum has simply enhanced this tendency, largely out of devotion to Torah (e.g., 53:3 [Eng. 53:2]) and deep respect for the patriarchs and other heroes of the faith (e.g., 105:17).

One might also mention the curious epithet "first Adam," which occurs in other targumic literature and so cannot be said to be distinctive of *Targum Psalms*. There are a handful of interesting occurrences, which will be discussed below, but it is unlikely that this locution constitutes a theme.

And finally, the kingdom of God is a theologoumenon that is of special importance in the Targumim of the Prophets, not least *Targum Isaiah*.[51] The locution "kingdom of God" does not occur in *Targum Psalms*, but a few passages seem to contribute to this theme. They will be considered below.

Date of Targum Psalms

On the basis of *Tg. Ps.* 108:11, Bacher suggested a late-fifth-century date as the terminus ad quem:[52]

> Who will bring me to the fortified city? Who will lead me to Edom? (RSV)

> And now because I sinned, who will lead me to the fortress of wicked Rome? Who led me to Constantinople of Edom? (Targ.)

Churgin, however, wonders if the reference to Constantinople in this verse is a late gloss and therefore not indicative of the true terminus ad quem.[53] I am inclined to agree. The older, original exegesis is the identification of Edom with Rome. When, in the fourth and fifth centuries, the power shifted to Constantinople, it was necessary to update the text with a gloss. On linguistic grounds,

---

[50] Díez Merino, "Haggadic Elements," 132, 134.

[51] On this locution, see the chapter in this volume by Chilton. See also B. D. Chilton, "Regnum Dei Deus est," *SJT* 31 (1978): 261–70; idem, *Glory of Israel*, 77–81.

[52] Bacher, "Targum zu den Psalmen," 471.

[53] Churgin, *Targum to Hagiographa*, 59.

Gustaf Dalman argues for the fourth and fifth centuries C.E., a somewhat earlier date.[54] Díez Merino agrees, adding the evidence of *Tg. Ps.* 69:3, 15, 16, where the description of the ongoing exile seems to reflect the dominance of the Roman Empire (i.e., the Roman Empire still existed). Díez Merino also makes the pertinent observation that *Targum Psalms* contains no reference to Mohammed and Islam (as do some of the later Targumim).[55] This silence supports a terminus ad quem prior to the end of the sixth century. An Amoraic stamp on the final form of *Targum Psalms* seems apparent. Dalman's date is probably as early as *Targum Psalms* can be dated. But are there indications that some of the material in this Targum reaches back to the Tannaitic period?

Díez Merino has recommended analysis of the Greek and Latin loan words,[56] for their appearance in *Targum Psalms* suggests that Greek was still in use in Palestine at the time the Targum was composed. This observation is consistent with an Amoraic date. The Greek terminology used for Roman officials, however, may also give some indication of an earlier date as well as a more specific provenance.

Targum Psalms contains about twenty Greek and Latin loan words.[57] The Greek words are not derived from the LXX. Although detailed study of these words will have to be undertaken elsewhere, a few comments here will be helpful. Several of the words are conventional, such as אוכלום (from ὄχλος, "crowd" or "army"; cf. *Tg. Ps.* 89:7 [Eng. 89:6]), אכסדרא (from ἐξέδρα, "porch" [in Greek contexts] or "parlor" [in Roman contexts]; cf. 104:3), אפותיקי (from ἀποθήκη, "storehouse" or "store"; cf. 33:7), פלטיותא (from πλατεῖα, "open street," "square," or "highway"; cf. 55:12 [Eng. 55:11]), and פרגמטיא (from πραγματεία, "business"; 121:8). קוסטל (from *castellum*, "strong tower" or "castle"; cf. 61:4 [Eng. 61:3]) is the one certain Latin loan word. Other loan words are more intriguing, such as אנגליא (from ἄγγελοι, "angels"; cf. 50:4), ברברין (from βάρβαρος, "foreigner" or "barbarian"; cf. 114:1), נמוס/נימוס (from νόμος, "law"; cf. 1:2), and קורים (κύρις/κύριος, "lord"; cf. 53:1 [Eng. Ps 53, superscription]).

The loan words that may provide indications of date and perhaps provenance are the words that refer to Roman officialdom. Because they continued to enjoy usage in the Byzantine period, they are not conclusive, but they may be suggestive. These terms are איפרכום (from ἔπαρχος, "eparch" or "prefect"; cf. *Tg. Ps.* 72:9, where the plural איפרכיא is used, from ἔπαρχοι), פלטרין (from πραιτώριον, from the Latin *praetorium*), and פלטין (from παλάτιον, from the Latin *palatium*,

---

[54] G. Dalman, *Grammatik des jüdisch-palästinischen Aramäisch, nach den Idiomen des palästinischen Talmud und Midrasch, des Onkelostargum (Cos. Socini 84), und der jerusalemischen Targume zum Pentateuch* (Leipzig: J. C. Hinrichs, 1894; repr., Darmstadt: Wissenschaftliche Buchgesellschaft, 1960), 34.

[55] Díez Merino, "Haggadic Elements," 136–37.

[56] Díez Merino, "Haggadic Elements," 137; Bacher, "Targum zu den Psalmen," 470. Bacher and Díez Merino do not mention Latin loan words, but there is at least one, possibly more.

[57] The number is approximate not only because of variants in the MSS but because some words may have Greek counterparts but are themselves derived from a Semitic source.

"headquarters," "residence," or "country seat"; cf. 68:13 [Eng. 68:12]). The use of איפרכיא suggests the Eastern empire of the Tannaitic period,[58] but this suggestion requires further study.[59]

Especially interesting is the targumic phrase "angels of the height." It may also suggest an early, eastern provenance. This phrase is thus potentially important for the question of date and provenance of *Targum Psalms:*

> He calls to the heavens above [מֵעָל] and to the earth, that he may judge his people. (MT 50:4)

> He will call to the heaven above [ἄνω] and and to the earth, to judge his people (LXX 49:4)

>> He will call to the angels of the height [לאנגלי מרומא] above [מלעיל], and to the righteous of the earth below, to extend judgment to his people. (Targ.)

> The heavens declare his righteousness, for God himself is judge. (MT 50:6)

> The heavens will declare his righteousness, for God is judge. (LXX 49:6)

>> And the angels of the height [אנגלי מרומא] will recount his righteousness, for God is the judge forever. (Targ.)

> You are gods [אֱלֹהִים], sons of the Most High, all of you. (MT 82:6)

> You are all gods [θεοί], even sons of the Most High. (LXX 81:6)

>> You are reckoned as angels [כמלאכיא], and all of you are like angels of the height [אנגלי מרומא]. (Targ.)

---

[58] There are many examples (mostly Greek) in Tannaitic-era literary sources, papyri, and inscriptions from Syro-Palestine (e.g., 1 Esd 6:3, 7, 18, 27; 8:67; 2 Macc 4:28) and Egypt (e.g., CRAI 1903; ILS 9370; P.Oxy. 237.8; 635; 1032.5–6; 1408.22; 1434.9; 1466.1 [Latin], 4 [Greek]; 1547.6), where a *praefectus*/ἔπαρχος (of either Syria or Egypt) is mentioned. Ἔπαρχος occurs several times in the LXX and in Josephus (e.g., *Ant.* 18.2.2 §33, in reference to Valerius Gratus, ἔπαρχος of Judea [15–19 C.E.]; 19.9.2 §363, in reference to Cuspius Fadus, ἔπαρχος of Judea [44–46 C.E.]; 20.9.1 §197 and *J.W.* 6.5.3 §§303, 305, in reference to Albinus, ἔπαρχος of Judea [62–64 C.E.]). After the death of Agrippa I in 44 C.E., Rome reorganized its administration of Palestine, appointing a series of procurators (beginning with Fadus). Normally the Greek equivalent of this rank is ἐπίτροπος, which also appears in the Targumim as a loan word in the form of אפיטרופוס (cf. *Tg. Neof.* Gen 39:4, 5; 41:40; 44:4; *Frg. Tg.* Gen 44:1; *Tg. Ps.-J.* Gen 41:34), though Greek writers (as we have seen in Josephus) sometimes use ἔπαρχος for this rank as well. I have found no Aramaic transliterations for the Latin words themselves (i.e., *praefectus* and *procurator,* as well as others, such as *tribunus* ["tribune"] and *praetor*). The Aramaic-speaking Jewish community's preference for Greek is consistent with an early and Eastern origin of the targumic diction. The reference in *1 Clement,* which dates to the end of the first century C.E., is not especially helpful, given its probable origin in Rome (cf. *1 Clem.* 37:3, "Not all are prefects [ἔπαρχοι] or tribunes or centurions or captains of fifty and so forth").

[59] Fresh study of Greek and Latin loan words in the Targumim is urgently needed; the older work by S. Krauss, *Griechische und lateinische Lehnwörter im Talmud, Midrasch, und Targum* (2 vols.; Berlin: S. Calvary, 1898–1899; repr., Hildesheim: Olms, 1987), is badly dated and not wholly reliable.

There is none like you among the gods [בָּאֱלֹהִים], O LORD, nor are there any works like yours. (MT 86:8)

There is none like you among the gods [ἐν θεοῖς], O LORD, nor are there any works like yours. (LXX 85:8)

> There is none besides you among the angels of the height [אנגלי מרומא], O LORD, and there is nothing like your deeds. (Targ.)

To these examples one can add Ps 6:1 (LXX 95:1), 97:6 (LXX 96:6), and 148:1 [Eng. 148:3]. In every occurrence of the phrase "angels of the height" the Greek loan word אנגלי/ἄγγελοι is used. The *meturgeman*, of course, is familiar with the Hebrew equivalent, and in fact employs the Aramaic מלאכי several times (cf. *Tg. Ps.* 8:6; 29:1; 57:6, 12; 68:11; 69:35; 78:25; 82:6; 89:7, 8; 91:11; 103:20; 148:2). But every time he adds the phrase "angels of the height," the Hebrew word for "angel" (מלאך) is not present in the Hebrew text that he is translating, and he uses the Greek loan word (אנגל). The impression one gains from this is that אנגלי מרומא is a set phrase.

Not only is אנגלי מרומא a set phrase; it seems to be a very old one, for its Hebrew equivalent appears in 4Q403, one of the fragmentary texts called the *Songs of the Sabbath Sacrifice:*[60]

> He will exalt the God of the angels of the height [אלוהי [מ]לאכי רום] seven times, with seven exalted words of wonder. (frg. 1, col. i, line 1)

> Praise the God of the heights [אלוהי מרומים], you who are exalted [הרמים, lit. "high"] among all the wise divine beings. (frg. 1, col. i, lines 30–31)

> Lift His exaltation to the heights, you godlike among the divine beings of the height [אלוהים מאלי רום]—His glorious divinity above all the heights of the height. Surely He [is the God of gods] over all the princes of the heights [ראשי מרומים], and King of king[s] over all the eternal councils. (frg. 1, col. i, lines 33b–34)

We might also cite 4Q392, which alludes to Ps 104:4 ("He makes his angels [מַלְאָכָיו / LXX 103:4 ἀγγέλους αὐτοῦ] winds and his ministers . . ."):

> For in the heights he makes winds and lightning [His angels and se]rvants of the holy of ho[lies]. (frg. 1, line 9)

The reconstruction is possible because of the allusion to Ps 104:4.[61] What is noteworthy is that the author associates the angels (מלאכי) with the expression "in the heights" (במרום), thus paralleling what is said of the angels in 4Q403.

---

[60] For text and notes, see C. Newsom, *Song of the Sabbath Sacrifice: A Critical Edition* (HSS 27; Atlanta: Scholars Press, 1985), 187, 189, 209–10, 214–17; J. H. Charlesworth and C. A. Newsom, eds., *Angelic Liturgy: Songs of the Sabbath Sacrifice* (vol. 4B of *The Dead Sea Scrolls: Hebrew, Aramaic, and Greek Texts with English Translations;* Princeton Theological Seminary Dead Sea Scrolls Project; Louisville: Westminster John Knox, 1999), 46, 50–52.

[61] For text, see B. Z. Wacholder and M. G. Abegg Jr., *A Preliminary Edition of the Unpublished Dead Sea Scrolls: The Hebrew and Aramaic Texts from Cave Four* (4 fascicles;

The phrase "angels of the heights" appears to be Semitic in origin; it does not occur in the LXX. Its appearance in 4Q403, which dates to 150–100 B.C.E.,[62] argues for an early date. Why the Targum prefers a Greek loan word for "angels" when a perfectly suitable Semitic word is available is not easy to answer.[63] This loan word is not employed in the Targumim of the Pentateuch or the Prophets, but it is found a few times in other Targumim of the Writings (e.g., *Tg. Job* 15:15; 20:27; 35:10; *Tg. Esth.* II 6:1).[64] The substitution of the loan word אנגלי for the Aramaic/Hebrew מלאכי may well be due to cultural influences, perhaps felt most in the Byzantine period. But the phrase itself, in its Semitic form, is quite old. Its appearance in 4Q403, itself a liturgical document, suggests that it entered the interpretive framework of the Aramaic Psalter at a very early date.

Finally, a few other arguments should be considered that have been made for the antiquity of some traditions in the Aramaic Psalter. Wilcox argues that there is present in the Aramaic Psalter material that is quite early, as seen in parallels with the NT, Justin Martyr, and Tertullian and in its close relationship to the Hebrew text (akin to the relationship seen in *Targum Onqelos*).[65] Wilcox cites an example from Psalm 68, presented here with parallels from Ephesians, Justin Martyr, and Tertullian:

> You ascended the high mount, leading captives in your train, and receiving gifts among man [בָּאָדָם] (Heb. 68:19 [Eng. 68:18])

> You ascend on high, you led captivity captive, you received gifts among man [ἐν ἀνθρώπῳ] (LXX 67:19)

>> You ascended to the firmament, O prophet Moses; you captured captives, you taught the words of Torah, you gave gifts to the sons of men [לבני אנש] (Targ.)

> Therefore it is said, "When he ascended on high he led a host of captives, and he gave gifts to people [τοῖς ἀνθρώποις]." (Eph 4:8)

> The words are these, "He ascended on high; he led captivity captive; he gave gifts to the sons of men [τοῖς υἱοῖς τῶν ἀνθρώπων]." (Justin, *Dial.* 39)

> "He ascended on high," that is, into heaven; "He led captivity captive," that is, death or servitude of man; "He gave gifts to the sons of men [*filiis hominum*]," that is, the gifts that we call *charismata*. (Tertullian, *Marc.* 5.8; cf. CSEL 47:598)

Washington, D.C.: Biblical Archaeology Society, 1991–1996), 2:38; F. García Martínez and E. J. C. Tigchelaar, trans., *The Dead Sea Scrolls: Study Edition* (2 vols.; vol. 1, New York: Brill, 1997; vol. 2, Boston: Brill, 1998), 2:788.

[62] Charlesworth and Newsom, *Angelic Liturgy,* 4–5.

[63] The suggestion that the Greek loan word אנגלי is part of a set phrase that predates the Targum, as seen in 4Q403, is consistent with the observation made years ago by Saul Lieberman, who concluded that "all Greek phrases in rabbinic literature are quotations." See S. Lieberman, *Greek in Jewish Palestine: Studies in the Life and Manners of Jewish Palestine in the II–IV Centuries C.E.* (New York: Jewish Theological Seminary of America, 1942), 6.

[64] Zunz (*Gottesdienstliche Vorträge,* 81) and Bacher ("Targum zu den Psalmen," 470) draw attention to the similar usage in *Targum Job* and *Second Targum of Esther.*

[65] Wilcox, "Aramaic Targum to Psalms," 143.

The targumic reading "to the sons of men" agrees with neither the Hebrew nor the LXX but finds an approximate parallel in Eph 4:8 and an exact parallel in Justin Martyr, a Palestinian writing in the middle of the second century C.E., and in Tertullian, a Latin church father writing ca. 200 C.E. This dictional coherence recommends an early date for the Aramaic reading. (The relevance of the targumic version for understanding the allusion to the passage in Eph 4:8 will be explored below.)

The evidence suggests that there are ancient traditions in *Targum Psalms,* even if the MSS that we have today, like all other targumic MSS excepting those found at Qumran (i.e., 4Q156, 4Q157, and 11Q10), give evidence of revisions and glosses dating as late as the Middle Ages. Some of the older material seems to reach back to the first century and in some instances even earlier. Accordingly, it is worthwhile to look for points of coherence between this Targum and the NT. Coherence with the NT will itself add further support to the conclusion thus far reached, that the extant *Targum Psalms* does indeed contain early Palestinian traditions.

The Aramaic Psalter and the New Testament

To date no study has appeared that I am aware of that systematically studies *Targum Psalms* and what light it might shed on the NT. A few studies along the way discuss possible examples; some of these will be taken into account in what follows.

It is lamentable that *Targum Psalms* has not figured more prominently in scholarship in the last fifty years, which has been rightly aware of the relevance of the targumic tradition for understanding better the teaching of Jesus and the writings of the NT. Our cursory survey of the exegetical and theological emphases of this Targum has found them to be rich, interesting, and in some cases probably pertinent to NT study. The following are examples where *Targum Psalms* might shed light on Jesus, the book of Acts, and the Pauline circle.

The Voice at the Baptism and the Transfiguration of Jesus

During both the baptism and the transfiguration of Jesus, a heavenly voice is heard:

> And a voice came from heaven, "Thou art my beloved [ἀγαπητός] Son; with thee I am well pleased." (Mark 1:11 RSV)

> And a cloud overshadowed them, and a voice came out of the cloud, "This is my beloved [ἀγαπητός] Son; listen to him." (Mark 9:7 RSV)

Most interpreters think the second-person construction of Mark 1:11 ("Thou art") is original and that the third-person construction of Mark 9:7 ("This is") is secondary, to make the point that Jesus' disciples, and not Jesus alone, heard the heavenly voice. This is probably what underlies Matthew's redaction, where the words spoken at the baptism in his account are also placed in the third person (cf. Matt 3:17, "This is my beloved Son" RSV). The Lukan evangelist, however, faithfully follows Mark's wording (cf. Luke 3:22, "Thou art my beloved Son" RSV).[66] Consequently, it is not too surprising that most commentators think the words of the heavenly voice allude to Ps 2:7:

> He said to me, "You are my son, today I have begotten you." (MT)

> The Lord said to me, "You are my son, today I have begotten you." (LXX)

Because there is no equivalent for Mark's "beloved" or "pleased," some commentators look to other passages, such as Isa 42:1 ("Behold my servant, whom I uphold, my chosen, in whom my soul delights" RSV) or Isa 44:2 ("Fear not, O Jacob my servant, Jeshurun whom I have chosen" RSV). Genesis 22:2 LXX has also been suggested because of the appearance of the adjective "beloved." The parallel otherwise is not especially close. The two Isaiah passages may well have contributed to Luke's form of the transfiguration voice: "This is my Son, my Chosen; listen to him" (Luke 9:35 RSV).

Regarding Mark's version, however, we do not have to choose between Ps 2:7 and Isa 42:1. It is probable that both have contributed to the wording of the voice at the baptism and that it is the Aramaic version of these passages that has done so. These passages are as follows, with the wording of Psalm 2 presented as literally as possible:

> He said: "Beloved as a son to a father you are to me, pure as if this day I had created you." (*Tg. Ps.* 2:7)

> "Behold my servant, I will bring him near, my chosen, in whom my Memra is pleased." (*Tg. Isa.* 42:1)

What makes the Aramaic version so appealing is that these passages offer the very elements otherwise missing in the two OT Scriptures that scholars have long thought underlay the utterance of the heavenly voice. *Targum Psalms*'s "beloved" (חביב)[67] and *Targum Isaiah*'s "pleased" (אתרעי, the *ithpe'el* of רעי, "to desire," "to be pleased with") are the very elements not found in either the Hebrew or the Greek forms of Ps 2:7 and Isa 42:1. It is difficult to escape the conclusion

---

[66] The second-person and third-person forms of the heavenly voice are conflated in *Gospel of the Ebionites* (cf. §4: "And a voice [came] from heaven, 'Thou art my beloved Son . . .' And again a voice from heaven [said] to him, 'This is my beloved Son . . .'"; from Epiphanius, *Pan.* 30.13.7–8). The second person is retained in *Gospel of the Hebrews*, though not without some interesting innovation (cf. §2: "the Holy Spirit descended upon him and rested on him and said to him, 'My Son, in all the prophets was I waiting for thee . . . For thou art my rest; thou art my first-begotten Son'"; from Jerome, *Comm. Isa.* 4 [on Isa 11:2]).

[67] For another, illustrative Aramaic example, see *Tg. Jer.* 31:9: " . . . My Memra will be to Israel as a Father, and Ephraim is beloved [חביב] before Me."

that the wording of the heavenly voice in the tradition of Jesus' baptism was shaped by the Aramaic form of the scriptural passages in question.[68]

Moreover, the Aramaic's innovative qualification, "as a son to a father you are to me"—doubtlessly motivated by a desire to avoid the anthropomorphism of the Hebrew text[69]—offers yet one more intriguing point of coherence with the Jesus tradition, in this case Jesus' distinctive manner of addressing God as "Abba" (אבא, "father"; cf. Mark 14:36; Rom 8:15; Gal 4:6).[70] We may have here an important clue that explains the choice of Scripture and wording in the formation of the baptismal utterance (whether it originated with Jesus—a possibility that should not be dismissed out of hand—or with his followers). That is, Jesus' fervent belief in, and commitment to, God as Father may well have resulted in the appropriation of Psalm 2, which speaks of the sonship of the Lord's Messiah but in the Aramaic speaks not only of the son as *beloved* but also of the Lord as *Father*.

The Temptation of Jesus

The Matthean and Lukan evangelists augment the Markan account of the temptation of Jesus (cf. Mark 1:12–13) with a block of material drawn from Q, in which Satan three times tempts Jesus (cf. Matt 4:1–11; Luke 4:1–13). In what is the second temptation in Matthew (or third in Luke's ordering), Satan urges Jesus, if (or since) he is the Son of God, to fling himself from the pinnacle of the temple. Jesus need not fear, for, after all, the Scripture assures,

"He will give his angels charge of you," and

"On their hands they will bear you up,
lest you strike your foot against a stone." (Matt 4:6 RSV)

Satan has quoted most of Ps 91:11–12. *Targum Psalms* renders these verses literally. But in the Aramaic context, they mean something far more sinister, something much more in keeping with the context of the Matthean and Lukan temptation narratives. Verses 11–12 are thrown into a new light when vv. 5–6 and

---

[68] See D. Plooij, "The Baptism of Jesus," in *Amicitiae Corolla* (ed. H. G. Wood; FS J. R. Harris; London: University of London Press, 1933), 239–52; T. W. Manson, "The Old Testament in the Teaching of Jesus," *BJRL* 34 (1952): 312–32, esp. 323–24. R. A. Guelich (*Mark 1–8:26* [WBC 34A; Dallas: Word, 1989], 34) discounts out of hand the Aramaic version of Ps 2:7 because the Targum is "late." This begs the question, however, for it is in the number of instances of coherence between the Targum and much earlier sources, such as the writings of the NT, that we begin to suspect that the Targum retains some early tradition. See the discussion in R. H. Gundry (*Mark: A Commentary on His Apology for the Cross* [Grand Rapids: Eerdmans, 1993], 52), who argues for Ps 2:7 and Isa 42:1 and is willing to explore the possibility of Aramaic influence.

[69] In the Greco-Roman world it would be impossible to speak of being "begotten" of God without conjuring up pagan mythology.

[70] Aramaic Isaiah may have contributed to this preferred manner of addressing God; see *Tg. Isa.* 8:4: "For before the child shall have knowledge to cry, 'My father [אבא], and My mother.'"

9–10 are taken into account. Again it is helpful to juxtapose the Hebrew and Aramaic versions:

> You will not fear the terror of the night, nor the arrow that flies by day, nor the pestilence that stalks in darkness, nor the destruction that wastes at noonday. (MT 91:5–6 RSV)

>> Be not afraid of the terror of demons who walk at night, of the arrow of the angel of death that he looses during the day; of the death that walks in darkness, of the band of demons that attacks at noon. (Targ.)

> Because you have made the LORD your refuge, the Most High your habitation, no evil shall befall you, no scourge come near your tent. (MT 91:9–10 RSV)

>> Solomon answered and said: "For you are my confidence, O LORD; in the highest dwelling place you have placed the house of your presence." The lord of the world responded and thus he said: "No harm shall happen to you; and no plague or demon shall come near to your tents." (Targ.)

In vv. 5–6 the Hebrew's "terror of the night" becomes in the Aramaic "the terror of demons who walk at night," and the Hebrew's "arrow" becomes in the Aramaic "the arrow of the angel of death." Also, the Hebrew's "destruction that wastes" becomes in the Aramaic a "band of demons that attacks." In vv 9–10 the Hebrew's "no scourge" becomes in the Aramaic "no plague or demon." And in keeping with *Targum Psalms*'s tendency to historicize, these verses are presented as dialogue between Solomon and the Lord.

The introduction of Solomon into what now is more prose than poetry (recall the observation of Bernstein discussed above) only enriches the demonological dimension of the psalm, for in late antiquity Solomon had the reputation of master exorcist. The tradition is quite old, antedating *Targum Psalms* by centuries. Josephus tells of one Eleazar, an exorcist who made use of incantations and various items said to be handed down from Solomon. Of Solomon the king, the Jewish historian and apologist writes,

> Now so great was the prudence and wisdom that God granted Solomon, that he surpassed the ancients, and even the Egyptians. . . . And God granted him knowledge of the art used against demons for the benefit and healing of people. He also composed incantations, by which illnesses are relieved, and left behind forms of exorcisms with which those possessed by demons drive them out, never to return. And this kind of cure is of very great power among us to this day, for I have seen a certain Eleazar, a countryman of mine, in the presence of Vespasian, his sons, tribunes, and a number of other soldiers, free men possessed by demons, and this was the manner of the cure: he put to the nose of the possessed man a ring that had under its seal one of the roots prescribed by Solomon, and then, as the man smelled it, drew out the demon through his nostrils, and, when the man at once fell down, adjured the demon never to come back into him, speaking Solomon's name and reciting the incantations that he had composed. (*Ant.* 8.2.5 §§45–47)

According to Josephus, Israel's famous king and patron of wisdom surpassed even the Egyptians. In context Josephus probably had in mind the

Egyptians' fame for magic and exorcism, a fame that grows out of passages such as Gen 41:8 and Exod 7:11 (cf. Wis 17:7; 18:13) and is exaggerated in later traditions (e.g., *b. Qidd.* 49b, "Ten measures of sorcery descended into the world; Egypt received nine, the rest of the world one"; *b. Šabb.* 104b, "Did not Ben Stada bring spells from Egypt?"; and esp. *Sepher ha-Razim*).[71] We are told that the Jewish exorcist Eleazar made use of a ring, under whose seal was a root, and incantations believed to have been composed by Solomon himself. The tradition of Solomon as exorcist and healer begins with 1 Kgs 4:29–34 and was embellished in later traditions, such as Wis 7:17–21 and *Testament of Solomon*. In the latter we are told that an angel gave Solomon a "ring, which had a seal engraved on precious stone" (*T. Sol.* 1:7). No doubt this ring with a seal is the very ring Eleazar claimed to possess. The tradition of the incantations said to have been composed by Solomon grew out of the story in which the king interrogated a host of demons, learning from them the ills they caused and how the demons could be thwarted (cf. the whole of the *Testament of Solomon*).[72] The root that Eleazar had under the seal of the ring is probably the Baaras root described elsewhere in Josephus. This root is said to be flame-colored and to emit a brilliant light, killing anyone who mishandled it: "it possesses one virtue for which it is prized; for the so-called demons . . . are promptly expelled by this root, if merely applied to the patients" (*J.W.* 7.6.3 §§180–186).

Solomon's fame was widespread in late antiquity, among non-Jews as well as among Jews. It is attested in scores of incantation texts, usually found inscribed on amulets or bowls.[73] Many of these incantations are written in Aramaic, Syriac, or Mandean,[74] and several refer to Solomon—for example, "Charmed and sealed is all sickness . . . by the seal of King Solomon, son of David";[75] "This is the seal-ring of King Solomon, the son of David. . . . Every demon . . . and all roof howlers, lilis [or liliths], and monsters, and all Satans, and idols, and curses . . . are bound and sealed . . . for all his house and all his dwelling, from this day and forever.

---

[71] See M. Margalioth, ספר הרזים (Book of the mysteries) (Jerusalem: American Academy for Jewish Research, 1966). Margalioth dates *Sepher ha-Razim* to the third century, but this is probably too early. See also D. C. Duling, "Solomon, Exorcism, and the Son of David," *HTR* 68 (1975): 235–52.

[72] And also the later *Sepher ha-Razim;* cf. Margalioth, ספר הרזים, 26.

[73] See C. C. McCown, "The Christian Tradition as to the Magical Wisdom of Solomon," *JPOS* 2 (1922): 1–24; L. R. Fisher, " 'Can This Be the Son of David?' " in *Jesus and the Historian* (ed. F. T. Trotter; FS E. C. Colwell; Philadelphia: Westminster, 1968), 82–97; J. H. Charlesworth, "Solomon and Jesus: The Son of David in Ante-Markan Traditions (Mk 10:47)," in *Biblical and Humane* (ed. L. B. Elder, D. L. Barr, and E. S. Malbon; FS J. F. Priest; Atlanta: Scholars Press, 1996), 125–51.

[74] For collections of texts, see Montgomery, *Aramaic Incantation Texts;* C. H. Gordon, "Aramaic Magical Bowls in the Baghdad Museum," *ArOr* 6 (1934): 319–34; E. M. Yamauchi, "Aramaic Magic Bowls," *JAOS* 85 (1965): 511–23; idem, *Mandaic Incantation Texts* (AOS 49; New Haven: American Oriental Society, 1967), esp. 153–305 (texts and translations).

[75] Montgomery, *Aramaic Incantation Texts,* 231–32. See also the discussion in Charlesworth, "Solomon and Jesus," 137–38.

Amen, Amen, Selah";[76] "Sealed with the seal-ring of El Shaddai, blessed be He, and with the seal-ring of King Solomon, the son of David, who worked spells on male demons and female liliths."[77]

Psalm 91 in the Aramaic presupposes this Solomonic exorcistic tradition and the demonology that went with it. What encourages us to date the demonological understanding of Psalm 91 to an early period is not only that it is associated with the story of Jesus' temptation but that this psalm has been found at Qumran grouped together with three other extracanonical exorcistic psalms (i.e., the *Apocryphal Psalms*^{a} [11Q11]).[78] The second extracanonical psalm is attributed to Solomon, the third is attributed to David and describes itself as an "incantation," and Qumran's version of Psalm 91 (the fourth exorcistic psalm in this scroll) is attributed to David and concludes with the words "Amen, Amen, Selah" (as in one of the Aramaic incantations mentioned above).

There is additional evidence of the antiquity of the demonological understanding of Psalm 91. According to Luke 10:17–20, the disciples return from their mission, saying, "Lord, even the demons are subject to us in your name!" Jesus replies, "I saw Satan fall like lightning from heaven. Behold, I have given you authority to tread upon [τοῦ πατεῖν ἐπάνω] serpents and scorpions, and over all the power of the enemy; and nothing shall hurt you" (vv. 18–19 RSV). The claim to have authority "to tread upon serpents and scorpions" almost certainly alludes to Ps 91:13: "you will trample down [LXX: καταπατήσεις] lion and serpent," a passage that probably underlies the patriarch's prophecy of the coming of a faithful priest. It will be a time when "Beliar shall be bound by him. And he shall grant to his children authority to trample [τοῦ πατεῖν] on wicked spirits" (*T. Levi* 18:12).

The appearance of Psalm 91 in the Matthean and Lukan versions of the temptation of Jesus is but one indication of many that the demonological orientation of this particular psalm in *Targum Psalms* derives from early, probably intertestamental tradition.

Jesus' Proclamation of the Kingdom of God

Chilton has shown that Jesus' proclamation that the "kingdom of God has drawn near" (Mark 1:15; cf. Luke 11:20) almost certainly reflects the

---

[76] Gordon, "Aramaic Magical Bowls," 322.

[77] Ibid.

[78] See J. P. M. van der Ploeg, "Un petit rouleau de psaumes apocryphes (11QPsAp^a)," in *Tradition und Glaube: Das frühe Christentum in seiner Umwelt* (ed. G. Jeremias et al.; FS K. G. Kuhn; Göttingen: Vandenhoeck & Ruprecht, 1971), 128–39 and pls. II–VII; E. Puech, "Les deux derniers psaumes davidiques du rituel d'exorcisme, 11QPsAp^a IV 4–V 14," in *The Dead Sea Scrolls: Forty Years of Research* (ed. D. Dimant and U. Rappaport; STDJ 10; New York: E. J. Brill, 1992), 64–89; F. García Martínez et al., *Qumran Cave 11, II: 11Q2–18, 11Q20–31* (DJD 23; Oxford: Clarendon, 1998), 181–205. For a convenient English translation, see M. G. Abegg, P. W. Flint, and E. Ulrich, *The Dead Sea Scrolls Bible: The Oldest Known Bible Translated for the First Time into English* (San Francisco: HarperCollins, 1999), 539–42.

emerging Aramaic paraphrase and interpretation of *Targum Isaiah* (see his chapter above).

Although the theologoumenon "kingdom of God" is not a characteristic of *Targum Psalms,* the *meturgeman* has translated and interpreted some statements that go beyond the Hebrew text. In Hebrew Ps 14:1 we are told that the fool says in his heart, "There is no God." In the Aramaic we find this interesting elaboration of the fool's words: "There is no rule of God on the earth [שולטנא דאלהא בארעא]." Although we do not have in *Targum Psalms* the exact diction of *Targum Isaiah*'s "the kingdom of (your) God" (as at *Tg. Isa.* 40:9, מלכותא דאל; *Tg. Isa.* 52:7, מלכותא דאלהיך), the sense of *Tg. Ps.* 14:1 is identical. Indeed, it may be said that *Targum Psalms*'s diction (שולטנא דאלהא בארעא = "the rule of God on earth") expresses more precisely the intended meaning of the theologoumenon in *Targum Isaiah.* Aramaic Isaiah's "kingdom of (your) God" in fact means the "rule of God (on earth)." It is this coherence with Jesus' declaration, "But if it is by the finger of God that I cast out demons, then the kingdom of God has come upon you" (Luke 11:20 RSV)—that is, the rule of God is present among humans on earth (cf. Mark 2:10, "the son of man has authority on earth")—that has led Chilton and others to conclude that the Aramaic language of Isaiah so helpfully clarifies the essence of Jesus' message.

Elsewhere in *Targum Psalms* God is said to be seated, in the midst of angels, "on the throne of glory [כורסי יקרא]" (89:8 [Eng. 89:7 RSV]) or sitting "on a throne of glory in heaven [כורסי יקרא בשמיא]" (123:1 RSV). These Aramaic expansions, however, in reality only intensify what is already implicit in the Hebrew Psalter. In the Hebrew, God is understood to be "enthroned in the heavens" (123:1). Indeed, the psalmist declares that the "LORD has established his throne in the heavens, and his kingdom rules over all" (103:19 RSV = Targ.), that therefore people "shall speak of the glory of thy kingdom . . . and the glorious splendor of thy kingdom" (145:11–12 RSV = Targ.), and that God's "kingdom is an everlasting kingdom," one that "endures throughout all generations" (145:13 RSV = Targ.).

The *meturgeman* has grasped well the theological thrust of the Psalter and has expressed it clearly, especially at 14:1, in targumic language. But just as often the *meturgeman* has not found it necessary to alter or augment the Hebrew text; for it says it well, too, just as it stands.

The Triumphal Entry and the Rejected Stone

When Jesus enters Jerusalem, enthusiastic disciples, pilgrims, and well-wishers cry out:

> "Hosanna! Blessed is he who comes in the name of the Lord!
>
> Blessed is the kingdom of our father David that is coming! Hosanna in the highest!" (Mark 11:9–10 RSV)

The allusion to Ps 118:25–26 is unmistakable:

> Save us [Heb. *hosanna*], we beseech thee, O LORD! O LORD, we beseech thee, give us success! (RSV)

> Blessed be he who enters in the name of the LORD! We bless you from the house of the LORD. (RSV)

In the Hebrew Psalter, however, there is no mention of David or of his kingdom. A little later in the Markan narrative, Jesus responds to the ruling priests who have challenged his authority to act and teach in the temple precincts; he does so by telling the parable of the Wicked Vineyard Farmers (Mark 12:1–9), which concludes with a citation of Ps 118:22–23:

> The very stone that the builders rejected has become the head of the corner; this was the Lord's doing, and it is marvelous in our eyes. (Mark 12:10–11 RSV)

Because the quotation of Ps 118:22–23 follows the LXX and because this passage plays a role in later Christology and apologetic, many critics assume that it has been added to the parable (thought by most to be an authentic parable of Jesus) by the Greek-speaking, LXX-reading Christian church. Perhaps, but before accepting this conclusion, the Aramaic Psalter should once again be considered.

Commentators recognize Psalm 118 as a thanksgiving liturgy, presented in the form of one who faced grave danger, sought God's help, was delivered, and now calls for praise. Although the principal in the Psalm is an individual, others, such as the keeper of the temple gates and the priest, participate in the liturgy. Accordingly, the psalm has an antiphonal structure, shifting from singular to plural.[79] The origin of this psalm and its original setting in the life of Israel are not important for our purposes. What is interesting is the life setting that the Aramaic Psalter has given it. Here is the second half of the psalm, according to the Aramaic, with departures from the Hebrew placed in italics:

19. Open to me the gates of *the city of* righteousness; I will enter them, I will praise Yah.

20. This is the gate of *the sanctuary of* the LORD; the righteous will enter by it.

21. I will give thanks in your presence, for you have *received my prayer,* and become for me a redeemer.

22. *The lad* that the builders *abandoned* was *among the sons of Jesse; and he was worthy to be appointed king and ruler.*

23. "This has come from *the presence of* the LORD," *said the builders;* "it is wonderful *before* us," *said the sons of Jesse.*

---

[79] See the summaries in Briggs and Briggs, *Critical and Exegetical Commentary,* 2:402–3; W. O. E. Oesterley, *The Psalms: Translated with Text-Critical and Exegetical Notes* (2 vols.; New York: Macmillan, 1939), 2:479–82; L. C. Allen, *Psalms 101–150* (WBC 21; Dallas: Word, 1983), 122–24.

24. "This day the LORD has made," *said the builders;* "let us rejoice and be glad in it," *said the sons of Jesse.*

25. "If it please you, O LORD, redeem us now," *said the builders;* "if it please you, O LORD, prosper *us* now," *said Jesse and his wife.*

26. "Blessed is he who comes in the name of *the word of* the LORD," *said the builders;* "they will bless you from the *sanctuary* of the LORD," *said David.*

27. "God, the LORD, has given us light," *said the tribes of the house of Judah;* "bind *the lamb* for a festal *sacrifice* with chains until *you sacrifice it, and sprinkle his blood* on the horns of the altar," *said Samuel the prophet.*

28. "You are my God, and I will give thanks in your presence; my God, I will *praise* you," *said David.*

29. *Samuel answered and said, "Sing praise, congregation of Israel,* give thanks in the presence of the LORD, for he is good, for his goodness is everlasting."

Many intriguing features present themselves. Most noticeable is the explicitness of the antiphonal structure. The speaking parts are clearly assigned. The psalm has been historicized, with the story of the selection of David as Israel's new king (cf. 1 Sam 16:1–13) melded with the original psalm. The assignment of the speaking parts reflects this new historical setting. Verses 19–22 set the stage for the drama, which begins with the call for the "city of righteousness" to be opened (v. 19), that is, the city of Jerusalem. Next comes the "gate of the sanctuary of the LORD" (v. 20), that is, the temple. The principal intends to give thanks, for his prayer has been heard and he has been redeemed (v. 21). Why is this? Verse 22 explains: "The lad that the builders abandoned was among the sons of Jesse; and he was worthy to be appointed king and ruler." This verse functions as the thesis for all that follows. The drama is now ready to unfold; the speakers now step onto the stage to play their respective parts.

The "builders," who in v. 22 rejected the lad, now acknowledge that his acceptance as king and ruler "has come from the presence of the LORD" (v. 23a). The sons of Jesse, who had been passed over in the selection of the new king, agree, adding, "It is wonderful before us" (v. 23b). The builders declare, "This day the LORD has made" (v. 24a). To this the sons of Jesse reply, "Let us rejoice and be glad in it" (v. 24b).

Now that the new king has been chosen, the community may call for deliverance. "If it please you, O LORD, redeem us now," say the builders (v. 25a). To this add Jesse and his wife: "If it please you, O LORD, prosper us now" (v. 25). Then the builders pronounce their beatitude, "Blessed is he who comes in the name of the word of the LORD" (v. 26a). David replies, "They will bless you from the sanctuary of the LORD" (v. 26b).

All the tribes (or families) of the house of Judah join in, saying, "God, the LORD, has given us light" (v. 27a). To this the venerable priest Samuel, who had initially not considered David, commands sacrifice, "Bind the lamb for a festal sacrifice" (v. 27b). David then confesses, "You are my God, and I will give thanks in your presence; my God, I will praise you" (v. 28). The psalm concludes with Samuel's injunction to the whole people: "Sing praise, congregation of Israel, give thanks in the presence of the LORD, for he is good, for his goodness is everlasting" (v. 29).[80]

The coherence between the Aramaic form of Psalm 118 and Jesus' entry into the city and into the temple precincts, where he engages in polemic with the ruling priests, is impressive. The transformation of the psalm into the story of David's recognition as king of Israel explains the interpretive allusion to Ps 118:25–26 in Mark's account of Jesus' entrance into the city, where people shout, "Blessed is the kingdom of our father David that is coming!" (Mark 11:10). Seen in the light of the Aramaic paraphrase, the allusion now makes sense. The Aramaic speaks of David, who is worthy to be king (מליך); the crowd welcomes the coming of David's kingdom (מלכות).

Moreover, concluding the parable of the Wicked Vineyard Farmers with the citation of Ps 118:22–23, which in the Aramaic speaks of a rejected child—Jesse's son David—now makes sense as the conclusion to a parable that tells of the violent rejection of the vineyard owner's son. It has been rightly pointed out that the shift from stone to child was accommodated by a wordplay in Hebrew between ha-eben ("the stone") and ha-ben ("the son").[81] Moreover, Aramaic Psalm 118 now makes it clear that the "builders" who rejected the child are none other than the priestly authorities.[82]

It should also be added that the Aramaic understanding of Psalm 118 is consistent with the Aramaic understanding of Isaiah's Song of the Vineyard (Isa 5:1–7), in which the Hebrew song, originally directed against a lawless and disobedient people (the Lord's vineyard), is redirected against the temple establishment. In Jesus' parable the vineyard is not the object of the Lord's displeasure; the farmers who care for it are.[83] It is no wonder that Mark narrates (entirely

---

[80] The closest rabbinic parallel to the structural arrangement that we have in *Targum Psalms* is found in *b. Pesaḥ.* 119a. The antiphonal arrangement is also attested in *Midr. Pss.* 118. Various rabbinic authorities in talmudic and midrashic literature interpret Psalm 118 eschatologically. See J. A. Sanders, "A Hermeneutic Fabric: Psalm 118 in Luke's Entrance Narrative," in C. A. Evans and J. A. Sanders, *Luke and Scripture: The Function of Sacred Tradition in Luke-Acts* (Minneapolis: Fortress, 1993), 140–53, esp. 143–48.

[81] The wordplay underlies the angry words of John the Baptist, who declares that God is able from *stones* to raise up *children* (or sons) to Abraham (cf. Matt 3:9 = Luke 3:8), and lies behind the otherwise curious comment of Josephus that when siege stones hurled against Jerusalem were seen approaching, the watchmen cried out, "the son is coming" (cf. *J.W.* 5.6.3 §272). In *Midr. Pss.* 118.20 (on Ps 118:22), Jacob, who begot the twelve tribes, is identified as the stone rejected by the builders.

[82] In the context of the parable of the Wicked Vineyard Farmers, the "builders" are the religious leaders, i.e., the ruling priests and their scribal allies. The same identification is found in Acts 4:11. In non-Christian Jewish literature, religious leaders are described as builders, either in a negative sense (as in CD 4:19; 8:12, 18) or in a positive sense (as in *b. Ber.* 64a; *b. Šabb.* 114a; *Exod. Rab.* 23.10 [on Exod 15:11]).

[83] The antiquity of the Aramaic interpretation is now attested by 4Q500. See J. M. Baumgarten, "4Q500 and the Ancient Conception of the Lord's Vineyard," *JJS* 40 (1989):

credibly) that the ruling priests "perceived that he had told the parable against them" (Mark 12:12).[84]

The specific point of coherence between *Tg. Ps.* 118 and the citation at the conclusion of the parable of the Wicked Vineyard Farmers is seen in the Aramaic's identification of the child (טליא) with David, the son of Jesse. The child is said to be worthy to be appointed "king and ruler" (למליך ושולטן). We have here the key elements (i.e., David and king[dom]) that the crowd has added to its allusions to Ps 118:25–26.[85] But the historicized version of Psalm 118 in the Aramaic coheres at other points with the entrance narrative and the ensuing controversy in the temple precincts, where Jesus enters the city, enters the temple precincts, and is challenged by the ruling priests, or "builders." Unlike the conclusion in the Aramaic version, the ruling priests do not in the end accept Jesus.

David's Son or David's Lord?

Targum Psalms offers three important points of coherence with Jesus' interpretation of Ps 110:1 in Mark 12:35–37. The pertinent part of the dominical utterance reads, "How can the scribes say that the Messiah is the son of David? David himself, inspired by the Holy Spirit, declared, 'The Lord said to my Lord . . .'" First, Jesus understands the psalm as composed by David; so does *Targum Psalms*, which begins, "Composed by David, a psalm." Second, Jesus says David was inspired by the Holy Spirit; so does *Targum Psalms*: "in the spirit of prophecy through David" (14:1); "David, who gave praise in prophecy in the presence of the LORD the words of this song . . ." (18:1). Third, Jesus understands Psalm 110 as messianic, and therefore the passage has relevance for the scribal opinion that the Messiah is "the son of David."

It was mentioned earlier that Samson Levey does not regard Psalm 110 as messianic. In the Aramaic, however, the psalm is understood as pertaining to

---

1–6; G. J. Brooke, "4Q500 1 and the Use of Scripture in the Parable of the Vineyard," *DSD* 2 (1995): 268–94. On the debate over how Septuagintal are the allusions to Isaiah 5 that are present in Mark 12, see J. S. Kloppenborg Verbin, "Egyptian Viticultural Practices and the Citation of Isa 5:1–7 in Mark 12:1–9," *NovT* 44 (2002): 134–59; and C. A. Evans, "How Septuagintal Is Isa 5:1–7 in Mark 12:1–9?" *NovT* 45 (2003): 105–10. Kloppenborg Verbin argues that the allusions to Isa 5:1–7 in Mark 12:1–9 are entirely Septuagintal. Evans acknowledges a measure of assimilation to the LXX but identifies Semitic (including targumic), non-Septuagintal elements.

[84] Psalm 118 exerted a remarkable influence on the Gospel of Luke, as seen especially in the use of the word "rejected." Besides Sanders, "A Hermeneutic Fabric," see J. R. Wagner, "Psalm 118 in Luke-Acts: Tracing a Narrative Thread," in *Early Christian Interpretation of the Scriptures of Israel: Investigations and Proposals* (ed. C. A. Evans and J. A. Sanders; JSNTSup 148; SSEJC 5; Sheffield, England: Sheffield Academic Press, 1997), 154–78.

[85] The phrase "the kingdom of our father David" is not a Jewish set phrase, nor is it a Christian confession. It is more likely a genuine reflection of what people were hoping for and boldly saying in public. In rabbinic literature we find "kingdom of the house of David" (*Mek.* on Exod 16:16–27 [*Vayassa'* §5 = J. Z. Lauterbach, *Mekilta de-Rabbi Ishmael* (3 vols., Philadelphia: Jewish Publication Society, 1933), 2:120]; *Tg. Jer.* 33:17; *Tg. Ezek.* 17:22).

David. Accordingly, David is told to "wait for Saul of the tribe of Benjamin to die" (v. 1). Of course, the primary reference is to the historical David, who succeeded Saul. But the Aramaic psalm has more in mind. According to v. 4, the Davidic king is "appointed leader *in the age to come*" (emphasis added) because he had been a "righteous king" (in place of the name Melchizedek). From this we realize that the David mentioned in v. 1 is not just the historical David but the David who will return "in the age to come." Rabbinic interpretation, at least as seen in *Midrash Psalms,* understood the Targum this way (cf. *Midr. Pss.* 110.4–5 [on Ps 110:1]).

Finally, it should be pointed out that in *Targum Psalms* the Messiah is said to have the "spirit of prophecy" (45:3 [Eng. 45:2]). Here we have a convergence of our second and third elements of coherence between Jesus' assumptions about Psalm 110 and its rendering in *Targum Psalms.*

Lament Psalms and the Passion

Some of the words and phrases quoted or alluded to from the Lament Psalms exhibit Aramaic traces. In one or two cases the Aramaic tradition finds expression in Jesus and the evangelists.

Shortly before dying, Jesus cries out on the cross, "*Elohi, Elohi, lama sabachthani,*" as the Markan evangelist transliterates and then rightly translates, "My God, my God, why hast thou forsaken me?" (Mark 15:34 RSV). The words are taken from the opening verse of Psalm 22 (v. 2 in the Hebrew; v. 1 in the English). The Lukan evangelist omits the quotation (substituting instead a quotation from Ps 31:6 [Eng. 31:5]). The Matthean evangelist retains the quotation of Psalm 22, transliterating a bit differently, "*Eli, Eli, lema sabachthani,*" but translating the same as does Mark.

Commentators usually assert that Mark's version does not reflect the Targum (because the transliteration does not match exactly the extant MSS of *Targum Psalms*) and that Matthew's transliteration reflects the Hebrew, at least with respect to the words "My God, my God." Both of these assertions require qualification.

First, it is true that Mark's transliteration does not match exactly the text of *Targum Psalms.* His transliteration assumes Aramaic that reads this way:

אלהי אלהי למה שבקתני

But the Aramaic of the extant *Targum Psalms* reads this way:

אלי אלי מטול מה שבקתני

Nevertheless, the Aramaic presupposed by Mark's transliteration is well represented in *Targum Psalms,* if not always at 22:2. Mark's "why" is *lama* (למה, which is better transliterated *lema,* as in the Matthean transliteration), while the Targum's "why" is the synonymous *metul ma* (מטול מה). However, the interrogative *lema* is found more than a dozen times elsewhere in *Targum Psalms,* as in

88:15: "Why, O Lord, have you forsaken [שבקתא] my soul?" In this example we not only have *lema;* we have the same verb (שבק) that is used in 22:2 and that appears elsewhere in *Targum Psalms* with the same function: "David said, 'O God [אלהא], you have forsaken us [שבקתנא]'" (60:3); "Is it not you, O Lord? You have forsaken us [שבקתנא]" (60:12).

Moreover, in the Targum "my God, my God" is rendered *eli, eli* (אלי אלי), which agrees with Matthew's transliteration, suggesting that the evangelist has not reverted to Hebrew at all.[86] *Eli* occurs frequently in *Targum Psalms;* so does *elohi* (אלהי). In fact, *elohi* appears later in *Tg. Ps.* 22, at vv. 3 ("My God, I call by day and you will not accept my prayer") and 11 ("from my mother's womb you are my God"). Sometimes *Targum Psalms* follows the Hebrew. At 22:2 the Hebrew reads *eli,* and so does the Targum. At 22:3 the Hebrew reads *elohai,* and the Targum reads the equivalent *elohi,* etc. The difference, then, between Mark's transliteration and the Aramaic of *Targum Psalms* is insignificant. Indeed, Mark's underlying Aramaic is thoroughly consistent with the language that we find in *Targum Psalms,* especially in Psalm 22. Mark has used *elohi,* which appears elsewhere in the Targum, including Psalm 22 itself. The Matthean evangelist revises his Markan source not to change it to Hebrew but to make it conform more precisely to the Aramaic of the specific verse that has been quoted.

The Aramaic version of Psalm 22 may also be reflected elsewhere in the passion narrative. Indeed, it may be the other way around: the events of the passion may have suggested looking to Psalm 22, especially as it was paraphrased and interpreted in Aramaic. The Hebrew of Ps 22:13 (Eng. 22:12) has "Many bulls encompass me, strong bulls of Bashan surround me," but in the Aramaic we find "The Gentiles have surrounded me, who are like many bulls." One may surmise that the handing of Jesus over to Gentile authorities may have encouraged meditation on Psalm 22. Of course, if the dying Jesus did in fact recite the opening line of Psalm 22, this would only further encourage study of this Psalm.

The Aramaic Psalter may also have colored the description of Judas' treachery, in that he shared food with Jesus shortly before betraying him to the ruling priests. According to Mark 14:20, the betrayer is "one of the twelve, one who is dipping bread into the dish with" (RSV) Jesus. We probably have here an allusion to Ps 41:10 (Eng. 41:9), which the Fourth Evangelist recognized and formally quoted: "I am not speaking of you all; I know whom I have chosen; it is that the scripture may be fulfilled, 'He who ate my bread has lifted his heel against me'" (John 13:18 RSV). In the Aramaic, Ps 41:10 reads, "whom I trusted, feeding him my meal—with cunning [חכמא] he has gained the advantage over me." One recognizes the root חכם, "to be wise," in this case, "with sophistry," or "with cunning." The detail of cunning may be reflected in the notation found in Mark 14:1b: "And the chief priests and the scribes were seeking how to arrest him by

---

[86] A point rightly made by J. Jeremias, *New Testament Theology: The Proclamation of Jesus* (New York: Scribner's, 1971), 5 n. 2: The "cry from the cross . . . has been transmitted *in toto* in Aramaic."

stealth [ἐν δόλῳ], and kill him." Δόλος means "deceit," but ἐν δόλῳ usually means "with stealth" or "with cunning" (cf. BAG).

Finally, we may have two points of coherence between the passion narrative and the Aramaic version of Psalm 69. John 15:25 says, "It is to fulfill the word that is written in their law, 'They hated me without a cause'" (RSV). The quotation comes from Ps 69:5 [Eng. 69:4]. In the Hebrew the full verse reads, "More in number than the hairs of my head are those who hate me without cause; mighty are those who would destroy me, those who attack me with lies. What I did not steal must I now restore?" In *Targum Psalms*, however, the verse is rendered, "More in number than the hairs of my head are those who hate me without cause; mighty are those who would vex me—my enemies, false witnesses [סהדי שקרא]. What I did not steal I must repay, because of their testimony [סהדותהון]." The Hebrew's "those who attack me with lies [or falsehoods]" has become in the Aramaic "my enemies, false witnesses." We may have coherence with the story of Jesus' hearing before the Jewish council, where *false witnesses* are said to have *testified* against Jesus (cf. Mark 14:56–57: τινες ἀναστάντες ἐψευδομαρτύρουν κατ' αὐτοῦ). Again, what was only hinted at in the older passion tradition is formally quoted in the Fourth Gospel (i.e., at John 15:25).

The second example from Psalm 69 is found in John. In 2:17, in response to his action in the temple precincts, the disciples of Jesus remember that it was written, "It is zeal for your house that has consumed me" (NRSV). The Scripture that was remembered is Ps 69:10 (Eng. 69:9). The Fourth Evangelist's quotation is unremarkable in that it follows the Hebrew and LXX closely. The subsequent comment attributed to Jesus in v. 19 ("Destroy this temple [ναός], and in three days I will raise it up" [NRSV]),however, brings to mind the Aramaic version of Ps 69:10: "Zeal for the Sanctuary house [בית מקדש] has consumed me" (NRSV). The quotation of Ps 69:10, to clarify the meaning of a dominical utterance making reference to a "sanctuary," strongly suggests that the Aramaic version of this passage played a part in the development of the tradition. Whether this tradition originated with Jesus himself or with early Aramaic-speaking disciples is not easy to decide.[87]

Examples of Targumic Coherence in Acts

The book of Acts contains several passages that appear to reflect the influence of the Aramaic Psalter. We shall look briefly at a few passages related to Peter, and one passage related to Paul.

In his Pentecost sermon, Peter appeals, "Save yourselves from this crooked generation!" (Acts 2:40 RSV). Most commentators think Peter's language draws

---

[87] The phrase "in three days" Jesus will be raised up (cf. Mark 8:31; 9:31; 10:33) itself reflects targumic tradition, in this case *Tg. Hos.* 6:2: "on the day of the resurrection of the dead he will raise us up" (cf. Heb. Hos 6:2: "He will revive us after two days; on the third day he will raise us up that we might live before him"). The point of origin of this tradition is probably dominical although it developed in somewhat different Synoptic and Johannine forms.

upon Deut 32:5 ("crooked and perverted generation") and/or Ps 78:8 ("crooked generation and rebellious generation"). There is, however, no equivalent for "save yourselves!" The Aramaic version of Ps 12:8 (Heb. "You, O LORD, protect us, guard us ever from this generation") may have contributed to Peter's language. The Targum reads, "You, O LORD, will keep *the righteous;* you will protect *them* from this *evil* generation forever" (with departures from the Hebrew placed in italics). The addition of "wicked" (בישא) in the Aramaic and the meaning of נצר ("to save" or "to rescue") in the Samaritan liturgy suggest that Peter may have alluded to Ps 12:8 as well as Deut 32:5 and Ps 78:8.

In two speeches Peter refers to utterances of David in the Psalter, and in all three Peter regards David as inspired of the Holy Spirit:

> Friends, the scripture had to be fulfilled, which the Holy Spirit through David foretold concerning Judas, who became a guide for those who arrested Jesus. (Acts 1:16–20; cf. Ps 69:26 [Eng. 69:25]; 109:8)

> For David says concerning him, "I saw the Lord always before me, for he is at my right hand so that I will not be shaken" . . . Since he was a prophet . . . David spoke of the resurrection of the Messiah. (Acts 2:25–31; cf. Ps 16:8–11)

Statements that the Holy Spirit "spoke beforehand by the mouth of David" or that David "was a prophet" are consistent with what we have seen in *Targum Psalms* (and reviewed above; cf. *Tg. Ps.* 14:1; 18:1).

We might also consider the community's word of praise in response to the report of Peter and John:

> "Sovereign Lord, who made the heaven and the earth, the sea, and everything in them, it is you who said by the Holy Spirit through our ancestor David, your servant: 'Why did the Gentiles rage, and the peoples imagine vain things? . . .'" (Acts 4:24–26; cf. Ps 146:6; 2:2)

The linkage of Ps 146:6 to Ps 2:2, which condemns the heathen for plotting against the Lord and against his Messiah, is intriguing when one remembers that the former text, along with words and phrases from Isaiah, is cited in the *Messianic Apocalypse* as part of an apocalyptic oracle foretelling the wonderful deeds of the Messiah: "[. . . For the hea]vens and the earth shall listen to His Messiah [and all t]hat is in them shall not turn away from the commandments of the holy ones . . . setting prisoners free, opening the eyes of the blind" (frgs. 2+4 ii 1–2, 8; cf. Ps 146:6–8). The early Christian community not only associates Ps 146:6 with the Messiah but understands Psalm 2 as Davidic (as in all probability Qumran did as well; cf. 1QSa 2:11–12: "when God will have begotten the Messiah among them").

And finally, the Paul of Acts may also reveal acquaintance with the Aramaic Psalter. Against the false prophet, Paul says, "And now listen—the hand of the Lord is against you, and you will be blind for a while, unable to see the sun" (Acts 13:11). The expression to be "blind and unable to see the sun" may allude to Ps 58:9 (Eng. 58:8): "Let them be like the snail which dissolves into slime, like the untimely birth that never sees the sun." This is a Semitic idiom, but it is only in the Targum that blindness and not being able to see the sun are linked: "Like the crawling snail whose way is slimy, like the abortion and the mole who are blind and do not see the sun." We may have here another example of dictional coherence.[88]

Targum Psalms and Paul

The present study draws to a close with three examples from Paul and his circle. The first example concerns a possible parallel with the apostle's comparison of Jesus with the "first Adam":

> Thus it is written, "The first man Adam became a living being"; the last Adam became a life-giving spirit. But it is not the spiritual which is first, but the physical, and then the spiritual. The first man was from the earth, a man of dust; the second man is from heaven. (1 Cor 15:45–47 RSV; cf. Gen 2:7)

Paul has quoted a portion of Gen 2:7, adding the words "first" and the proper name Adam. This manner of referring to Adam occurs at least five times in *Targum Psalms* (אדם קדמא; cf. 49:2; 69:32; 92:1; 94:10). All of these references are to the Adam of the creation story, who offered sacrifice (*Tg. Ps.* 69:32), uttered a song concerning the Sabbath (*Tg. Ps.* 92:1), and was taught knowledge by the Lord (*Tg. Ps.* 94:10). Paul's contrast between the first man, who is physical, and the second man, who is heavenly, has its counterpart in Philo (cf. *Alleg. Interp.* 1.31–32 [commenting on Gen 2:7]), but the locution "first Adam" is distinctly targumic.[89]

The second example is found in Eph 4:8: "Therefore it is said, 'When he ascended on high he made captivity itself a captive; he gave gifts to his people.'" The author has quoted Ps 68:19 (Eng. 68:18), which in the Hebrew reads, "You ascended the high mount, leading captives in Your train, and receiving gifts [לָקַחְתָּ מַתָּנוֹת] among people," but in the LXX reads, "You ascended to the height, having taken captive captivity, you received gifts [ἔλαβες δόματα] among people." Both the Hebrew and the Greek speak of God *receiving* gifts, but the quotation in Ephesians says "gave gifts to" people.

The paraphrase in Ephesians coheres with the wording of the Targum: "You ascended to the height, *O prophet Moses;* you captured captives, *you taught the words of Torah,* you *gave them as* gifts *to* the sons of men, and even the stubborn *who are converted turn in repentance*" (with italics indicating departures from the Hebrew). The Targum's *"gave"* (יהבתא), *"to"* (ל), and plural "sons of

---

88 Wilcox, "Aramaic Targum to Psalms," 147.

89 The epithet occurs four times in *Targum Psalms* and twice in *Targum Qoheleth* (cf. 6:10; 7:29) and twice in *Targum Pseudo-Jonathan* (cf. Gen 27:15; Exod 4:11). The occurrence in *Tg. Job* 15:7, which places the words in reverse order (קדמאי אדם), has simply followed the Hebrew (הראישון אדם). Thus, half of the occurrences are found in *Targum Psalms*.

man" (בני נשא) agree with the Ephesians version of the text (indeed, "to the sons of men" is attested in Tertullian, *Marc.* 5.8.5: *filiis hominum*). Moreover, introducing the theme of repentance and conversion thematically coheres with the Pauline understanding of the gifts in terms of apostles, prophets, and evangelists (cf. Eph 4:11), whose basic ministry concerns prompting people to repent and be converted.[90]

Finally, the author of 1 Timothy refers to the gift given to Timothy διὰ προφητείας, "by prophecy" (1 Tim 4:14). Προφητεία occurs nineteen times in the Greek NT, usually in reference to a specific prophecy. The adverbial "by prophecy" in 1 Tim 4:14 is unique. We may have here another instance of targumic diction. In *Targum Psalms* the expression occurs at least four times: "David, who sang in/by prophecy [בנבואה] in the presence of the LORD the words of this song" (18:1); "concerning those who sit in the Sanhedrin of Moses, which was spoken in/by prophecy [בנבואה] by the sons of Korah" (45:1); "Composed by Solomon, uttered in/by prophecy [בנבואה]. O God, give your just rulings to the King Messiah, and your righteousness to the son of King David" (72:1); and "Composed by David, spoken in/by prophecy [בנבואה]" (103:1). Because "prophecy" occurs in the Targum hundreds of times and the prepositional phrase "in/by prophecy" occurs dozens of times, it cannot be claimed that this phrase is distinctive to *Targum Psalms*. But there is a strong possibility that the phrase in 1 Timothy is targumic.[91]

Conclusion

Targum Psalms will take its place alongside the other Targumim that contain early traditions and, in places, shed light on interpretive and linguistic features in the NT. Its contributions, of course, are not limited to what it tells us about early Christianity; it will tell us much about Judaism of late antiquity, the rabbinic midrashic tradition, and several other matters, such as the text of the Psalter and what role the Psalter played in the life of the synagogue and in the lives of the faithful. *Targum Psalms* presents many difficulties and will prove to be a challenge for interpreters. Nevertheless, its investigation will yield rewards. May the results of the present essay encourage further study of this important Targum.

---

[90] Wilcox, "Aramaic Targum to Psalms," 144–45; M. McNamara, *The New Testament and the Palestinian Targum to the Pentateuch* (2d ed., AnBib 27A; Rome: Pontifical Biblical Institute Press, 1978), 78–81. McNamara is correct to point out the similar targumic exegesis of Deut 30:12–14 that underlies Rom 10:6–8.

[91] The parallel at Ezra 6:14a ("And the elders of the Jews built and prospered, through the prophecy [בנבואת / ἐν προφητείᾳ] of Haggai the prophet and Zechariah the son of Iddo"), the only biblical parallel, is Aramaic, thus attesting the expression well before the emergence of the Targum. For approximate Greek parallels in intertestamental literature, see Sir 46:1, 20; *T. Levi* 8:2; *T. Benj.* 3:8.

Immanuel: Virgin Birth Proof Text or Programmatic Warning of Things to Come (Isa 7:14 in Matt 1:23)?

Rikk E. Watts

Introduction

In the first occurrence of his characteristic fulfillment formula, Matthew writes,

> "She [Mary] will bear a son, and you are to name him Jesus, for he will save his people from their sins." All this happened to fulfill what had been spoken by the Lord through the prophet:

> "Look, the virgin shall conceive and bear a son, and they shall name him Emmanuel," which means, "God is with us." (1:21–23 NRSV)

Although it is widely recognized that Isa 7:14 does not appear to predict a virginal conception, that as far as we can tell the oracle was not understood messianically in contemporary Judaism, and that Jesus' miraculous origin is hardly of major concern in the NT, the general opinion is that this has not prevented Matthew from ingeniously reading the Immanuel oracle as a prophecy of Jesus' virgin birth. Matthew, after all, pays scant attention to the contexts of his OT citations.[1] But although it is still a somewhat controversial issue, a number of recent studies affirm C. H. Dodd's contention that the NT authors were more aware of the contexts of their OT citations than is generally accepted.[2] D. Instone-Brewer's work on pre-70 C.E. rabbinic method suggests that the rabbis took account of the larger scriptural context although their interpretive horizon was one of legal precedent.[3] Likewise Darrell Bock's work on Luke, my own on Mark, Richard Hays's and Florian Wilk's on Paul, and Greg Beale's recent monumental commentary on

---

[1] E.g., S. V. McCasland, "Matthew Twists the Scripture," *JBL* 80 (1961): 143–48; cf. K. Stendahl, *The School of St. Matthew and Its Use of the Old Testament* (2d ed.; Philadelphia: Fortress, 1968).

[2] C. H. Dodd, *According to the Scriptures* (London: Nisbet, 1952).

[3] D. Instone-Brewer, *Techniques and Assumptions in Jewish Exegesis before 70 C.E.* (TSAJ 30; Tübingen: J. C. B. Mohr [Paul Siebeck], 1992).

Revelation, to name just a few, are representative of a growing number of scholars who contend that the NT authors frequently assumed the larger context of their OT citations and allusions.[4]

Against the background of the original intent of Isaiah's oracle and in the light of a near parallel at Qumran, this essay will argue that (a) Matthew's citation of Isa 7:14 not so much serves as a proof text supporting Jesus' miraculous birth as constitutes a warning of the dire consequences should Israel respond faithlessly to the salvation he inaugurates and (b) the twofold naming—Jesus (salvation) and Immanuel (potential disaster if Yahweh's intervention is met with unbelief)—is programmatic for the gospel's larger literary and theological schema.[5]

Isaiah 7:14–17

The difficulties surrounding Isa 7:14 are well known, with scholars taking widely differing positions and frequently interpreting identical material in diametrically opposed ways. Not uncommonly, troublesome materials are excised because they fail to cohere with the "true" meaning of the oracle and must therefore be later additions by less perceptive scribes. Given our Matthean horizon, we will have to deal with the coherence of the text as it stands.

The larger setting is Isaiah's call to effect judicial sanction upon idolatrous Judah. As Beale has demonstrated, since both leaders and people have

---

[4] D. Bock, *Proclamation from Prophecy and Pattern: Lucan Old Testament Christology* (JSNTSup 12; Sheffield, England: JSOT Press, 1987); Rikki E. Watts, *Isaiah's New Exodus and Mark* (WUNT 2.88; Tübingen: J. C. B. Mohr [Paul Siebeck], 1997; reprinted as *Isaiah's New Exodus in Mark*, BSL; Grand Rapids: Baker, 2000); R. B. Hays, *Echoes of Scripture in the Letters of Paul* (New Haven: Yale University Press, 1989); Florian Wilk, *Die Bedeutung des Jesajabuches für Paulus* (FRLANT 179; Göttingen: Vandenhoeck & Ruprecht, 1998); G. K. Beale, *The Book of Revelation* (NIGTC; Grand Rapids: Eerdmans, 1999). See also L. Hartman, *Prophecy Interpreted: The Formation of Some Jewish Apocalyptic Texts of the Eschatological Discourse Mark 13 Par.* (ConBNT 1; Uppsala: Gleerup, 1966); and, more recently, idem, "Scriptural Exegesis in the Gospel of St. Matthew and the Problem of Communication," in *L'évangile selon Matthieu: Rédaction et théologie* (ed. M. Didier; BETL 29; Gembloux, Belgium: Duculot, 1972), 131–52. On this passage in particular, see also Warren Carter, "Evoking Isaiah: Matthean Soteriology and an Intertextual Reading of Isaiah 7–9 and Matthew 1:23 and 4:15–16," *JBL* 119 (2000): 503–20.

[5] If Matthew has indeed been inspired by Mark, then this would be his equivalent of Mark 1:1–3, which, I have argued elsewhere, also serves a similar function (Watts, *New Exodus*, 53–90). Matthew has recently been charged with anti-Semitism. From the perspective of the reading proposed here, the charge is misplaced because it fails to realize the extent to which Matthew's perspective is rooted within his own Jewish prophetic tradition. See further Scot McKnight, "A Loyal Critic: Matthew's Polemic with Judaism in Theological Perspective," in *Anti-Semitism and Early Christianity* (ed. Craig A. Evans and Donald A. Hagner; Minneapolis: Fortress, 1993), 55–79; and Fredrick W. Danker, "Matthew: A Patriot's Gospel," in *The Gospels and the Scriptures of Israel* (ed. Craig A. Evans and W. Richard Stegner; JSNTSup 104; Sheffield, England: Sheffield Academic Press, 1994), 94–115.

rejected Yahweh's word (Isa 5:24), they are, *lex talionis,* to be created in the images of the gods they serve: they will be as blind and as deaf as their idols (cf. Psalms 115, 135).[6] The subsequent encounter with Judah's King Ahaz, structured around the meaning of the three name-parable oracles (cf. Isa 8:18), functions as the inaugural implementation of that judgment whereby the prophetic word reveals and crystallizes Ahaz's, and thus the nation's, rebellious stance.

The process begins with Isaiah's taking Shear-jashub to meet with the king. Regardless of how one understands the "remnant" language—whether of Judah or, as I believe, of the shattered remains of the Syro-Ephraimite coalition[7]—Yahweh declares that the conspiracy against Ahaz will not stand. But equally, neither will the king if he does not believe and desist from soliciting Assyrian assistance. Isaiah then comes a second time to Ahaz to reaffirm Yahweh's word, inviting him to ask for any sign he might wish, "whether it be as deep as Sheol or as high as heaven" (7:10–11).[8] There is no reason to doubt that Yahweh's offer is genuine. But not surprisingly, given Judah's thoroughgoing rebellion evident in chs. 1–5, Ahaz's less-than-eager response merely reveals the depth of his refusal to trust and his idolatrous determination to pursue his own agenda. That he cloaks this in a false piety only heightens the offence (v. 12). Isaiah is scarcely taken in (v. 13) and in righteous indignation pronounces the Immanuel oracle (vv. 14–17, 18–25).

Many scholars hold that vv. 14–17 primarily constitute a word of judgment.[9] Verse 9b's dire warning against faithlessness, combined with Isaiah's subsequent rebuke (v. 13), suggests that v. 14's לָכֶן introduces for Ahaz, his house, and Judah impending disaster the likes of which has not been seen since the secession of the ten tribes (vv. 14–17).[10]

---

[6] G. K. Beale, "Isaiah vi 9–13: A Retributive Taunt against Idolatry," *VT* 41 (1991): 257–78; also Watts, *New Exodus,* 188–94.

[7] See R. E. Clements, *Isaiah 1–39* (NCB; Grand Rapids: Eerdmans, 1980), 83; followed by John Day, "'Shear-Jashub' (Isaiah vii 3) and 'the Remnant of Wrath' (Psalm lxxvi 11)," *VT* 31 (1981): 76–78.

[8] The consecutive form of the verb obviously indicates that vv. 10ff in some way flow out of the preceding.

[9] E.g., K. Budde, "Das Immanuel-Zeichen und die Ahaz-Begegnung Jesaja 7," *JBL* 52 (1933): 25; E. J. Kissane, *The Book of Isaiah* (2 vols.; Dublin: Browne & Nolan, 1941–1943); G. Fohrer, "Zu Jes. 7. 14 im Zussamenhang von Jes. 7.10–22," *ZAW* 68 (1956): 54–56; Joseph Jensen, "The Age of Immanuel," *CBQ* 41 (1979): 220–39; Marvin A. Sweeney, *Isaiah 1–39* (FOTL 16; Grand Rapids: Eerdmans, 1996), 150–63; H. G. M. Williamson, "The Messianic Texts in Isaiah 1–39," in *King and Messiah in Israel and the Ancient Near East* (ed. John Day; JSOTSup 270; Sheffield, England: Sheffield Academic Press, 1998), 253; cf. J. J. Stamm, "Die Immanuel-Weissagung: Ein Gespräch mit E. Hammershaimb," *VT* 4 (1954): 20–33; and Clements, *Isaiah 1–39,* 89.

[10] Cf. E. G. Kraeling, "The Immanuel Prophecy," *JBL* 50 (1931): 292–93, who regards vv. 10–16 as a midrashic interpolation between the warning and threat of vv. 9b and 17; and S. Blank, "Immanuel and Which Isaiah?" *JNES* 13 (1954): 83–86, who must either omit or relocate vv. 9b and 13 in order for Immanuel to be a promise of deliverance.

Various objections, however, have been put forward. First, לָכֵן does not always introduce a threat and so should not be assumed to do so here.[11] Second, the child should be identified with a royal or messianic figure, and this naturally presages a bright future.[12] Moreover, since the background to these verses is the Syro-Ephraimite threat and since Isaiah encouraged Ahaz to ask for a sign, Immanuel would make more sense if it was positive;[13] after all, if judgment was intended, then surely something like Ichabod would have been more appropriate (1 Sam 4:21).[14] And since it is untenable for Immanuel to be a double sign—indicating both deliverance and judgment—it can only have a positive significance.[15] Third, the diet of curds and honey—perhaps seen as the food of the gods[16]—suggests prosperity,[17] and Isa 7:16's promised desolation of the coalition's territory can only mean good news for Judah. Finally, it has been argued that the days envisaged in v. 17 refer not to the dire condition of Judah after the departure of the ten northern tribes but instead to the prosperity experienced at the height of Solomon's reign.[18] Some have found these considerations so compelling that they see the Immanuel oracle as one of promise and support.[19] A larger number of commentators, impressed but not quite so convinced, have argued for some version of a both-and approach.[20]

---

[11] See William McKane, "The Interpretation of Isaiah VII 14–25," *VT* 17 (1967): 209, and those cited therein.

[12] E.g., J. J. Scullion, "An Approach to the Understanding of Isaiah 7 10–17," *JBL* 87 (1968): 214, who invokes the general background of Egyptian birth stories, the Ras Shamra poems, and Mesopotamian and Ugaritic texts. For McKane, "Isaiah VII 14–25," Isaiah simply means that Immanuel will become a popular name after Yahweh's deliverance of his people.

[13] B. Duhm, *Das Buch Jesaja* (HKAT 3.1; Göttingen: Vandenhoeck & Ruprecht, 1892), cited approvingly and further developed in McKane, "Isaiah VII 14–25," 211.

[14] McKane, "Isaiah VII 14–25." See also J. J. Stamm, "La prophétie d'Emmanuel," *RTP* 32 (1944): 120–22.

[15] McKane, "Isaiah VII 14–25," 212.

[16] See the discussion in Scullion, "An Approach," 296, citing Exod 3:8, 17; Deut 6:3; 11:9; 26:9.

[17] McKane, "Isaiah VII 14–25," 217.

[18] E.g., Scullion, "An Approach," 298–99; John H. Hayes and Stuart A. Irvine, *Isaiah, the Eight Century Prophet: His Times and Preaching* (Nashville: Abingdon, 1987), 133.

[19] E.g., E. Hammershaimb, *Some Aspects of Old Testament Prophecy from Isaiah to Malachi* (Copenhagen: Rosenkilde og Bagger, 1966), 19–20; McKane, "Isaiah VII 14–25"; Scullion, "An Approach"; J. Høgenhaven, *Gott und Volk bei Jesaja: Eine Untersuchung zur biblischen Theologie* (ATDan 24; New York: E. J. Brill, 1988), 87–93; S. A. Irvine, *Isaiah, Ahaz, and the Syro-Ephraimitic Crisis* (SBLDS, 123; Atlanta: Scholars Press, 1990), 164–71; Hayes and Irvine, *Isaiah,* 136. Frequently, however, scholars holding this view resort to excising varying amounts of contrary material that they regard as arising from editorial misunderstanding (e.g., Isa 7:15, 17d; 18–20).

[20] E.g., G. H. A. von Ewald, F. Delitzsch, A. B. Davidson, K. Marti, J. Skinner, O. Procksch, K. Budde, J. J. Stamm, L. G. Rignell, J. Coppens, O. Kaiser, and G. von Rad (see the full bibliographical details in McKane, "Isaiah VII 14–25," 210 n. 3), and more recently Hans Wildberger, *Isaiah 1–12: A Commentary* [trans. Thomas H. Trapp; 2 vols.; CC; Minneapolis: Fortress, 1991–], 1:312–13).

The literature here is enormous, and it is impossible to cover every nuance of each alternative.[21] Nevertheless, the central thrust of these objections can be addressed. First, it is indeed true that לָכֵן can introduce a positive word. But as J. Lust has argued, in every case where it follows a warning or rebuke, the effect is negative, and this, significantly, includes Isaiah (e.g., 1:21–24; 5:10–14, 16–25 [bis]; 8:6–7).[22]

Turning to Immanuel, the central matter, a number of issues arise. First is the question of his identity, for which at least eight proposals have been offered.[23] It might be, in light of the designation of the first and last children as Isaiah's off-spring (7:3; 8:3), that the absence of any similar remark concerning Immanuel implies that the readers already knew something of his identity (cf. the definite article in "the young woman," which might indicate that both Ahaz and Isaiah knew her). It might also be that Immanuel is a royal scion who will learn, unlike Ahaz, to reject evil and to choose the good (cf. 1:3, 16b–20, 24; 5:13, 19, 21, 24; 8:6).[24] But the fact remains that the text as it stands offers nothing specific. If the identification of the child was crucial to interpreting the oracle, why does the writer or final editor remain silent on the matter? Instead, the overriding concern, as the bulk of the material makes clear (7:16–25), is how the name relates to the nature of the circumstances being described. This is consistent with the other name oracles where the meaning of the names rather than the identity of the children is of primary interest. It is also worth noting that if Shear-jashub is not himself the remnant, nor Maher-Shalal-Hash-Baz the spoiler, then it is unlikely that this second child is himself somehow "God with us."

So what is the significance of "Immanuel"? There is little question that the expression can imply salvation (e.g., Ps 48:8, 12), support for faithful David (2 Sam 7:3), and even Yahweh's response to repentance (e.g., Amos 5:14; Zeph 3:15). But in this context such a positive reading faces one fatal objection: Ahaz is hardly either faithful or repentant. The concentration on the house of David (Isa

---

[21] See, e.g., the extensive literature cited in McKane, "Isaiah VII 14–25"; Jensen, "Age of Immanuel"; and J. Lust, "The Immanuel Figure: A Charismatic Judge-Leader," *ETL* 47 (1971): 464–70.

[22] Lust, "Immanuel Figure," 467; see also, e.g., 10:15–16; 16:6–7; 28:11–14; 29:13–14; 30:6b–7, 8–14; cf. Stamm, "Weissagung," 31. On the other hand, in 26:12–15, 27:7–9, 29:17–22, and 30:15–18, לָכֵן, preceded by positive words, introduces favorable outcomes.

[23] Lust, "Immanuel Figure," 465f, lists Ahaz's son Hezekiah, a messianic figure for the remote future, a miraculous child (appealing to ancient Near Eastern mythology), a collective interpretation involving all the sons born during this period, Isaiah's own son, and a mysterious savior before offering his own proposal: a charismatic judge. Gene Rice, "A Neglected Interpretation of the Immanuel Prophecy," *ZAW* 90 (1978): 220–27, suggests that the remnant, namely, Isaiah's children and disciples (8:13, 18), are collectively Immanuel.

[24] See, e.g., Wildberger, *Isaiah,* 1:313, and Jensen, "Age of Immanuel," 227–37, for whom even an ideal, messianic, though not necessarily eschatological figure is implied; but cf. Williamson, "Messianic Texts," 253–54, who argues that Isaiah is committed only to a divinely appointed leader, not necessarily of Davidic descent. For the view that he is a son of Isaiah (cf. 8:18), see Day, " 'Shear-Jashub,' " 78 n. 3.

7:2, 13) and the threat of v. 9b—"if you [pl.] do not stand firm in faith, you [pl.] shall not stand at all" (NRSV), itself probably an allusion to a proverbial form of Nathan's promise—only make the contrast between David and Ahaz even starker.[25] One also notes the shift from "your God" (v. 10) to "my God" (v. 13),[26] and Isaiah's שִׁמְעוּ־נָא (v. 13a), which nearly always implies hostile intent.[27]

Second, it is not at all obvious that Yahweh's presence always means bless-ing. In the paradigmatic saving event—the exodus—it also entailed judgment when Israel rebelled or refused to trust (e.g., Num 14, 16). Likewise, in 1 Samuel 4, the material sign of Yahweh's presence, the ark of the covenant (1 Sam 4:3–5), meant disaster for a presumptuous and faithless Israel (vv. 10–11, 18, 20–22; cf. Mic 3:11). Closer to home, in the account immediately preceding Isaiah 7, it is again Yahweh's presence (in the temple) that occasions Isaiah's call and the sub-sequent devastation of idolatrous Judah (Isa 6:1, 9–12). A similar idea is also found later in Malachi, where the coming of Yahweh of Hosts threatens de-struction (3:1–5; 4:1–6 [Eng.]).

It is noteworthy that a number of scholars have proposed that behind the Immanuel language and other motifs in Isaiah 7–8 stands the Zion tradition. Of particular importance is Psalm 46, in which the exaltation (אָרוּם) of God over his enemies is twice celebrated with the refrain "Yahweh of Hosts is with us" (יְהוָה צְבָאוֹת עִמָּנוּ, vv. 8, 12 MT).[28] Strikingly, these themes pervade the very chapters preceding our passage. "Yahweh of Hosts" occurs eleven times in Isaiah 1–6, in-cluding twice in Isaiah's call, and the idea of Yahweh's exaltation occurs three times.[29] But over whom is Yahweh exalted? In each instance it is the proud and rebellious in Judah (שׂגב, 2:9–14, 17; 5:11–17; cf. 1:21–26, 28, 31; 3:12–15; 6:1; 12:4). The same kind of ironic critique is found in Mic 3:11, where, in spite of the boast "the LORD is in our midst" (יְהוָה בְּקִרְבֵּנוּ), corrupt Judah and Jerusalem will be destroyed. All this suggests that if the presence of Yahweh of Hosts implies the humbling of Ahaz and Judah and if Isaiah can speak of his children as signs and symbols from Yahweh of Hosts (8:18), then Immanuel seems primarily to have ominous implications.[30]

---

[25] Hence the plural; see 2 Sam 7:16; cf. 2 Sam 7:3, mentioned above, and further 1 Sam 25:28; 1 Kgs 11:38; Ps 89:29, 38 [Eng. 89:28, 37]; Isa 55:3; see Williamson, "Messi-anic Texts," 251.

[26] See also Lust, "Immanuel Figure," 466; and likewise the shift from "my people" in 1:3; 3:12, 15; and 5.13 to "this people" in 6:9, 10; 8:6, 11, 12; and 9:16.

[27] As in most instances in the MT; cf. F. Zimmermann, "The Immanuel Prophecy," *JQR* 52 (1961/1962): 158.

[28] So, e.g., Day, " 'Shear-Jashub,' " 77, and the literature cited therein.

[29] Respectively, Isa 1:9, 24; 2:12; 3:1; 5:4, 16, 24; 6:3, 5; and 2:11, 17; 5:16. This is compared, in Isaiah 7–8, to twice for the former (8:13, 18) and not at all for the latter.

[30] See also Bernhard W. Anderson, " 'God with Us'—in Judgment and in Mercy: The Editorial Structure of Isaiah 5–10(11)," in *Canon, Theology, and Old Testament Inter-pretation* (ed. Gene M. Tucker, David L. Peterson, and Robert K. Wilson; Philadelphia: Fortress, 1988), 243; Andrew H. Bartelt, *The Book around Immanuel: Style and Structure in Isaiah 2–12* (Biblical and Judaic Studies from the University of California 4; Winona Lake, Ind.: Eisenbrauns, 1996), 115: "The presence of God will no longer be active in protection

Along the same lines and remembering that Israel's exodus was, par excellence, the time of Yahweh's presence among his people, the repeated references to Yahweh's outstretched hand recall Yahweh's judgments on Egypt. But in keeping with Yahweh's exaltation over Judah's arrogant leaders and people, his hand is now extended against them (יָד נטה, Isa 1:25; 5:25; 9:12, 16, 21; 10:4; cf. Exod 3:19, 20; 7:4f; 8:5f, 17; 9:22; 10:12, 21f; 14:16, 21, 26). It is surely not surprising, given the thoroughgoing Deuteronomic covenant language in Isaiah 1,[31] that the presence of the Holy One of Israel in all his כָּבוֹד ("glory," Isa 6:3) among a rebellious people כָּבֵד ("heavy," 1:4) with iniquity means judgment.[32]

But what about the promised devastation of the coalition? Does not this demonstrate a positive element to Immanuel? Not necessarily. In 1 Samuel 4 Yahweh's presence meant judgment on faithless Israel as well as pagan Philistia. So too here. As the Shear-jashub oracle indicated, the Syro-Ephraimite coalition will indeed be reduced to a mere remnant. This circumstance will not change regardless of Ahaz's decision. But this destruction does not inevitably mean salvation for Judah: its own idolatrous faithlessness will be its undoing. Immanuel, then, means judgment for both.[33] That this is the case is further suggested by the two other Immanuel references in Isaiah 8. The first, in Isa 8:8, is associated with Judah's judgment (vv. 6–8),[34] and the second, in v. 10, apparently describes the shattering of the Syro-Ephraimite coalition (vv. 9–10).[35]

Turning to the next consideration, we find that the significance of the child's diet is not immediately clear.[36] True, curds and honey appear to echo the descriptions of the promised land's flowing bounty (Exod 3:8, 17; Deut 6:3; 11:9; 26:9)

---

and deliverance but rather in summoning up Assyria as a means of destruction and punishment (vv. 18–25)."

[31] A number of commentators have noted parallels with Deuteronomy's account of covenant renewal on the plains of Moab. Isaiah 1:2's "hear O heavens and earth" recalls Deut 32:1, cf. 31:28; the term "sons" (Isa 1:4) is typical of father-son covenant terminology used of suzerain and vassal (cf. Deut 32:5–6, 19–20); particularly appropriate in this context is "rebellion" (Israel is first called Yahweh's "son" in Exod 4:12; cf. Hos 11:1; Jer 3:19; and in Deut 21:18–21 rebellious sons are stoned). "Forsake" and "abandon" (Isa 1:4) bespeak apostasy and covenant unfaithfulness (cf. Deut 28:20; 29:25, 26; 31:16, 20; 32:19; etc.), and "not know or understand" echoes Deut 32:28. Isaiah 1:5–9 seems to pick up the curses and ailments of Deut 28:16, 22, 25–33, 51–52, 62–63; 29:23. That Yahweh appears in his palace/temple—the place where the treaty was kept between the feet of the Deity so that he could be reminded of it—to pass sentence further suggests that Isaiah is interpreting events within a covenantal horizon. Cf. L. G. Rignell, "Isaiah Chapter 1: Some Exegetical Remarks with Special Reference of the Relationship between the Text and the Book of Deuteronomy," *ST* 2 (1957): 140–58; J. J. M. Roberts, "Isaiah in Old Testament Theology," *Int* 36 (1982): 130–43; and S. Niditch, "The Composition of Isaiah 1," *Bib* 61 (1981): 509–29.

[32] Cf. Rolf Rendtorff, "Zur Komposition des Buches Jesaja," *VT* 34 (1984): 312, where קְדוֹשׁ־יִשְׂרָאֵל is primarily associated with judgment.

[33] As also noted by Carter, "Evoking Isaiah," 150–51.

[34] E.g., Day, "'Shear-Jashub,'" 78, n. 3.

[35] E.g., Clements, *Isaiah 1–39*, 97.

[36] See, e.g., the helpful summary of alternatives in Gene Rice, "The Interpretation of Isaiah 7:15–17," *JBL* 96 (1977): 363–69.

or, for some, even divine food that marvelously brings wisdom.[37] But given the threatening nature of much of the preceding material, and particularly the threatening overtones of Immanuel and the poignant use of the "outstretched hand" motif, the suggestion that *eating* curds and honey be taken ironically has merit.[38] As Jensen and others have shown, the imagery would not normally be applied to settled life in Canaan and is better understood to refer to the relative superabundance consequent to the extensive destruction of cities and towns, dislocation of settled agriculture, and depopulation of the land.[39] As a result, much of the land will be overgrown and the ruined cities serve as pasture. But this will be more than sufficient for the insignificant herds (one young heifer, two sheep), such that they will easily sustain the even more reduced human population (Isa 7:20–25). This explains the abundance of milk (and thus curds) and the presence of wild honey presumably gathered from bees' nests in the burgeoning brambles (cf. vv. 18b–19). The child might eat the food of the gods but only, ironically, as the aftermath of God's judgment. It is by experiencing Yahweh's discipline that Immanuel (whoever he might be) will come to know how to make right choices (cf. Deut 8.3).[40] There is, then, some measure of hope, and it may well be that it is to this that the prophet later turns in Isa 9:1–7; 10:12–27; 11:1–16. But in this passage it is only a mere glimmer. Ironically, then, Yahweh of Hosts' holy presence means judgment on idolatrous Ahaz and Judah.

Finally, in 7:17, as several scholars have shown, the hiphil of בא with the preposition על and YHWH as subject consistently implies a threat.[41] The comment of CD 7:11–12 on this verse also takes it this way. If Isaiah had intended the time before the traumatic division of the kingdom, then we might have expected something like the "time of David and [his son] Solomon" (cf. 2 Chron 11:17; 33:7; Neh 12:45).[42] Instead the time of the breach appears to be the best understanding (cf. *Tg. Isa.* 7:17) and may be echoed in the prophet's own subsequent withdrawal from the ways of Judah (Isa 8:11–18).[43]

---

[37] So, e.g., P. G. Duncker, " 'Ut sciat reprobare malum et eligere bonum,' Is VII 15b," *Sacra Pagina: Miscellanea biblica* (ed. J. Coppens, E. Descamps, and E. Massaux; 2 vols.; BETL 12, 13; Gembloux: J. Duculot, 1959), 1:408–9; and Scullion, "An Approach," 297.

[38] Rice, "Isaiah," 365, citing E. M. Good, *Irony in the Old Testament* (Philadelphia: Westminster, 1965), 123–24. M. McNamara, "The Emmanuel Prophecy and Its Context," *Scr* 14 (1962): 122, remarks that there is a distinction between (a) a land that flows with milk and honey and (b) eating curds and honey. Perhaps.

[39] See Jensen, "Age of Immanuel," citing G. Fohrer, *Das Buch Jesaja* (3 vols.; vols. 1 and 2, 2d ed.; vol. 3, 1st ed.; ZBK; Zurich: Zwingli, 1964–1967), 2:115–16; and Rice, "Isaiah." Prosperity in settled Canaan was usually seen in terms of the abundance of corn, wine, and oil.

[40] See further Jensen, "Age of Immanuel"; cf. Scullion, "An Approach," 297–98. Jensen argues persuasively that v. 15b's "refuse the evil and choose the good" refers not only to sophisticated moral discernment but also to making the right choice. This suggests an age of around twenty (cf. Num 1:3, 20, 22, 24, etc.; and 14:29–30).

[41] Rice, "Isaiah," 367, citing R. Kilian, *Die Verheissung Immanuels, Jes. 7, 14* (SBS 35; Stuttgart: Katholisches Bibelwerk, 1968), 45–46; and Wildberger, *Isaiah,* 1:326.

[42] Rice, "Isaiah," 367.

[43] Ibid.

Given our interest in Matthew, the question inevitably arises: did Isaiah envisage this as a miraculous virgin birth? It is now widely agreed that he did not and, had it not been for Matthew's use of this text, it is extremely doubtful if anyone would ever have read it so. The data seem quite clear. The word עַלְמָה is a broad term meaning a young or immature woman of marriageable age, often a virgin but not necessarily.[44] At the time of the LXX's translation, παρθένος apparently did not always mean "virgin," any more than the Hebrew עַלְמָה.[45] And here again, in spite of the considerable scholarly attention devoted to the identity of the young woman in question, in the immediate context it seems of no particular significance.[46]

As to her condition, the use of the adjective in a verbless clause signifies either past or present action, and so, given the presence of the qal active participle (יֹלֶדֶת), which usually means an action in progress or about to begin, it seems that the young woman is currently pregnant and anticipating the birth in the near future.[47] Moreover, the prediction of offspring is apparently a stock expression in marriages,[48] and as two uses of the Ugaritic cognate of עַלְמָה, ǵlmt—one parallel to ʾatt ("wife") and the other as a young woman is embraced, "See, a young woman shall bear a son" (hl ǵlmt tld bn)—suggest, there is nothing particularly extraordinary here.[49] And apparently neither Ahaz nor Isaiah nor any Jewish tradition ever felt it so. This is further confirmed by an examination of Yahweh's giving "signs" in similar contexts (Exod 3:12; 1 Sam 2:34; Jer 44:29f; 2 Kgs 19:29):

---

[44] This is a relatively rare word in the MT, but two references make the meaning clear: young women in a harem (Song 6:3) and the recipient of man's sexual attention (Prov 30:19). John Walton, "Isa 7.14: What's in a Name?" *JETS* 30 (1987): 291–93.

[45] "παρθένος," 2, LSJ 1339; "παρθένος," *TDNT* 5:827, 829–33.

[46] For options, see, e.g., Wildberger, *Isaiah*, 1:308–10; and the summary in Michael E. W. Thompson, "Isaiah's Sign of Immanuel," *ExpTim* 95 (1983): 67–71, who lists the prophet's wife, Ahaz's wife, Mary (as per Matthew), a child-bearing Zion, a symbol of Israel, a young woman perhaps representative of many young women who will soon so name their sons. On the basis of Gen 24:43, Exod 2:8, and Prov 30:19, Christoph Dohmen ("Das Immanuelzeichen: Ein jesajanisches Drohwort und seine inneralttestamentliche Rezeption," *Bib* 68 [1987]: 305–29) thinks that the emphasis lies on a woman who is foreign to both Ahaz and Isaiah; cf. *Num. Rab.* 9.14 (on Num. 5:17), commenting on Song 6:8, where the rabbis see עלמות as implying a woman of unknown origin. For Gillis Gerleman ("Die sperrende Grenze: Die Wurzel עלם im Hebräischen," *ZAW* 91 [1979]: 338–49), she is a woman who, knowing nothing of Isaiah's words, will call her son Immanuel.

[47] See GKC 141–42, 116a; and compare with Gen 16:10 (Hagar) and Judg 13:3 (Samson's mother), both of which use a verbless clause but differ in that the birth verb is a *wāw*-consecutive perfect, suggesting a more future birth, and so these women might not yet be pregnant; Walton, "Isa 7.14," 290–91; W. Weren, "Quotations from Isaiah and Matthew's Christology (Mt 1, 23 and 4, 15–16)," in *Studies in the Book of Isaiah* (ed. J. van Ruiten and M. Vervenne; FS Willem A. M. Beuken; BETL 132; Leuven: Leuven University Press and Peeters, 1997), 448.

[48] John Gray, *The Krt Text in the Literature of Ras Shamra* (2d ed.; Leiden: E. J. Brill, 1964), 57; cited in Herbert M. Wolf, "A Solution to the Immanuel Prophecy in Isaiah 7:14–8:22," *JBL* 91 (1972): 450.

[49] Keret 128 ii 21–22 and Hymn to Nikkal (*UT* 77.7); cited in Scullion, "An Approach," 292–93; Wolf, "A Solution," 450; and Walton, "Isa 7.14," 291–92.

rarely, if ever, are they supernatural in themselves, and their intent is not to over-awe with supernatural power.[50]

Returning to the central question of the Immanuel oracle, the overall emphasis on judgment is also supported by the context of the material as it currently stands. The opening lawsuit in Isaiah 1 lays out Yahweh's coming judgment. Chapters 2–4, with minor incursions of hope, constantly reiterate warnings and threats. They apparently go unheeded, and the juridical parable song of the vineyard provokes the people of Judah and Jerusalem into passing judgment on themselves (5:1–7).[51] The following woes see Judah reduced to chaos (5:30), and in ch. 6 Yahweh's presence and Isaiah's call set in motion the wheels of judgment. In the very next scene Ahaz's refusal to trust in the parable name Shear-jashub, because of his determination to pursue his own idolatrous realpolitik, means that God-with-us signifies dreadful desolation. In other words, and this needs to be heard clearly, Immanuel is the name that heralds the judgment announced in Isaiah 6.

Consequently, Assyria, in whom Ahaz has instead trusted, will become Yahweh's "axe" by which the idolatrous tree of Jesse will be reduced to a stump (cf. 6:13; 10:15; 11:1), with only a remnant surviving (8:6–8).[52] As the Divine Warrior declares in the introduction to the book (1:24–25):

> Therefore says the Sovereign, the LORD of hosts, the Mighty One of Israel:
>
> Ah, I will pour out my wrath on my enemies, and avenge myself on my foes!
>
> I will turn my hand against you; I will smelt away your dross as with lye and remove all your alloy. (NRSV)

This is Yahweh's alien and wonderful plan (cf. 28:21; 5:19).[53] Yahweh has not abandoned his covenant, nor has he abandoned his purpose that Jerusalem should become a light to the nations (2:1–4; cf. 4:2–6). He still intends that the mountain of his house, his temple, be established as the highest mountain, to which all nations will come. It is his goal that many peoples be taught his ways and walk in his paths, that instruction go forth from Zion and his word from Jerusalem. But it will happen through a strange and mysterious work. His people must first pass through the cleansing fire of his presence among them. Yahweh of Hosts himself will become "a stone one strikes against; . . . a rock one stumbles over—a trap and a snare for the inhabitants of Jerusalem. . . . Many among them shall stumble; they shall fall and be broken; they shall be snared

---

[50] Walton, "Isa 7.14," 294–95. This "in similar contexts" is important. The exodus event, for example, does not meet this criterion.

[51] G. A. Yee, "A Form-Critical Study of Isaiah 5:1–7 as a Song and a Juridical Parable," *CBQ* 43 (1981): 30–40; and G. T. Sheppard, "More on Isaiah 5, 1–7 as a Juridical Parable," *CBQ* 44 (1982): 45–47.

[52] Also O. Steck, "Bermerkungen zu Jesaja 6," *BZ* 16 (1972): 188–206; and Clements, *Isaiah 1–39*, 89.

[53] For this and much of the following, see Anderson, " 'God with Us,' " 243.

and taken" (8:14–15 NRSV). But for those who, believing, perceive the signs, including that of Immanuel, and who wait for Yahweh and hope in him (8:17), there is the promise of participating in the restoration when "the root of Jesse shall stand as a signal to the peoples; the nations shall inquire of him, and his dwelling shall be glorious" (11:10 NRSV). Then they will "make known his deeds among the nations, and proclaim that his name is exalted . . . (let this) be known in all the world . . . for great in your midst is the Holy One of Israel" (12:4b–6).

Isaiah 7:14 in Matthew

Matthew's genealogical listing, with its three groups of fourteen generations structured around Abraham, David, and the deportation, prepares his hearers/readers to anticipate the coming of messianic salvation,[54] a new exodus from exile.[55] After all that begetting, it is fitting that he should meet this expectation by beginning his story proper with the announcement of the birth of Jesus, the one who will preside over Israel's restoration. Several observations can be made. First, although it is generally recognized as a birth narrative, several scholars have challenged this designation because of the absence of any reference to the birth itself.[56] The rather understated and matter-of-fact manner in which Mary's virginal conception is introduced suggests that it is not the principal issue.[57] Instead the story is primarily concerned with two things: dealing with the questionable circumstances surrounding the child's nativity and, more important, explaining his significance as expressed, not unlike Isaiah's parable children, through his two names: Jesus and Immanuel.

---

[54] As is widely affirmed; e.g., W. D. Davies and D. C. Allison Jr., *A Critical and Exegetical Commentary on the Gospel according to Saint Matthew* (3 vols.; ICC; Edinburgh: T&T Clark, 1988–1997), 1:187; Donald A. Hagner, *Matthew 1–13* (WBC 33A; Dallas: Word, 1993), 7.

[55] This claim has been contested, but see Watts, *New Exodus*, 67, 82ff, and esp. 73 n. 111, citing Pinkhos Churgin, "The Period of the Second Temple—An Era of Exile," *Horeb* 8 (1944): 1—16 (Heb), in L. Smolar and M. Auerbach, *Studies in Targum Jonathan to the Prophets* (LBS; New York: Ktav, 1983), xxv, who notes the absence of any biblical feast to celebrate the return from exile; see also N. T. Wright, *The New Testament and the People of God* (Christian Origins and the Question of God 1; Minneapolis: Fortress, 1992), 215–338; and now Craig A. Evans, "Jesus and the Continuing Exile of Israel," in *Jesus and the Restoration of Israel* (ed. Carey E. Newman; Downers Grove, Ill.: InterVarsity, 1999), 77–100.

[56] E.g., Krister Stendahl, "Quis et Unde? An Analysis of Mt. 1–2," in *Judentum-Urchristentum-Kirche* (ed. W. Eltester; FS J. Jeremias; BZNW 26; Berlin: Töpelman, 1964), 97–105; H. C. Waetjen, "The Genealogy as the Key to the Gospel according to Matthew," *JBL* 95 (1976): 205–30.

[57] So, e.g., Stendahl, "Quis," 56; Charles Thomas Davis, "Tradition and Redaction in Matthew 1:18–2:23," *JBL* 90 (1971): 415; and Ulrich Luz, *Matthew 1–7* (trans. Wilhelm C. Linss; Minneapolis: Fortress, 1989), 127.

The questionable circumstances surrounding Jesus' birth probably explain the inclusion of Tamar, Ruth, and Bathsheba in Matthew's genealogy.[58] They show that the house of David is no stranger to scandalous unions.[59] This may also explain why Joseph himself is designated a son of David—the only individual other than Jesus so labeled—and why Matthew emphasizes his righteousness. It helps defuse potential criticism, especially when this righteous man realizes that Mary's condition is Yahweh's doing. A similar apologetic might well motivate the twofold mention of the Spirit (vv. 18, 20). Not only is the Spirit clearly important; the description of the Spirit as "Holy" appears to be a Matthean accent, thus stamping this moment as God's work (and only again in 28:19).[60]

The names are the other concern. That this is Matthew's first use of his distinctive fulfillment formula and that it is in his first narrative unit strongly suggest that he regards them as programmatic. For Mark Powell, "You are to name him Jesus, for he will save his people from their sins" (1:21) sets up the gospel, which then goes on to explain how this will happen,[61] and for John Nolland, "the name Emmanuel presages a future in connection with this child in which the presence of God will be known and experienced in a decisive manner. It is the unfolding of Matthew's story that must tell the rest."[62]

Jesus, being the Greek form of Joshua, which in popular etymology derived from יָשַׁע, "to save," is apparently considered self-explanatory and straightforward.[63] This Jesus, in saving his people from their sins, will end their exile (Isa 40:2; 43:25; 59:2).[64] But what are we to make of Immanuel? That the language of the surrounding material is so heavily influenced by the Isaiah citation indicates

---

[58] Rahab, understood as the woman of Jericho, has often been included here, but her identity is open to question; cf. R. Bauckham, "Tamar's Ancestry and Rahab's Marriage: Two Problems in Matthew's Genealogy," *NovT* 37 (1995): 313–29.

[59] Raymond E. Brown, *The Birth of the Messiah* (ABRL; New York: Doubleday, 1977), 73–74.

[60] Although the Spirit is mentioned eleven times in Matthew (1:18, 20; 3:11, 16; 4:1; 10:20; 12:18, 31, 32; 22:43; 28:19), including once in a citation (Isa 42:1–4 in Matt 12:18), the adjective "Holy" only appears on five of these occasions (Matt 1:18, 20; 3:11; 12:32; 28:19). Of these five, two, the baptism (4:1) and the Beelzebul controversy (12:32), appear to be traditional, leaving only the two references in Matt 1 and the one at the Great Commission as clearly Matthean contributions.

[61] M. A. Powell, "The Plot and Subplots of Matthew's Gospel," *NTS* 38 (1992): 187–204, where he builds on the work of Edwards, Matera, and Kingsbury and proposes that "Matthew's narrative can be best understood as embodying one main plot (God's plan and Satan's challenge) and at least two sub-plots (Jesus and the religious leaders, Jesus and the disciples). The religious leaders' success at bringing Jesus to the cross and the disciples' failure in preventing this brings about the fulfillment of God's plan of salvation" (as summarized in *NTA* 36, no. 3 [1992], 333).

[62] J. Nolland, "No Son of God Christology in Matthew 1.18–25," *JSNT* 62 (1996): 12.

[63] Davies and Allison, *Matthew,* 1:209, cite Philo, *Names* 121, as evidence that this was known outside Palestine.

[64] See further Wright, *Jesus and the Victory of God* (vol. 2 of *Christian Origins and the Question of God;* Minneapolis: Fortress, 1996), 268–74.

that the story as we have it was composed with the Isaiah text in mind. Matthew has told this story in order to prepare for the Immanuel citation.[65]

Technically, Matthew's citation is largely Septuagintal, the only variation being his change from "you will call" to "they will call" (cf. MT: "she will call").[66] Though not of particular concern for our argument, Matthew may be following a Greek text unknown to us—the various versions diverging here. Or if Chris Stanley is correct, Matthew is simply engaging in the standard practice of making "exegetical" alterations so that his understanding of the point of the original text can be heard.[67] If so, then perhaps Matthew intends that although Jesus would not actually bear this name, it would, in time, be recognized that his role as Savior would also include whatever Immanuel signified.[68]

So, why has Matthew appealed to this text? What does he think Immanuel means? Generally, it is argued either (a) that he wanted to show that Jesus' origin—born of a virgin, and of the house of David—was in keeping with the scriptures; (b) that Immanuel provides an additional christological title with which he can work (cf. 28:20); or (c) that he might have intended to provide apologetic ammunition for his audience.[69] But how convincing are these putative reasons?

Concerning the first and third suggestions, as far as we know, there is no Jewish tradition that appealed to Isa 7:14 in expectation of a miraculous, let alone virgin, birth. And as already noted, Matthew seems more interested in the Immanuel motif than Mary's virginity. It is there, but he hardly emphasizes it. In this, Matthew seems no different from the other NT writers, for whom Jesus' virgin birth seems not to play a major role.

Nor is there any evidence that Isa 7:14 was ever understood in terms of a future messianic hope. It is true that in some rabbinic traditions Immanuel

---

[65] Again Stendahl, "Quis," and Hagner, *Matthew 1–13*, 15, noting:

LXX Isa 7:14 = Matt 1:23	Matthew 1
ἐν γαστρὶ ἕξει	ἐν γαστρὶ ἔχουσα (v. 18)
καὶ τέξεται υἱόν	τέξεται δὲ υἱόν (v. 21)
	ἔτεκεν υἱόν (v. 25)
καὶ καλέσεις (LXX)/καλέσουσιν (Matt)	καὶ καλέσεις τὸ ὄνομα αὐτοῦ Ἰησοῦν (v. 21)
τὸ ὄνομα αὐτοῦ Εμμανουηλ	καὶ ἐκάλεσεν τὸ ὄνομα αὐτοῦ Ἰησοῦν (v. 25)

[66] Matthew's ἕξει follows ℵ, A, and Q. See the discussion in Stendahl, *School of St. Matthew,* 97–99; Robert Horton Gundry, *The Use of the Old Testament in St. Matthew's Gospel* (NovTSup 18; Leiden: E. J. Brill, 1967), 89–91; and George M. Soares Prabhu, *The Formula Quotations in the Infancy Narrative of Matthew* (AnBib, 63; Rome: Biblical Institute, 1976), 229ff.

[67] C. D. Stanley, *Paul and the Language of Scripture: Citation Technique in the Pauline Epistles and Contemporary Literature* (SNTSMS 74; New York: Cambridge University Press, 1992), 343ff.

[68] See, e.g., Gundry, *St. Matthew's Gospel,* 89–91.

[69] See, e.g., Brown, *Birth of the Messiah,* 149–50; Davies and Allison, *Matthew,* 1:213.

was understood to be Hezekiah, whom other traditions associated with the Messiah.[70] But what evidence is there that Matthew was himself making this somewhat convoluted connection? On the contrary, it appears not only that kingship is not a theme in 1:18–25, whereas it is in 2:1–23,[71] but that any suggestion that Jesus is a messianic son of David derives instead from the opening sentence (1:1), the genealogy's concentration on David (vv. 6, 17), and, in that light, Joseph also being a son of David (v. 20).

Further, when one remembers that Matthew is almost universally considered to be writing to an audience of Jewish background—hence he offers no linguistic explanation of the name Jesus[72]—how convincing would an apologetic move of this kind be? It might work for later Gentile Christians who came to their LXX via their Christian heritage, but as the valiant efforts of Justin and the early Fathers suggest, it would hardly wash with informed Jewish readers. Immanuel is unable to bear the Davidic-messianic weight placed upon it. All in all, I doubt if Matthew's citation would have done much to further his audience's faith in a messianic Jesus' virgin birth. On the contrary, it appears that this much is simply assumed. It seems highly unlikely, at least to me, that Matthew had either agenda (a) or agenda (c) in mind when he composed this narrative.[73]

This leaves us with suggestion (b), that Immanuel functions as a christological title. Contrary to one proposal, the two references in 18:20 and in 28:20 hardly suffice to demonstrate that the comforting presence of Jesus, "God with us," is a major Matthean motif.[74] W. D. Davies and Dale Allison mention two other possibilities, namely, that Matthew is explicitly calling Jesus God or simply indicating that God is somehow active in Jesus.[75] Since Matthew elsewhere never explicitly calls Jesus God, it seems unlikely that he meant such an overt designation here. If he wanted to do so, he could have altered the form of the Greek to make Jesus' identification with God clearer, but he stays with the LXX. One might note again that the name Immanuel, like most such namings in the OT, is not speaking about the ontological status of the individual as much as about what God is doing. This is not to deny that at a deeper level Matthew might also give us a nudge and a wink, "Immanuel indeed!" After all, he is writing some time after

---

[70] E.g., Justin, *Dial.* 43; *Exod. Rab.* 18.5 (on Exod 12:29); *Num. Rab.* 14.2 (on Num 7:48); and the linkage in some rabbinic texts between Hezekiah and the Messiah; *b. Sanh.* 94a; *b. Ber.* 28b; cf. *b. Sanh.* 98b–99a.

[71] D. R. Bauer, "The Kingship of Jesus in the Matthean Infancy Narrative: A Literary Analysis," *CBQ* 57 (1995): 306–23.

[72] Davies and Allison, *Matthew,* 1:209; and Philo, *Names* 121.

[73] The issues here are two: In the current understanding of Matthew's use of these texts, it is almost impossible to understand why he might have composed his infancy narrative around them. As is generally admitted, the essential story must have come to him. But if he started with the story, why use these strange texts, which apparently nobody associated with the Messiah? See M. J. Down, "The Matthaean Birth Narratives: Matthew 1[18]–2[23]," *ExpTim* 90 (1978/1979): 51–52.

[74] *Pace* J. A. Ziesler, "Matthew and the Presence of Jesus," *Epworth Review* 11 (1984): 55–63, 90–7, it is not clear that Matt 10:20 or 25:31–46 fit the bill either.

[75] Davies and Allison, *Matthew,* 1:217.

Paul and in all likelihood shares a similar Christology: not only was Jesus a sign of Yahweh's delivering presence; he was, in some strange and mysterious way, himself the very presence of God with us. Nevertheless, as Nolland has argued, there is very little warrant here for an explicit Son of God Christology.[76]

Instead, as is clearly indicated by his introductory formula, it seems that some kind of eschatological fulfillment is in mind. According to various Jewish traditions, there was an expectation that just as God had been with his people in the past, so too he would be with them, especially in the messianic future (Isa 43:5; Ezek 34:30; 37:27; Zech 8:23; 11QTemple[a] 29:7–10; Jub. 1:17, 26).[77] This surely has more warrant, although the idea that God was somehow at work in Jesus is hardly controversial: can anyone doubt that Matthew is convinced that God was, in a very special and mysterious way, active in Jesus?[78] The question is why he should explicitly choose Immanuel and the Isaiah citation. And why, if his audience was familiar enough with Jewish tradition to forgo explaining the name Jesus, he explains Ἐμμανουήλ.

Two points can be made. First, it appears that Matthew is keen, for the sake of emphasis, to retain the original Immanuel form.[79] Second, his explanation of Immanuel is drawn not from Isa 7:14 but from Isa 8:8, 10. That he also later appeals to Isa 8:23b–9:1 in Matt 4:15–16, itself a key transition point in his gospel's literary structure,[80] indicates that he is aware of the larger Isaianic context.[81] All this suggests that Matthew has in mind the presence of God with his people precisely as Isaiah viewed it, and hence his unshakable emphasis on Immanuel. That, above and beyond all expectation, Mary was in fact a virgin is certainly felicitous, but as already argued, it hardly seems the point of his appeal. Instead this Jesus who, positively, will save his people from their sins is

---

[76] Nolland, "No Son of God Christology," 3–12. The reference to the Holy Spirit merely indicates that Yahweh is at work, and without clearer contextual indicators, proposed further allusions to Gen 1:1–2, the servant, etc., outrun the data. Matthew 1:22's "by the Lord through the prophet" is indeed prolix but is more likely intended to show that the strange work that Immanuel signifies is from God. Does Matthew expect his audience to recognize the source, as suggested by Carter, "Evoking Isaiah," 506–7? Perhaps, although it might be his equivalent of Heb 2:6, "someone has testified somewhere"—an equally Jewish document.

[77] Davies and Allison, Matthew, 1:218.

[78] Craig S. Keener, A Commentary on the Gospel of Matthew (Grand Rapids: Eerdmans, 1999), 97; and, e.g., Barry Blackburn, Theios aner and the Markan Miracle Traditions (WUNT 2.40; Tübingen: J. C. B. Mohr [Paul Siebeck], 1991), where some of Jesus' mighty deeds suggest an assimilation to God; cf. Jack Dean Kingsbury, Matthew: Structure, Christology, Kingdom (Philadelphia: Fortress, 1975), 40–83; and Ronald Thiemann, "The Promising God: The Gospel as Narrated Promise," in Why Narrative? Readings in Narrative Theology (ed. Stanley Hauerwas and L. Gregory Jones; Grand Rapids: Eerdmans, 1989), 322–38.

[79] See also Luz, Matthew 1–7, 121.

[80] As per J. D. Kingsbury, "The Structure of Matthew's Gospel and His Concept of Salvation-History," CBQ 35 (1973): 451–74; and D. R. Bauer, The Structure of Matthew's Gospel: A Study in Literary Design (JSNTSup, 31; Sheffield, England: Almond Press, 1988).

[81] Cf. Weren, "Quotations from Isaiah"; and Carter, "Evoking Isaiah," 507.

also, negatively, the fulfillment, the final and complete expression in Israel's history, of the Immanuel principle.[82]

If this suggestion is correct, then Matthew deliberately chooses Isa 7:14 not only because Israel's God is uniquely present in Jesus—which is a considerable shift, since, as noted earlier, the name Immanuel in Isaiah does not mean that Immanuel himself is "God with us" but instead indicates what the presence of God will mean for rebellious Judah—but because he wants primarily to highlight that this very presence means disaster to those who refuse to respond to him in faith.[83] For Matthew, Jesus is both the sign and the reality.

But are there any further data to indicate that this is what Matthew has in mind? Several lines of evidence suggest as much.

Jewish Tradition

Although, to the best of my knowledge, the term Immanuel does not appear in either talmudic or midrashic literature,[84] there are several references to Isa 7:17—the outcome of Immanuel—in the *Damascus Document* (CD-A 7:9–13; cf. 13:21–14:1 [= 4Q266 f9iii.18; 4Q267 f9v.4]). Looking to Yahweh's future intervention, the writer speaks of the destruction of the wicked "when God visits the earth" and "when there comes the word which is written in the words of Isaiah, son of Amoz, the prophet." He then cites Isa 7:17 and goes on to describe a division in Israel, with the righteous escaping and the renegades being given over to the sword.[85] Finally he goes on to speak of an interpreter of the Law (itself seen as the fallen tent of David), the leader of the nation, who will preside over this coming judgment (CD-A 7:15–21).

Several items are noteworthy. First, although I do not want to suggest that the writer of the *Damascus Document* has no role for a messianic figure in his larger eschatological schema, it is significant that his use of Isaiah does not occasion any mention of such. Second, clearly for him at least, this part of the Immanuel oracle meant a division in Israel and particularly judgment on the wicked. This is in keeping with the opening of the work, where the writer reminds his readers of when God previously judged his people, destroyed their sanctuary, and sent a remnant into exile (CD-A 1:1–6)—which theme is also important to Matthew as he prepares for his opening reference to Immanuel (cf. μετοικεσίαν ["deportation"] in Matt 1:12, 17b). In his mercy, after the time of wrath, God

---

[82] The idea of a dual opening—blessing yet potential judgment—is not new. I have argued elsewhere that Mark introduces his gospel with a combined appeal to the Jewish scriptures—Isaiah and Exodus/Malachi—to make exactly this point: Yahweh has acted in Jesus, but what matters is how Israel responds; Watts, *New Exodus,* 53–90.

[83] This is in contrast to Luz, *Matthew 1–7,* 123, for whom the Immanuel citation is intended to show us the grace that occurs through Jesus.

[84] L. Blau, "Immanuel," in *The Jewish Encyclopedia* (12 vols., New York: Funk & Wagnalls, 1901–1906), 5:562; H. L. Ginsberg, "Immanuel," *EncJud* 8:1293.

[85] F. García Martínez and E. J. C. Tigchelaar, trans., *The Dead Sea Scrolls: Study Edition* (2 vols.; vol. 1, New York: Brill, 1997; vol. 2, Boston: Brill, 1998), 2:561.

caused "to arise from Israel and from Aaron a shoot of the planting" (CD-A 1:7, שורש מטעת . . . ויצמח; cf. Isa 11:1)[86] and sent them the Teacher of Righteousness, who made clear God's bringing the covenant curses on the wicked in the last generation (CD-A 1:12–18a). Matthew's apparent awareness of the larger context of Isaiah 7 at least suggests the possibility that he shares a similar outlook: Immanuel entails both salvation and judgment. Third, these events are to be accompanied by the coming of an interpreter of the Law. It might be significant, then, that Matthew presents Jesus, son of David, as the ultimate interpreter of the Law (e.g., Matt 5:17–20; 22:34–46). Given these similarities, we cannot but ask whether there is any evidence of this kind of division in Matthew.

Herod and the Magi

The immediately following account in Matt 2:1–18 appears to be just this and might partly explain his inclusion of the story at this juncture. Most modern commentators agree that Matthew is interested in the contrast between Herod and the Magi. Herod, representative of the Jewish leaders, and "all of Jerusalem with him" are, as Matthew dryly puts it, "stirred up."[87] And yet, although the religious authorities have been informed, it is only the Gentile Magi who in faith seek Jesus (cf. Abraham in Matt 1:1; Gen 12:2). But why even bother to include this story? As Davies and Allison note, this contrast well suits not only Matthew's interest in universal mission but also his critique, especially of the Jewish leaders who have rejected Yahweh's offer in Jesus.[88] This would make even more sense if Immanuel in the Isaianic understanding was programmatic for his presentation of Jesus. The unbelieving response of Herod and Jerusalem bodes ill for the future of the nation.

It might also explain the presence of several interesting conceptual parallels with the Ahaz account.[89] First, there is the motif of the fear of the faithless king. Just as in Isa 7:2 "the heart of Ahaz and the heart of his people shook as the trees of the forest shake before the wind" (NRSV), so too in Matthew, "When King Herod heard this, he was frightened, and all Jerusalem with him" (Matt 2:3 NRSV). Herod, inquiring as to the child's whereabouts feigns piety (2:8), as does Ahaz (Isa 7:12). And Herod, like Ahaz, is clearly an unjust and oppressive ruler, hardly the kind of shepherd king that Yahweh intended for his people. Ironically,

---

[86] Cf. 4Q161 3.11–35; 4Q285 f5 1–5; Isa 4:2; 11:1, 10; 27:6; 37:31.

[87] Luz, *Matthew 1–7*, 135–36, sees Matthew as unrealistically uniting all of Jerusalem with Herod. On the other hand, given the proclivities of the Romans and of Herod, one can understand why the thought of the birth of a messianic king would cause Jerusalem "to be stirred up" (my translation). No doubt for different reasons, but stirred up all the same.

[88] Davies and Allison, *Matthew*, 1:228.

[89] A. M. Dubable, O.P., "La conception virginale et la citation d'Is., vii, 14 dans l'évangile de Matthieu," *RB* 85 (1978): 368–69. One might also note that whereas Ahaz, a son of David, rejected the offer of a sign, righteous Joseph, also a son of David, responds in faith.

Herod eventually becomes a kind of Nebuchadnezzar, driving Israel's deliverer into exile—this I believe is partly the point of Matthew's allusion to Jer 31:5 (Rachel weeping for her children) in Matt 2:18. Both kings respond to their fear by attempting to secure their realms through reliance on their own devious wisdom. And both will ultimately fail. In addition, in Isaiah's narrative Ahaz has only just been invited to "ask a sign from the LORD your God; let it be deep as Sheol or high as heaven" (Isa 7:11 NRSV). Without wanting to make too much of this, I find it interesting that a sign as high as the heaven is precisely what the Magi, Herod, and all Jerusalem are given (Matt 2:2, 7, 9–10).

From the very beginning of Matthew's story, then, we have division. Some respond with faith and others with hostility to the salvation promised in Jesus. Already a dark and foreboding shadow is cast over the good news. The terse remark in 2:29 shows that Herod the Great's son Herod Archelaus was no different.

Matthew's Structure

Elements of Matthew's larger literary structure also point in this direction. Bacon's original suggestion has not found much favor, largely because he overextended the parallels.[90] The fact remains, however, that Matthew seems to have five collections of extended teaching, as nearly every commentator recognizes. If we leave aside the potential red herring of how we label what precedes and follows these materials, N.T. Wright is, I think, on to something when he argues for a Deuteronomic "two-ways," "blessing-curse" pattern such that the Sermon on the Mount (chs. 5–7), beginning with its nine blessings, matches the Eschatological Discourse, which begins with a series of seven curses (chs. 23–25).[91] I would add that the whole appears to form a chiasm around the pivotal ch. 13 (on which see below):

chs. 5–7   blessings of the new Torah (111 verses)

  ch. 10   mission as summons to the community (outward focus) (38 verses)

    ch. 13   parables of the Kingdom (50 verses)

  ch. 18   life in the community (inward focus) (33 verses)

chs. 23–25   curses and warnings about the future (136 verses)

From this perspective, God has raised up a deliverer, Jesus, as a new Moses[92] to save his people from their sins (cf. Isa 40:2–3; 43:25; 44:22). But there

---

[90] Benjamin W. Bacon, *Studies in Matthew* (London: Constable, 1930).

[91] Wright, *People of God,* 386–90. There is some debate over whether the eschatological discourse should begin with ch. 23. In my view, Matthew's eschatology at this point is primarily, if not exclusively, focused on the fate of Jerusalem and thus warrants the inclusion of ch. 23 as the opening salvo.

[92] On this typology in Matthew, see D. C. Allison Jr., *The New Moses* (Minneapolis: Fortress, 1993).

is the possibility that Israel will not respond in faith.[93] And once again, although the blessing of return from exile is offered, the rejection of salvation in Jesus ultimately results in a curse. This, of course, is precisely what Immanuel implies. Yahweh has come among his people, but because the nation's leaders have refused to accept his offer, they will instead experience judgment.

Further Matthean Motifs

Following Matthew's presentation of Jesus as the new Moses promulgating the eschatological Torah on the mountain (Matt 5–7; cf. Isa 2:1–5?),[94] we have what looks like ten mighty deeds, which probably should also be understood in terms of the new-Moses and new-exodus motifs.[95] I would also argue that many of these mighty deeds can be traced back to OT archetypes whose occurrences imply the saving presence of Yahweh (e.g., calming the sea, Matt 8:23–27).[96] One cannot help but notice the contrast in responses. While Matthew's crowds are amazed—but that appears to be all (9:33)—his Pharisees denounce this activity as satanic (9:34). On the other hand, an apparently Gentile centurion responds with a faith the like of which Jesus has not seen, not in all Israel (8:10). Tellingly, and echoing the contrast between Herod and the Magi, only Matthew has Jesus' subsequent declaration, "I tell you, many will come from east and west and eat with Abraham and Isaac and Jacob in the kingdom of heaven, while the heirs of the kingdom will be thrown into the outer darkness, where there will be weeping and gnashing of teeth" (8:11–12 NRSV). God is present among his people. The crucial issue is how they respond.

Elements of Matthew 10 work on the same basis. When sent out on mission to Israel, the disciples are enjoined not to take any supplies with them. Although this is sometimes taken to mean that they are to rely on faith, it seems more likely that this is to force the situation such that they can only stay if they are accepted and offered hospitality (cf. vv. 40–42; 25:31–46). If not, they must move on. But in so doing, they are to shake the dust of their feet, thereby declaring that this village not only is no longer to be regarded as Jewish (10:11–15) but will suffer a worse fate than Sodom or Gomorrah (10:16; a metaphor used several times in Isa 1:9, 10; 3:9).[97] In 10:34–35 Matthew's Jesus announces, "I have not come to bring

---

[93] For the suggestion that this had happened before, see R. E. Watts, "Consolation or Confrontation? Isaiah 40–55 and the Delay of the New Exodus," *TynBul* 41 (1990): 31–59.

[94] See also Allison, *New Moses*, 172–207.

[95] See also ibid., 207–13, though with caveats.

[96] E.g., J. P. Heil, *Jesus Walking on the Sea: Meaning and Gospel Functions of Matt 14:22–33, Mark 6:45–52, and John 6:15b–21* (AnBib, 87; Rome: Pontifical Biblical Institute, 1981), 84–103.

[97] T. W. Manson, *The Sayings of Jesus, as Recorded in the Gospels according to St. Matthew and St. Luke* (part 2 in *The Mission and Message of Jesus*; ed. H. D. A. Major, T. W. Manson, and C. J. Wright; London: I. Nicholson & Watson, 1937; [repr., London: SCM Press, 1950]), 76; cf. *m. Ohol.* 2:3.

peace on the earth but a sword," which division is also implied in his answer to John—"Blessed . . . scandalized" (11:6)—and comes to full expression in his upbraiding of Chorazin, Bethsaida, and Capernaum. This is precisely the kind of division the writer of the *Damascus Document* envisioned.

Hostility toward Jesus comes to something of a climax in the Beelzebul controversy in Matthew 12 and 13, the latter of which I earlier suggested forms the hinge around which Matthew's other blocks of teaching are arranged. I have argued elsewhere that Mark's understanding of Jesus' parables cannot be separated from the preceding account of the denunciation and rejection of Jesus in the Beelzebul controversy.[98] The same relation obtains for Matthew. In Isaiah it was idolatrous Judah's rebuff of Yahweh (Isaiah 5) that led to its being blinded and deafened (Isaiah 6), which judgment was effected through Isaiah's proclamation of the three child name-parables (cf. Immanuel, Isaiah 7). Likewise, the Beelzebul controversy crystallizes the Pharisees' rejection of God's saving activity in Jesus (Matt 12:24; cf. v. 23, "can this be the Son of David?"). If Matthew intends Jesus' names to have a programmatic function, then to reject Jesus is to invite the judgment implied by Immanuel (v. 32; note also Matthew's expansions in vv. 34–37, 39–45). Bearing in mind that Immanuel in Isaiah heralds the judgment of Isaiah 6, it makes excellent sense, in describing for the first time the rationale for his parabolic speech, that Matthew's Jesus should cite Isaiah 6, declaring,

> With them indeed is fulfilled the prophecy of Isaiah that says:
>
> You will indeed listen, but never understand,
>   and you will indeed look, but never perceive.
> For this people's heart has grown dull,
>   and their ears are hard of hearing,
>   and they have shut their eyes. (Matt 13:14–15 NRSV)

Jesus speaks as he does because the hearts of the Pharisees are hard.[99] This is precisely the situation of Judah that the Immanuel prophecy addressed. The leadership of Jesus' day, as had Ahaz and the leaders of Judah before them, refused to accept Yahweh's offered word of salvation and so came under the judgment intimated by Immanuel.

This motif continues in ch. 15 when once again Jesus is confronted, this time by authorities from Jerusalem. As in Mark, Matthew's Jesus appeals to Isaiah 29, which arguably describes the effects of an already implemented Isaiah 6.[100] If so, then what we have here is the unfolding of the process of division and

---

[98] Watts, *New Exodus*, 183–209.

[99] Much is often made of the differences between Mark and Matthew, with Matthew seen as softening Mark by making the hardness of heart the raison d'être of the parables. But this is a false dichotomy. In Isaiah the peoples' hearts are already idolatrous, and Isaiah's call is simply to form the people in the image of the gods they worship; see Beale, "Isaiah vi 9–13," citing Ps 115:4–8; 135:15–18; also Watts, *New Exodus*, 188–94.

[100] Watts, *New Exodus*, 213–18.

judgment. It might not be coincidental that Jesus' response to the Pharisees focuses on their failure to honor their parents (vv. 4–6). Since this was the first
commandment with promise—that you might live long in the land (Eph 6:2; cf.
LXX Exod 20:12 and Deut 5:16)—to break it invites destruction and exile.

The same pattern recurs when Jesus finally confronts Israel's leaders on
their own turf. The entire thrust of Matthew 21's account of the Jerusalem hier-
archs' refusal to attend Jesus' "entry," his subsequent "cleansing" of the temple,
the cursing of the fig tree, his question about their refusal to accept John, and the
parable of the Tenants is that of impending doom.[101] The whole concludes with
the famous stone saying in 21:43–44: "Therefore I tell you, the kingdom of God
will be taken away from you and given to a people that produces the fruits of the
kingdom. The one who falls on this stone will be broken to pieces; and it will
crush anyone on whom it falls" (NRSV) The language is familiar. Yahweh of Hosts
himself had once declared, in connection with the Immanuel name-parable, that
he would become "a stone one strikes against; . . . a rock one stumbles over—a
trap and a snare for the inhabitants of Jerusalem. . . . Many among them shall
stumble; they shall fall and be broken; they shall be snared and taken" (Isa
8:14–15 NRSV).

This brings us to the last block of teaching, which, along with Wright, I see
as encompassing Matthew 23–25. Standing over against 5:1–11, ch. 23 marks a
complete turnaround. Instead of nine words of proffered blessing, we find seven
curses. The rejection of Jesus means that Immanuel, "God-with-us," leads finally
to a series of woes and a stinging denunciation of Jesus' generation (vv. 35–38).
His concluding "See, your house is left to you, desolate" (v. 38 NRSV) is, hardly by
accident, immediately followed by Matthew's recounting of Jesus' prophecy of
the temple's destruction (ch. 24). And even here the language of desolation recalls the outcome of Isaiah's message—"Then I said, 'How long, O Lord?' And he
said: 'Until cities lie waste without inhabitant, and houses without people, and
the land is utterly desolate'" (Isa 6:11 NRSV)—which, because of Judah's unbelief,
Immanuel entails (cf. Isa 1:7; 5:9, 17).

Matthew and Yahweh's Plan

But this is not the end. In Isaiah's day, as we saw earlier, Yahweh's intention
was that his people would be a source of blessing to the nations. Matthew has not
forgotten this—Jesus is after all, son of David, son of Abraham (Matt 1:1). Yahweh
would still make known his glory. He would yet cause the root of Jesse to stand as a
banner to the peoples. And if Jerusalem refused to become the place to which the
nations could come, no matter. He would send his people to the nations:

> Now the eleven disciples went to Galilee, to the mountain to which Jesus had di-
> rected them. When they saw him, they worshiped him; but some doubted. And

---

[101] E.g., Keener, *Matthew*, 495–516; and to the extent that Matthew follows Mark,
Watts, *New Exodus*, 304–49, and the extensive literature cited therein.

Jesus came and said to them, "All authority in heaven and on earth has been given to me. Go therefore and make disciples of all nations, baptizing them in the name of the Father and of the Son and of the Holy Spirit, and teaching them to obey everything that I have commanded you. And remember, I am with you always, to the end of the age." (Matt 28.16–20 NRSV).

Conclusions

As noted earlier, several scholars have suggested that Matthew's account of Jesus' naming has programmatic significance for his gospel. I would concur in that both names—Jesus and Immanuel—set the agenda for the gospel. But if we take the original Isaianic setting into account, as I have argued Matthew appears to have done, they evoke different aspects of that story—salvation and judgment— with Immanuel primarily constituting a dire warning for those who reject this salvation. As in Qumran, the Immanuel oracle foreshadows a coming division in Israel.

For Matthew, just as Isaiah had proclaimed Yahweh's offer of salvation, so now God had acted in Jesus to save his people—hence the highly structured genealogy, which anticipates Israel's deliverance from exile. But here too, as in Isaiah, the crucial issue was trust. If the offer was not met with faith, the end result was judgment. Moreover, if Jesus is the one in whose life Immanuel comes to its ultimate and final or fulfilled form, then we ought not be surprised that, for those who reject Jesus as the agent of God's blessing to the nations, it means their ultimate and final end. Consequently, although Matthew begins with an announcement of eschatological blessing, in the end Israel's leaders are the subject of unrelenting woes, the temple and Jerusalem are delivered over to destruction, and Yahweh's vineyard is given into the hands of others—namely, an Israel reconstituted around Jesus, through whom Yahweh's intention for the nations will go forward.

This study also says something about Matthew's use of fulfillment language. In this case, at least "fulfillment" seems better understood in paradigmatic terms: as Yahweh had acted in the past, so he would act again. Matthew sees Isa 7:14 not as a proof text for some long foretold virgin birth, which in any case apparently no one ever expected, but instead as a scriptural elucidation of the significance of Jesus, which elucidation works only if Jesus is already believed to be the climax of Israel's history. From this perspective, Matthew's use of Isaiah 7 is not so much apology as it is explanation and theology.[102]

---

[102] See also, e.g., Prabhu, *Formula Quotations*, 17.

⊛ *4*

The Gospels and the Text of the Hebrew Bible: Micah 5:1 (Matt 2:6) in Tatian's Diatessaron

Robert F. Shedinger

This essay poses the following question: How useful can the NT be as a source of evidence in text-critical discussions of the HB?[1] Emanuel Tov's standard introduction to the textual criticism of the HB ignores citations of the HB in the NT among the witnesses to its textual history, an omission that is entirely understandable given the fact that HB citations in the NT generally follow already known textual witnesses (such as the MT and the LXX) while those that differ from these witnesses seem to differ as a result of the exegetical interests of the NT writers.[2] But by using the discipline of NT textual criticism, it may be possible to reconstruct an earlier form of some HB citations in the Gospels, a procedure that may allow us to uncover textual issues in these citations relevant for the textual criticism of the HB. This, of course, does not mean that use of the discipline of NT textual criticism will transform the Gospels into a significant source of text-critical evidence relating to the HB, but I do intend to show that HB citations in the Gospels should not be completely ignored in this regard.

Specifically, this study will analyze the citation of Mic 5:1 (Eng. 5:2) in Matt 2:6, since it has already been argued in the literature that the text of Mic 5:1 as it stands in the MT is corrupt and in need of some type of emendation. The questions is: Can the Matthean citation of this text shed any light on the legitimacy of such proposed emendations, particularly if an earlier form of the Matthean citation can be reconstructed than that which stands in the Greek MS tradition of the Gospel? After answering the question in the affirmative, this study will briefly consider two other places where a similar dynamic may be at work.

In 1929, Ernst Sellin, in his commentary on the Minor Prophets, puzzled over the clause in Mic 5:1 ממך לי יצא להיות מושל בישראל ("from you will come forth

---

[1] An earlier version of this article was a paper presented in the Textual Criticism of the Hebrew Bible section at the annual meeting of the Society of Biblical Literature, Nashville, November 2000.

[2] See E. Tov, *Textual Criticism of the Hebrew Bible* (Minneapolis: Fortress, 1992).

for me one to be a ruler in Israel"). First, he observed that לִי must, according to the context, have God as its referent but that God is always referred to in the third person throughout the rest of this prophecy.[3] Thus he questioned whether לִי could be considered a part of the original text. Second, Sellin argued that metrical considerations in the poetry required an explicit subject for the verb יֵצֵא, a point he felt was confirmed by the appearance of the explicit subject ἡγούμενος in Codex Alexandrinus of Mic 5:1.[4] Sellin correctly observed that ἡγούμενος translates מֶלֶךְ in Ezek 43:7, 9, and certainly מֶלֶךְ would fit the context well as a subject of יֵצֵא, but Sellin did not follow this route. Instead he observed that in Mic 5:2 (Eng. 5:3) we read that Israel would be given up until the time when "she who is in labor has brought forth" (יוֹלֵדָה יָלָדָה). To Sellin, this meant that the ruler promised in v. 1 would come in the form of a child, a point confirmed by the prophecy in Isa 9:5 (Eng. 9:6), "For us a child is born, to us a son is given." From all this Sellin confidently concluded, "Aber als ursprüngliches Wort dürfte nach v. 2 sicher יֶלֶד statt לִי anzunehmen sein vgl. auch Jes 9, 5,"[5] leading him to translate the clause in question as, "Aus dir soll *ein Kind* hervorgehn."[6] Sellin ingeniously accounts for the troublesome לִי and the lack of an explicit subject for יֵצֵא in one move, but his methodology for supporting this conjectural emendation will, obviously, not be convincing to most textual critics of the HB. He did, however, correctly observe that this clause as it stands in the MT is problematic.

In 1956, Joseph Fitzmyer revisited this issue and proposed a more satisfying emendation.[7] He agreed with Sellin that the לִי was grammatically problematic and that the meter of the verse seemed to require an explicit subject for יֵצֵא. According to Fitzmyer, לִי as an ethical dative, which in this case must refer to God, nowhere ever occurs before the verb as it does here. Thus Fitzmyer proposes to view the *yôd* as dittography of the following *yôd* in יֵצֵא, but to retain the *lāmed* and view it as an emphatic particle attached to יֵצֵא, a particle akin to the Arabic *la* or Akkadian *lu*.[8] For an explicit subject for יֵצֵא, Fitzmyer proposes מֶלֶךְ as the most likely choice. Fitzmyer points out that if מֶלֶךְ was originally in this verse, its disappearance can be explained as haplography, as a scribe's eye skipped from the final

---

[3] D. E. Sellin, *Das Zwölfprophetenbuch* (2 vols.; 2d and 3d rev. ed.; KAT 12; Leipzig: A. Deichert, 1929–1930), 1:335.

[4] Ibid., 1:336.

[5] Ibid.

[6] Ibid., 1:331 (my emphasis).

[7] See J. A. Fitzmyer, "*lᵉ* as a Preposition and a Particle in Micah 5,1 (5,2)," *CBQ* 18 (1956): 10–13.

[8] Ibid., 13. Reference should be made here to the interesting variant in a small fragment of Micah included in 4QXII^f (4Q81), which appears to read מִמֵּךְ לִי לֹא יֵצֵא. See E. C. Ulrich, et al., *Qumran Cave 4.X: The Prophets*, (DJD 15; Oxford: Clarendon, 1997), 270. The לֹא, if read as a negative particle, makes little sense in the context. Russell Fuller ("4QMicah: A Small Fragment of a Manuscript of the Minor Prophets from Qumran, Cave IV," *RevQ* 61 [1993]: 201) therefore reads it as a conditional particle expressing a wish ("would that one would come forth for me . . ."). But the question must be raised whether this לֹא might not be an alternative rendering of the emphatic particle theorized by Fitzmyer, though this would still leave the problematic לִי.

kāp of מִמְּךָ to the final *kāp* of מֶלֶךְ. A consonant cluster such as מִמְכָמֹלֶךְ could have led a scribe to omit the מֶלֶךְ in the middle.[9] With these emendations, then, Fitzmyer would read the clause in question as מִמְּךָ מֶלֶךְ לִיצֵא לִהְיוֹת מוֹשֵׁל בְּיִשְׂרָאֵל ("from you will indeed come forth a king to be a ruler in Israel").

Fitzmyer's emendation seems likely, but it remains a conjectural emendation. There is no known text of Micah that supports the reading מֶלֶךְ unless one views the reading of ἡγούμενος in Codex Alexandrinus as reflecting a *Vorlage* reading מֶלֶךְ. This appears to be unlikely. First, Alexandrinus is not followed by any other LXX witness; Vaticanus and Sinaiticus, for example, both reflect the Hebrew of the MT with their ἐκ σοῦ μοι ἐξελεύσεται τοῦ εἶναι εἰς ἄρχοντα ἐν τῷ Ἰσραήλ. Second, it seems a stretch to view ἡγούμενος as a translation of מֶלֶךְ. Although it is true that the former seems to translate the latter in Ezek 43:7, 9, there are over 1,500 instances where מֶלֶךְ is rendered by the more precise βασιλεύς. Moreover, in these two references in Ezekiel where ἡγούμενος does seem to translate מֶלֶךְ, there is every reason to believe that the LXX translators did not mean for ἡγούμενος to be a precise rendering of מֶלֶךְ, as a consideration of the context will demonstrate.

In Ezekiel 43 we find a vision of the glory of God returning to the rebuilt temple. Ezekiel is then told that the temple is God's throne and footstool and that therefore the house of Israel would no longer defile God's name; neither the Israelites nor their kings (מְלָכִים) would any longer engage in such defilement. Because this text looks toward the future from Ezekiel's perspective—it describes conditions of the Second Temple period—the reference to the kings of Israel would have been puzzling to the LXX translators, given the political reality that the kingship of Israel had not yet been reconstituted.[10] It appears that the LXX translators substituted ἡγούμενοι here so that the exhortation to no longer defile the name of God could apply to the "leaders" of the Jewish community broadly conceived and not specifically to the kings of a reconstituted Israelite monarchy that did not exist.

Thus there appears not to be a single instance in the LXX where מֶלֶךְ is rendered intentionally by ἡγούμενος. Alexandrinus does not appear to be a likely textual witness for Fitzmyer's emendation. A better candidate is found in the citation of Mic 5:1 in Matt 2:6, though not in the standard canonical Greek text of Matthew, which also reads ἡγούμενος, but rather in the text of Matthew that can be extracted from the second-century gospel harmony known as Tatian's *Diatessaron*.[11]

---

[9] Fitzmyer, "*lᵉ* as a Preposition," 12.

[10] I am assuming here a date for LXX Ezekiel prior to the establishment of the Hasmonean dynasty. Even if LXX Ezekiel is later, it is not at all clear if the Hasmonean kings would have been considered a legitimate reconstitution of the Israelite monarchy that Ezekiel seems to be envisioning.

[11] The most likely explanation for the appearance of ἡγούμενος in Codex Alexandrinus of Mic 5:1 is that Alexandrinus has been assimilated to the text of Matt 2:6 appearing in fifth-century MSS of the Gospel. By the fifth century, the authoritative status of the Gospels would likely have influenced the text of HB citations appearing therein.

Working with the text of the *Diatessaron* presents the researcher with many difficult challenges, challenges that some might think to be insuperable. Although contemporary scholarship generally supports the idea that Tatian wrote his gospel harmony in Syriac, no Syriac text of the harmony survives.[12] What do survive are a number of other texts and harmonies in a variety of languages that have been influenced in their development by the Syriac text of Tatian's harmony. Although this does indeed present a real challenge, the difficulties are not insuperable, and when used critically and cautiously, information from the various vernacular witnesses to Tatian's *Diatessaron* can be employed to reconstruct the likely original Syriac reading of the harmony. In my work on this text, I am indebted to the methodology articulated by William L. Petersen for reconstructing original Diatessaronic readings, a methodology I will summarize here.

As mentioned above, it is now widely acknowledged that the original language of the *Diatessaron* was Syriac. It is further acknowledged that this original Syriac harmony was disseminated widely throughout the area of Syriac-speaking Christianity, a position from which it influenced the text of the Old Syriac Gospels and to a lesser extent the Peshitta Syriac Gospels,[13] as well as biblical citations in Syriac patristic sources and the medieval Arabic and Persian harmonies.[14] Parts of this original Syriac also survive in the fourth-century commentary written by Ephraem Syrus, a prolific writer and theologian of the Syriac church, on the *Diatessaron*.[15] It is also widely acknowledged that Tatian's Syriac harmony was early translated directly into Latin, possibly for use by Manicheans in North Africa, and that this Latin harmony went on to influence the text of the Old Latin Gospels as well as a number of vernacular harmony texts in Old High German, Middle High German, Middle Dutch, Middle Italian, and even Middle English,

---

[12] For arguments relating to the original language of the *Diatessaron*, see C. Kraeling, *A Greek Fragment of Tatian's Diatessaron from Dura* (SD 3; London: Christophers, 1935), 18, who argues for a Greek original; Daniel Plooij, *Traces of Syriac Origin of the Old-Latin Diatessaron* (Amsterdam: Koninklijke Akademie van Wetenschappen, 1927); and W. L. Petersen, "New Evidence for the Question of the Original Language of the Diatessaron," in *Studien zum Text und zur Ethik des Neuen Testaments* (ed. W. Schrage; BZNW 47; Berlin: de Gruyter, 1986), 325–43; both of the latter argue for a Syriac original.

[13] The Syriac Gospels are now available in a convenient form in G. A. Kiraz, ed., *Comparative Edition of the Syriac Gospels: Aligning the Sinaiticus, Curetonianus, Peshitta, and Harklean Versions* (4 vols.; Leiden: Brill, 1996). For a critical edition of the Peshitta MSS, see P. E. Pusey and G. H. Gwilliam, eds., *Tetraeuangelium Sanctum juxta simplicem Syrorum versionem ad fidem codicum, Massorae, editionum denuo recognitum* (Oxford: Clarendon, 1901).

[14] For the text of the Arabic harmony, see A. S. Marmardji, ed., *Diatessaron de Tatien* (Beirut: Imprimerie Catholique, 1935). For the Persian harmony, see G. Messina, ed., *Diatessaron persiano* (BibOr 14; Rome: Pontifical Biblical Institute, 1951).

[15] For the Syriac text of Ephraem, see L. Leloir, ed., *Saint Ephrem, Commentaire de l'évangile concordant, texte syriaque* (2 vols.; vol. 1, Dublin: Hodges Figgis, 1963; vol. 2, *Folios additionnels*, Leuven: Peeters, 1990). An English translation is C. McCarthy, trans., *Saint Ephrem's Commentary on Tatian's Diatessaron* (JSSSup 2; Oxford: Oxford University Press, 1993).

among others.[16] Thus, witnesses to Tatian's *Diatessaron* can be categorized in two distinct groups: Eastern witnesses, those that can be traced back to the original Syriac harmony, and Western witnesses, those that can be traced back to the early Latin translation of the Syriac harmony.

Each of these individual Diatessaronic witnesses has its own complex textual history that must be accounted for. It appears that all of these texts went through a process of "vulgatization." That is, Eastern witnesses were over time brought into greater conformity with the text of the Peshitta Gospels, the standard gospel text of the later Syriac church, whereas Western witnesses were assimilated to the text of the Latin Vulgate Gospels, the standard gospel text of the Western church. This process of vulgatization had the effect of erasing from the tradition authentic variant readings that originally stood in Tatian's *Diatessaron*, the very readings we are interested in. Thus, it is highly problematic to accept a variant as authentic to the *Diatessaron* if it stands in only a single Diatessaronic witness; variants could have crept into Diatessaronic witnesses from a variety of sources with no connection to the original text of the *Diatessaron*. But Petersen argues that if a variant reading is supported by at least one witness from each branch of the Diatessaronic tradition, Eastern and Western, it is likely that this reading is authentic to the *Diatessaron* in the absence of any other obvious explanation for the unique agreement of Eastern and Western witnesses. There is little evidence of later cross-fertilization between Eastern and Western witnesses because of obvious barriers of language and geography. Thus, if Eastern and Western witnesses agree in a variant against all other textual witnesses in a gospel passage, this variant is likely to stem from Tatian's original Syriac harmony.[17]

Returning now to the citation of Mic 5:1 in Matt 2:6, we will apply this methodology to the Diatessaronic witnesses to Matt 2:6. One problem is that Matthew's citation is not a simple citation of Mic 5:1. Rather, Matthew has combined a portion of Micah with a phrase from 2 Sam 5:2 to create a more focused prophetic prediction of Jesus' Bethlehem origins. That is, Matthew is dependent upon Mic 5:1 for his καὶ σὺ Βηθλέεμ, γῆ Ἰούδα, οὐδαμῶς ἐλαχίστη εἶ ἐν τοῖς ἡγεμόσιν Ἰούδα· ἐκ σοῦ γὰρ ἐξελεύσεται ἡγούμενος, but here the

---

[16] For a thorough survey of the development of Diatessaronic studies, see W. L. Petersen, *Tatian's Diatessaron: Its Creation, Dissemination, Significance, and History in Scholarship* (VCSup 25; New York: E. J. Brill, 1994). For brevity, I will only cite references here for the Western Diatessaronic witnesses that I cite later in this study. For the Old Latin Gospels, see A. Jülicher, ed., *Itala: Das Neue Testament in altlateinischer Überlieferung* (4 vols.; Berlin: de Gruyter, 1938–1963). For the Middle Italian harmonies, see V. Todesco, P. A. Vaccari, and M. Vattasso, eds., *Il Diatessaron in volgare italiano* (Studi e testi 81; Vatican City: Biblioteca Apostolica Vaticana, 1938). For a recent critique of the theory of an Old Latin harmony, see U. B. Schmid, "In Search of Tatian's Diatessaron in the West," *Vigiliae Christianae* 57 (2003): 176–99.

[17] Petersen's criteria for isolating authentic variant readings in the *Diatessaron* were first articulated in W. L. Petersen, "Romanos and the Diatessaron: Readings and Method," *NTS* 29 (1983): 490, and later repeated in Petersen, *Tatian's Diatessaron*, 373.

citation of Micah breaks off and Matthew's final phrase, ὅστις ποιμανεῖ τὸν λαόν μου τὸν Ἰσραήλ, stems from 2 Sam 5:2, where the people of Israel address David with these words: "The LORD said to you: you will shepherd my people Israel, you will be a ruler [LXX: ἡγούμενον] over Israel."[18] For the part of this passage that is dependent upon Mic 5:1, however, it appears that the *Diatessaron* read "king" in place of the ἡγούμενος of the Greek text of Matthew, as the following evidence illustrates.

Among Eastern witnesses to the Diatessaronic tradition, both MSS of the Old Syriac Gospels (Sinaitic and Curetonian), along with all MSS of the Peshitta, read here,

menekī gēr nepōq malkā ("for from you will come forth <u>a king</u>").

This is in contrast to the Harklean Syriac, which reads *mdabranā* ("leader," "governor") in place of the *malkā* of the Old Syriac and Peshitta. Since the Harklean Syriac is known to be a slavishly literal translation of the Greek Gospels, its choice of *mdabranā* to render ἡγούμενος is not surprising. But the *malkā* of the other Syriac texts is unexpected if they are also looking at a *Vorlage* reading ἡγούμενος. Along with the Syriac Gospels, support for this reading comes also from the Arabic harmony with its

minka yakhruju malik ("from you will come forth <u>a king</u>")[19]

and possibly also from the Persian harmony with its

da te apparirà il re ("from you will come forth <u>the king</u>")[20]

On the Western side, one MS of the Old Latin Gospels (it^a) reads,

ex te enim exiet rex ("for from you will come forth <u>a king</u>")

in contrast to all other Old Latin texts, which read either *dux* or *princeps,* in closer conformity to the Greek text of Matthew.

Thus, we have support from both sides of the Diatessaronic tradition for the more specific reading "king." This reading occurs elsewhere in the Matthean textual tradition only in the Ethiopic text of the gospel,[21] a text that is unlikely to have influenced the Latin, Syriac, Arabic, and Persian witnesses to the *Diatessaron*. We may therefore conclude that the original text of the *Diatessaron* read *malkā* and that, given the appearance of this same variant in the Ethiopic Gospels, Tatian probably took this reading from the Greek text of Matthew that he knew in the

---

[18] The fact that David is referred to by ἡγούμενον here may explain the appearance of ἡγούμενος in the Greek tradition of Matt 2:6, a point I will return to below.

[19] Marmardji, *Diatessaron de Tatien,* 22.

[20] Messina, *Diatessaron persiano,* 24. This is according to the Italian translation of Messina. The Italian *il re* translates the Persian *pādišāh.*

[21] According to the apparatus in S. C. E. Legg, ed., *Evangelium secundum Matthaeum* (vol. 1 of *Novum Testamentum Graece: Secundum textum westcotto-hortianum;* Oxford: Clarendon, 1940).

middle of the second century, a text tradition that also influenced the Ethiopic text of Matthew. If a text of Matthew existed very early with the reading βασιλεύς, we may postulate that this reading, not ἡγούμενος, was original to Matthew's Gospel, and that Matthew received the reading βασιλεύς from a text of Mic 5:1 reading מלך, the very emendation proposed by Fitzmyer for this text. Thus, at least a portion of Fitzmyer's conjectural emendation of Mic 5:1 finds external support in the citation of Micah occurring in Matt 2:6 in its Diatessaronic form.

This, of course, leads to a question: if, as I have argued, Matthew's Gospel originally read βασιλεύς, why was the reading changed to ἡγούμενος by a later scribe? It is clear from the gospel accounts that Jesus is nowhere pictured as someone who fulfills Jewish political messianic expectations as they are expressed in a text such as *Psalms of Solomon* 17. He does not destroy Rome; rather, he is destroyed by Rome. In the context of early Christian-Jewish debates about the messianic status of Jesus, it may have been necessary for the church to distance Jesus somewhat from too close an association with militant Davidic political messianism, an association that βασιλεύς would most certainly have elicited. The change to ἡγούμενος allowed the church to effect this distancing while still retaining a Davidic identification, since David is referred to by the term ἡγούμενον in LXX 2 Sam 5:2 and ἡγούμενος occurs in LXX Gen 49:10, a text with obvious messianic connotations in early Judaism.[22]

If what I have argued here is correct and the *Diatessaron* does preserve an earlier form of the Gospels than the Greek MS tradition, might the Gospels contain other citations of the HB in which the Diatessaronic form of the citation contains evidence that might be useful for the textual criticism of the HB? I will briefly consider two additional examples where this might be the case, but in neither case is the evidence particularly clear.

In Matt 1:23, the writer cites the famous passage from Isa 7:14, "behold a virgin/young woman will conceive and bear a son and she will call his name Immanuel," ostensibly as a prophetic prediction of the virgin birth of Jesus. There is, however, some confusion over the identity of the person or persons who will call this child Immanuel. According to the Greek text of Matthew, it is the people of Israel in general who will call the child Immanuel (καὶ καλέσουσιν τὸ ὄνομα αὐτοῦ Ἐμμανουήλ), but in the MT of Isaiah, it is the young woman (וקראת שמו עמנואל). The LXX is different again with its second person singular "you will call" (καλέσεις),[23] which in the context could only refer to king Ahaz. Moreover, a fourth possibility appears in the Qumran Isaiah MS Isaiah[a] (1QIsa[a]), which reads

---

[22] The LXX personifies Gen 49:10 by rendering "scepter" as ἄρχων and "staff" as ἡγούμενος. Homer Heater has argued for Matt 2:6 as being a "cumulative exegesis" of Mic 5:1, 2 Sam 5:2, and Gen 49:10. See H. Heater, "Matthew 2:6 and Its Old Testament Sources," *JETS* 26 (1983): 395–97.

[23] The LXX has apparently read קראת as קָרָאתָ a second-person masculine singular, rather than the MT's vocalization קָרָאת, an unusual form of the third-person feminine singular normally written קראה. For a discussion of this unusual form, see GKC §44f. Codex Sinaiticus of the LXX renders the Masoretic Hebrew correctly with its καλέσει.

an apparent qal third person singular masculine וְקָרָא. This reading is difficult contextually, since there is no obvious male presence in the verse to serve as an implied subject for וְקָרָא. But the Qumran reading could be vocalized as the pu'al וְקֹרָא, which would yield the passive "and his name will be called."[24]

When one turns to the Diatessaronic witnesses at Matt 1:23, there is some evidence that the *Diatessaron* originally read the passive *netqri*. Among Eastern witnesses, the passive occurs in the Curetonian Syriac Gospel, a citation of Matt 1:23 in the *Demonstrations* of Aphrahat (17.9), both of which read *netqrī šmeh 'amanū'īl* ("and his name <u>will be called</u> Immanuel"),[25] and the Persian harmony (*e il suo nome <u>sarà chiamato</u> Emmanuele* ["and his name <u>will be called</u> Immanuel"]).[26] Among Western witnesses, the Middle Italian Tuscan harmony supports the passive with its *e <u>sarà chiamato</u> il nome suo Emanuel* ("and his name <u>will be called</u> Immanuel").[27] It is therefore possible that the *Diatessaron* preserves the original text of Matthew, which arose as a result of Matthew consulting a Hebrew text of Isaiah with the Qumran reading קרא, read correctly or incorrectly as a pu'al.[28] Certainty on this is impossible, given that the passive verb in the

---

[24] The pu'al of קרא occurs elsewhere in Isaiah in 48:8; 58:12; 61:3; 62:5; 65:1, though in each case the syntax differs from what we find in the Qumran text. E.g., in Isa 48:8 the pu'al is used impersonally, followed by the prepositional phrase לְךָ with the literal sense "it is called to you." This same syntax is used with every other occurrence of the pu'al in Isaiah as well as in the only other occurrence of the pu'al in the HB, in Ezek 10:13. Thus it is questionable whether קרא can legitimately be read as a pu'al in 1QIsaiahᵃ. J. de Waard understands this reading as a qal used in an impersonal way in accordance with Matthew's impersonal καλέσουσιν. See J. de Waard, *A Comparative Study of the Old Testament Text in the Dead Sea Scrolls and in the New Testament* (STDJ 4; Leiden: Brill, 1965).

[25] Aphrahat's citation of the passage presents something of a problem. At first look, it appears he is citing from Isaiah rather than the gospel (whether a Syriac text of Matthew alone or a Syriac harmony), since he introduces the citation with *wad-yalda metiled 'eša'ya tub'emar* ("and of the child being born Isaiah again said"). But after the citation Aphrahat includes the gloss on Immanuel "that is, God with us," which clearly comes from the gospel text. Aphrahat could only be citing from the OT Peshitta form of Isaiah, but he varies in wording from this text, as the discussion below shows. Thus we must conclude that Aphrahat has taken this citation from a gospel text, his reference to Isaiah reflecting the ascription of this citation to Isaiah in the gospel. For the text of Aphrahat, see R. Graffin, I. Parisot, F. Nau, and M. Kmoskó, eds., *Patrologia Syriaca* (3 vols.; Paris: Firmin-Didot et Socii, 1894–1926), vols. 1, 2.

[26] In Persian the verb is *khavāndah šavad*. See Messina, *Diatessaron persiano*, 16.

[27] In addition to the Tuscan harmony, the Middle Dutch Liège, Haaren, and Cambridge harmonies and the Middle High German Zürich harmony all read, "and his name will be Immanuel," which may also support the tradition that explicitly employs the passive verb.

[28] According to A. Baumstark ("Die Evangelienzitate Novatians und das Diatessaron," *OrChr* 27 [1930]: 7), Novatian (*Trin.* 24) reads the verb in the second person plural (*et vocabitis nomen eius*, "and you [pl.] will call his name"), which Baumstark thought was the reading of the *Diatessaron* on the basis of the *watad'unasmahu* ("and you [pl.] will call his name") he found in one MS of the Arabic harmony. Whatever one makes of this agreement between Novatian and a MS of the Arabic harmony, one must reject this as the reading of the *Diatessaron* in the absence of corroboration from any other Diatessaronic witness. It should also be noted that the OT Peshitta also reads the passive *netqri* with the

Diatessaron could just be a rendering of Matthew's impersonal third person plural καλέσουσιν. But there is one other piece of evidence that might help determine which scenario is more likely.

Justin Martyr seems to differ from all other textual witnesses when he introduces the future middle form καλέσεται into his citation of Matt 1:23.[29] The future middle would have the same passive force as the Diatessaronic reading but would differ from a true passive by having a durative connotation.[30] That is, his name will be called Immanuel *for all time*. Certainly, Justin may have made this change for theological reasons, but it is also possible that Justin preserves the original reading of Matthew, which is based on a Hebrew *Vorlage* reading קרא, and that the reading καλέσεται also gave rise to the passive verb in the *Diatessaron*.[31] This durative meaning would serve Matthew very well. Matthew is not citing Isaiah as predicting the naming of the child, in which case the true passive κληθήσεται would be appropriate; he is citing Isaiah as predicting the significance of this child for Israel for all time. He will forever be experienced as "God with us," a point that would be underscored by the use of καλέσεται. Since this use of the future middle is rare, however, later scribes may have made the change to καλέσουσιν to make more explicit that it is the people whom this child will save from their sins (Matt 1:21) who will "call" him Immanuel. If this is correct, it would demonstrate that the variant in the Qumran Isaiah MS occurred in other Hebrew MSS of Isaiah in the first century and is not a singular reading in Isaiah[a].

One more example comes from the citation of the Shema in Mark 12:29. The *Diatessaron* seems to shorten the introductory clause of the Shema to "Hear, O Israel, the LORD our God is one." That is, it omits the repetition of "LORD" from the familiar Shema formula, "Hear, O Israel, the LORD is our God, the LORD

Diatessaron, a point that raises the possibility that the *Diatessaron* is following the Syriac OT, not Matthew. This possibility is mitigated by the fact that Tatian shows little evidence of having used the OT Peshitta in the creation of the *Diatessaron*. For a discussion, see R. F. Shedinger, "Did Tatian Use the Old Testament Peshitta? A Response to Jan Joosten," *NovT* 41 (1999): 265–79; R. F. Shedinger, *Tatian and the Jewish Scriptures: A Textual and Philological Analysis of the Old Testament Citations in Tatian's Diatessaron* (CSCO 591, Subsidia 109; Leuven: Peeters, 2001). For the argument that Tatian did use the OT Peshitta, see J. Joosten, "The Old Testament Quotations in the Old Syriac and Peshitta Gospels: A Contribution to the Study of the Diatessaron," *Textus* 15 (1990): 55–76; idem, "Tatian's *Diatessaron* and the Old Testament Peshitta," *JBL* 120 (2001): 501–23. More likely the OT Peshitta has assimilated to the text of the Old Syriac Gospels, or it is a witness to a Hebrew text reading וקרא.

29 Justin, *Dial.* 43.5.

30 For the future middle of καλέω with a passive durative meaning, see H. W. Smyth, *Greek Grammar* (Cambridge: Harvard University Press, 1920), §§809, 1738.

31 R. Gundry (*The Use of the Old Testament in St. Matthew's Gospel: With Special Reference to the Messianic Hope* [NovTSup 18; Leiden: Brill, 1967], 90) has suggested that Justin's καλέσεται and Matthew's καλέσουσιν are alternative ways of rendering the Hebrew קרא read as a pu'al. But it seems problematic to imply that Justin was reading a Hebrew source.

is one."[32] This omission occurs also in one MS of the Vulgate of Deut 6:4. Perhaps this is coincidental. But perhaps the Vulgate of Deuteronomy and the *Diatessaron* of Mark are alerting us to a variant form of the Shema in early Hebrew MSS of Deuteronomy. Despite the formulaic character of the Shema, small variations in its text could occur, as is demonstrated by the Nash Papyrus, which adds the third person masculine pronoun הוא between the second יהוה and אחד.[33]

It would be significant if a Hebrew text with this omission could be found, and a candidate does exist in a phylactery fragment found at Wadi Murabba'at.[34] In the initial publication of this fragment, the editors placed dots above the final three letters, the הוה, of the second occurrence of the divine name, alerting us to the fact that these letters are uncertain in the MS. And a check of the photographs of this phylactery fragment does show that the text is very difficult to read at just this place.[35] The existence of the second occurrence of the divine name is not certain, though its omission is not certain either. So it remains unclear if the Diatessaronic form of Mark 12:29 preserves a variant form of the Shema, a variant also supported by one Vulgate text of Deuteronomy and perhaps by a phylactery fragment from Wadi Murabba'at. But it remains an intriguing possibility.

All of the foregoing arguments depend on the notions that there was a greater amount of textual fluidity in the first two centuries of the transmission of the NT text than is usually allowed for by textual critics and that the *Diatessaron* is

---

[32] This omission occurs in the Sinaitic Syriac Gospel, Ephraem Syrus's *Commentary on the Diatessaron* (13.11, 15.2), the *Liber graduum* (22.21), the Old Latin Gospels (MSS a, b, k), and the Middle Italian Tuscan harmony (302) and on this basis can be considered Diatessaronic. For the text of the *Liber graduum*, see Graffin, Parisot, Nau, and Kmoskó, *Patrologia Syriaca*, vol. 3. This omission is not, however, unique to the *Diatessaron*, for it occurs also in two Greek MSS of Mark (F *l*184), two MSS of the Latin Vulgate of Mark, one MS of the Bohairic Coptic, and one recension of the Georgian Gospel. These texts cannot explain the occurrence of this omission in all the Diatessaronic witnesses. The Georgian Gospel is generally believed to have been influenced by the *Diatessaron* and may be considered as further Eastern support for the reading. See B. M. Metzger, *The Early Versions of the New Testament: Their Origin, Transmission, and Limitations* (Oxford: Clarendon, 1977), 190–94. The Bohairic Coptic dates from no earlier than the ninth century and so cannot have influenced the early Diatessaronic sources. The same is true for the Greek sources, and indeed, C. S. C. Williams ("Tatian and the Text of Mark and Matthew," *JTS* 43 [1942]: 42) has argued that Lectionary 184 of Mark's Gospel has been influenced by the text of the *Diatessaron* rather than the reverse. The two MSS of the Vulgate could have influenced the Tuscan harmony, but certainly not the Syriac witnesses. Thus it is likely that early MSS of Mark included the omission and independently influenced the Diatessaronic tradition and the other witnesses to Mark.

[33] On the Nash Papyrus, see W. F. Albright, "A Biblical Fragment from the Maccabean Age: The Nash Papyrus," *JBL* 56 (1937): 145–76; F. C. Burkitt, "The Hebrew Papyrus of the Ten Commandments," *JQR* 15 (1903): 392–408.

[34] This phylactery is designated MurPhyl and was first published in P. Benoit, J. T. Milik, and R. de Vaux, eds., *Les grottes de Murabba'at* (2 vols.; DJD 2; Oxford: Clarendon, 1961), vol. 2.

[35] See R. H. Eisenman and J. M. Robinson, *A Facsimile Edition of the Dead Sea Scrolls* (2 vols.; Washington, D.C.: Biblical Archaeology Society, 1991). This text is catalogued as PAM 40.356.

a valid source for recovering a portion of this early textual fluidity. In conclusion, it will be helpful to briefly support these two points.

William Petersen has argued that when one looks at the evidence from the *Diatessaron* along with the evidence of Gospel quotations in Justin, Marcion, Clement, and Irenaeus, one finds "incontrovertible proof" that the text of the four Gospels was in a state of flux in the second century. The text of the *Diatessaron*, then, provides us with a snapshot of the state of the Gospel text in the middle of the second century.[36] As to why the second-century text was in such a state of flux, Petersen elsewhere suggests that this text was not always friendly to later Christian orthodoxy and that some early readings were removed or changed by the emerging orthodox church for theological reasons.[37] That this "orthodox corruption of scripture" was still occurring in the third and fourth centuries has been adequately demonstrated by Bart Ehrman.[38] There is thus no reason to reject out of hand the idea that such "corruption" began much earlier, in a proto-orthodox stage.[39] Finally, Helmut Koester has accused NT textual criticism of having been "deluded by the hypothesis that the archetypes of the textual tradition which were fixed ca. 200 CE—and how many archetypes for each Gospel?—are (almost) identical with the autographs. This cannot be confirmed by any external evidence."[40] Actually, Koester believes that what evidence exists serves to support the opposite view, that "substantial revisions of the original texts have occurred during the first hundred years of their transmission."[41]

The argument presented in this paper, that some HB citations in the Gospels originally stood in forms different from what is preserved in the later Greek MS tradition, fits well with this view that there was considerable textual fluidity in the Gospel texts over the first two centuries of their transmission. If this is the case, then the *Diatessaron* is really our only witness to the state of the Gospel texts as early as the middle of the second century, and variant readings in the

---

[36] Petersen, "New Evidence," 328.

[37] W. L. Petersen, "What Text Can New Testament Textual Criticism Ultimately Reach?" in *New Testament Textual Criticism, Exegesis, and Early Church History: A Discussion of Methods* (ed. B. Aland and J. Delobel; Kampen, Neth.: Pharos, 1994), 150.

[38] B. Ehrman, *The Orthodox Corruption of Scripture: The Effect of Early Christological Controversies on the Text of the New Testament* (New York: Oxford University Press, 1993).

[39] This has been argued also by J. N. Birdsall ("The New Testament Text," in *From the Beginnings to Jerome* [ed. P. R. Ackroyd and C. F. Evans; vol. 1 of *The Cambridge History of the Bible*; Cambridge: Cambridge University Press, 1970], 339), who states that "the early second century was a time when the text was subject to alteration and corruption on doctrinal grounds arising from the theological unification of an originally heterogeneous tradition."

[40] H. Koester, "The Text of the Synoptic Gospels in the Second Century," in *Gospel Traditions in the Second Century: Origins, Recensions, Text, and Transmission* (ed. W. L. Petersen; Notre Dame: University of Notre Dame Press, 1989), 37. For an opposing view, see F. Wisse, "The Nature and Purpose of Redactional Changes in Early Christian Texts: The Canonical Gospels," ibid., 39.

[41] Koester, "Text of the Synoptic Gospels," 37.

Diatessaron that can be reconstructed via a careful and judicious use of Diatessaronic witnesses must be given greater credence in text-critical discussions of the NT than is usually the case, unless we are to conclude that variant readings in the *Diatessaron* are the result of editorial work by Tatian and not reflective of his gospel sources. This last point is, of course, possible, but most who have worked on the text of this gospel harmony have concluded otherwise. For example, in his work on Ephraem Syrus's *Commentary on the Diatessaron*, Louis Leloir recognized that many of Ephraem's variant readings "sont problement tatianiques, non en ce sens que Tatien en serait le créateur—beaucoup lui sont antérieures, ou ont existé dans des traditions parallèles à Tatien."[42] Not all "Tatianisms" stem from Tatian, and perhaps most do not. Therefore the *Diatessaron* is an important witness to the state of the gospel texts in the middle of the second century.

If this is the case, then the Diatessaronic form of citations from the HB might well be a source of evidence for textual critics of the HB. The NT, or at least the Gospels, will not, of course, become a major source of evidence for such text-critical inquiries. But under certain conditions, conditions in which an earlier form of the citation can be reconstructed than that which stands in the Greek text tradition of the Gospels, the Gospels may become a source of evidence for the textual criticism of the HB. The fruits of NT textual criticism may indeed shed light on problems posed by the textual criticism of the HB.

---

[42] L. Leloir, *Le témoignage d'Éphrem sur le Diatessaron* (CSCO 227, Subsidia 19; Louvain: Imprimerie Orientaliste, 1962), 237. A similar point is made by A. F. J. Klijn (*A Survey of the Researches into the Western Text of the Gospels and Acts, Part Two: 1949–1969* [NovTSup 21; Leiden: Brill, 1969], 11), who explains the agreement observed between the *Diatessaron* and the *Gospel of Thomas* on the theory that both texts quoted from a similar canonical text of the Gospels, one that had many unusual readings.

5

Torah, Life, and Salvation: Leviticus 18:5 in Early Judaism and the New Testament

Simon J. Gathercole

Leviticus 18:5b deals with the responsibilities of everyday existence, the Torah and God's promise of the reward of life. Because such broad and weighty subject matter is encapsulated so neatly in one short phrase ("the one who does these things shall live by them"), it is small wonder that the phrase became an oft-quoted text in early Judaism.[1] Again because of its subject matter, the way it is used sheds light on the particular practices and priorities of the groups that produced the documents citing it.

The aim of this essay is to challenge the understanding of Lev 18:5 advocated by E. P. Sanders, J. D. G. Dunn, and N. T. Wright and, more particularly, their understanding of its *Nachleben* in early Judaism and the NT.[2] It is generally agreed that Galatians 3 and Romans 10, which cite Lev 18:5, are central texts for the understanding of Paul's "doctrines" of Torah and justification, so the early interpretive history of Lev 18:5 not only is of interest to scholars of the use of Scripture in Second Temple (and later) Judaism, but also is of great importance to NT scholars. Like most texts that encroach on the territory of Paul's understanding of Torah and justification, it is hotly debated, and there is no sign of consensus. Dunn talks of the "the puzzle of Paul's use of Lev. 18.5."[3] This essay aims to study neglected evidence that has not been harnessed for the debate, so as to point in the direction of a solution to "the puzzle."

---

[1] I am grateful to J. D. G. Dunn for his comments on sections of this article as well as to the New Testament Seminar, University of Aberdeen, and the Scripture in Early Judaism and Christianity Group at the annual meeting of the Society of Biblical Literature, Nashville, November 2000, for helpful observations and feedback.

[2] This understanding of Lev 18:5 goes back to G. E. Howard, "Christ the End of the Law: The Meaning of Romans 10.4ff," *JBL* 88 (1969): 331–37.

[3] J. D. G. Dunn, *The Theology of Paul the Apostle* (Edinburgh: T&T Clark, 1998), 153. Similarly, N. T. Wright on Gal 3:10–14 writes, "There are several passages of which one might say . . . that 'this one of the most complicated and controverted passages in Paul.' But Galatians 3:10–14 must surely be well up the list in the battle for any such accolade" (*Climax of the Covenant* [Edinburgh: T&T Clark, 1991], 137).

Dunn makes explicit the understanding of Lev 18:5 contested here:

> "he who does these things shall live by them" (Lev. 18:5). Paul seems to understand the passage in its most obvious sense—that keeping the statutes and ordinances of the law was the way of living appropriate to the covenant, which the covenant required. Moses did *not* say, and Paul did not understand him to say, that keeping the law was a means of earning or gaining life (in the future . . .). Rather the law prescribes the life which is to be lived by the covenant people (cf. Hab 2:4). The life sustained by God is life in accordance with the regulations and institutions of the law.[4]

In Dunn's view, this applies not only to Moses and Paul but also to the Jewish understanding of the text in the postbiblical period. Citing texts from Deuteronomy through *Psalms of Solomon* to *4 Ezra*, Dunn writes that "Lev. 18.5 can be regarded as a typical expression of what Israel saw as its obligation and promise under the covenant."[5]

Two problems come to the fore here. The first is Dunn's interpretation of "live" in the verse. Dunn excludes (generally) the aspect of an eternal life not yet attained,[6] and this is in part a function of focusing on the meaning of the original context of Lev 18:5 and the "first commentary" on it in Ezekiel 20.[7] Further, Dunn initially points to two elements in Lev 18:5: the regulatory aspect, and the deuteronomic promise of "lengthening of days." But it is only the first that really has an impact on the interpretation of the Jewish and Pauline usage. Thus Dunn can conclude that what Paul is ruling out is that *life* should be *governed or regulated* by the Torah. We shall see that Wright reads Gal 3:12 in a similar manner.

The second problem, and the focus of the study here, is that Dunn's interpretation of the texts that he sees as referring to Lev 18:5 is somewhat inaccurate and incomplete. (It is, however, more comprehensive than that of Howard, who generalizes about "Tannaitic Judaism" and Paul's "contemporaries" on the basis of one line from *Sipra*).[8] We will examine here the use of Lev 18:5 from the second century B.C.E. to the second century C.E.. Dunn focuses on the original context of the Pentateuch and its interpretation in Ezekiel 20 at the expense of later interpretations of the text. His situation of the verse in the context of deuteronomic theology is sound, but his focus on the regulatory aspects of the law in these texts is considerably overplayed. This leads to an essentially tautologous

---

[4] J. D. G. Dunn, *Romans 9–16* (WBC 38B; Waco: Word, 1988), 612.

[5] Ibid., 601.

[6] Although, in his exegesis of Gal 3:12, J. D. G. Dunn (*Galatians* [BNTC; London: A. & C. Black, 1993], 175) concedes the possibility of reference to eternal life, this aspect does not crop up again; that is, it does not affect his understanding of Lev 18:5 in Gal 3:12 or Rom 10:5.

[7] Dunn, *Theology of Paul*, 152–53.

[8] Howard, "Christ the End of the Law," 334–35, understands the focus to be not upon "perfection, but rather in terms of making Yahweh's law the foremost aspect of one's life," which he takes from *Sipra Lev.* §193 (on Lev 18:5). Since *Sipra* dates from the third century C.E., this essay will leave it out of consideration.

meaning of Lev 18:5[9] and does not make sense of the meaning of Ezekiel 20 (also Ezekiel 33 and Nehemiah 9:29), which refers to *deuteronomic lengthening of days* rather than to the regulatory function of Torah.[10]

Philo, *Prelim. Studies* 86–87:
Regulatory Understanding of Lev 18:5

Dunn's interpretation of Lev 18:5 is correct for Philo, *Prelim. Studies* 86–87. Here Philo identifies the Greco-Roman ideal of the good life with keeping the commandments of God, a deduction that he makes from Lev 18:1–6:

> Therefore, real true life, above everything else, consists in the judgments and commandments of God, so that the customs and practices of the impious must be death.

So here there is clear reference to the kind of *regulatory* understanding of (probably) Lev 18:5, such that it is what the "good life" consists in that is at issue for Philo. Philo is using Lev 18:1–6 to answer the kinds of questions posed by the Greek and Roman philosophical traditions.[11] As mentioned above, this is an example of the way the use of Lev 18:5 sheds light on the special concerns of the author because of the wide-ranging and general religious topics in its purview. But although Philo's exegesis is worthy of study in its own right, the questions of what constitute "life" that determine Philo's discussion are quite unique. We shall see that all the other intepretations are quite different. Philo's distance from Palestine means that in many cases his exegesis is radically different from what goes on in texts that hail from in and around Jerusalem. And when it comes to relating early Jewish and Pauline texts, Dunn rightly emphasizes the lack of relevance of Philo for an understanding of Paul's exegesis of Scripture.[12]

Red Herrings: Bar 4:1 and *Let. Aris.* 127

Other passages to which Dunn makes reference are Bar 4:1 and *Let. Aris.* 127. But it is difficult to see how these texts can refer to Lev 18:5. *Letter of Aristeas* 127 talks in terms very similar to those of Philo, about the nature of the good or noble life: τὸ γὰρ καλῶς ζῆν ἐν τῷ τὰ νόμιμα συντηρεῖν εἶναι. Again, it consists in the

---

[9] Thus, "the one who does these things does them," or "the one who lives by these things lives by them." I owe this observation to F. B. Watson.

[10] Also noteworthy is Ezek 20:25, which refers to law that Israel will *not* live by.

[11] See, e.g., the introduction to Michael Grant., ed. and trans., *Cicero, On the Good Life* (Harmondsworth, England: Penguin, 1971), 7–44.

[12] See Dunn, *Romans 1–8* (WBC 38A; Waco: Word, 1988), 202, in the discussion of Abraham's faith in Philo and Romans: "As usual, Philo's exegesis is determined by his own apologetic religious and philosophic concerns and shows no other contact with Paul."

keeping of the commandments, but there is no similarity to Lev 18:5, only the infinitive τὸ ζῆν, as compared with the future indicative ζήσεται in the LXX.

Baruch 4:1 refers to the promissory, not the regulatory, function of the Torah: "all those who hold to it [the book of the commandments] will live, while those who abandon it will die" (πάντες οἱ κρατοῦντες αὐτῆς εἰς ζωήν, οἱ δὲ καταλείποντες αὐτὴν ἀποθανοῦνται). There is no reference here to our verse, however. The text contains some of the key concepts in Lev 18:5—the commandments and "life"—but there is no verbal similarity. So it is hard to see how reference to these sections of the *Letter of Aristeas* and Baruch can be brought in to support an interpretation specifically of Lev 18:5.

Since, to my knowledge, there are no other quotations of passages as long as that of Lev 18:1–6 in Philo's *On the Preliminary Studies,* we will need to establish criteria for assessing when Lev 18:5b is being referred to. Clearly Bar 4:1 and *Let. Aris.* 127 provide too little evidence; they each contain (perhaps) one element of Lev 18:5. One of Rabbi Ishmael's exegetical principles was, "I shall draw an analogy on the basis of three shared traits from one matter to another";[13] I propose to be a little less demanding and to claim that a text referring to two elements of Lev 18:5b constitutes part of its interpretive history.[14] The elements are ποιήσετε αὐτά, or ποιήσας αὐτά; ἄνθρωπος; ζήσεται; and ἐν αὐτοῖς; we can be flexible as to tense, number, mood, and so on, of these elements.

Deferred Eschatology and the Interpretation of Lev 18:5

Some background to the history of interpretation of Lev 18:5 that will be proposed here is appropriate. It has long been a commonplace that particularly in the second to first centuries B.C.E., the promised vindication of Israel and punishment of the nations were increasingly deferred to the age to come. At the beginning of the twentieth century, Albert Schweitzer referred to a "Transzendentierung" of the Jewish hope for vindication,[15] which current scholarship calls "deferred eschatology" or the like. Harrington describes how, in the postbiblical period, "God's justice is deferred until the time of death and/or the last judgment."[16]

---

[13] *Sipre Num.* §6 (on Num 5:9–10). J. Neusner, *Sifré to Numbers: An American Translation and Explanation* (BJS 118; Atlanta, GA: Scholars, 1986), 1:78.

[14] I am avoiding the more refined gradings of, e.g., citation/allusion/echo provided by Richard Hays (*Echoes of Scripture in the Letters of Paul* [New Haven: Yale University Press, 1989]), which are very productive in other areas of interpretation but are not so relevant here, where we are looking specifically at the interpretive history of a definite text.

[15] A. Schweitzer, *Von Reimarus zu Wrede: Eine Geschichte der Leben-Jesu-Forschung* (Tübingen: Mohr/Siebeck, 1906), 244; ET *The Quest of the Historical Jesus* (trans. W. Montgomery; London: Unwin Brothers, 1910), 246.

[16] See, e.g., D. J. Harrington, *Invitation to the Apocrypha* (Grand Rapids: Eerdmans, 1999), 61 and also 75, and the contrasts drawn between the eschatologies of Sirach and Wisdom of Solomon in A. A. Di Lella, "Conservative and Progressive Theology: Sirach and Wisdom," *CBQ* 28 (1966): 139–54, esp. 143–46, 150–54.

What is perhaps not so well appreciated, however, is the impact of this deferral on the interpretation of specific scriptural texts. Joachim Schaper points out this tendency in the subsequent interpretation of Ps 1:5 through the LXX into the Mishnah:

> So when judgment comes, the wicked shall not stand firm;
>   sinners shall not stand [לֹא־יָקֻמוּ] in the assembly of the righteous.

Schaper notes that "The Septuagint provides us with an interesting interpretation of יָקֻמוּ"; it is translated as ἀναστήσονται.[17] The use of ἀναστήσονται would certainly lend itself to being understood in terms of a final resurrection; the translation may even have been prompted by such reflection (compare the use of the same word in Dan 12:2, T. Jud. 25:4, Pss. Sol. 3:11–12).[18] Schaper points to many translational moves similar to this.[19] But he further links LXX Ps 1:5 here to its use in m. Sanh. 10.3 in the catalogue of groups who will not inherit the world to come:

> The generation of the Dispersion have no share in the world to come, for it is written, *So the Lord scattered them abroad from thence upon the face of all the earth. So the Lord scattered them abroad*—in this world; *and the Lord scattered them abroad from thence*—in the age to come.
>
> The men of Sodom have no portion in the world to come, for it is written, *Now the men of Sodom were wicked and sinners against the Lord exceedingly (Gen. 13:13); wicked* in this world, *and sinners* in the world to come. But they will stand in judgment.
>
> R. Nehemiah says: Neither of them [that is, both these (the generation of the dispersion) and those (the men of Sodom)] shall stand in judgment,
>
> for it is said, *Therefore the wicked shall not stand in judgment, nor sinners in the congregation of the righteous (Ps. 1:5)*
>
> *Therefore the wicked shall not stand in judgment*—this refers to the generation of the flood.
>
> *Nor sinners in the congregation of the righteous*—these are the men of Sodom. (Trans. Danby.)

So there is an exegetical tradition here, where Psalm 1 has moved from a reference to the historical punishment of the wicked and toward a mention of resurrection and punishments in the world to come. This tendency can be seen throughout this section of *Sanh.* 10 and elsewhere in the Mishnah.[20] These

---

[17] J. Schaper, *Eschatology in the Greek Psalter* (Tübingen: Mohr, 1995), 46.

[18] On the other hand, the word is very frequent in the LXX.

[19] E.g., Ps 15(16):9f; 21(22):30–32; 45(46):9; 47(48):15; 48(49):12; 55(56):9.

[20] On Num 14:37 [Danby's translation—verses are cited in the Mishnah], " 'Even those men who brought up an evil report of the land died by the plague before the Lord,' it is said, '*Died*—in this world. *By the plague*—in the world to come.' Again, 'the party of Korah is not destined to rise up, for it is written, *And the earth closed upon them*—in this

examples from (possibly the Greek Psalter and) the Mishnah show an "eschatologizing" tendency, in particular in their treatment of future tenses.

Second, LXX Job teaches explicitly a doctrine of the future resurrection that is not clear in the Hebrew text. The clearest statement of this comes in a (translationally speaking) unaccountable afterword to the book.[21] The Hebrew text ends at Job 42:17 with וימת איוב זקן ושבע ימים. This is translated straightforwardly into the Greek: καὶ ἐτελεύτησεν Ιωβ πρεσβύτερος καὶ πλήρης ἡμερῶν. But there is an addition: γέγραπται δὲ αὐτὸν πάλιν ἀναστήσεσθαι μεθ' ὧν ὁ κύριος ἀνίστησιν. Spittler comments that there are other references to a doctrine of resurrection scattered through the book as well.[22] And there is also an eschatologizing tendency elsewhere in LXX Job. In MT Job 34:9 the wicked person talks of the lack of benefit in trusting in God; in the Greek he speaks about the lack of judgment that God exercises—most likely eschatological judgment.[23]

Third, the Hebrew text of Sirach gives no clear evidence for personal immortality, resurrection, or afterlife of any kind, but a doctrine of punishment after death found its way into the Greek translation (c. 117 B.C.E.)[24]—for example, in the transition from the Hebrew "for the expectation of mortals is worms" (Sir 7:17b) to "for the punishment of the ungodly is fire and worms" in the Greek. Here is reference to a postmortem punishment for the wicked. And there is a possible reference to an afterlife for the righteous in LXX Sir 48:11: Job adds, after a discussion—common to the Hebrew and Greek texts—of the appointed time of divine wrath and its final fury (48:10), "For we will indeed live in life" (καὶ γὰρ ἡμεῖς ζωῇ ζησόμεθα). It is not just the addition itself but the context of a final tribulation ("divine wrath," "final fury") that would naturally lead the reader to understand the text in an eschatological light.

---

world. *And they perished from among the assembly*—in the world to come'" (*m. Sanh.* 10.3). Mishnah *Abot* 4.1 has a similar example: "Who is rich? He who is happy in what he has, as it is said, *When you eat the labor of your hands, happy you will be, and it will go well with you* (Ps. 128:2). (*Happy will you be*—in this world, *and it will go well with you*—in the world to come)." H. Danby, *The Mishnah* (Oxford: Clarendon, 1933; repr. Oxford: Oxford University Press, 1985), 397–98, 453.

[21] Assuming that the Hebrew *Vorlage* does not contain the extra sentence.

[22] R. P. Spittler, "Testament of Job," *OTP* 1:841 n. 4c.

[23] Eschatological judgment is the usual meaning of ἐπισκοπή (cf. its equivalent פקד in the Dead Sea Scrolls), contra the understanding of H. Heater, *A Septuagint Translation Technique in the Book of Job* (CBQMS 11; Washington, D.C.: Catholic Biblical Association of America, 1982). See references to פקד/ἐπισκοπέω in, e.g., CD 7.9; 1QS 3.18; 4.11, 26; 4Q417 2 i 7 = 4Q418 43–45 i 5; *Wis.* 3:7, 3:13, 4:15; Luke 1:78; 1 Pet 2:12.

[24] Again, the Greek text of Sir 11:26 is susceptible to an interpretation of postmortem punishment; and see 48:11b. Di Lella, "Conservative and Progressive Theology," 146: "This should cause no surprise, for Sirach's grandson made the translation in Alexandria shortly before the author of the Wisdom of Solomon spelt out the truth of a blessed immortality for the righteous and a miserable fate for the wicked."

We can see in these cases the wider theological developments in early Jewish thought impinging (not surprisingly) on the exegesis of individual texts—in this case, an "eschatologizing" exegetical tendency. This is precisely what is also at work in the interpretation of Lev 18:5.

Pss. Sol. 14

Salvation in *Psalms of Solomon* is not confined to eschatological vindication but certainly includes it. Reference to resurrection in *Psalms of Solomon* abounds.[25] Perhaps the most explicit reference comes in *Pss. Sol.* 3:11–12:

> The destruction of the sinner is forever,
>   and he will not be remembered when God visits the righteous.
> This is the share of sinners forever,
>   but those who fear the Lord shall rise up to eternal life,
>   and their life shall be in the Lord's light, and it shall never end.
> [οἱ δὲ φοβούμενοι τὸν κύριον ἀναστήσονται εἰς ζωὴν αἰώνιον
> καὶ ἡ ζωὴ αὐτῶν ἐν φωτὶ κυρίου καὶ οὐκ ἐκλείψει ἔτι.]

This eschatological scheme and theology of salvation as future reward can be seen in *Pss. Sol.* 14, which refers to the future life as an inheritance: οἱ δὲ ὅσιοι κυρίου κληρονομήσουσιν ζωὴν ἐν εὐφροσύνῃ ("the holy ones of the Lord will inherit life with joy") (14:10). The discontinuity is assumed, so we see a life not yet attained. How will the righteous inherit this life? The righteous are equated with "those who walk in the righteousness of his commandments, in the Torah" (14:2):[26]

> τοῖς πορευομένοις ἐν δικαιοσύνῃ προσταγμάτων αὐτοῦ,
> ἐν νόμῳ, ᾧ ἐνετείλατο ἡμῖν εἰς ζωὴν ἡμῶν.
> ὅσιοι κυρίου ζήσονται ἐν αὐτῷ εἰς τὸν αἰῶνα. (14:2–3)

Even M. Winninge, who defends Sanders's reading of *Psalms of Solomon* in *Paul and Palestinian Judaism*, acknowledges uncharacteristically that "their righteousness is connected with the demands of living according to the Torah."[27] The

---

[25] M. Winninge, *Sinners and the Righteous: A Comparative Study of the Psalms of Solomon and Paul's Letters* (Stockhom: Almqvist & Wiksell International, 1995), 132, notes (contributing to his argument for a Pharisaic context for the Psalms) *Pss. Sol.* 2:31; 3:12; 13:11; 14:9f; 15:12f. R. B. Wright, "Psalms of Solomon," *OTP* 2:644–45, refers primarily to 2:31 and 3:12.

[26] The righteous one is again defined in terms of his actions in *Pss. Sol.* 5:17 (Winninge, *Sinners and the Righteous*, 133: "Righteousness is a positive achievement of the pious Jew") and 15:4. But Herbert Braun goes overboard saying "Ja, dies Lob Gottes ist dann eben doch eine Tat . . . eine Tat, die dem Täter, die rechte Bewahrung vor allen Strafen durch Gott einträgt" ("Von Erbarmen Gottes über den Gerechten: Zur Theologie der Psalmen Salomos," in *Gesammelte Studien zum Neuen Testament und seiner Umwelt* [3d ed.; Tubingen: Mohr, 1971], 33).

[27] Winninge, *Sinners and the Righteous*, 119. He leaves vague the question of how they are connected, however.

psalmist describes the "us" in 14:3 as having been instructed in the Torah by the Lord "for our life" / "unto life" (εἰς ζωὴν ἡμῶν). This is unlikely to denote duration of time ("for all their lives"); εἰς does not describe duration but has the more prospective sense of "unto."

Leviticus 18:5 comes into play in *Pss. Sol.* 14:3, "the holy ones of the Lord will live by it forever [ζήσονται ἐν αὐτῷ εἰς αἰῶνα]."[28] Here we have two elements of Lev 18:5: the future tense of ζάω and the preposition ἐν with αὐτῷ. The future tense of ζήσονται accords with the description of the future inheritance we have just seen. Ἐν is often taken to be locative[29] but is more likely to be instrumental; the previous line indicates that God commanded Torah εἰς ζωὴν ἡμῶν. So future life comes ἐν αὐτῷ; it is dependent on obedience to the Torah. Εἰς αἰῶνα is also ambiguous, however; but since the later part of the psalm (14:10) assumes the inherited, future character of "life," this earlier section is probably also working within that framework. This runs counter to Dunn's understanding of *Pss. Sol.* 14:2–3 in terms of "a *way* of life, and not of a life yet to be achieved or attained."[30]

Winninge tries to assert here that *Pss. Sol.* 14:2–3 "does not imply righteousness by works, because the mercy of God is basic for their life and salvation."[31] The expression of this antithesis is a frequent problem in current scholarship on Judaism: inability to see the frequent tension in Jewish literature that salvation is based both on obedience and on gracious divine election at the same time.[32] Winninge refers the reader to *Pss. Sol.* 15:12f and the relevant page in *Paul and Palestinian Judaism*,[33] but Lev 18:5 is being alluded to here in the same sense, that doing Torah is the precondition of a future life. And the holy ones of the Lord will live by it (ζήσονται ἐν αὐτῷ) forever, as a consequence of their Torah observance. Although I agree with Dunn that Lev 18:5 is in evidence here, it is difficult to see how he can use it to support his position.

1QS 4

The other passage that Dunn notes as supporting his understanding of Lev 18:5 is 1QS 4:6–8. This is a strange choice for two reasons. First, the

---

[28] Cf. also a possible (though not as clear) reference to Lev 18:5 in *Pss. Sol.* 15:4: the righteous one is ὁ ποιῶν ταῦτα.

[29] As translated by R. B. Wright, "Psalms of Solomon," *OTP* 2:630–70 (663), and taken by Dunn, *Theology of Paul the Apostle*, 153 n. 126.

[30] Dunn, *Theology of Paul*, 152–53.

[31] Winninge, *Sinners and the Righteous*, 119 n. 75.

[32] See above all discussion of the rabbinic literature on this question by F. Avemarie, *Tora und Leben: Untersuchungen zur Heilsbedeutung der Tora in der frühen rabbinischen Literatur* (Tübingen: Mohr, 1996). For treatment of this issue in the earlier, Second Temple literature, see my *Where Is Boasting? Early Jewish Soteriology and Paul's Response in Romans 1–5* (Grand Rapids: Eerdmans, 2002).

[33] Sanders, *Paul and Palestinian Judaism* (Minneapolis: Fortress, 1997), 393.

allusion to Lev 18:5 is extremely vague: only the phrase "all those who walk in it" (כול הולכי בה) could have any connection with the verse, and that would be a somewhat tangential one (the "it" in question being the "spirit of the sons of truth"). Second, the theological content of 1QS 4:6–8 is at odds with Dunn's argument that the role of the Torah was merely that of regulating, marking, and prolonging a life already possessed. 1QS 4 gives here a symmetrical description of how the deeds of the righteous and the wicked are determinative for their destiny both in the immediate and in the eternal future. After a long list (lines 2–6) of the qualities and virtues of the sons of truth—such as intelligence, wisdom, purity from idols, and the like—the end result of these virtues is described, as García Martínez's translation demonstrates:[34]

> These are the foundations of the spirit of the sons of truth in the world. And the reward (פקודת) of all those who walk in it will be healing, plentiful peace in a long life, fruitful offspring with all everlasting blessings, and eternal enjoyment with endless life (ושמחת עולמים בחיי נצח), and a crown of glory with majestic raiment in eternal light (באור עולמים). (1QS 4:6–8; cf. also 4Q257 2 i 3–6)

M. Philonenko sees reference here to a vision of world history, an earthly eschatology, in juxtaposition with individual futuristic eschatology: "les récompenses terrestres promises aux justes . . . puis les récompenses éternelles."[35] This fits the text much better than Nickelsburg's emphasis on the eternal life as already possessed but that death will not terminate. In 1QS 4:6–8 the emphasis is very much on divine intervention (not merely maintenance of an already possessed life), as is indicated by פקודת.[36] All the standard translations render the sentence in the future,[37] and Nickelsburg's description that the share of the righteous already consists of the benefits listed is unsatisfactory.[38] In 1QS 4, we do not see eternal life as something already attained; although such an understanding is found frequently at Qumran, another soteriological model is at work here.

---

[34] Cf. CD-B 20:27–34: "But all those who hold fast to these precepts, going and coming in accordance with the Law . . . they shall rejoice and their hearts shall be strong, and they shall prevail over all the sons of the earth, God will forgive them and they shall see his salvation because they took refuge in his holy name."

[35] M. Philonenko, "L'apocalyptique qoumrânienne," in *Apocalypticism in the Mediterranean World and the Near East* (ed. D. Hellholm; Tübingen: Mohr/Siebeck, 1983), 214.

[36] The -ל before the elements of the content of the reward is prospective. On פקד, see above, n. 23.

[37] F. García Martínez and E. Tigchelaar, *The Dead Sea Scrolls Study Edition* (2 vols.; vol. 1, New York: Brill, 1997; vol. 2, Boston: Brill, 1998), 1:77; G. Vermes, *The Dead Sea Scrolls in English* (4th ed.; Harmondsworth, England: Penguin, 1995), 74; M. Wise, M. Abegg, and E. Cook, trans., *The Dead Sea Scrolls: A New Translation* (San Francisco: HarperCollins, 1995), 130. Likewise Preben Wernberg-Møller's translation and commentary, *The Manual of Discipline* (Leiden: Brill, 1957), 26.

[38] G. W. E. Nickelsburg, *Resurrection, Immortality, Eternal Life* (London: Oxford University Press, 1972), 156.

CD 3:14–16

There is, however, evidence for the way the Qumran community (or at least their parent community) did use Lev 18:5. An important passage in the *Damascus Document* contributes to the question of the nature of the reward of life.[39] Here, for the first time since Philo, we have the five key words cited in correct sequence, as we do in Paul. This passage in the *Damascus Document* is ignored by Dunn as well as by Oegema in his treatment of the interpretation of Lev 18:5[40] but has been discussed at length by Danny Schwartz.[41] The Genizah manuscripts of D begin with an account of the unfaithfulness of Israel, her rejection of God, and persecution of those who pursue the way of perfection. To the faithful remnant, however, God has revealed his secret will, the substance of which is contained in this document and which the author commands the community to heed. At this point in CD 3:14–16, there is an interesting gloss of Lev 18:5 that challenges Dunn's assumption that Torah primarily regulates life or refers to a deutero-nomic "lengthening of days"; rather, it appears that obedience to Torah leads to the reward of eternal life (however this is understood). The text begins with an explanation of the importance of the halakic rulings of the community; they are the means by which the community can produce the works of Torah that are pleasing to God and thus receive the eschatological reward:

> [García Martínez:] . . . the hidden matters in which all Israel had gone astray: his holy sabbaths and his glorious feasts, his just stipulations and his truthful paths, the wishes of his will *which man must do in order to live by them* [אשר יעשה האדם וחיה בהם]. He disclosed [these matters to them] and they dug a well of plentiful water; *and whoever spurns them shall not live* [ומואסיהם לא יחיה].[42]

> [Davies:] . . . the hidden things in which Israel had gone astray—His holy sabbaths, and his glorious festivals, His righteous testimonies and His true ways, and the de-sires of His will, *which a man should do and live by.* He opened to them and they dug a well of copious water. [And those who despise it shall not live.][43]

On the smaller syntactic point of the object of ומואסיהם, the García Martínez version is the odd translation out, taking the catalogue of synonyms for the community's teachings as the grammatical object of the "spurning." Other

---

[39] See, e.g., Dunn, *Theology of Paul,* esp. 153–55.

[40] G. S. Oegema, "Die verschiedenen Auslegungen von Lev. 18,5," *Für Israel und die Völker: Studien zum alttestamentlich-jüdischen Hintergrund der paulinischen Theologie* (NovTSup 95; Leiden: Brill, 1998), 95–101.

[41] See D. R. Schwartz, *Leben durch Jesus versus Leben durch die Torah: Zur Religions-polemik der ersten Jahrhundert* (Franz-Delitzsch-Vorlesung 2; Münster: Institutum Judai-cum Delitzschianum, 1993).

[42] García Martínez and Tigchelaar, *Dead Sea Scrolls,* 1:555.

[43] P. Davies, *The Damascus Covenant: An Interpretation of the "Damascus Docu-ment"* (Sheffield, England: Sheffield Academic Press, 1983), 241.

translators line up with Davies here,[44] and the "abundant waters" (מים רבים) might seem more likely to be the object, being the last plural noun mentioned. The catalogue of lines 14–15, however, have constituted a strong element in the discourse and are combined with the reference to Lev 18:5. So the parallelism works better if one takes the negated form of Lev 18:5 ("they shall *not* live") to refer to those who despise these same community teachings. But this is not of decisive importance.

Where Davies is certainly wrong is in taking the וחיה ("and live") as regulative rather than as a promise. Here other translators oppose him.[45] The regulative reading ignores the parallelism with the following sentence, which Davies unaccountably places in angle brackets in his translation. The first half of the contrast is a direct quotation from Leviticus 18:5. If this first half were left standing alone, the meaning could refer to regulation. The contrast is not, however, between obedience and disobedience (living by them and not living by them) but rather life and not life (reward and punishment). Here the contrast is stark. This is no mere regulation of life: Torah observance leads to eternal life, but the one who rejects the Torah as the community understands it shall not live.

Further support for this reading of CD 3 comes from a fragment of the *Damascus Document* from cave 4, where the text talks of the precepts being given "so that man could carry them out and live," omitting the phrase at issue, "by them," and thus (at least for the modern reader) clarifying the meaning:

> You chose our fathers and gave their descendants your truthful regulations and your holy precepts, so that (a) man could carry them out and live [אשר יעשה האדם וחיה].[46]

Here the emphasis is entirely on the promissory side of the statement; the regulatory aspect, which may be a part of the original context of Lev 18:5, has disappeared with the disappearance of בהם.

Going back to the Genizah manuscript, the "life" in CD 3 is not merely lengthened life in this age. Schwartz picks up on this text in his discussion of Lev 18:5. He is arguing against the usual usage of Lev 18:5 in later Jewish tradition as a prohibition of martyrdom: by definition, if the purpose of doing the commandments is to gain life by them, then martyrdom does not achieve this.[47] Schwartz's arguments are relevant here, though directed at different opponents. He argues that in Ezekiel 20 (probably wrongly), the LXX, and Philo, *Prelim. Studies* 86–87, it is uncertain whether the reference is to life in this world (in which case, Schwartz argues, it refers to lengthened life) or to life in the age to come. But he is certainly right to argue that in CD 3 the reference is to eternal life. "Hier also wird ganz deutlich angenommen, daß unser Leviticus-Vers Leben als Lohn für Einhalten der Torah verspricht, und hier ist weiter auch ausdrücklich gesagt, daß das Leben,

---

44 See Vermes, *Dead Sea Scrolls*, 99; and Wise, Abegg, and Cook, *Dead Sea Scrolls*, 54.
45 Ibid.
46 4QD[a] 11 11–12. Cf also statements such as "the path to life" in 4Q185 1–2 ii 1–2.
47 Schwartz, *Leben durch Jesu*, 5: "Dieser Vers dient als Hauptbeweis dafür, daß man kein Märtyrer sein darf."

das hier versprochen ist, das ewige Leben ist (חיי נצח - CD III, 20)."[48] This final point is a key observation; the חיה in lines 14–16 is partly explained by line 20, where the reference is indisputably to "eternal life."

Sanders, in his reading of the passage, starts by asserting that this is "gratuity," not "self-salvation." He says of this passage that "human obedience, though necessary, does not initially open the path of salvation, for God brings man into the right path by pardoning his transgressions and building 'a sure house in Israel' (3.18–19)."[49] To say nothing of the false either/or of thoroughgoing grace or autosoterism, Sanders has set up the question to get the desired answers. He is right that "human obedience though necessary does not *initially open the path of salvation.*" But the point is rather that obedience to the commands here does secure the final end of salvation and eternal life.

Targum Ezekiel

It is interesting that *Targum Onqelos* and *Targum Jonathan* "translate" Lev 18:5 as referring to eternal life, but the evidence from the Targumim on the Pentateuch cannot be assumed to reflect particular early traditions. Some of the editors of the new Aramaic Bible series, however, do date some of the other Targumim early. Levey, for example, dates *Targum Ezekiel* to immediately after 70 C.E., as one of the documents produced in the wake of the crisis of the destruction of Jerusalem.[50] He defines its social context as "basically Pharisaic-rabbinic." Ribera dates the Targum less precisely but no less early: "It appears to be situated chronologically between the second century B.C.E. and the second century C.E., that is, before what is known as rabbinic literature."[51] Similarly, Robert Gordon dates *Targum Jonathan* to the Minor Prophets to after, but not long after, 70 C.E..[52] Again, *Targum Ruth* is reported to be Tannaitic: "It may not be out of place to recall that the Tosafists, in contradicting Rashi's statement that there was no Targum of the writings, observed that it was made in the time of the Tannaim. That is the oldest known opinion on the origin of this Targum, and it may very well be right."[53] There is certainly no internal evidence to push the date later. In addition, some other Targumim are very early, but they will be of less interest to

[48] Ibid., 9.

[49] Sanders, *Paul and Palestinian Judaism,* 295.

[50] S. H. Levey, *The Targum of Ezekiel* (ArBib 13; Wilmington, Del.: Glazier, 1987), 4.

[51] J. Ribera, "The Image of Israel according to Targum Ezekiel," in *Targumic and Cognate Studies: Essays in Honour of Martin McNamara* (ed. K. J. Cathcart and M. Maher; Sheffield, England: Sheffield Academic Press, 1996), 121.

[52] See also R. P. Gordon, "The Targumists as Eschatologists" in *Congress Volume: Göttingen, 1977* (VTSup 29; Leiden: Brill, 1978), 113–30, on the dating of the Targumim.

[53] D. R. G. Beattie, *The Targum of Ruth* (ArBib 19; Edinburgh: T&T Clark, 1994), 12. Beattie (pp. 11–12) supplies other arguments in favour of the Targum's antiquity, including law that perhaps predates the Mishnah, and exegesis that might be earlier than that of *Ruth Rabbah.*

138

Simon J. Gathercole

us because they are also the most literal translations and so do not give us so much evidence of development in theology upon the Hebrew Bible.[54]

We will confine our attention here to *Targum Ezekiel*, where it is clear, to quote Levey, that "the righteous, by observing Torah, will be rewarded with eternal life (20.11, 13, 21)" whereas the destiny of the wicked is hell (1:8; 26:20; 31:14, 16; 32:18–32).[55] Or as Smolar and Aberbach put it, "Eternal life in the world to come is granted to those who observe the statues and ordinances given by God."[56] The interpretation of Lev 18:5 is at issue here, since the Hebrew text of canonical Ezekiel refers to Lev 18:5 at 20:11, 13, 21 and at 33:16, 19. Crucially, whereas the MT reads, "[statutes and ordinances] by whose observance a man shall live," *Targum Ezekiel* has in chs. 20 and 33, "if a man observes them, he shall live an everlasting life through them." This is almost identical to *Targum Onqelos* and *Targum Jonathan* Lev 18:5 as well as to CD 3:14–16.

4 Ezra 7:21

There is a much less of a close parallel in *4 Ezra*.[57] I include this reference for the sake of completeness and because it would have been written around the time of *Targum Ezekiel* if Levey and Ribera are correct about the dating. The reference to Lev 18:5 is somewhat dubious, and it is also uncertain whether the reference is to a future "length of days" or whether there is any reference to the age to come:

> For God strictly ordained for those entering the world when they should come, what they should do to live, and what to do to avoid punishment.

> Mandans enim mandavit Deus venientibus quando venerunt,
> quid facientes viverent et quid observantes non punirentur. (*4 Ezra* 7:21)

The contrast between *viverent* and *punirentur* indicates that the reference is not to regulation here. But the "life" here may be life in this age, as Ezra and the angel have been discussing the question of why Israel has not received the world as her possession. The text and its surrounding context are unclear.

m. Mak. 3.15

In Mishnah *Makkot* we see a complicated argument that incorporates the only reference in the Mishnah to Lev 18:5:

---

[54] E.g., *Targum Jonathan* to the Former Prophets and *Targum Proverbs*.

[55] Levey, *Targum of Ezekiel*, 12.

[56] L. Smolar and M. Aberbach, *Studies in Targum Jonathan to the Prophets* (LBS; New York: Ktav 1983), 180 (note also n. 335).

[57] Noted by Avemarie, *Tora und Leben*, 376.

All they that are liable to Extirpation, if they have been scourged are no longer liable to Extirpation, for it is written *And thy brother seem vile unto thee* (Deut. 25:3)—when he is scourged then he is thy brother.[58] So R. Hanina b. Gamaliel.

Moreover, R. Hanina b. Gamaliel said If he that commits one transgression thereby forfeits his soul, how much more, if he performs one religious duty, shall his soul be restored to him! R. Simeon says From the same place we may learn [the same], for it is written *Even the souls that do them shall be cut off. . .* (Lev. 18.29); and it says *Which if a man do them he shall live by them* (Lev. 18.5).

Thus to him who sits and commits no transgression is given a reward, as is the case with one that performs a religious duty (*m. Mak.* 3.15). (Trans. Danby.)

The sayings of Rabbi Hanina ben Gamaliel (*fl.* c. 80–120 C.E.) and Rabbi Simeon ben Yochai (*fl.* c. 140–165 C.E.) describe the process of *extirpation:* God's abrupt termination, by disaster or disease, of the life of one who commits specific kinds of wickedness. *M. Meg.* 1.5, *m. Yebam.* 4.13, and *m. Ketub.* 3.1 all contrast punishment exacted through the judicial process of the court with punishment exacted through "extirpation at the hand of heaven." This is usually reserved for deliberate sins, whereas the same sin committed in error can be atoned for through presenting a sin offering.[59]

The argument of *m. Mak.* 3.15 begins by asserting that the person who has been punished through the channels of the judicial system is not subject to this heavenly punishment. This is a common Jewish idea,[60] which is backed up by the play on words in the reference to Deut 25:3, "your brother seems vile to you." (Reverse ק and ל, and the verse reads, "the one scourged is your brother"). This introduces another saying of Rabbi Hanina, but it is difficult precisely to determine the significance of the reference to Lev 18.5 here. The verse is clearly introduced as a scriptural proof-text of Hanina's proposition that "how much more, if he performs one religious duty, shall his soul be restored to him." If one stresses the symmetry of extirpation and restoration, then Lev 18.5 might refer to life in this world; conversely, one might stress the asymmetry implied in the "how much more," and the common Rabbinic motif of the asymmetry of divine reward and punishment, in which God's reward for righteousness always outweighs his punishment of wickedness. We know from *Sifra Leviticus* that other Tannaim understood Lev 18.5 as referring to the age to come. *Ahare Mot* §8 (i.e., *Sipra Lev.* §193 [on Lev 18:5]) actually polemicises against the "this-worldly" understanding,[61] while *Ahare Mot* §13 (i.e., §194 [on Lev 18:6]), by contrast, uses the text as a prohibition of martyrdom.[62]

---

[58] The key to understanding the play on words here is the similarity between לקה ("to be scourged") and קלה ("to be vile"). Thus Danby, *The Mishnah,* 408 n. 5.

[59] See *m. Ker.* 1.2, 2.6, 6.3; *m. Sanh.* 7.8, *m. Hor.* 2.3, 2.6. Only the scapegoat can atone for sins that merit extirpation (*m. Šeb.* 1.6).

[60] See, e.g., the concept in *T. Ab.* 14:15; passim in Pseudo-Philo, *Liber antiquitatum biblicarum;* and discussion in Sanders, *Paul and Palestinian Judaism,* 168–74.

[61] J. Neusner, *Sifra: An Analytical Translation* (Atlanta: Scholars, 1988) 3:74.

[62] Neusner, *Sifra,* 3:80.

Luke 10:25–37

We can also turn to the Gospels for evidence, earlier than Mishnah *Makkot*, that is also not used in current debates concerning Lev 18:5 in Paul.[63] The parable of the Good Samaritan is one text that, at least within the rhetorical world of the gospel, gives us an insight into the Jewish theology of final judgment according to works. In Luke 10, a teacher of the law comes to ask Jesus, "What must I do to inherit eternal life?" (10:25 NRSV). The view of the *nomikos* is extremely clear: he assumes that inheriting eternal life results from obedience to the two great commandments. This is his interpretation of Torah, as is clear from v. 26. And Jesus says to him, "Do this, and you will live" (10:28 NRSV).

The use of Lev 18:5b in Luke 10:25 and 10:28 here is not quite as explicit as the formulation in the *Damascus Document*. But the differences between the Lukan and the original Leviticus text by no means militate against a connection between Lev 18:5 and Luke 10. What has happened is in accordance with what we have seen elsewhere. There is a deferral of promises to a future eschatology: the ambiguous (in the sense of reference to *this* life or *future* life) ζήσεται becomes ζωὴν αἰώνιον κληρονομήσω, about which there can be no doubt. Furthermore, there is an "eternalization" of the life that, in its original context in Leviticus, would have been understood in terms of lengthened life and prosperity of one's descendants and the nation as a whole. As well as eternalization, then, it is also an individualization. There are also smaller changes of tense and person. First, the form of words in Luke 10:25 in the question of the *nomikos* retains the aorist participle ποιήσας, but ζήσεται is expanded into ζωὴν αἰώνιον κληρονομήσω, which is also a shift to the first person. Also, when Jesus replies in 10:28, ποιήσετε becomes the singular imperative ποίει, and ζήσεται is adapted from the third person to the second person, ζήσῃ. Thus:

LXX Lev 18:5b: καὶ ποιήσετε αὐτά, ἃ ποιήσας ἄνθρωπος ζήσεται ἐν αὐτοῖς·

Luke 10:25: τί ποιήσας ζωὴν αἰώνιον κληρονομήσω;

Luke 10:28: τοῦτο ποίει καὶ ζήσῃ.

The importance of Lev 18:5 for this whole section (Luke 10:25–37) becomes more apparent when one notes Nolland's observation that "Luke creates an inclusio around the episode by using again at the end of v 28 ποιεῖν, 'to do,' and the ζάω root ('life/live'), which have occurred in the opening verse (v 25). The challenge will be reiterated in v 37 at the termination of the linked parable, where the same imperative form of ποιεῖν will recur."[65] It has been argued that

---

[63] Though see Dunn, *Romans 9–16*, 601: "Luke 10:28 should not be overlooked!" In Dunn's exegesis it is not discussed, however, and has no influence on the interpretation.

[64] Cf. ὁ ποιήσας αὐτὰ ἄνθρωπος ζήσεται ἐν αὐτοῖς (Rom 10:6); Ὁ ποιήσας αὐτὰ ζήσεται ἐν αὐτοῖς (Gal 3:12) for contemporary versions of Lev 18:5.

[65] J. Nolland, *Luke 9:21–18:34* (WBC 35B; Waco: Word, 1993), 582.

the parable of the Good Samaritan is a kind of midrash on Lev 18:5. This is developed by Earle Ellis and W. R. Stegner. Ellis "has shown how Leviticus 18:5 establishes the unity of the pericope."[66] Ποιεῖν is repeated not just in the concluding imperative (Πορεύου καὶ σὺ ποίει ὁμοίως) but also in the answer of the νομικός to Jesus' question; the neighbor to the one who fell among thieves was Ὁ ποιήσας τὸ ἔλεος μετ᾽ αὐτοῦ (Luke 10:37).

It is not only the imperative ποίει that recurs at the end of the pericope, as Nolland noted above, but also the aorist participle ποιήσας. Stegner develops his argument further by arguing that Luke 10:25–37 taps into an existing exegetical tradition along typical rabbinic lines,[67] focusing on the words ποιήσας and ἄνθρωπος: he mentions that *Sipra*, *Targum Onqelos*, and *Targum Jonathan* all apply Lev 18:5 to the world to come.[68] Obviously there is no demonstrable literary dependence here; rather, "Jesus [and his interlocutor] probably followed the conventional exegesis of this passage that was later incorporated into the Sifra and the Targums."[69]

Luke 10 is usually omitted from discussions of the relation between Torah observance and "life." The emphasis among most "new perspective" scholars is to see Torah as regulating life and not so much in terms of leading to future life. Again, against Dunn, Luke 10 contributes evidence to the contrary understanding of Lev 18:5.

Mark 10:17–22

Very similar theologically but without the use of Lev 18:5 is the triple tradition in Mark 10:17–22 and parallels. Jesus replies to an *archōn* who comes to him and asks, τί ποιήσω ἵνα ζωὴν αἰώνιον κληρονομήσω; ("What must I do to inherit eternal life?" NRSV). His question and that of the *nomikos* in Luke 10 show that the concern with one's destiny in the age to come was clearly an issue for at least two people in the lifetime of Jesus, as Horbury notes.[70] Again, the fact that the life here is in the future is implied by the verb κληρονομήσω. The bifurcation of "this age"/"the age to come" that is basic to rabbinic thought is also ingrained in

---

[66] W. R. Stegner, "The Parable of the Good Samaritan and Leviticus 18:5," in *The Living Text* (ed. D. Groh and R. Jewett; FS E. W. Saunders; Washington, D.C.: University Press of America, 1985), 29; see E. E. Ellis, *The Gospel of Luke* (NCB; London: Marshall, 1974), 161.

[67] According to Stegner, "Parable of the Good Samaratin," 29, following a pattern that Peder Borgen, *Bread from Heaven* (NovTSup 10; Leiden: Brill, 1965), 28–58, has noted in Philo, John, and the Palestinian midrashim.

[68] Stegner, "Parable of the Good Samaritan," 31. *Targum Neofiti* apparently does not mention future life.

[69] Stegner, "Parable of the Good Samaritan," 32.

[70] W. Horbury, "Paul and Judaism: Review of E.P. Sanders, *Paul and Palestinian Judaism*," *ExpTim* 89 (1977/1978): 117. C. E. B. Cranfield, *Mark* (Cambridge: Cambridge University Press, 1959), 327, notes that the *archōn* "at least asks the question that really matters"!

the thinking of Jesus and his contemporaries.[71] There is also an individualism implicit in the question.[72] In any case, Jesus replies, on the *archōn*'s own soteriological terms, in the language of Second Temple orthodoxy, "You know the commandments: 'Do not commit adultery, do not murder, do not steal, do not bear false witness, honor your mother and father'" (Mark 10:19). Again, obedience to the commandments is the way to inherit life in the age to come. As we saw in Luke 10, works are related to the attainment of an individual, future, eternal life. The difference in this passage lies in Jesus' additional stipulation that the *archōn* follow him and sell all his possessions. Jesus does not reject reward theology but reconfigures it as (or incorporates into it) reward for service to himself and the kingdom.

Rom 10:5 and Gal 3:12

Of the passages examined in this essay, Rom 10:5 and Gal 3:12 seem to be the hardest to deal with; whether this is because of the inherent density and difficulty of the texts or because of the mountainous commentary on them is hard to determine. But two reasons indicate why the Jewish texts we have cited thus far should be used to illuminate the meaning here in Paul. (There is, of course, no reason why Paul's interpretation should necessarily be the same as that of the texts we have cited.) First, Paul is summing up in the verses the theology of the Sinai covenant, which his opponents observe. This is particularly implied by Rom 10:5, where Paul contrasts the righteousness described by Moses with the righteousness that comes by faith. Second, stronger evidence comes from the way Paul uses Lev 18:5 to gloss in Rom 10:5 the phrase "the righteousness that is from Torah" (τὴν δικαιοσύνην τὴν ἐκ [τοῦ] νόμου)—the same phrase Paul uses to describe his own primary concern before his Damascus road experience.[73] And within Paul's Pharisaic theology, obedience to Torah would have had an eschatological orientation, looking forward to the reward of resurrection. But we should not prejudge the issue. There is not space here to explore comprehensively these two passages, which have generated such an extensive interpretive history; we will focus on the specific issue at hand in both Rom 10 and Gal 3.

---

[71] For the "this age"/"the age to come" antithesis in the teaching of Jesus, see Mark 10:30 (and possibly 3:29); Matt 12:32; Luke 18:30; Luke 20:34–35. Cf. also "this world" (with a more spatial sense, though clearly in antithesis to "eternal life"), John 12:25; 16:33. Paul also refers to "this age" (though without the corresponding "age to come") in 1 Cor 1:20, 28; 3:18; 2 Cor 4:4. As W. D. Davies and D. C. Allison note (*A Critical and Exegetical Commentary on the Gospel according to St. Matthew* [3 vols.; ICC; Edinburgh: T&T Clark, 1988–1997], 2:348), systematic formulations of the dichotomy only come later, however.

[72] J. Gnilka, *Das Evangelium nach Markus* (2 vols.; EKKNT 2; Zurich: Benziger, 1979), 2:85, highlights this.

[73] The phrase comes in Phil 3:9, where Paul describes his life before his encounter with Christ.

First is Rom 10:5: Μωϋσῆς γὰρ γράφει τὴν δικαιοσύνην τὴν ἐκ [τοῦ] νόμου ὅτι ὁ ποιήσας αὐτὰ ἄνθρωπος ζήσεται ἐν αὐτοῖς. Here I will concentrate on Dunn's interpretation; Wright's throws up a wholly different set of questions that cannot be dealt with here.[74] As mentioned, Dunn's interpretation of Lev 18:5 saw that the "obvious sense" of the passage was "that keeping the statutes and ordinances of the law was the way of living appropriate to the covenant" and that "Moses did *not* say, and Paul did not understand him to say, that keeping the law was a means of earning or gaining life (in the future . . .)."[75] Neither, according to Dunn, did Paul's Jewish contemporaries take Lev 18:5 to refer to future life.[76] We have seen, however, that Lev 18:5 has, in numerous places in Jewish literature, been concerned with an obedience to the Torah that aims to receive eternal life in the future.

Paul is contrasting two understandings of what leads to final vindication, the eschatological salvation that Paul in Rom 11:26 sees will come to all Israel. This is the same σωτηρία that Paul desires and prays for in 10:1 and that is Paul's repeated concern in 10:9, 10, 11, and 13. Even if one argued that some of these were logical rather than eschatological futures, 10:11 (οὐ καταισχυνθήσεται) certainly must refer to final vindication at the eschaton. So if Paul is speaking of eschatologically oriented righteousness by faith, it makes sense that he contrasts it with eschatologically oriented righteousness by obedience to Torah. We can see, then, that it is coherent to see Paul as understanding Lev 18:5 in a way that mirrors the interpretation of his contemporaries, Philo excepted.

The second passage is Gal 3:11–12, which contrasts Lev 18:5 with Hab 2:4:

ὅτι δὲ ἐν νόμῳ οὐδεὶς δικαιοῦται παρὰ τῷ θεῷ δῆλον, ὅτι Ὁ δίκαιος ἐκ πίστεως ζήσεται· ὁ δὲ νόμος οὐκ ἔστιν ἐκ πίστεως, ἀλλ᾽ Ὁ ποιήσας αὐτὰ ζήσεται ἐν αὐτοῖς.

In Dunn's and Wright's readings of Galatians 3, the picture is similar to what we have just seen. Here I will focus on Wright's interpretation, which (as we saw with Dunn above) focuses on the original context of Leviticus 18 and its surrounding chapters. "The context of Leviticus 18, from which Paul quotes v. 5, is the warning that, unless Israel keeps the covenant charter properly, the land itself will eject those who are polluting it. This is emphasized in 20:20–5, 26:14–43."[77] Seeing this context as determinative for Paul's understanding again has the effect of diverting the discussion away from the "deferred eschatology" that was so prominent in the Second Temple period, not least in the NT (e.g., in Luke 10). Thus the possibility that the verse has undergone a transformation from "lengthening of days" to "eternal life" does not receive proper consideration.[78]

---

[74] See Wright, *Climax of the Covenant*, 239–46.

[75] Dunn, *Romans 9–16*, 612.

[76] Ibid., 601.

[77] Wright, *Climax of the Covenant*, 150.

[78] See Wright's dismissal of the view (expressed by Gundry), ibid., 139 n. 5. The "eternal" view of life is also argued by W. C. Kaiser, "Leviticus 18:5 and Paul: Do This and You Shall Live (Eternally?)," *JETS* 14 (1971): 19–28.

The focus, for Wright, is rather on the doing of Torah as the boundary-marking practice that sets Jew off over against Gentile. Galatians 3:11–12 "simply asserts that the Torah *as it stands* is not the means of faith, since it speaks of 'doing,' which is best taken in the sense of 'doing the things that mark Israel out,' and hence cannot be as it stands the boundary marker of the covenant family."[79] Or again, "Habakkuk is saying that covenant membership is not demarcated by Torah, because that would set up the 'doing of the law' as the covenant boundary marker, which would then mean ultimately that the covenant was determined by race."[80] In other words, for Wright (as Dunn), obedience to Torah is not the means to salvation but rather marks out covenant membership, in the Jewish perspective.

This comes in (partly understandable) reaction to ahistorical understandings of Gal 3:10–14. Wright notes that Paul is not "offering an abstract account of 'how one gets saved.' . . . For Paul, then, the covenant is not detached from the realities of space and time, and of the this-worldly orientation which was characteristic of Israel's covenant."[81] This contrast, however, between covenant life, whose boundaries are marked by Torah, and abstract systems of eternal salvation is an entirely counterproductive one for the interpretation of Paul and Judaism. Eschatological salvation and eternal life need not be "abstract" or "detached from the realities of space and time," and to talk of way of life, or of existence within the covenant, as being discrete from final vindication makes little sense in the Jewish or Pauline perspective. The interpretation of Lev 18:5 that we have seen in the period from 200 B.C.E. to 200 C.E. has shown just that.

Conclusion

Paul is not simply in dialogue with the Deuteronomic picture of covenant theology (or an exclusivistic misunderstanding of that covenant), as Dunn and Wright have maintained. Paul is in dialogue with a Judaism that thought in terms of obedience, final judgment, and eternal life, not a Judaism merely organized around sin–repentance–forgiveness or sin–exile–restoration. This is most evident from Romans 2, where Paul talks to his interlocutor as one who holds to a theology of final vindication on the basis of works, resulting in eternal life:[82]

> God "will give to each person according to what he has done." To those who by persistence in doing good seek glory, honor, and immortality, he will give eternal life. But for those who are self-seeking and who reject the truth and follow evil, there will be wrath and anger. There will be trouble and distress for every human being

---

[79] Wright, *Climax of the Covenant*, 150.

[80] Ibid., 149.

[81] Ibid., 150.

[82] I would argue that Paul (as well as his interlocutor) also holds to this scheme expressed in Rom 2:6–10, as he is himself building on this in his argument as common ground.

who does evil first for the Jew, then for the Gentile; but glory, honor, and peace for everyone who does good first for the Jew, then for the Gentile. (Rom 2:6–10)

This is what Paul presupposes his interlocutor to believe. This is not an ahistorical medieval theology read back into first-century Judaism but rather a proper appreciation of the Judaism with which Paul is in debate. The scheme of a final judgment followed by an age to come of eternal life was a scheme that Paul and his Jewish contemporaries shared. So there are three reasons for rejecting the understanding of Lev 18:5 in early Judaism and Christianity as merely referring to the identification of Israel in its life under the Torah. The first reason, then, is the broader thought-world of both Judaism and Christianity—that is to say, an understanding of final judgment and eternal life in the age to come that is not necessarily less covenantal than Deuteronomic theology but rather that includes and goes beyond that Deuteronomic theology.[83] Second, we have plenty of evidence that these broader theological developments in eschatology led to fresh, "eschatologizing" interpretations of individual texts. Third, there is ample evidence for an understanding, both pre- and post-70 C.E., of Lev 18:5 as talking in terms of eternal life. And this understanding was, furthermore, on the increase.[84]

---

[83] Notwithstanding Schiffmann's criticism of Sanders that the covenant did not embrace the sphere of the age to come in Tannaitic literature. See L. Schiffman, "The Rabbinic Understanding of Covenant," *RevExp* 84 (1987): 289–98. There is no reason to suspect that in the Second Temple literature the reward and punishment in this life lay in the sphere of the covenant and that eternal life did not.

[84] See Oegema, *Für Israel und die Völker*, 95–101; and Avemarie, *Tora und Leben*, esp. 104–16.

6

The Significance of Signs in Luke 7:22–23 in the Light of Isaiah 61 and the Messianic Apocalypse

Michael Labahn

Preliminary Remarks

The meaning of eschatology in the proclamation of Jesus and its early records is quite controversial in current scholarship. The classical analysis, made in 1907 by Adolf Harnack, of the source common to Matthew and Luke, called Q, claims that the value of Q among the earliest records of the words and proclamation of Jesus is seen in its modest interest in eschatological elements in the sayings of Jesus. For Harnack, this caution fits well with the preaching of the historical Jesus himself: "Above all, the tendency to exaggerate the apocalyptic and eschatological element in the proclamation of Jesus, and to subordinate to this the purely religious and ethical elements, will ever find its refutation in Q."[1]

There are some parallels to this point of view in recent research.[2] During the last decades, Q is no longer taken as a mere collection of heterogeneous sayings of Jesus. Exegetical interest has changed to redaction-critical methods that try to separate various strata within the document. Eschatological and apocalyptic elements were taken as important indicators for identifying later parts or layers of Q. Since the work of Dieter Lührmann and other scholars, research into the

---

[1] A. Harnack, *The Sayings of Jesus: The Second Source of St. Matthew and St. Luke* (New Testament Studies 2; New York: Putnam's Sons, 1908), 250–51 (the translation here is slightly adapted to reflect the German more literally). The original German is found in A. Harnack, *Sprüche und Reden Jesu: Die zweite Quelle des Matthäus und Lukas* (Beiträge zur Einleitung in das Neue Testament 2; Leipzig: Hinrichs, 1907), 173: "Vor allem . . . die Übertreibung des apokalyptisch-eschatologischen Elements in der Verkündigung Jesu und die Zurückstellung der rein religiösen und moralischen Momente hinter jenes immer wieder ihre Widerlegung durch die Spruchsammlung finden."

[2] Still, one should not overlook the emphasis on eschatology in the preaching of Jesus raised by the influential works of Johannes Weiss and Albert Schweitzer; cf., e.g., J. S. Kloppenborg, "Symbolic Eschatology and the Apocalypticism of Q," *HTR* 80 (1987): 287–303, here 288.

eschatology of Q is mostly concerned with apocalyptic predictions of the final judgment at the time of return of the Son of Man, with whom Q identifies Jesus. The way of interpreting Jesus and his proclamation of the kingdom of God by apocalyptic hints of the final judgment is taken as a reliable criterion for identifying redaction in Q.[3] Apocalyptic traits have been regarded as late phenomena in the literary strata of Q, phenomena that impress the entire document.[4] The relationship of apocalyptic traditions within Q toward matters of wisdom forms a main subject of recent research in scholarship.[5] One may compare, for example, John S. Kloppenberg's stratigraphical differentiation between a sapiential layer and an apocalyptic layer in Q, to which narrative material was added in order to transform Q into a biographical genre.[6]

The analysis made by Siegfried Schulz, however, may be recalled as an exception of sorts.[7] He claims that there are words of Jesus available in Q showing an imminent apocalyptic expectation (*Naherwartung*) that belongs already to an early layer of Q. Present time is understood as time of decision whereas the Q group represents the eschatological community.[8] The spirit of God is present in the domain of the Q community that is aware of the eschatological salvation in its midst.[9] Thus Schulz regards the post-Easter enthusiasm of the group as a criterion to differentiate between early traditions belonging to early Palestinian Jewish Christian circles and later layers from Hellenistic Jewish Christian circles in Syria. The later parts take into account the delay of the Parousia. Other scholars, however, deny the importance of apocalyptic strands in Q.[10] We may agree with

---

[3] Cf., e.g., D. Lührmann, *Die Redaktion der Logienquelle* (WMANT 33; Neukirchen-Vluyn: Neukirchener Verlag, 1969), 69, 96–97.

[4] Cf. J. S. Kloppenborg, *Excavating Q: The History and Setting of the Sayings Gospel* (Minnesota: Fortress, 2000), 118: "The threat of judgment is a major editorial theme of Q."

[5] Cf. the introductory remarks by M. Ebner, *Jesus—ein Weisheitslehrer? Synoptische Weisheitslogien im Traditionsprozeß* (Herders Biblische Studien 15; New York: Herder, 1998), 2–21, who limits the role of eschatology in the preaching of Jesus while regarding him as a teacher of wisdom. The importance of wisdom motifs as well as eschatological motifs, by an "interaction of the themes," is highlighted by R. A. Edwards, *A Theology of Q: Eschatology, Prophecy, and Wisdom* (Philadelphia: Fortress, 1976), 78–79 (quotation, 80); see also 147–55.

[6] J. S. Kloppenborg, *The Formation of Q: Trajectories in Ancient Wisdom Collections* (2d ed.; SAC; Harrisburg, Pa.: Trinity Press International, 1999); idem, *Excavating Q*, 143–53. See also B. L. Mack, "Q and the Gospel of Mark: Revising Christian Origins," *Semeia* 55 (1992): 15–39 (esp. 16), with far-reaching consequences for research on the historical Jesus and early Christianity.

[7] Cf. Kloppenborg, "Symbolic Eschatology," 289, who relates the work of Siegfried Schulz to the research done by Philipp Vielhauer and Ernst Käsemann.

[8] S. Schulz, *Q: Die Spruchquelle der Evangelisten* (Zürich: Theologischer Verlag, 1972), 63.

[9] Ibid., 65.

[10] A. D. Jacobson, "Apocalyptic and the Synoptic Sayings Source Q," in *The Four Gospels* (ed. F. Van Segbroeck, C. M. Tuckett, G. van Belle, and J. Verheyden; FS F. Neirynck; BETL 100; Leuven: Leuven University Press, 1992), 403–19, esp. 417–19.

the arguments affecting limits of apocalyptic interpretations, but we should not deny completely any eschatological elements in Q.

As an alternative or as a supplemental method to stratigraphical investigations, socio-rhetorical analyses can be mentioned, interpreting Jesus as well as eschatological texts in Q in a noneschatological way. Eschatology is thereby not understood conventionally as dealing with final events known from Jewish eschatological imagery; rather eschatology means an alternative interpretation of presence with strong sociological impacts defining group boundaries or the self-understanding of a particular circle.

I would like to offer two examples: John S. Kloppenborg proposes a symbolic interpretation of eschatology in Q.[11] The rhetorical aims are twofold: (1) "Q takes over the images of judgment and catastrophic destruction and redeploys other traditional apocalyptic *topoi* as corollary to its 'antistructural ethic.'" Eschatology in Q serves to establish an ethos that is opposed to the *communitas*. (2) "Apocalyptic language also afforded a useful means to a social end, namely, the demarcation of sharp group boundaries within which such an ethic may be observed and fostered and within which shape and substance may be provided for community existence."[12] There are some similarities to the interpretation of the kingdom of God by Leif E. Vaage. The kingdom of God represents an "ethical concept, serving to promote a certain way of being in the world."[13] Vaage differentiates between the first layer of Q and its later redaction. In its eschatological parts, the first layer is characterized by a social vision that is "anarchic." There is to be found a "transvaluation" of present needs of daily supply by agreeing with an ascetic-Cynic way of life.[14] The redaction of Q adds polemical passages that intend to strengthen group boundaries (Q 7:28; 16:16; 13:28–9).[15]

More recently there is also a narrative approach to Q attempting to understand Q as an entire literary document with a narrative plot.[16] In an important article Arto Järvinen defines the narrative strategy of Q by pointing to the eschatological expectation of the return of the Son of Man: "The 'Son of man' functions as an important symbol that helped the Q community to interpret

---

[11] Kloppenborg, "Symbolic Eschatology," 304, 306.

[12] Ibid., 306.

[13] L. E. Vaage, "Monarchy, Community, Anarchy: The Kingdom of God in Paul and Q," *TJT* 8 (1992): 52–69, here 60.

[14] Cf. ibid., 61–67, and Vaage's summary, 68.

[15] Ibid., 60–61. In accordance with recent scholarly practice I quote Q-texts by their Lukan position prefaced by "Q". This is not a decision for the Lukan wording or the Lukan position as original in Q.

[16] E.g., M. Hüneburg, *Jesus als Wundertäter in der Logienquelle: Ein Beitrag zur Christologie von Q* (Arbeiten zur Bibel und ihrer Geschichte 4; Leipzig: Evangelische Verlagsanstalt, 2001); A. Järvinen, "The Son of Man and His Followers: A Q Portrait of Jesus," in *Characterization in the Gospels: Reconceiving Narrative Criticism* (ed. D. Rhoads and K. Syreeni; JSNTSup 184; Sheffield, England: Sheffield Academic Press, 1999), 180–222; and E. Sevenich-Bax, *Israels Konfrontation mit den letzten Boten der Weisheit: Form, Funktion, und Interdependenz der Weisheitselemente in der Logienquelle* (Münsteraner Theologische Abhandlungen 21; Altenberge, Germany: Oros, 1993).

the rejection and failure of its mission to Israel. Jesus' role as the scorned Son of man and his glorious *parousia*—two quite contradictory phenomena—provided the Q community with applicable analogues to their own situation."[17]

The various proposals indicate that the eschatological or so-called eschatological texts and motifs *are dealing with the present time of the speakers or the readers and reinterpret provocatively the present time*. The eschatological texts and motifs serve as rhetorical aims and establish an alternative understanding of presence. I am not convinced, however, that we can deny the existence of any eschatological elements in the texts of Q.

Before we proceed further, we need some kind of definition for the crucial term "eschatology" itself.[18] In short, "eschatology" contains conceptions and expectations concerning the final events of history,[19] including judgment, as well as salvation established by God or his envoy. The "last things" (ἔσχατα) may limit the course of history and carry out new actions done by God as they are expected by Jewish and early Christian eschatological imagery. The narrators of these things may obtain a different position toward eschatological events: eschatological events may already begin to happen in the current time of the narrators, or the events may be expected from the near or far future.[20]

Both kinds of eschatology can be found in Q: futuristic eschatology and present eschatology; both do not necessarily have to be separated from each other by ascribing them to various layers.[21] Rather, both kinds of eschatology recall elements of Jesus' preaching in which he combines features of futuristic as well as present eschatology.[22]

---

[17] Järvinen, "Son of Man," 182.

[18] For a discussion of the term "eschatology," see, e.g., S. Hjelde, *Das Eschaton und die Eschata: Eine Studie über Sprachgebrauch und Sprachverwirrung in protestantischer Theologie von der Orthodoxie bis zur Gegenwart* (BEvT 102; Munich: Kaiser, 1987), 15–30; and G. Sauter, *Einführung in die Eschatologie* (Die Theologie; Darmstadt: Wissenschaftliche Buchgesellschaft, 1995), 1–26.

[19] Cf. J. Frey, *Die eschatologische Verkündigung in den johanneischen Texten* (vol. 3 of *Die johanneische Eschatologie;* WUNT 117; Tübingen: Mohr Siebeck, 2000), 3–4.

[20] Cf. ibid., 4.

[21] M. Sato, "Wisdom Statements in the Sphere of Prophecy," in *The Gospels behind the Gospels: Current Studies on Q* (ed. R. A. Piper; NovTSup 75; Leiden: Brill, 1995), 139–58, esp. 147, stresses the correspondence of present eschatology and futuristic eschatology, but his statement that this fact was "generally acknowledged" can only be regarded as a rhetorical remark rather than a description of recent research. Cf. also C. M. Tuckett, *Q and the History of Early Christianity: Studies on Q* (Peabody, Mass.: Hendrickson, 1996), 139. See also the mediating position of D. Zeller, "Der Zusammenhang der Eschatologie in der Logienquelle," in *Gegenwart und kommendes Reich: Schülergabe Anton Vögtle zum 65. Geburtstag* (ed. P. Ziegler and D. Zeller; Stuttgart: Katholisches Bibelwerk, 1975), 67–77, who focuses on three ways of interpreting eschatology: expectation of future judgment, imminent apocalyptic expectation, and present eschatology.

[22] Thus I disagree with Joel Marcus's theory that the preaching of Jesus can be divided into two phases characterized by different kinds of eschatology, the change taking place at a certain point in Jesus' life. See J. Marcus, "The Beelezebul Controversy and the Eschatologies of Jesus," in *Authenticating the Activities of Jesus* (ed. B. D. Chilton and C. A.

One particular saying of Jesus and its reception in Q is to be stressd here which indicates that the present time is the time of fulfillment of eschatological hopes: Jesus' answer to John the Baptist, Q 7:22–23. The saying points to the present as the time of fulfillment of OT predictions by combining different texts from the book of Isaiah (Isa 26:18–9; 35:5–6; 61:1). For illustrating the present eschatology in Q 7:22 a significant parallel in Qumran should to be mentioned: the *Messianic Apocalypse* (4Q521), which presents a combination of various elements of salvific expectations originally also belonging to the book of Isaiah. The thesis here is as follows: *By taking up words from the historical-Jesus tradition, the Sayings Gospel combines (1) the knowledge of the closeness of eschatological salvation by God in Jesus, which is continued in the Q group's own life and proclamation, and (2) the expectation of the cosmological realization of this salvation through the final judgment by the coming Son of Man; this expectation is still alive, facing the refusal of the community's own preaching of salvation, or—it may be—is newly awakened by facing the devastating experience of the Jewish War against the Romans.*[23]

Jesus' Answer to the Baptist's Question, Q 7:18–23: An Expression of Fulfilled Hope of Salvation and a Serious Warning

A Play of Question and Answer

Reception of Q and Reader Directive in the Synoptic Gospels

The episode of the Baptist's question and Jesus' answer is part of a larger paragraph (Matt 11:2–19; Luke 7:18–35) dealing with different aspects of the relationship between John the Baptist and Jesus:

In the Gospel of Matthew, the episode of John the Baptist follows the missionary instruction, after a short summary narrating Jesus' new teaching and preaching in "their cities" (Matt 11:1). The catchword "cities" is taken up again in v. 20, where the cities become witnesses for Jesus' miracles (cf. v. 2) but punishment is announced because of their refusal of the Savior.[24] The woe in v. 21 presents an interpretation of v. 6: those who deny repentance and refuse Jesus, although they have witnessed his deeds, judge themselves as offending Jesus and will bring final judgment onto themselves. The gospel did not allude to the names of the two cities, Chorazin and Bethsaida, earlier, but Matthew takes them over from Q (cf. Q 10:13–15) and integrates them into the immediate

---

Evans; NTTS 28/2; Boston: Brill, 1999), 247–77. According to Marcus, the change took place at Jesus' baptism (Mark 1:9–11 par.) and his vision of Satan's fall (Luke 10:18); cf. J. Marcus, "Jesus' Baptismal Vision," *NTS* 41 (1995): 512–21.

[23] P. Hoffmann, "QR und der Menschensohn: Eine vorläufige Skizze," in *Tradition und Situation: Studien zur Jesusüberlieferung in der Logienquelle und den synoptischen Evangelien* (NTAbh NF 28; Münster: Aschendorff, 1995), 243–78.

[24] Cf. U. Luz, *Das Evangelium nach Matthäus* (4 vols.; 3d ed.; EKKNT 1; Zürich: Benzinger, 1985–2002), 2:162.

context in his gospel.[25] When the Baptist refers to the works of the Messiah (ἔργα τοῦ Χριστοῦ, Matt 11:2), Matthew alludes, at first glance, to the speech given by Jesus in Matthew 10. The link in the context, however, reaches back still further. The reader of Matthew already knows the miracles alluded to in Matt 11:5 from two previous chapters dealing with miracles, Matthew 8–9. A further link can be drawn to the proclamation of the Sermon on the Mount.[26] Thus the Gospel of Matthew presents a clear narrative christological link within its literary structure.

The pericope from Q is also woven into the entire narrative context of the Gospel of Luke but in a slightly different way. The question of the Baptist concerning the coming one is not directly answered by Jesus. The relatively open answer of Jesus raises for Luke a christological problem that he solves twice. As a first literary key, Luke prepares the following scene by means of a narrator's commentary that replays the question of the Baptist's envoys (Luke 7:20).[27] The omniscient narrator adds a reference to Jesus' deeds seen by the Baptist's disciples: "Jesus had just then cured many people of diseases, plagues, and evil spirits, and had given sight to many who were blind" (v. 21 NRSV). Besides this redundant introduction to v. 22 by the narrator, the overall narrative context provides a further christological hint for the implied reader. Luke does not need to mention the resurrection of the dead in v. 21 because he has already reported the raising of the widow's son (vv. 10–17). Therefore the narrator claims that Jesus has performed different healings (cf. also the healings already reported in chs. 4–6) when Jesus is asked by the disciples of John, although the content of the list in v. 22 does not completely agree with the reported miracles in the list. Nevertheless, there is

---

[25] It was probably Matthew who changed the order of the pericopes from that in Q, which presented the vow oracles, Q 10:13–15, after the response to a town's rejection, Q 10:10–2; cf. e.g., W. D. Davies and D. C. Allison, *A Critical and Exegetical Commentary of the Gospel according to Saint Matthew* (3 vols.; ICC; Edinburgh: T&T Clark, 1988–1997), 2:236–37.

[26] J. Gnilka, *Das Matthäusevangelium* (2 vols.; HTKNT 1; Freiburg: Herder, 1986), 1:406; Luz, *Matthäus* 2:162; J. M. Robinson, "The Sayings Gospel Q," in *The Four Gospels* (ed. F. Van Segbroeck, C. M. Tuckett, G. van Belle, and J. Verheyden; FS F. Neirynck; BETL 100; Leuven: Leuven University Press, 1992), 362–88, 364–65. According to Davies and Allison, *Matthew,* 2:240, "works of Christ" alludes also to the Sermon on the Mount and therefore contains at least a hint of all the deeds and preaching reported in Matt 4:23–11:2 (see also Luz, *Matthäus,* 2:167). The fact that the Baptist queried Jesus from prison, which is noticed in Matt 4:12, supports his view (cf., e.g., Gnilka, *Matthäusevangelium,* 1:405; Luz, *Matthäus,* 2:164).

[27] One can easily recognize Lukan compositional technique in the elaboration of the story with the motif of legation and in the typical Lukan style and language; cf. J. Jeremias, *Die Sprache des Lukasevangeliums: Redaktion und Tradition im Nicht-Markusstoff des dritten Evangeliums* (KEK: Sonderband; Göttingen: Vandenhoeck & Ruprecht, 1980), 161–62; see also, e.g., K. Backhaus, *Die "Jüngerkreise" des Täufers Johannes: Eine Studie zu den religionsgeschichtlichen Ursprüngen des Christentums* (Paderborner theologische Studien 19; Paderborn: Schöningh, 1991), 116; J. A. Fitzmyer, *The Gospel according to Luke* (2 vols.; AB 28, 28A; Garden City, N.Y.: Doubleday, 1981), 1:667; J. Nolland, *Luke 1–9:20* (WBC 35A; Dallas: Word, 1989), 329–30.

some historical determination of the following indirect answer of Jesus; by pointing to the fulfillment of eschatological expectations by Jesus' deeds, the narrator by implication leads the reader to the decision that Jesus is to be identified with the coming one. This option presupposes, however, that the reader shares the same cultural code and the same horizon of eschatological hopes with the narrator. The narrative context impresses on Jesus' answer an explicit christological trait. With this feature the narrator surpasses the Jewish cultural code, for the "coming one" is not a classical Jewish messianic title[28] and Jewish eschatology does not expect miracles to be performed by the Messiah.[29] Therefore Christian messianic interpretation is presupposed here. The proclamation of good news leads back behind the actual narrative context and points toward the Lukan Sermon on the Plain (6:20) or even to Luke's account of Jesus' inaugural preaching in 4:14–30 with the citation of Isa 61:1–2 in Luke 4:18. The Lukan story of the Baptist's question refers back to 6:20–7:17 or even to the overall narrative in 4:14–7:17.

Besides a few minor overlaps with the Gospel of Mark, only Matthew and Luke report the passage on John and Jesus, and the texts of both gospels have most of the words in common, so that these pericopes can be traced back to Q.[30]

Salvation and Judgment—the Interpretation of the Baptist's Expectation in Q

In the reconstruction of Q, some questions arise concerning the original narrative context of Q 7:18–23 and concerning stratigraphy. What is the literary relationship of the Baptist's question to the story of the healing of the centurion's son/slave? Do the passages on John and Jesus form an original unity or present a later collection of separate traditions?[31] Or are they perhaps a later addition to an earlier layer of Q,[32] or is the figure of the Baptist an original part of the earliest stratum of Q, so that only some later supplements may be identified? Without

---

[28] Cf., e.g., F. Hahn, *Christologische Hoheitstitel: Ihre Geschichte im frühen Christentum* (3d ed.; FRLANT 83; Göttingen: Vandenhoeck & Ruprecht, 1966), 393. Differently Nolland, *Luke*, 328–29, who reports a variety of explanations and claims that "the use of the term is a means of bringing to expression in a nonspecific manner the essence of all Jewish eschatological hope."

[29] Cf., e.g., M. Karrer, *Der Gesalbte: Die Grundlagen des Messiastitels* (FRLANT 151; Göttingen: Vandenhoeck & Ruprecht, 1990), 272 n. 179, 323.

[30] Cf. J. S. Kloppenborg, *Q Parallels: Synopsis, Critical Notes, and Concordance* (FF Reference Series; Sonoma, Calif.: Polebridge, 1988), 52.

[31] E.g., M. Dibelius, *Die urchristliche Überlieferung von Johannes dem Täufer* (FRLANT 15; Göttingen: Vandenhoeck & Ruprecht, 1911), 6–8; J. Ernst, *Johannes der Täufer: Interpretation–Geschichte–Wirkungsgeschichte* (BZNW 53; New York: de Gruyter, 1989), 55; Kloppenborg, *Formation of Q,* 115: "variety of traditions and layers of tradition"; Tuckett, *Q and the History of Early Christianity,* 126.

[32] Cf., e.g., Kloppenborg, *Formation of Q,* 166–70: Q²; W. Cotter, " 'Yes, I Tell You, and More Than a Prophet': The Function of John in Q," in *Conflict and Invention: Literary, Rhetorical, and Social Studies on the Sayings Gospel Q* (ed. J. S. Kloppenborg; Valley Forge, Pa.: Trinity Press International, 1995), 135–50, here 135.

giving a detailed answer to all these questions, it is evident that there is a serious composition of texts dealing with John the Baptist in the reconstructed text of Q. Our analysis will use two methodological approaches. First is a synchronic analysis of the composition of the final Q document.[33] Later a diachronic interpretation will lead us back to the historical Jesus and to his preaching.

The reference to the coming one in the question of John in Q takes up eschatological expectations from the Baptist's own proclamation of the final judgment (cf. Q 3:16b:[34] "the one to come after me is more powerful than I").[35] There is, however, some change in perspective. Jesus' reply does not form a direct answer to the question of the Baptist. The Baptist expects final judgment[36]—this identification of John's expectation remains true regardless of the much disputed question whether the Baptist awaits judgment by an agent of God[37] or, more probably, by God himself.[38] Jesus provides an indefinite answer.[39] This seems to be a rhetorical signal, as whether Jesus is the coming one cannot be answered by a clear yes or no.[40] In contrast to the expectation of the coming judge, present time

---

[33] According to my point of view, Q 7:18–23 belongs to the earliest part of Q. I cannot find any compelling reason to regard all of the tradition on the Baptist as later additions to Q.

[34] Unless otherwise mentioned, I follow the reconstruction by J. M. Robinson, P. Hoffmann, and J. S. Kloppenborg, eds., *The Critical Edition of Q: Synopsis Including the Gospels of Matthew and Luke, Mark and Thomas with English, German, and French Translations of Q and Thomas* (Hermeneia; Minneapolis: Fortress, 2000). The translations in this article are also taken from this critical edition.

[35] Cf. D. C. Allison, *The Intertextual Jesus: Scripture in Q* (Harrisburg, Pa.: Trinity Press International, 2000), 109; Backhaus, *Jüngerkreise*, 120; Kloppenborg, *Formation of Q*, 94; idem, *Excavating Q*, 66–67, 122; Sevenich-Bax, *Konfrontation*, 324.

[36] Cf., e.g., W. Zager, *Gottesherrschaft und Endgericht in der Verkündigung Jesu: Eine Untersuchung zur markinischen Jesusüberlieferung einschließlich der Q-Parallelen* (BZNW 82; Berlin: de Gruyter, 1996), 114–36.

[37] Cf. R. L. Webb, *John the Baptizer and Prophet: A Socio-historical Study* (JSNTSup 62; Sheffield, England: Sheffield Academic Press, 1991), 261–306, who differentiates two levels, a "celestial/theological level," referring to God, and a "terrestrial/historical level," alluding to God's judgment done "by Yahweh's agent" (304). G. Theissen and A. Merz, *Der historische Jesus: Ein Lehrbuch* (Göttingen: Vandenhoeck & Ruprecht, 1996), 189–90, agree with this position. J. C. O'Neill, *Messiah: Six Lectures on the Ministry of Jesus* (Cambridge, England: Cochrane, 1980), 2–3, points out that the Baptist names Jesus the coming one, for which reason he identifies Jesus with God.

[38] Cf., e.g., Backhaus, *Jüngerkreise*, 319; Ernst, *Johannes*, 48–55; M. Reiser, *Die Gerichtspredigt Jesu: Eine Untersuchung zur eschatologischen Verkündigung Jesu und ihrem frühjüdischen Hintergrund* (NTAbh NF 23; Münster: Aschendorff, 1990), 171–72; M. Tilly, *Johannes der Täufer und die Biographie der Propheten: Die synoptische Täuferüberlieferung und das jüdische Prophetenbild zur Zeit des Täufers* (BWA[N]T 137; Stuttgart: Kohlhammer, 1994), 42, 77; Zager, *Gottesherrschaft*, 134–36.

[39] A clear positive christological determination of Jesus' answer is just given by the narrative links in both Gospels (see section immediately above this, "Reception of Q and Reader Directive in the Synoptic Gospels"); cf. Tilly, *Johannes*, 85.

[40] I take up observations presented by Cotter, "More Than a Prophet," 140–42, stressing different points. See also, with different exegetical arguments and pleas, J. I. H. McDonald, "Questioning and Discernment in Gospel Discourse: Communicative Strategy

is characterized by deeds of divine salvation. We may leave the question open whether Q shares the same christological aim as the gospels of Matthew and Luke. Q 7:1–10 alone narrates a miracle—the healing of the Roman centurion's slave—that can only by force be included in the catalogue of end-time signs hinting at salvation in Q 7:22.[41] Although this observation may not point to a missing interest of Q in the miracles of Jesus,[42] it marks a strong difference to the literary compositions of Matthew and Luke. Therefore it seems probable that Q is more concerned with the last part of the catalogue in Q 7:22, the proclamation of the gospel to the poor.[43] On the intratextual level, this kind of preaching has been fulfilled by Jesus' beatitude of the poor in 6:20.[44] When Jesus calls the poor people blessed, he reinterprets their specific social status in the light of the kingdom of God. By calling the poor blessed, Jesus proclaims that God's salvation does already form a reality in their present life. They already belong to the arriving kingdom, and therefore salvation is already present. Both Jesus and Q share the same concept of the presence of salvation; we can find this eschatological conception in other parts of Q as well.

Nevertheless, there is a difference between Jesus and Q in understanding what is meant by the term "poor" (πτωχοί). In the proclamation of Jesus, it forms a social characterization for economically poor people. Within the narrative of Q, this term points toward the sociological identity of the Q group. The beatitudes that start with blessing the poor in Q take aim at the communities' own situation; cf. Q 6:22–23, which is related to people who are persecuted in the name of Christ.[45]

With the double perspective in adjusting and accepting the proclamation of the Baptist, the narrator does not establish a polemic purpose against a group

---

in Matthew 11:2–19," in *Authenticating the Words of Jesus* (ed. B. D. Chilton and C. A. Evans; NTTS 28/1; Boston: Brill, 1999), 333–61, 344: "John's disciples and, indeed, John himself, are not given a direct or 'assertive' answer by Jesus but inducted by questioning into an interpretative and discerning frame of mind." Sevenich-Bax (*Konfrontation*, 325–26) identifies a rhetorical question applied to affirmation.

[41] Contrary to Robinson, "Sayings Gospel," 365: "Q 7,22 thus serves to define Jesus' Inaugural Sermon and his Healing of the Centurion's Boy as validating the ascription to him of the title ὁ ἐρχόμενος." But the second miracle, an exorcism, which is presented in Q 11:14–23, stands also in tension with the catalogue of salvation in Q 7:22. This fact calls for the assumption of tradition in v. 22.

[42] Cf. Hüneburg, *Jesus*.

[43] Contrary to Allison, *Jesus*, 111, who regards Q 7:22 as an extratextual reference. Christian tradition knew that Jesus had performed the reported miracles. This knowledge is not, however, stressed in Q, unlike Matthew and Luke; this circumstance leads us to interpret Q predominately on the level of the Q text itself, which can be successfully done with the reference in Q 6:20.

[44] Cf. Sevenich-Bax, *Konfrontation*, 324.

[45] Robinson, "Sayings Gospel," 366–68. Robinson considers the term πτωχοί to be self-identification of the early Christian community. Further, it may be assumed that the term "the poor" is not exclusively an honorary designation of the community of Jerusalem (so Gal 2:10; Rom 15:26).

of followers of John the Baptist.[46] The figures of the narrative world serve the narrator's purpose to reflect historical events and to provoke an awareness for current problems.[47] Correction and acceptance of already narrated events and of questions and answers of narrative figures try to reinterpret and to broaden the understanding of the text-external readers—perhaps in a dialogue with their own christological conceptions:[48] Jesus is the coming one, for God is present in Jesus, who has come by performing saving deeds (v. 22). At the same time, he is the one to come, who secures the boundaries of the group, for he will return to judge people's behavior toward the preachers of Jesus (v. 23). Therefore there are some social implications in the tension between knowledge of salvation and hope in the final realization of the expectation. Endangered by people outside the group, the community itself is strengthened knowing that the group provides a sphere of eschatological salvation that separates the members of the group from outsiders who do not share their belief. Socio-rhetorical interpretation has pointed to the sociological aims of eschatological matters. These aspects, however, present only one element within the interpretation of the entire eschatological phenomenon, to which christological and theological implications need also to be attached.

Experience of Salvation by Jesus and by the Agents of Q in Dispute

Q 7:22 does not stand alone with its portrait of salvation in Q. The Beatitudes in Q are not pointing into a far future, announcing only a radical change. On the contrary, they affirm present salvation. The present tense ἐστιν, which many exegetes interpret to have a future sense,[49] has to be taken seriously as a new classification of the addressees.[50] With the statement of a new reality in the beatitude, an eschatological reinterpretation of the addressees has taken place.

The rhetorical pragmatism of the Beatitudes differs from the Cynic parallels. The reality of simple life, of poverty, is called "blessed" in the light of a new perception of the presence of the kingdom of God. This new perception of its presence does not propagate a new ethos. Moreover the Beatitudes proclaim a

---

[46] Cf., e.g., R. Bultmann, *Die Geschichte der synoptischen Tradition* (9th ed.; FRLANT 29; Göttingen: Vandenhoeck & Ruprecht, 1979), 22. See also P. Stuhlmacher, *Das paulinische Evangelium, I: Vorgeschichte* (FRLANT 95; Göttingen: Vandenhoeck & Ruprecht, 1968), 219–21; D. R. Catchpole, *The Quest for Q* (Edinburgh: T&T Clark, 1993), 240. The polemical interpretation is seriously criticized by Backhaus, *Jüngerkreise*, 127–34.

[47] With another exegetical aim argues Tilly (*Johannes*, 87), who calls the Baptist an ideal questioner.

[48] Cf., e.g., P. Hoffmann, *Studien zur Theologie der Logienquelle* (NTAbh NF 28; Münster: Aschendorff, 1972), 215.

[49] Cf. Tuckett, *Q and the History of Early Christianity*, 141 with n. 9 (literature).

[50] According to Leif E. Vaage, the Beatitudes aim at the present audience so that the presence of the kingdom is realized by a Cynic lifestyle: "Ethical discourse is in its own right a second-order reflection on the embodied understanding of existence realized in the social practice of a group" ("Q and Cynicism: On Comparison and Social Identity," in *The Gospels behind the Gospels: Current Studies on Q* [ed. R. A. Piper; NovTSup 75; Leiden: Brill, 1995], 199–229, here 220). Vaage ("Monarchy," 61) refers to Pseudo-Crates (of Thebes), *Ep.* 11 and 18, as a parallel.

new reality resulting from God's recent activity. The new interpretation of the presence of the kingdom does not actually change the specific social misery. There is, however, also a change of social status from the inner perspective of the marginalized person: it is affirmed that the poor are not poor in the view of God's kingdom, and this message also changes the self-perception of the addressees so that it also causes a change of social reality.

There are some further texts in Q illustrating the presence of salvation. According to Q 10:9, the messengers of the mission instruction (Matt 9:35–11:1) perform healings, which can be seen in the light of Q 7:22.[51] The arrival of the kingdom of God or perhaps the kingdom itself is executed by their healings.[52] By the performance of healings, the presence of the kingdom is visible and effective,[53] although the kingdom cannot be completely identified with these deeds. Like Q 11:20,[54] the saying in 10:9 underlines the effective proximity of the kingdom. The messengers are linked with the eschatological claim and the refusal of Jesus (10:13).[55] There is still a remarkable difference between their activity and that of Jesus, for the work of the messengers is not combined with the christological claim of the Baptist's quest—Jesus' messengers are not asked to be the "coming ones."

The Lord's Prayer (Q 11:2b–4), which can be read in the light of the yearning for the arrival of the kingdom (11:2b), is continued in 11:9–13 with sapiential argumentation which intends to characterize the certitude with which the Q group prays to the Lord.[56] That God turns toward the pious petitioner is a well-known motif and part of his care for the world. A special motivation of recent hope for God's attention lies, however, in the expectation of the arriving kingdom. Similarly 12:22–31,[57] with its call to seek God's kingdom first and the warning not to be concerned with one's own life, is more than just a sapientially founded remark of a deep trust in God. Rather, 12:31 combines confidence in God's provision of everyday necessities with one's own search for God's kingdom: which is an answer to God's invitation into his

---

[51] Cf., e.g., Zeller, "Zusammenhang," 72.

[52] The call to heal (θεραπεύετε) combines healings and exorcisms; cf. B. Kollmann, *Jesus und die Christen als Wundertäter: Studien zu Magie, Medizin, und Schamanismus in Antike und Christentum* (FRLANT 170; Göttingen: Vandenhoeck & Ruprecht, 1996), 317.

[53] H. Weder, *Gegenart und Gottesherrschaft: Überlegungen zum Zeitverständnis bei Jesus und in frühen Christentum* (BTS 20; Neukirchen-Vluyn: Neukirchener Verlag, 1993), 49: "In den Heilungen reicht die Gottesherrschaft bis in die Häuser Galiläas".

[54] Cf. M. Labahn, "Jesu Exorzismen (Q 11,19f) und die Erkenntnis der ägyptischen Magier (Ex 8,15): Q 11,20 als bewahrtes Beispiel für Schrift-Rezeption Jesu nach der Logienquelle," in *The Sayings Source Q and the Historical Jesus* (ed. A. Lindemann; BETL 158; Leuven: Peeters, 2001), 617–33, esp. 621–23.

[55] Cf. Zeller, "Zusammenhang," 72.

[56] Cf. Ebner, *Jesus*, 311–15.

[57] Vaage, "Monarchy," 66, claims again Cynic texts to be the nearest parallels: Dio Chrysostom, *Or.* 10.15–16; 6.31–34. The Cynic parallels, however, propagate the liberation of oneself from depending on material matters, pointing to analogies from nature.

kingdom. God's salvation is present in the community that has entered the kingdom, to the degree that they accept the authority of the proclamation of God's kingdom.

Therefore, the composition of Q, which combines the Baptist's question and Jesus' reply, contains a double eschatological orientation, as do other passages in Q. Present time is marked by the presence of eschatological salvation—a salvation that is already perceptible in the present by those who are guided by the proclamation of Jesus and his followers. At the same time, a reaction of the addressees is expected corresponding to their awareness of the presence of salvation in the present time. Whoever takes offence at Jesus and rejects this reinterpretation of present time will be indicted in the judgment at the return of the Son of Man. According to Q, the warning is not a potential one; it is a distressing reality for "this generation" (cf. Q 7:31; 11:29–32, 51). "This generation" refuses the offer of salvation presented by Jesus and now mediated by the Q messengers, and the Q document hints at repression suffered by members of the Q group (e.g., 6:22–23; 12:4, 11–12). On the final literary level, 7:23 functions as a literary-sociological link. On the negative side, 7:23 is directed against "this generation,"[58] which takes offence at Jesus, and reacts to its attitude with the motif of judgment (cf. 11:30–32, 50–51). On the positive side, the beatitude strengthens the group, which acknowledges itself to be safe and secure in the light of the promise of salvation; such a view is comparable to that of the pious, to whom the promises of salvation in the *Messianic Apocalypse* (4Q521) are addressed (cf. below). Still, the eschatological gifts of salvation are not expected to come in the future, as in the Qumran texts. Rather the present community is the locale where eschatological salvation becomes real. The beatitude pushes the members of the Q group to stay within the community as the sphere of salvation.

The expectations of the final judgment are closely connected with the expectation of the final realization of salvation: the same salvation that is already present within the preaching and the deeds of Jesus and in those of his followers will ultimately be established universally.

The Message of the Pre-texts: Jesus' Answers, Q 7:22, 23

On the one hand, Q 7:18–23 forms a rhetorical and pragmatic unit in its literary context.[59] On the other hand, we can find literary seams and traits of reworking, so that we may have to reckon with both traditions and later additions as well.[60] Q 7:18–23 presupposes a complicated prehistory, and the original

---

[58] Cf. Sevenich-Bax, *Konfrontation,* 331.

[59] Cf., e.g., R. Cameron, " 'What Have You Come Out to See?' Characterizations of John and Jesus in the Gospels," *Semeia* 49 (1990): 35–70, regarding Q 7:18–35 as an entire unit in accordance with the ancient *chreia.*

[60] Differently, e.g., Backhaus, *Jüngerkreise,* 118–19 (cf. the authors mentioned in 118 n. 19); Kloppenborg, *Formation of Q,* 107, who pleads for a literary unity and traces the pericope back to the early Christian community.

connection between the Baptist's quest and 7:22 is doubtful[61] because his quest is for a person and the answer deals with events of the present, not with any particular person. The Baptist's quest is carefully connected with the Baptist's portrait in Q and belongs stratigraphically to the context of Q's composition dealing with John the Baptist. Aside from its last part, Jesus' answer shows no specific affinity to other Q passages. The command to hear and to see receives a narrative supplementation from the narrators of the gospels, especially from Luke. There is no such narrative elaboration in Q, and therefore the command seems not to be part of Baptist-*plot*, to which it is connected in the reconstructed Q text.[62] Furthermore, Q 7:23 and 7:22 were probably not connected before the composition of Q;[63] on the other hand, we have already mentioned that Luke 7:20–21 and probably 7:18 originate, to a large extent, from the hand of Luke's composition.

Because the question of the Baptist that frames the present narrative originally belonged to the plot of the Q document, our interest in the analysis of the pre-texts is especially concerned with the saying of Jesus in Q 7:22. Jesus' remark does not contain any explicit messianic claim;[64] it connects, at best, indirectly the mentioned eschatological events with Jesus' own work, in that his own preaching and his own deeds are part of the eschatological events[65] in which God acts.[66]

Surprisingly, the catalogue of Q 7:22 does not mention exorcisms. They are listed in Matt 10:8—an instruction to the disciples that is somewhat parallel to Q 7:22. Hints at Jesus' exorcisms can be found in nearly every layer of early Christian Jesus tradition, from the pre-Markan tradition through a pre-Q tradition

---

[61] Cf., e.g., H.-W. Kuhn, *Enderwartung und gegenwärtiges Heil: Untersuchungen zu den Gemeindelieder von Qumran mit einem Anhang über Eschatologie und Gegenwart in der Verkündigung Jesu* (SUNT 4; Göttingen: Vandenhoeck & Ruprecht, 1966), 195–96 with n. 5; Tuckett, *Q and the History of Early Christianity*, 126. The Baptist's quest and Jesus' reply, together with the beatitude, are regarded as a historical tradition, e.g., by Davies and Allison, *Matthew*, 2:244–46; J. D. G. Dunn, *Jesus and the Spirit: A Study of the Religious and Charismatic Experience of Jesus and the First Christians as Reflected in the New Testament* (NTL; London: SCM, 1975), 56–60; W. G. Kümmel, "Jesu Antwort an Johannes den Täufer: Ein Beispiel zum Methodenproblem in der Jesusforschung," in G. Kümmel, *Heilsgeschehen und Geschichte: Gesammelte Aufsätze, 1965–1977* (2 vols.; vol. 2, ed. E. Grässer and O. Merk; Marburger theologische Studien 16; Marburg: Elwert, 1965–1978), 2:177–200, esp. 195–200; McDonald, "Questioning," 349–50; Nolland, *Luke*, 326–27; F. Mussner, "Der 'historische' Jesus," in F. Mussner, *Jesus von Nazareth im Umfeld Israels und der Urkirche: Gesammelte Aufsätze* (ed. M. Theobald; Tübingen: Mohr Siebeck, 1999), 43–61, 49; "War Jesus von Nazareth für Israel erkennbar?" in ibid., 116–34, esp. 120; Webb, *John*, 281–82. This is taken into account by Luz, *Matthäus*, 2:166.

[62] Differently F. Neirynck, "Q 6,20b–21; 7,22 and Isaiah 61," in *The Scriptures in the Gospels* (ed. C. M. Tuckett; BETL 131; Leuven: Peeters, 1997), 27–64, 61–62: only the catalogue, "a description of the time of salvation," forms a separate tradition.

[63] Cf. F. Bovon, *Das Evangelium nach Lukas* (3 vols.; EKKNT 3; Zürich: Benzinger, 1989), 1:370. Differently, e.g., Hoffmann, *Studien*, 202–4; Kuhn, *Enderwartung*, 196.

[64] Cf. Theissen and Merz, *Jesus*, 272.

[65] Ibid., 197.

[66] Cf. J. Becker, *Jesus von Nazaret* (de Gruyter Lehrbuch; New York: de Gruyter, 1996), 138–39.

(Q 11:14–23) to the Gospels in narrative texts as well as in various discourses. Therefore the lack of exorcisms is indeed striking and difficult to explain if Q 7:22 were an early Christian formulation;[67] this is so even though we have an example of a Jesus narrative without exorcisms in the Gospel of John dating several decades later.[68]

Because of the lack of direct christological claims, it may be assumed that Q 7:22 can be ascribed to the historical Jesus. The assumption is supported by a high "plausibility of context." Q 7:22 expresses Jesus' claim that the kingdom is effectively near, within present time. This claim is expressed with Isaian terminology that appears in the Synoptic Gospels significantly often in the sayings of Jesus.[69] The narrators of the written documents express a christological interpretation of the catalogue by means of their narrative context; Q by forming the Baptist's quest, the gospels of Matthew and Luke by narrating miracles in the entire literary context and including clear signals to guide the reader. Nevertheless, there is some uncertainty in bridging the gap between oral Jesus traditions and written gospel texts.[70] The transformation of tradition into the Greek language may have caused some friction, perhaps influenced by the language of the LXX.[71] Still, in any attempt to reconstruct the teaching of the historical Jesus, Q 7:22 ought to be included.

Q 7:22: Eschatological Salvation

Jesus does not directly answer the question of the Baptist but simply alludes to the events that happen in his public ministry: "Go report to John what you hear and see."[72] The events that the Baptist and his envoy see (and hear) form, in the narrative context of Q (and further elaborated in the gospels of Matthew and

---

[67] Cf. Kümmel, "Antwort," 198.

[68] Cf. M. Labahn, *Jesus als Lebensspender: Untersuchungen zu einer Geschichte der johanneischen Tradition anhand ihrer Wundergeschichten* (BZNW 98; New York: de Gruyter, 1999), 483–84. For a recent exploration of the problem, cf. R. A. Piper, "Satan, Demons, and the Absence of Exorcisms in the Fourth Gospel," in *Christology, Controversy, and Community: New Testament Essays in Honour of D. R. Catchpole* (ed. D. G. Horrell and C. M. Tuckett; NovTSup 99; Leiden: Brill, 2000), 253–78.

[69] Cf. the survey by C. A. Evans, "From Gospel to Gospel: The Function of Isaiah in the New Testament," in *Writing and Reading the Scroll of Isaiah: Studies of an Interpretative Tradition* (ed. C. C. Broyles and C. A. Evans; 2 vols.; VTSup 70, Formation and Interpretation of Old Testament Literature 1; Leiden: Brill, 1997), 2:651–91, esp. 667–74.

[70] On the problem of continuity and discontinuity in oral tradition, cf. Labahn, *Jesus*, 89–99.

[71] This is an important criterion for criticizing the authenticity of the saying Q 7:22: A. Vögtle, "Wunder und Wort in urchristlicher Glaubenswerbung (Mt 11,2–5 / Lk 7,18–23)," in *Das Evangelium und die Evangelien* (KBANT; Düsseldorf: Patmos, 1971), 219–42, here 238; Kloppenborg, *Formation of Q*, 108. It is not evident that the LXX actually influenced the Greek version of Q 7:22. The Greek of the LXX is not significantly different from the Hebrew text; cf. J. Becker, *Johannes der Täufer und Jesus von Nazareth* (BibS[N] 63; Neukirchen-Vluyn: Neukirchener Verlag, 1972), 84.

[72] The Matthean sequence seems to be original, as the Lukan order fits the general Lukan tendency to place doing before hearing; cf. Bovon, *Lukas*, 1:369.

Luke), the answer to the question. Within the two gospels, the announced events are identified with the words and deeds of Jesus, and in Q especially with Jesus' words (Q 6:20). It is not the aim of Jesus' words, however, to propose that the Baptist's disciples follow Jesus to see what he is doing—as it is implied in the received Lukan narrative. Jesus' call to see and to hear is a strong rhetorical invitation to perceive the present reality through the eyes of the speaker. The second part of Jesus' reply reveals his interpretation of the present reality, which he wants to share with his audience: recent time is a time in which eschatological events already begin to take place.

It is difficult, however, to identify the original addressees of Jesus' rhetorical command. They may be found among the Galilean audience of Jesus' proclamation and may be connected with the critical questions of people who asked where the kingdom of God proclaimed in Jesus' parables was visible and at work.

According to Jesus' argumentation, these events characterize the present as an eschatological time. This means for the narrators, who connect this remark with the Baptist's quest, that Jesus identifies himself with the coming one.[73] Jesus himself, however, has not exclusively identified the miracles and the proclamation of the end time with his own activity.[74] It is thus affirmatively stated that the miracles of the end time already happen during the time of Jesus' preaching. The claim presupposes two different assumptions of Jesus' preaching activity: (1) his awareness of working in the time of God's arriving kingdom and (2) his own activity as God's tool and therefore his performance of God's miracles of the end time (cf. Q 11:20).

Q 11:19–20 varies this picture by regarding Jesus' exorcisms as hints of God's rising kingdom; Jesus is God's tool by exorcizing with the "finger of God." Nevertheless, Jesus' exorcisms are not unique insofar as the in-breaking kingdom not only is present in his own exorcisms but also occurs in the exorcisms of the Jewish exorcists who also act as tools of God for the arrival of the kingdom.[75] This interpretation can be drawn from the apodosis of the second εἰ sentence in Q 11:20.[76]

Within the semantic world of the proclamation of Jesus, however, this saying belongs to the words that describe the kingdom of God as a kingdom that arrives and has already been realized where its salvation takes place or is proclaimed. In the presence of Jesus' preaching, eschatological salvation is realized

---

[73] E.g., D. J. Harrington, *The Gospel of Matthew* (SP 1; Collegeville, Minn.: Liturgical Press, 1991), 160.

[74] Differently, e.g., B. F. Meyer, "Appointed Deed, Appointed Doer: Jesus and the Scriptures," in *Authenticating the Activities of Jesus* (ed. B. D. Chilton and C. A. Evans; NTTS 28/2; Boston: Brill, 1999), 155–76, esp. 159: "Jesus is saying that his own public activity in Israel must be read as the superabundant fulfillment of eschatological promises."

[75] The objection of E. P. Sanders, *Jesus and Judaism* (3d ed.; Philadelphia: Fortress, 1987), 137–41, against ascribing this saying to the historical Jesus as he is not the only and exclusive miracle worker in his surroundings, fails to see that Q 7:22 does not express a direct and exclusive messianic claim.

[76] Cf. Labahn, "Jesu Exorzismen," 621–22.

by God. The miracles and the proclamation in present time establish the reality of salvation definitely establishing God's peace on earth. Indeed, the hint at the raising of the dead illuminates the present in the light of the coming end of history because the fact of the raising of the dead makes God's final intervention significantly visible. The remark does not necessarily indicate that it depends on the well-known resurrection narratives of Jesus.[77] This part of the catalogue may form a utopian element in Jesus' expectation. Perhaps we find here the seed for Jesus' expectation that is expressed in his so-called saying of the cup (cf. Mark 14:25 par.). Because the kingdom of God is arriving, resurrection of the dead by God will happen immediately so that people may be asked to open their eyes to see.

God's kingdom appears within the current events; the kingdom with its salvation reaches into the present and gives a new face to it. It is not connected exclusively with Jesus' own deeds; rather, Jesus interprets the events in his circumstances anew and appeals to his audience to join his interpretation.

Q 7:23: Blessed Is the One Who Recognizes the Signs of the Time before It Is Too Late

In its literary context Q 7:23 serves an apologetic purpose that may be a part of the Q-plot criticizing the attitude of "this generation" toward Jesus. It is by no means certain, however, that the saying is a late formulation and was invented by the narrator of Q. Jesus does not introduce himself as the subject of eschatological events. Still, the circumstances of the arriving kingdom happen during his proclamation, and he is himself a tool of God, through which God establishes his reign. This is a fundamental presupposition for the beatitude about those who do not take offense in the teaching of Jesus. The content of the beatitude can be seen in the proclaimed presence of salvation. Whoever accepts the proclamation of the arriving kingdom belongs to the side of salvation. The social reality is not directly changed by proclaiming salvation; the promise stands under the eschatological proviso of the reversal of the current order by a final act of God. The present-tense verb (ἐστιν), however, promises to the audience that they are already living in the light of the final reversal and therefore in the light of salvation, although the definite change will be a part of the future that will come soon.

A similar observation can be made concerning the blessing of the eyewitnesses in Q 10:23–4: "Blessed are the eyes that see what you see. For I tell you: Many prophets and kings wanted to see what you see, but never saw it, and to hear what you hear, but never heard it." Both beatitudes are connected by the term μακάριος ("blessed") and the semantic word field "to see." Blessed are those who see what they see; what the blessed see may be deduced from Q 7:22. It may be asked as whether the "hearing" of Q 10:23, which is not mentioned in the shorter blessing, is a secondary addition and refers to the circumstances of the Q

---

[77] Cf. H. Merklein, *Die Gottesherrschaft als Handlungsprinzip: Untersuchungen zur Ethik Jesu* (3d ed.; FB 34; Würzburg: Echter, 1984), 162 n. 585.

group's proclamation. Seeing and hearing the recent events[78] receive a significant eschatological quality; whoever sees the eschatological acts of God, of which Jesus is God's tool, is called blessed. Therefore "seeing" has a deeper meaning than just the viewing of something; rather it means seeing and comprehending the signs of the times, so that seeing leads into a new perception of one's own reality. Whoever sees the present in the light of the eschatological events becomes part of God's final acts and therefore will became part of the eschatological salvation proclaimed by the beatitude.

There are some analogies to Q 7:23 that also deal with the presence of eschatological salvation, which is promised to those who do not take offence in Jesus and therefore do not lack salvation. In the context of the Q document, we can take v. 23 together with the polemic against "this generation"; their refusal of Jesus is threatened by the coming judgment performed by the "Son of Man."

If Q 7:23 is taken as an isolated saying, it clarifies the alternative of salvation and judgment, which is brought about by one's attitude toward the proclaimer who is a representative of the kingdom of God. Therefore this remarkable claim need not be read as an expression of early Christian Christology. No one besides God seems to be the judge, and the authority of the proclaimer is connected with the content of his proclamation. Q 7:23 may be regarded as a reflection of the claim of the historical Jesus and his self-consciousness as being the sent proclaimer of the arriving kingdom of God. According to the christological conception of Q, it is Jesus who will return to execute judgment as the "Son of Man." Whoever believes in Jesus as the "Son of Man" receives the promise of salvation, a promise that can be interpreted eschatologically in the light of Q 7:22. Therefore Q can not only be interpreted as containing a hope that expects salvation from the Parousia in the future.[79] During the present time, salvation is at work in the proclamation of the Q group, that is, the people who believe in Q's preaching and take part in salvation. Although Q is clearly affected by the refutation of its preaching and the present time is understood as a time of refusal, the claim of the presence of salvation is still maintained.

---

[78] In contrast to, e.g., *Pss. Sol.* 17:44; 18:6, the seeing of the eschatological acts in Q 7:22 is not a matter of the expected future but happens in the presence of the speaker and gives an eschatological connotation to the beatitude in Q 7:23; cf. also M. Reiser, "Eschatology in the Proclamation of Jesus," in *Jesus, Mark, and Q: The Teaching of Jesus and Its Earliest Records* (ed. M. Labahn and A. Schmidt; JSNTSup 214; Sheffield, England: Sheffield Academic Press, 2001), 216–38, esp. 232.

[79] E.g., Lührmann, *Redaktion*, 96–97. He points to 1 Thess 1:9–10, a text that is sometimes viewed as close to the theology of Q and its Son of Man Christology. The affinities to the title "Son of Man," which are said to derive from 1 Thess 1:9–10, are, however, not convincing; cf. A. Labahn and M. Labahn, "Jesus als Sohn Gottes bei Paulus: Eine soteriologische Grundkonstante der paulinischen Christologie," in *Paulinische Christologie—Exegetische Studien: Festschrift für H. Hübner zum 70. Geburtstag* (ed. U. Schnelle, T. Söding, and M. Labahn; Göttingen: Vandenhoeck & Ruprecht, 2000), 97–120, esp. 106–7.

Q 7:22 and Jewish Eschatological Hope as Fulfillment of Scripture

It is well known that Jewish eschatological and messianic hope contemporary to the NT has been worked out from Scriptures.[80] Early Christian texts also engage in an exegetical process, partly innovating, partly depending upon, Jewish tradition. Biblical traditions and their eschatological hopes are elementary for Jesus' interpretation of his own work and his understanding of the kingdom of God.[81]

In a few recent studies, the *Messianic Apocalypse* (4Q521) has been regarded as a very close parallel to Q 7:22,[82] which, according to Klaus Koch, lies "closer to the messianic image of the Gospels than does any other Qumran text."[83] More interesting than the subject of literary dependence, for which different models of direct or indirect relationship between the *Messianic Apocalypse* and Q 7:22 are presented,[84] are questions about how eschatological time is described in the

---

[80] Cf., e.g., K. Koch, "Heilandserwartungen im Judäa der Zeitenwende," in *Die Schriftrollen von Qumran: Zur aufregenden Geschichte ihrer Erforschung und Deutung* (ed. S. Talmon; Regensburg: Pustet, 1998), 107–35, esp. 112; J. Zimmermann, *Messianische Texte aus Qumran: Königliche, priesterliche, und prophetische Messiasvorstellungen in den Schriftfunden von Qumran* (WUNT, 2 Reihe, 104; Tübingen: Mohr Siebeck, 1998), 377–78.

[81] Cf. B. Chilton and C. A. Evans, "Jesus and the Scriptures," in *Studying the Historical Jesus: Evaluations of the State of Current Research* (ed. B. Chilton and C. A. Evans; 2d ed.; NTTS 19; Boston: Brill, 1998), 281–335; cf. also the literature on Jesus' interpretation of Torah, ibid., 298–99 n. 43. On this subject, cf. also Theissen and Merz, *Jesus*, 319–32; Meyer, "Deed."

[82] For the much disputed text, cf., besides the literature already mentioned by Zimmermann, *Texte*, 343 n. 84, K.-W. Niebuhr, "Die Werke des eschatologischen Freudenboten (4Q521 und die Jesusüberlieferung)," in *The Scriptures in the Gospels* (ed. C. M. Tuckett; BETL 131; Leuven: Peeters, 1997), 637–46, É. Puech, "Some Remarks on 4Q246 and 4Q521 and Qumran Messianism," in *The Provo International Conference on the Dead Sea Scrolls: Technological Innovations, New Texts, and Reformulated Issues* (ed. D. W. Parry and E. Ulrich; STDJ 30; Leiden: Brill, 1999), 545–65, esp. 551–63; Zimmermann, *Texte*, 343–89. For an edition of the text, cf. É. Puech, "4QApocalypses messianique," in *Qumrân grotte 4, XVIII: Textes hébreux (4Q521–4Q528, 4Q576–4Q579)* (DJD 25; Oxford: Clarendon, 1998), 1–38. For photographs, see ibid., plates I–III. For the relationship to NT texts, cf. Evans, "From Gospel," 661–62; C. A. Evans, "Jesus and the Dead Sea Scrolls from Qumran Cave 4," in *Eschatology, Messianism, and the Dead Sea Scrolls* (ed. C. A. Evans and P. W. Flint; Studies in the Dead Sea Scrolls and Related Literature; Grand Rapids: Eerdmans, 1997), 91–100, here 96–97; C. A. Evans, "The New Quest for Jesus and the New Research on the Dead Sea Scrolls," in *Jesus, Mark, and Q: The Teaching of Jesus and Its Earliest Records* (ed. M. Labahn and A. Schmidt; JSNTSup 214; Sheffield, England: Sheffield Academic Press, 2001), 163–83, 171–73; Allison, *Jesus*, 111–13.

[83] Koch, "Heilandserwartungen," 116: " . . . dem Messiasbild des Evangelien näher als jeder andere Qumrantext."

[84] A direct dependence is considered by J. J. Collins, "The Works of the Messiah," *DSD* 1 (1994): 98–112, here 107: "It is quite possible *that the author of the Sayings source knew 4Q521;* at least he drew on a common tradition" (my emphasis). See also J. D. Tabor and M. O. Wise, "4Q521 'On Resurrection' and the Synoptic Gospel Tradition: A Preliminary Study," *JSP* 10 (1992): 149–62, esp. 161, concerning common eschatological traditions. Both positions are cited by G. J. Brooke, "Luke-Acts and the Qumran Scrolls: The

Qumran text, what kind of changes will happen during the end time, who will effect the change, and what is the temporal placement of the narrator in relation to
the narrated eschatological events. Answering these questions helps to understand
more fully the narrative pragmatic of Q 7:22 and the peculiarity of Jesus' teaching.

The *Messianic Apocalypse,* written ca. 100 B.C.E., depends on a Hebrew proto-
Essene or Essene text from the second half of the second century B.C.E.[85] The *Messianic Apocalypse* proclaims eschatological events. Fragment 2, which is of special
interest for NT research, deals with the eschatological salvation of the pious (frg. 2 ii
5–14[?]), who have been admonished to be strong and to seek the Lord (line 3).
The passage appeals to the addressees to increase their piety; the appeal is but-
tressed with promises of salvation that are narrated in the following text.[86]

Between lines 4 and 5 there is a change in subject, which may represent a
signal within the structure of the text. The Lord (אדני) will address himself to
pious adherents to honor them. According to line 11, wonderful things without
analogy are expected from the Lord. The content of these wonderful things is expressed in the fragmentary lines 12–13: healing the badly wounded and—parallel
to it—giving life to the dead, the proclamation of good news to the meek (there
follows an uncertain passage), leading (back?) the exiled, and making rich the
hungry.[87] The motifs of raising the dead and proclamation of good news to the
poor form an impressive similarity between the *Messianic Apocalypse* and Q 7:22.

4Q521 frg. 2 ii 12	Q 7:22
cf. line 8 (פוקח עורים)[88]	τυφλοὶ ἀναβλέπουσιν,
–	χωλοὶ περιπατοῦσιν,
–	λεπροὶ καθαρίζονται
–	καὶ κωφοὶ ἀκούουσιν,
ומתים יחיה	νεκροὶ ἐγείρονται,
ענוים יבשר	πτωχοὶ εὐαγγελίζονται.

Cave of MMT," in *Luke's Literary Achievement: Collected Essays* (ed. C. M. Tuckett;
JSNTSup 116; Sheffield, England: Sheffield Academic Press, 1995), 72–90; on p. 76
Brooke favors the position of Tabor and Wise. See also M. Becker, "4Q521 und die
Gesalbten," *RevQ* 18 (1997): 73–96, esp. 93.

[85] Puech, "Remarks," 552. G. Vermes, "Qumran Forum Miscellanea I," *JJS* 43
(1992): 303–4, argues against an Essene background of the manuscript. C. A. Evans,
"Qumran's Messiah: How Important Is He?," in *Religion in the Dead Sea Scrolls* (ed. J. J.
Collins and R. A. Kugler; Studies in the Dead Sea Scrolls and Related Literature; Grand
Rapids: Eerdmans, 2000), 135–49, esp. 137 n. 17, disagrees with Vermes by pointing to
numerous parallels in language between the *Messianic Apocalypse* and Essene texts.

[86] Cf. É. Puech, "Une apocalypse messianique (4Q521)," *RevQ* 15 (1992): 475–519,
esp. 514.

[87] My presentation of the text depends on Zimmermann, *Texte,* 344–47 (with
explanations).

[88] Nearly a literal citation of Ps 146:8. It is remarkable that the motif also occurs in
Isa 35:5, to which Q 7:22 is closely connected. The reference on Isa 35:5 should not,
however, be imported into 4Q521 frg. 2 ii (against Zimmermann, *Texte,* 359). On the

The language of the *Messianic Apocalypse* is replete with biblical terminology and motifs.[89] The text describes the activity of God during the beginning of the "kingdom of God."[90] Here we have reached the central question of the passage: who performs the eschatological events—the Messiah or God himself?[91] The Messiah or the messiahs are mentioned for the last time in line 1, but their number is still debated.[92] In line 5 אדני ("the Lord") is the acting subject of the text, and the word is repeated in line 11. Therefore it is not convincing to assume a change of subject in lines 9–10[93]—a passage that cannot definitely be reconstructed. The assumption that God is acting in the entire line 12 is supported by his deed in making the dead alive. Raising the dead is, according to late biblical literature and according to Jewish literature, an act done by God alone.[94] The extraordinary motif of the proclamation of good news by God and not by his envoy, however, stands in contrast to Isa 61:1–2 and opens a discussion concerning the role of the Messiah in this passage. John J. Collins connects the authority of God and the work of the Messiah: "God acts through the agency of a prophetic messiah in line 12."[95] After line 1, however, the Messiah is not mentioned again in the undisputed part of the text, and the only acting subject in lines 5–12 is אדני. Therefore God must also be acting in line 12, and not God's Messiah. In Isaiah 61,

---

other hand, it is obvious that the healing of the blind is one of the traditional acts expected during the end time. The mention of the blind is not to be understood metaphorically (in contrast to H. Kvalbein, "The Wonders of the End-Time: Metaphoric Language in 4Q521 and the Interpretation of Matthew 11.5 par.," *JSP* 18 [1998]: 87–110; R. I. Denova, *The Things Accomplished among Us: Prophetic Tradition in the Structural Pattern of Luke-Acts* [JSNTSup 141; Sheffield, England: Sheffield Academic Press, 1997], 135, considers a double function "both metaphorical and literal").

[89] Zimmermann, *Texte*, 388. *Messianic Apocalypse* frg. 2 ii presents a form of intertextuality found in Q 7:22, where pre-texts may be discovered. But it is difficult to describe exactly their extent. Probably it is not an adequate understanding of the text to discover limited pre-texts, but rather to read it as an allusion to the eschatological events as they are foretold in the Scriptures. Puech ("Remarks," 556) is right to say that there is not a clear citation from Scripture. Cf. Niebuhr, "Werke," 637.

[90] Cf. Zimmermann, *Texte*, 388.

[91] In favor of a messianic interpretation are Tabor and Wise, "4Q521," 157–58; Evans, "Jesus," 97. In favor of a prophetic Messiah, Elijah, or a prophet like Elijah, is Collins, "Works," 100–102; J. J. Collins, *The Scepter and the Star: The Messiahs of the Dead Sea Scrolls and Other Ancient Literature* (ABRL; New York: Doubleday, 1995), 118–20; idem, *The Apocalyptic Imagination: An Introduction to Jewish Apocalyptic Literature* (2d ed.; Biblical Resource Series; Grand Rapids: Eerdmans, 1998), 165–66; Kloppenborg, *Excavating Q*, 123, thoroughly depends, in his interpretation of Q 7:22, on the observations by Collins. In favor of God are Becker, "4Q521," 90–92; Frey, *Die eschatologische Verkündigung*, 359–60 n. 152; Koch, "Heilandserwartungen," 116; Niebuhr, "Werke," 640; Puech, "Remarks," 556, 558 ("God [not a messiah] is clearly the author of all the eschatological works"); Zimmermann, *Texte*, 363–64.

[92] Cf. Zimmermann, *Texte*, 385–86; Becker, "4Q521," 75–78, e.g., argues for the plural.

[93] Cf. Neirynck, "Q 6,20b–21," 53.

[94] E.g., Frey, *Die eschatologische Verkündigung*, 357–59; Collins, "Works," 101, pointing to *2 Bar.* 30; *4 Ezra* 7.

[95] Collins, "Works," 100; idem, *Scepter,* 118 (cf. also 132 n. 85).

God is the true subject of the eschatological activity, standing behind the proclamation of the envoy of good news.[96]

Comparing the statements of the *Messianic Apocalypse* with Q 7:22, there is a small but significant measure of agreement. Thus both texts show a complex connection of different biblical pre-texts.[97] The reception of Scripture in both texts wavers between allusion and citation. In both texts we can find the motifs of resurrection of dead, proclamation of good news to the poor (in the same sequence), and giving sight to the blind (in a different order).

There is no significant difference between Q 7:22 and the *Messianic Apocalypse* in the way they use Scripture. In Q 7:22 Jesus refers back to his view and experience of reality and tries to lead people to the same assessment of reality so that all share the same perception.[98] For Jesus, the signs and miracles of the eschatological religious tradition and expectation of his people takes place in present time. Jesus considers his own service part of the eschatological realization of God's will of salvation. Although the kingdom of God takes place in present time, Jesus does not evoke a *realized* eschatology; he still expects the future and universal breakthrough of God's kingdom to come as it is expressed, for example, in the parable of the Growing Seed (Q 13:18–9, 20–1).

There are also important differences between both statements. The *Messianic Apocalypse* eagerly awaits the final action of God in the future whereas, according to the saying of Jesus, the divine activity is already present in recent time[99]—not just in Jesus' deeds and proclamation but also in events in the Jewish environment. Jesus understands his work as a part of the eschatological activity of God.[100] The *Messianic Apocalypse* motivates the pious to persevere, pointing to God's compensation at the end of time. Q 7:22 is silent at this point. Without going too far, it may be assumed that piety is not a precondition for the people to become part of the coming kingdom. Moreover, the kingdom is offered to the people who live on the edge of society without preconditions, as can be shown by the beatitude of the poor, hungry, and grieving, Q 6:20b–21.

---

[96] Cf. Niebuhr, "Werke," 638.

[97] This is highlighted in the recent study by G. J. Brooke, "Shared Intertextual Interpretations in the Dead Sea Scrolls and the New Testament," in *Biblical Perspectives: Early Use and Interpretation of the Bible in Light of the Dead Sea Scrolls* (ed. M. E. Stone and E. G. Chazon; STDJ 28; Leiden: Brill, 1998), 35–57, esp. 46. He thus underscores the difference between both catalogues.

[98] Cf. in C. Perelman, *The Realm of Rhetoric* (Notre Dame: University of Notre Dame Press, 1982), 81–105: "Arguments Based on the Structure of Reality".

[99] According to C. Mearns, "Realized Eschatology in Q? A Consideration of the Sayings in Luke 7.22, 11.20, and 16.16," *SJT* 40 (1987): 189–210, esp. 203, the miracles are "not necessarily demonstrations of its [i.e., the kingdom's] presence." In the light of the interpretation of the *Messianic Apocalypse,* Mearns's opinion strikes me as wholly unconvincing.

[100] Tabor and Wise, "4Q521," 160–61, connect the cleaning of the leper and the resurrection of the dead with the Elijah/Elisha traditions (1 Kgs 17:17–24; 2 Kgs 4:18–37; 5:1–14) and claim the expectation of a new Elijah (Mal 4:5–6) as the main background of Q 7:22. In this case, the saying would proclaim the fulfillment of the expectation.

Likewise, Q 7:22 and the *Messianic Apocalypse* agree with one another in that the eschatological events are worked out by God himself and not by an envoy, such as his Messiah.[101] A further parallel to both texts can be found in 11QMelch 2:15–20, which also belongs to the reception history of Isa 61:1–2 (and Isa 52:7), expecting the proclamation of good news in the end of time: "This is the day of [peace about which God] spoke [of old through the words of Is]aiah the prophet, who said [Isa 52:7], 'How beautiful upon the mountains are the feet of the messenger who announces peace, of the mess[enger of good who announces salvation,] saying to Zion: "Your God reigns"'" (11QMelch 2:15–16).[102] In contrast to 4Q521 frg. 2 ii 12 and Q 7:22, the proclaimer of good news in 11QMelch 2:15–20 is distinguished from God as his anointed prophet. God is, however, the source of his herald's proclamation. It may be concluded that the findings of Qumran clearly indicate that the eschatological expectation of preaching the good news[103] is not an original Christian formulation, as was proposed in some previous studies.[104]

Conclusion

The proclamation of the presence of salvation in Q 7:22 is not an isolated occurrence in the final Q document; the connection in language with Q 6:20 has to be taken seriously: Salvation is presented to the poor, who from now on belong to the arriving kingdom of God. In the Q document, this claim probably has to be read as referring to the Q community, so that the community is the locale in which eschatological salvation is already present. Therefore we can find elements of present eschatology in Q—a certitude of salvation, whose portrait is elaborated with pictures and motifs of the traditional early Jewish eschatological expectation.

Salvation is present.[105] But the final and universal breakthrough of God's reign is still a subject of the community's hope and connected with the expectation of the Parousia of the Son of Man. The dynamic and local elements of Jesus' proclamation of the arriving kingdom seem to become less important in contrast to the presence of salvation in the community. The community passes on the gift of salvation by proclaiming the kingdom of God and by healing. The refusal of its preaching attains an eschatological quality. Whoever accepts the proclamation of the kingdom becomes a recipient of the promise of salvation. Q shares this point of view with Jesus. But there is an important difference. Jesus proclaims salvation

---

[101] Cf. Becker, "4Q521," 93–94.

[102] The translation is from F. García Martínez, *The Dead Sea Scrolls Translated: The Qumran Texts in English* (Leiden: Brill, 1994), 140.

[103] For the proclamation of good news originating in God's will, cf. also 1QH[a] 23:14 (*olim* 18:14).

[104] Contrary to Kümmel, "Antwort," 198–99.

[105] It is somewhat artificial and not justified by NT texts when Mearns ("Eschatology," 191) claims that "first generation Christian eschatology was primarily realized, and second generation Christianity . . . was predominantly futuristic."

to social and religious outsiders—without preconditions. The Q-group, however, develops another social rhetoric. The proclamation of the presence of salvation does not aim at a reinterpretation for outsiders in Israel so that they become part of God's kingdom; rather it aims at a self-definition and boundary-making in the light of God's activity. In the definition of group boundaries, the social rhetoric is comparable to the *Messianic Apocalypse,* which serves a related idea. In the Qumran text, the futuristic expectation of salvation serves as a self-insurance for the pious.

Q 7:23 contains also a warning. In the literary context of Q, the saying criticizes a refusal of the Q proclamation that seems to be accompanied by an active resistance (Q 10:10–6; 6:22–3). The opponents of the Q group are threatened by the final judgment, which the coming of Son of Man will bring on. This motif represents another christological trait that distinguishes Q from the eschatological thought of Jesus. Jesus expected that *God* would carry out his reign universally and that its final appearance would necessarily follow the present eschatological events. In Q Jesus himself is connected with the final act. Judgment accompanies the final consummation of the kingdom; in the final layer of Q, "this generation" is confronted with judgment because they refuse the proclamation of salvation by the Q group.

We can uncover a twofold eschatological scheme in Q,[106] which divides into the present promise of salvation and the final establishment of God's universal reign. In contrast to Jewish apocalyptic schemes,[107] both stages are connected with the appearance of the Messiah. Jesus, as the one who has already come, stands in the center of Q as the one who has proclaimed eschatological salvation, in which the community partakes. This present salvation stands under the proviso of the Parousia of the Son of Man and the universal arrival of God's reign.

In contrast to OT and Jewish tradition, early Christian thought identifies the eschatological activity of God with Jesus' words and deeds. Within an explicit Christology, Jesus is recognized as the giver of eschatological salvation. Jesus' activity, especially his miracles and exorcisms, realize eschatological salvation. The new *aiōn* that is to come is already present in the deeds of Jesus, with christological consequences. This is clarified by reading Q 7:23 in connection with 7:22. In Jesus' teaching, the order not to take offence in Jesus has its origin in the authority of his proclamation and finally in the One to whom Jesus refers back, in *God.* In Q and in the gospels of Matthew and Luke, the term ἐν ἐμοί ("at me") is underscored insofar as stress is laid on behavior toward the person who proclaims the kingdom of God: *Jesus.*

---

[106] See also the remarks by Meyer, "Deed," 163, who states that, for both Jesus and the early Christian communities, "there were two facets of the eschatological consciousness: first a consciousness of eschatological promise/prophecy 'already fulfilled'; second, the complementary consciousness of promise/prophecy 'still to be fulfilled.'" This attractive description, however, resembles—as far as I can see—a too fixed scheme of promise and fulfillment.

[107] Cf. Koch, "Heilandserwartungen," 122ff.

✲ *7*

"No One Has Ever Seen God": Revisionary Criticism in the Fourth Gospel

A. J. Droge

No text, secular or religious, fulfills another text.—Harold Bloom[1]

At the conclusion of the prologue to the Fourth Gospel comes the narrator's pronouncement: θεὸν οὐδεὶς ἑώρακεν πώποτε (John 1:18a). And juxtaposed to this assertion of the Deity's invisibility—that is to say, unknowability—stands the claim that μονογενὴς θεὸς ὁ ὢν εἰς τὸν κόλπον τοῦ πατρὸς ἐκεῖνος ἐξηγήσατο (1:18b).[2] To say that the Fourth Gospel is adamant on this point would be an understatement; it is hammered home again and again by the narrative's main character, and almost always in a polemical context. "No one has seen the Father," the Revealer declares, "except the one who is from God; this one has seen the Father" (6:46). "You have never heard his voice [φωνή] or seen his form [εἶδος], and you do not have his word [λόγος] abiding in you" (5:37b–38a NRSV). "The one who sent me is true; him you do not know. I know him" (7:28b–29a). "You know neither me nor my Father. If you knew me, you would also know my Father" (8:19). "You do not know him, but I know him" (8:55a). These paired assertions of invisibility and visibility, ignorance and knowledge, concealment and revelation work like a kind of Johannine striptease or dance of the seven veils. In the second half of the narrative, indeed, one of the characters becomes so aroused that he demands to see it all. "Show us the Father," Philip pleads, "and satisfy us!" To this the hero responds, in language reminiscent of the prologue, "He who has seen me has seen the Father" (14:8–9; cf. 12:45)—a perfect example of the Fourth Gospel's hermeneutical circle and its essentially contentless revelation.

---

[1] H. Bloom, " 'Before Moses Was, I Am': The Original and the Belated Testaments," *Poetics of Influence: New and Selected Criticism* (New Haven, Conn.: Henry R. Schwab, 1988), 404.

[2] The absence of direct and indirect objects is only one of several challenges presented by the second half of this line.

On the face of it, there is nothing particularly remarkable about these repeated assertions. Claims about the unknowability of god(s) are as common in the religious discourse of late antiquity as claims of epiphanies and divine revelation. Indeed, the two seem to require each other. Consider this excerpt of a spell from the *Papyri Graecae Magicae*:

> I summon you, Headless One, who created heaven and earth, who created night and day, / you who created light and darkness; you are Osoronnophris, *whom none has ever seen* [ὃν οὐδεὶς εἶδε πώποτε]; you are Iabas; you are Iapos; you have distinguished the just and the unjust; you have made male and female. . . . / I am Moses, your prophet, to whom you have transmitted your mysteries / celebrated by Israel; . . . hear me.

Then the revelation follows in the form of a series of "I am" sayings:

> I am the Headless Daimon with my sight in my feet; [I am] the Mighty One, the Immortal Fire; I am the Truth who hates the fact that unjust deeds are done in the world [etc.].[3]

Think also of Marcion's *fremder Gott* or the ἄγνωστος θεός of so-called Gnosticism and the Hermetica. Like the Deity of the Fourth Gospel, this being is the God beyond the so-called god(s) of this world, unseen and unknown apart from revelation.

Consider, too, the strategic advantages of pairing up a claim of revelation with an assertion of the Deity's heretofore invisibility and unknowability: the more the latter is emphasized, the more impressive and unique the claim to revelation and its content becomes. Yet this is not how most modern commentators have chosen to understand this theme in the Fourth Gospel. Rather than contextualize the assertion about the Deity's invisibility in terms, say, of the history of late antique religions, most interpreters insist that this idea is entirely in accord with "a general Old Testament assumption . . . that God is invisible"[4] and that "not even the greatest representatives of Israel have seen God."[5] Confirmation for this is sought in one verse, Exod 33:20, where Moses' request to see the divine glory *(kabod)* is denied: "You cannot see my face; for no one shall see me and live."[6] One of this generation's preeminent commentators on Exodus asserts the following about the prohibition placed on seeing God:

---

[3] *PGM* 5.96–110, 145–149, in H. D. Betz, ed., *The Greek Magical Papyri in Translation, Including the Demotic Spells* (Chicago: University of Chicago Press, 1986), 1:103 (trans. D. Aune).

[4] C. K. Barrett, *The Gospel according to St. John* (2d ed.; Philadelphia: Westminster, 1978), 169.

[5] R. Brown, *The Gospel according to John* (2 vols.; AB 29, 29A; New York: Doubleday, 1966–1970), 1:36. Cf. R. Bultmann, *The Gospel of John: A Commentary* (trans. G. R. Beasley-Murray et al.; Philadelphia: Westminster, 1971), 81: "We have here in a radical form the oriental and OT idea of the sovereignty and absoluteness of God."

[6] Cf. Exod 19:21 and Lev 16:2 for a similar warning.

[Moses'] request to have God reveal himself in an unmediated form is . . . denied. There are limits placed even on God's chosen mediator. No man can experience God and live. But a partial concession is made. . . . Moses is allowed to catch a fleeting glimpse of the "back" of God. Of course, a tremendous anthropomorphism is involved, but the extreme caution with which it is used is an eloquent testimony to the Hebrew understanding of God.

This commentator goes on to say that

The refusal of God to comply in full with Moses' request for a revelation of himself called forth a similar reaction from . . . the classic Jewish and Christian commentators . . . [who] were fully agreed that no mortal man can see the essence of God and live. . . . *Obviously the Old Testament is unambiguous at this point.*[7]

Now, nothing could be further from the truth. In fact, there is enormous ambiguity on this point, both in biblical and in so-called postbiblical literature. To begin with, Exod 33:20 does not preclude a vision of the Deity; it merely states that the Deity's "face" may not be seen (although note that Moses had only requested to see his "glory"). Yet even this qualification stands in unresolved tension—if not outright contradiction—with a host of other passages indicating that "seeing" the Deity (or his "face") was a rather *common* experience. A casual survey of biblical texts reveals that Abraham,[8] Hagar,[9] Jacob,[10] Moses,[11] Aaron, Nadab, Abihu and the seventy elders,[12] Gideon,[13] the parents of Samson,[14]

---

[7] B. S. Childs, *The Book of Exodus: A Critical, Theological Commentary* (Philadelphia: Westminster, 1974), 595–96, 598 (my emphasis).

[8] "YHWH appeared to [Abraham] by the terebinths of Mamre" (Gen 18:1).

[9] "So [Hagar] named YHWH who spoke to her, 'You are El-Roi'; for she said, 'Have I really seen God and remained alive after seeing him?'" (Gen 16:13).

[10] "So Jacob called the place Peniel [i.e., the face of god], saying, 'For I have seen God face to face, and yet my life is preserved'" (Gen 32:30).

[11] "Thus YHWH used to speak to Moses face to face [LXX: ἐνώπιος ἐνωπίῳ], as one speaks to a friend" (Exod 33:11); "YHWH descended in the cloud and stood with [Moses] there, and proclaimed the name, 'YHWH.' YHWH passed before him" (Exod 34:5–6); "And [YHWH] said, 'Hear my words: When there are prophets among you, I YHWH make myself known to them in visions; I speak to them in dreams. Not so with my servant Moses; he is entrusted with all my house. With him I speak face to face [LXX: στόμα κατὰ στόμα]—clearly, not in riddles; and he beholds the form [LXX: δόξα] of YHWH'" (Num 12:6–8); "Never since has there arisen a prophet in Israel like Moses, whom YHWH knew face to face [LXX: πρόσωπον κατὰ πρόσωπον]" (Deut 34:10); see also the following note.

[12] "Then Moses and Aaron, Nadab and Abihu, and seventy of the elders of Israel went up, and they saw the God of Israel [LXX: "the place where the God of Israel stood there"]. . . . They beheld God [LXX: "and they appeared in the place of God"], and they ate and drank" (Exod 24:9–11).

[13] "Help me, Lord God! For I have seen the messenger of YHWH face to face" (Judg 6:22; cf. 2:1 for the identification of the "messenger of YHWH" with YHWH himself).

[14] "And Manoah said to his wife, 'We shall surely die, for we have seen God.' But his wife said to him, 'If YHWH had meant to kill us, he would not have accepted a burnt offering and a grain offering at our hands, or shown us all these things, or now announced to us such things as these'" (Judg 13:22–23).

Elijah,[15] Micaiah,[16] Amos,[17] Isaiah,[18] Ezekiel,[19] and Job[20] are all said to have "seen," had a "vision of," or had "appear" to them YHWH, G(g)od, or the divine "glory."[21] (This list would increase considerably if we added "auditions" to the accounts of visions of the Deity and if we opened the survey to include so-called postbiblical texts.) Especially worthy of note are the claims not only that Moses spoke with YHWH on a regular basis—"face to face"—but also that Moses and his fellow mountain climbers even celebrated a meal with the Deity (see nn. 11 and 12).

There are (as indicated in the notes) instances in which the Greek translators, apparently troubled by the human, all-too-human character of the theophanies, deliberately tampered with the texts. Even so, the majority of these anthropomorphic theophanies in the Hebrew texts are still found in the Greek translation.[22] Were we to presume that the author of the Fourth Gospel was familiar with these passages, especially those concerning Moses, then we would have every reason to think that the assertion "No one has ever seen God" is not only *not* in accord with "a general Old Testament assumption" but also that it is an outright and deliberate *subversion* of a general OT assumption (if I may use that expression) that God may be—and has been—seen. And if we recall that this assertion itself follows on the heels of a claim that "the Law was given through Moses, grace and truth through [the Revealer]" (1:17), then we might begin to

---

[15] "[YHWH] said, 'Go out and stand on the mountain [Horeb, the mount of God] before YHWH, for YHWH is about to pass by.' Now there was a great wind, so strong that it was splitting mountains and breaking rocks in pieces before YHWH, but YHWH was not in the wind; and after the wind an earthquake, but YHWH was not in the earthquake; and after the earthquake a fire, but YHWH was not in the fire; and after the fire a sound of sheer silence. When Elijah heard it, he wrapped his face in his mantle and went out and stood at the entrance of the cave. Then there came a voice to him" (1 Kgs 19:11–13).

[16] "Then [Micaiah] said, 'Therefore hear the word of YHWH: I saw YHWH sitting on his throne, with all the host of heaven standing beside him to the right and to the left of him'" (1 Kgs 22:19).

[17] "I saw YHWH standing on the altar" (Amos 9:1).

[18] "I saw YHWH sitting on a throne, high and lofty" (Isa 6:1); "My eyes have seen the King, YHWH of hosts!" (Isa 6:5).

[19] "I saw visions of God" (Ezek 1:1). "And above the dome over their [i.e., the living creatures'] heads there was something like a throne, in appearance like sapphire; and seated above the likeness of a throne was something that seemed like a human form. Upward from what appeared like the loins I saw something like gleaming amber, something that looked like fire all around; and downward from what looked like the loins I saw something that looked like fire, and there was splendor all around. Like the bow in a cloud on a rainy day, such was the appearance of the splendor all around. This was the appearance of the likeness of the glory of YHWH" (Ezek 1:26–28).

[20] "I had heard of you by the hearing of the ear, but now my eye sees you" (Job 42:5).

[21] Perhaps mention should also be made of Daniel's dream vision (Dan 7:9). I leave aside instances where a worshipper is enjoined to seek the "face" of YHWH (Ps 27:8–9) or longs to see the "face" of God (Ps 42:2).

[22] See C. T. Fritsch, "A Study of the Greek Translation of the Hebrew Verbs 'to See,' with the Deity as Subject or Object," *ErIsr* 16 (1982): 51–56.

wonder whether the Fourth Gospel wasn't perhaps espousing a position analogous to that of Marcion.[23] Whoever it was who spoke with Moses "face to face" and "ate and drank" with him, it certainly was not God (i.e., the God beyond the god of this world). Nor was this God the authorizing voice behind the Mosaic law. But if not God, then who is it who appears and speaks in the Scriptures?

On two occasions in the Fourth Gospel, the Revealer addresses his adversaries directly and refers to "your Law" (8:17 [Deut 19:15]; 10:34 [Ps 82:6]); on another occasion, speaking to the members of his own entourage, he refers to "their Law" (15:25 [Ps 35:19?; 69:4?]). Moreover, in two of these instances, the specific textual references appear to be the Psalms, so that "Law" (νόμος) here would designate not simply the books of Moses but a much broader collection of writings. The use of the second and third person in these passages puts distance not just between the Revealer and his adversaries but between himself and a collection of texts that he and they might otherwise be supposed to share.

But there is more. In an altogether stunning announcement, the Revealer declares, "All who have come [before me] are thieves and robbers; but the sheep did not listen to them" (10:8). "The thief comes only to steal, slaughter, and destroy; I came that they may have life" (10:10). Just who these "thieves and robbers" are is not specified, and had we time, I could regale you with the ingenious attempts of commentators, ancient and modern, to identify them. On the face of it, though, the unconditional nature of the declaration would seem to include among these "thieves and robbers" none other than "Moses and the prophets," to say nothing of the other so-called heroes of the scriptural tradition. What we seem to have here is not an evolutionary schema or a pattern of prophecy and fulfillment, so familiar from the Synoptics as well as from other writings of the Jesus movement; rather we have disjunction and opposition, broadly thematized in the Fourth Gospel as a dualism of falsehood and truth, pretenders and the real thing, death and life. At the level of texts, this dualism seems to place in opposition counterfeit texts and genuine Scriptures: "The Law came through Moses; grace and truth through [the Revealer]" (1:17); that is, "grace and truth" as mediated exclusively through the Scripture of the Fourth Gospel. Passages such as these would tend toward the conclusion that the Fourth Gospel is unequivocal about the Scriptures *falsely so called:* they are unreliable, riddled with falsehoods, dangerous, evil. They are, in short, one of the instrumentalities by which the thieves and robbers steal, slaughter, and destroy.

---

[23] The absence of a conjunctive particle in 1:17 sharpens the juxtaposition, implying conflict and perhaps even supersession rather than fulfillment; cf. J. Ashton's apt remarks: "We may compare John [*sic*] with Matthew [*sic*] here, for whom Jesus was a second Moses, refining and purifying the law, but not replacing it. . . . John, by contrast, puts the law aside, offering instead, in the name of Jesus Christ, 'grace and truth' (1:17). The deliberate replacement of one founder-figure by another (the same step would be taken six centuries later on behalf of Mohammed) is effectively the proclamation of a new religion" (*Understanding the Fourth Gospel* [Oxford: Clarendon, 1991], 473).

My point is this: to interpret the Fourth Gospel's claim that "no one has ever seen God" as consistent with "a general Old Testament assumption" is not only to misunderstand the nature of that claim; it is also to miss entirely the significance that claim has for the Fourth Gospel's exegetical strategy toward a collection of texts that biblical scholars routinely refer to as the "Old Testament" but that the Fourth Gospel refers to, variously, as "the Law of Moses" (1:17; 7:19),[24] "[Moses'] writings" (5:46–47), "your Law" (8:17; 10:34, the latter quoting Ps 82:6; cf. the reference to "their Law" in 15:25, alluding to Ps 35:19?; 69:4?), "the Law and the Prophets" (1:45), "the Prophets" (6:45),[25] or simply "the scriptures" (5:39).[26] Now, I would insist that we do not have access to these texts except insofar as they are mediated through the Fourth Gospel—a text, moreover, that is itself riddled with textual problems. This raises a methodological issue of considerable consequence. It would surely be anachronistic to presume that one of the many modern printed versions of the Bible can be identified with an assortment of texts the Fourth Gospel references in a variety of ways. But it would be equally anachronistic to presume for the Fourth Gospel a knowledge of something like the MT or the so-called Septuagint, or both. In fact, in the period when the Fourth Gospel was being constructed, there was no "Bible" (singular). There was certainly no "book" (that is to say, no codex), since this technology had not yet been widely disseminated. We must take seriously, I submit, the recognition that "the Scriptures" (pl.) were neither collectively fixed nor individually stable but were continually subjected to alterations and revisions. Indeed, the Fourth Gospel itself presents compelling evidence for this messy, complicated textual history.

To the best of my knowledge, no consensus has yet been achieved on whether the author of the Fourth Gospel consulted "the Scriptures" in Hebrew, or one or more of the Aramaic or Greek versions, or all three. However that question may be finally answered, and it may not be possible to answer it definitively (e.g., how do we know that a relatively early text such as the Fourth Gospel doesn't preserve an "original" reading?), it bears strongly on a related but secondary question: has the author of the Fourth Gospel modified his quotations of, or references to, these "Scriptures"? The answer to this question seems to be a resounding yes! To summarize the results of Maarten Menken's *Old Testament Quotations in the Fourth Gospel*:

> The evangelist modified his quotations in various ways and for various reasons. . . .
> He replaced a word by another word having a parallel position in a parallel line (1:23); he supplied a word from a parallel line to make a quotation fit better into the context (6:31; 19:36), or he wove several parallel lines into each other to arrive at a text that suited his purposes (7:38). . . . He added, omitted, or changed

---

[24] Note what the hero's adversaries assert in 9:29, "We know that God has spoken to Moses" (NRSV).

[25] Occasionally there is a reference to an individual "prophet" (1:23 [Isa 40:3]; 12:38 [Isa 53:1], 39–40 [Isa 6:10]; cf. 12:14–15).

[26] By contrast, the references to γραφή ("scripture," sg.) are always to a specific passage (see 2:22; 7:38, 42; 10:35; 13:18; 17:12; 19:24, 28, 36, 37; 20:9; cf. 15:25, ὁ λόγος).

elements on the basis of analogous OT passages to adapt a quotation to his general ideas or to the specific context of the quotation in the gospel, or to make it more comprehensible (6:31; 7:38; 12:15, 40; 13:18; 19:36). . . . He shortened his text by a few words to give it a universal meaning (6:45); he omitted elements he did not need in the gospel context (12:15, 40). He chose an alternative translation of a word to make the quotation suit the gospel context better (12:15, 40), or changed the sequence of lines for the same reason (12:40). He vocalized and translated his Hebrew text in such a way that the quotation suited his [Christology and theology] (7:38; 12:40).[27]

Granted, one may take issue with one or another of these conclusions of Menken; but if he is correct in his general characterization of "Old Testament quotations in the Fourth Gospel," then I submit there is much to be said in favor of Krister Stendahl's judgment that "on the whole John's [sic] way of quoting the O.T. [sic] is consistent in its inconsistency."[28] Menken finds Stendahl's remark "significant but unjustified,"[29] attributing the "editorial changes" to the evangelist's Christology while insisting that "the changes are *legitimate* insofar as they stay within the boundaries of the common practices of explanation and alteration of texts in John's Jewish milieu."[30] Against those who would characterize the Fourth Gospel's "treatment of the OT as free," Menken insists that "it is at best *relatively* free."[31]

The hesitancy of scholars to characterize the Fourth Gospel's exegetical strategy as "free" without qualification is more than a little curious. Another recent book on this topic asserts the following: "John [sic] feels *free* to subject the OT [sic] passages he cites to *certain limited non-essential alterations* in order to adapt them to the new and uniquely Johannine contexts in which he places them."[32] Now, how the author can claim this and then later say (of the citation at John 15:25) that "it is not possible to ascertain precisely the OT referent"[33] escapes me—as does his concluding remark that "in the majority of cases . . . John introduces into his citations *textual materials external to the passages he actually cites.*"[34] If this isn't unqualified exegetical freedom, then I'd like to know what is.

---

[27] M. J. J. Menken, *Old Testament Quotations in the Fourth Gospel: Studies in Textual Form* (CBET 15; Kampen, Neth.: Pharos, 1996), 206–7.

[28] K. Stendahl, *The School of St. Matthew and Its Use of the Old Testament* (Philadelphia: Fortress, 1954), 163.

[29] Menken, *Old Testament Quotations,* 206 n. 2. (The meaning of this remark escapes me.)

[30] Ibid., 207 (alluding, for example, to so-called pesher exegesis and the technique of *qal we-homer,* 208).

[31] Ibid., 209 (my emphasis).

[32] B. Schuchard, *Scripture within Scripture: The Interrelationship of Form and Function in the Explicit Old Testament Citations in the Gospel of John* (SBLDS 133; Atlanta: Scholars Press, 1992), 52 (my emphasis).

[33] Ibid., 123.

[34] Ibid., 151–52 (my emphasis).

Without minimizing the contributions of Menken and others, I would say that we still have a considerable set of problems on our hands. How do we know, for example, that a relatively early text such as the Fourth Gospel does not preserve in its scriptural quotations an "original" reading, or at least a reading earlier than any of the biblical manuscripts we possess? That is, how can one measure the degree of deviation without knowing what the fixed point is? On the other hand, if the exegetical strategy of the Fourth Gospel is to be understood in light of the contemporary rules of the exegetical game, as Menken and others have tried to demonstrate, I would say that it appears that Stendahl may well have been right after all. The only exegetical rule is that there are no rules. In order for these rules to be rules, one, ideally, would like to see a negative—an example of the violation of one of them. To the best of my knowledge, I do not recall anyone claiming that the Fourth Gospel's "use of the Old Testament" ever violates the rules of the exegetical game. On the contrary, we are continually reassured that, whatever alterations the Fourth Gospel has made in its *Vorlage,* they are "legitimate," "limited," and "nonessential" changes. But who is in the position to make such an Olympian pronouncement? Isn't this really a theological, and not a historical, claim? In my view, these are apologetic stratagems that distract attention from a more intellectually interesting and important set of questions for the study of exegesis.

I submit that the problems surrounding the Fourth Gospel's appropriation of the Scriptures will not be solved along the traditional lines of inquiry—for example, "Did the author of the Fourth Gospel use the Hebrew or Greek text of the Old Testament?" or "Are the author's exegetical techniques consistent with his Jewish milieu?" Although these are not unimportant questions, more attention needs to be paid to what I would call the problematics of exegetical conflict and to the often improvisational and innovative strategies deployed in order to contest the meaning of "the Scriptures." I have in mind a situation like that described notoriously by Paul in 2 Corinthians 3–4 but in evidence in almost every text associated with the Jesus movement. What is required in the case of the Fourth Gospel is a recognition (1) that its "use of the Old Testament" is nothing less than a revolutionary attempt to usurp the meaning of "the Scriptures" and (2) that this usurpation requires a carefully worked out theory about the Scriptures. Of interest to me, then, is not so much the *what* of exegesis as the *how;* not the meaning the Fourth Gospel gives to this or that "scripture" as the theorizing about "the Scriptures" on which its individual exegetical claims may be said to depend.

No interpretation is transparent, of course, but what is often overlooked, at least with respect to the subject of my concern, is that the act of interpreting a text always involves the constitution of a text. To quote T. E. Lawrence, "Nothing is written." Strictly speaking, there is no datum separable from the interpretation of it. This is certainly true of modern commentaries on the Fourth Gospel. Critics as widely different as a Bultmann and a Brown each present a theory of the text allegedly before the act of interpreting it. Yet their radically different constitutions of the text are inextricably linked with their radically different interpretations of it. May we say that something similar was the case with the Fourth Gospel and the texts in relation to which its author was concerned to set his own narrative? Wayne Meeks has described this relationship—the relationship between the law, or writings of Moses, and the Revealer and text of the Fourth Gospel—as "emphatically ambiguous,"[35] and this, in my view, is a good first step in trying to understand the Fourth Gospel's complicated stance toward the Scriptures. In the short time I have this afternoon, let me consider a few examples.

In John 10 the Revealer's adversaries charge him with blasphemy "because," they say, "although you are a mere human you make yourself a god" (10:33). To this the hero offers the following reply: "Is it not written in your Law [ἐν τῷ νόμῳ ὑμῶν], 'I said, "You are gods"'? If he called 'gods' those to whom the word [ὁ λόγος] of God came—and this scripture [ἡ γραφή, i.e., "this passage"] cannot be annulled—do you say of the one the Father sanctified and sent into the world, 'You blaspheme,' because I said, 'I am the Son of God'?" (10:34–36). Now several things should be noted here. First, the quotation from "your Law" comes from Ps 82[LXX 81]:6a, indicating that "Law" in the Fourth Gospel can be used to refer to a broad collection of texts. Second, the Revealer insists that "this scripture"—that is, this passage in Psalm 82—cannot be "annulled" (λυθῆναι). He does not say that "the scriptures" in general—αἱ γραφαί—cannot be annulled. In the Fourth Gospel, the singular γραφή always refers to a specific passage (what we would call, since Stephanus, a "verse"); the plural γραφαί, to a collection of texts (John 5:39). Why is it that this passage of Psalm 82 cannot be annulled? No explicit answer is given, but one may be inferred. The Revealer asserts that this passage derives from the authorizing voice of the Deity's λόγος and may therefore be relied upon as authentic. This would also leave open the possibility that there are other passages in the collection that are not so authorized and may be annulled. Is there evidence in the Fourth Gospel that would support such a view?

Let me point out two instances where "a scripture"—or, from the point of view of the Fourth Gospel, "a scripture falsely so called"—appears to be annulled. In John 6 the miracle-seeking crowds in Galilee demand, "What sign are you going to do, so that we might see (it) and believe you? . . . Our fathers ate the manna in the wilderness, as it is written, 'He gave them bread from heaven to eat'" (6:30–31). This is an obvious allusion to Exodus 16, although the quotation comes from Ps 78[LXX 77]:24 (possibly Ps 105[LXX 104]:40 as well). The Revealer's response, however, calls this "scripture" into question: "I swear to you, it was not Moses who gave them the bread from heaven, but it is my Father who gives you the true bread from heaven" (6:32). This response not only undermines the authority of Moses and the authenticity of the manna miracle; by implication it also casts doubt on the authority and authenticity of the so-called scriptural basis on which they both may be said to depend. Put differently, both

---

[35] W. Meeks, *The Prophet-King: Moses Traditions and the Johannine Christology* (SNT 14; Leiden: Brill, 1967), 288.

the historical episode itself and the text by which it is mediated are annulled or, we might say, abrogated, suppressed, superseded.

We find a similar interpretive move being made regarding the alleged scriptural basis for the Messiah's place of origin and the question of the identity of the Revealer in the Fourth Gospel. Some among the festival-goers in John 7 ask, "Has not the scripture [again ἡ γραφή] said that the Anointed One comes from the seed of David and from Bethlehem, the village where David lived?" (7:42, referring to Mic 5:2[LXX 1]). Their question is left dangling, without an explicit answer, for, from the point of view of the Fourth Gospel, there is no need to comment on it. It is patently wrong. The Revealer of the Fourth Gospel is not of Davidic descent, nor does he come from Bethlehem. Here again, I contend, we have the annulment or supersession of another γραφή, another counterfeit or corruption that has found its way into the Scriptures.

To understand better the Fourth Gospel's "emphatically ambiguous" stance toward the Scriptures, consider the analogous exegetical strategy set forth in Ptolemy's *Letter to Flora,* a text roughly contemporary with the Fourth Gospel and a Valentinian handbook, so to say, on how to read the law of Moses:[36] "It is left to me . . . to give you an accurate description both of the nature of the Law itself and of its author, the Lawgiver. I shall prove my assertions from the words [λόγοι] of our Savior, which are the only sure guide to the perception of truth. . . . Not all of that Law in the pentateuch [πεντάτευχος] of Moses has been made by one Lawgiver. That is, it is not made by God alone. Some of its provisions are made by men, and the words of the Savior teach us that there are three divisions in it" (*Flor.* 3.8; 4.1). Relying on "the words of the Savior" (as they are found in what would later come to be called the Gospel according to Matthew) as his "canon," or criterion of authenticity, Ptolemy proceeds to analyze the pentateuchal collection (indeed, this is the first occurrence of the term "Pentateuch" to refer to the Law of Moses) to distinguish what in that collection is from God (strictly speaking, from the "Demiurge" or the "Mesotes"),[37] what materials were added by Moses ("*not* as God legislates through him"), and what by the elders (for "they too have inserted certain commandments of their own").

Similar to this is the textual theory of the great Alexandrian Christian exegete Origen, who in his *Epistula ad Africanum* claims that those responsible for transmitting the Scriptures had tampered with them by removing all the passages that reflected negatively on the history of Israel: "Insofar as they were able, the experts [σοφοί = rabbinic authorities?] have removed from the knowledge of the

---

[36] *Apud* Epiphanius, *Pan.* 33.3.1–33.7.10; see G. Quispel, *Ptolémée, Lettre à Flora* (2d ed.; Paris: Cerf, 1966).

[37] I.e., not from "the perfect God himself" (see *Flor.* 7.3–7). Ptolemy begins his treatise by setting his own exegetical theory in relationship to two others: "Some say [the Law] was given by God the Father, but others [Marcionite Christians] . . . by our adversary the Devil, author of corruption—as, indeed, they ascribe the creation of the world to him" (3.2). In fact, Marcion appears to have distinguished between Yahweh and Satan; the former was the Demiurge.

people all passages containing accusations of their elders, rulers, and judges, some of which have been preserved in the apocrypha." Origen's parade example of suppression is their removal of the tradition—well known from Origen's "New Testament"—that Israel always murdered its prophets.[38] This accusation is put into the mouth of Jesus in the gospels of "Matthew" and "Luke," but Origen is a careful enough reader to know that no such evidence exists within the pages of his "Old Testament" to warrant such a charge. Moreover, Origen alleges that this is only one among many differences between the Hebrew (Jewish) and Greek (Christian) Bibles. "Must not whatever the Savior said be understood to be true, *even if the scriptures that confirm what he recounted are not to be found?"* (*Ep. Afr.* 13–15). Like Ptolemy, Origen utilizes the sayings of Jesus as his "canon" to correct (in this case, restore) the otherwise corrupt textual condition of the Scriptures.

Going further afield, we might even look to the Qur'an, and Islamic tradition about the Qur'an, as yet another analogy for comparison. I mean the Qur'anic critique of the Jewish and Christians Scriptures as corrupt because of human and Satanic mischief: "We have sent no messenger or apostle before you with whose recitations Satan did not tamper. Yet God abrogates what Satan interpolates; he confirms his revelations, for God is all-knowing, all-wise. This is in order to make the interpolations of Satan a test for those whose hearts are diseased and hardened" (Qur'an 22:52–53). Recall as well the stunning and extraordinarily complex admission made by the Islamic tradition that there are "Satanic verses" within the Qur'an itself and the equally striking admission that the Qur'an is incomplete: "Let none of you say, 'I have got the whole of the Qur'an.' How does he know what all of it is? For much of the Qur'an is gone. Let him say instead, 'I have got what has survived.'"[39]

The fabrication of a claim or the invention of a tradition that alleges there are problems in the transmission of a text might be seen as an exegetical liability. In fact, it serves the exegete's purposes only too well, for the exegete simply cannot afford to be seen in possession of a text that has come down intact. The link between the text and the putative author to whom it had been revealed has, at all costs, to be broken. The claims to imperfect transmission, textual corruptions, "Satanic verses," and the like are the creation of an exegete attempting to create space for his interpretation. The exegetical fiction is that this theorizing about the text is separate from the interpretation of it; the exegetical reality, however, is that the process of interpretation is already well under way in the exegete's "fixing" of the text. I call these fabrications of textual transmission "native" or "indigenous higher criticism," different only in degree, I submit, from its modern counterpart

---

[38] Citing Heb 11:37; Matt 23:29–38; Acts 7:52; 1 Thess 2:14–16.

[39] See F. E. Peters, *A Reader on Classical Islam* (Princeton: Princeton University Press, 1994), 161–65, 177–84; H. Gätje, *The Qur'an and Its Exegesis* (trans. A. T. Welch; Oxford: Oneworld, 1996), 57–59; and esp. J. Burton, *The Collection of the Qur'an* (Cambridge: Cambridge University Press, 1977), 117–37.

in biblical studies (cf., e.g., the *Quellenkritik* of a Wellhausen, Schwartz, or Bultmann on the Fourth Gospel).

Now, the Fourth Gospel is neither a systematic treatise nor a commentary in the conventional sense. The "Scriptures" (variously referred to) function in a manner similar to the other characters in the narrative. This means that we can only infer from the Fourth Gospel its theory of, and exegetical strategy toward, the Scriptures. Like Ptolemy, Origen, and the Qur'an, the Fourth Gospel's perspective on the Scriptures is ambiguous and critical because the very nature of these texts requires the interpreter to distinguish what is authentic in them from what is inauthentic or counterfeit, or in some cases to restore what has been lost. Furthermore, the dualism so characteristic of the Fourth Gospel seems to imply that these corruptions and counterfeits are not simply the result of human error or invention; like the Qur'an, the Scriptures themselves contain "Satanic verses."

I have described one technique of the Fourth Gospel's appropriation of the Scriptures as "abrogationist" or "supersessionist." In the two cases cited earlier, those having to do with the manna miracle and the question of the place of the Messiah's origin, both "scriptures" have been superseded.[40] But this is not the only technique the Fourth Gospel employs; it also adopts two others that I will call "revisionist" and "restorationist" strategies of textual appropriation. These three strategies should not be thought of as entirely separate or discrete, as there are times when they overlap, if not in the manner of their execution, then at least in terms of their function. Again, a few examples will have to suffice.[41]

As an example of the Fourth Gospel's revisionist strategy, consider the famous opening lines of the prologue: "In the beginning was the *Logos,* and the *Logos* was with God, and the *Logos* was God. . . . All things came into being through it," and so on (John 1:1–3). This is not simply a rejection or supersession of the Genesis account of creation; this is a revision of it, a rewriting of the ἀρχή. The author plays a game of one-upmanship with the scriptural narrative, frontloading the account of creation by placing the *Logos*-God "in the beginning." Note, too, that it is the *Logos,* in contrast to all the other would-be scriptural claimants, who is in the unique position to "exegete" the Deity: "No one has ever seen God; (the) unique God-who-is-in-the-breast-of-the-Father, that one has

---

[40] Compare the complex Islamic notion of *naskh* ("abrogation," "suppression," "replacement") with respect to certain passages in the Qur'an; see Burton, *Collection of the Qur'an,* 131–37.

[41] In the interest of time I mention only two instances of textual "restoration": both 7:38b ("as the scripture said, 'Rivers of living water will flow out of his belly'") and 15:25 ("But the word that is written in their law must be fulfilled: 'They hated me without a cause'") have no known textual referents. Each, I contend, is an instance of "scriptural restoration" (read invention). Cf. 17:12 and 19:28, which have quotation formulas but no apparent quotations. In fact, the former passage appears to be the "fulfillment" of the hero's own statement (λόγος) in 6:37, 39, prompting W. Sproston to identify this as the otherwise unknown "scripture" (" 'The Scripture' in John 17:12," in *Scripture—Meaning and Method: Essays Presented to Anthony Tyrrell Hanson* [ed. B. P. Thompson; Hull, England: University of Hull Press, 1987], 24–36).

given an account (of him)."[42] The choice of the verb ἐξηγεῖσθαι here rather than, say, ἀποκαλύπτειν is significant. Without denying the revelatory role of the *Logos*, it also adds a narrative dimension (ἐξήγησις) to the revelation that is crucial for establishing a proprietary relationship between the Fourth Gospel and "the Scriptures." "It is the [W]ord which gives . . . the only authentic account or 'exegesis' of God."[43] The conception seems to be something like this: the *Logos*, as divine intellect or mind (note its metaphorical location in the physical place of intellection, "the Father's breast"), is both the authorizing voice that speaks in "the Scriptures" and hence the only agency capable of (re)establishing their authority and expounding their true meaning *(as this is mediated exclusively by the Fourth Gospel!).*

For another instance of the Fourth Gospel's revisionist strategy of scriptural appropriation, consider the tortured exchange that takes place between the Revealer and his adversaries in John 5. The polemic reaches a rather high pitch when the Revealer charges, "You have never heard his [the Father's] voice or seen his form, and you do not have his word dwelling in you, because the one whom he sent you do not believe" (5:37–39). The resemblance between this accusation and the description of the theophany at Horeb in Deut 4:12 cannot be coincidental: "And the Lord spoke to you [pl.] from the midst of the fire; you heard the voice of the words but did not see the likeness, only the voice." The Revealer's accusation, then, would seem to be a revision—again, a rewriting—of the theophany account, insisting that, not only was there no vision, there was no audition either. But this accusation is not simply a revision of the text; it is also a sinister anthropological statement. His adversaries do not have "his [the Father's] word [τὸν λόγον αὐτοῦ] dwelling in them." That is, they do not have the "word as text" in their possession, nor are they possessed of the "word as *logos*." Not only *did* they not hear the "voice"; they *could* not hear the voice—then or now. Again, this is not a rejection of the text but a correction or rewriting of it. It is also a statement of what is required in order for the text to be read correctly (hermeneutics and anthropology seem to be inextricably related in the Fourth Gospel). First, the Revealer must correct the text, and second, the reader/hearer must possess the *logos*, which makes interpretation possible. It is a dramatic, proleptic enactment of a principle that the narrator makes explicit in his concluding remarks on the action in the first half of the narrative:

> They were not believing in him, in order that the word [λόγος] of Isaiah the prophet might be fulfilled, which he said, "Lord, who has believed our report? And to whom has the arm of the Lord been revealed?" [Isa 53:1]. For this reason *they could not believe,* because again Isaiah said, "He has blinded their eyes, and he has hardened their heart, so that they might not see with their eyes and understand with their heart and turn, and I would heal them" [Isa 6:10]. Isaiah said these things because he saw his glory and spoke about him. (John 12:38–41)

---

[42] This admittedly tortured translation is an attempt to reflect the difficulties presented by the Greek at 1:18b.

[43] Ashton, *Understanding the Fourth Gospel,* 529.

By what means does the author of the Fourth Gospel claim the authority
to usurp the Scriptures in this manner? In a fashion similar to that of Ptolemy
and Origen, the Fourth Gospel takes as its canon the "words" (λόγοι, ῥήματα)
of the Revealer as the hermeneutical place on which to stand and the exclusive
place from which the Scriptures may be reconstituted and appropriated. Indeed, the same fulfillment formula that introduces quotations from Scripture,
"This happened in order to fulfill the scripture . . . ," is applied twice to the
Revealer's own words (18:9, 32), indicating that his λόγοι have the same authority as "the Scriptures."[44] Recall as well the final statement of the episode
cited earlier, where what the Revealer says is placed on a par with the Scriptures:
"If you do not believe [Moses'] writings, how will you believe my words?"
(5:47). But equally important, if not more so, are the author's claims about the
preexistent *Logos*, set forth in the prologue and alluded to in various ways
throughout the narrative, which allow the author to usurp the biblical materials, reject some of it, restore and revise other parts, and thereby transform
them into "Johannine" texts. Put differently, at the level of exegetical strategy, it
is the Fourth Gospel's use of the *Logos* that not only allows for the correction
and restoration of "the Scriptures" but also sets forth the manner in which they
must be read.

To swipe a term from the deconstructionists and invest it with a distinc-
tively Johannine meaning, we might say that the Fourth Gospel is "logocentrist."
To play with this term still further, we might say that the narrative world created
by the Fourth Gospel is "logocentrite"—indeed, "rabidly logocentrite." Philo of
Alexandria is an instructive analogue here (leaving aside for the moment the
much debated question of direct Philonic influence on the Fourth Gospel).
Philo's theory of the *logos*, especially as it relates to his understanding of the biblical theophanies (and especially those concerning Moses) and the importance of
the *logos* to his theory of the Scriptures, may be employed as both positive and
negative points for comparison with the Fourth Gospel. Philo would have agreed
entirely with the Fourth Gospel's claim that "no one has ever seen God." For
Philo, all of the biblical theophanies were "logophanies."[45] So also in the religious
imagination of the Fourth Gospel: what the various heroes of the Scriptures saw
was not the Deity itself, but the preexistent *Logos*. This is why the Revealer can say
of Abraham that "he rejoiced to see my day; he saw and was glad" (John 8:56),
and of Moses that "he wrote about me" (5:46). This is also why the narrator can
claim that Isaiah "saw his [viz., the preexistent *Logos*'s] glory and spoke of him"
(12:41). Recall, too, how the Revealer's "I am" sayings mimic the discourse of the
Deity in the biblical theophanies.

What sets Philo apart from the Fourth Gospel, however, is the confidence Philo displays in the *text* of the Scriptures. Although aware that Hebrew is

---

[44] Note that 18:32 is a reference back to 2:22, where "the scripture" (ἡ γραφή) and
"the word [ὁ λόγος] which Jesus spoke" are linked. The Revealer's λόγοι are γραφαί.

[45] The references, too numerous to list here, are discussed by C. H. Dodd, *The Interpretation of the Fourth Gospel* (Cambridge: Cambridge University Press, 1953), 68–70.

the *lingua sacra* and that the Scriptures were originally written in that language, Philo nevertheless has an unbridled confidence in the accuracy of the Greek Scriptures with which he works. This is not because Philo was a Hebraist who could judge the accuracy of the Greek translation. In fact, he seems not to have known any more Hebrew than was necessary to give a certain *recherché* appearance to his commentaries and theological treatises. Philo's confidence in the Greek Scriptures depends, rather, on his own theory of the text, namely, that the work of the seventy translators was divinely guided: their seventy separate translations agreed word for word.

> Sitting here in seclusion with none present save the elements of nature, earth, water, air, and heaven, the genesis of which was to be the first theme of their sacred revelation, for the laws begin with the story of the world's creation, they became as it were possessed, and, under inspiration, wrote, not each several scribe something different, but *the same word for word, as though dictated to each by an invisible prompter.* Yet who does not know that every language, and the Hellenic especially, abounds in terms, and that the same thought can be put in many shapes by changing single words and whole phrases and suiting the expression to the occasion? This was not the case, we are told, with this Law of ours, but *the Hellenic words used corresponded literally with the Chaldean, exactly suited to the things they indicated.* (Philo, *Moses* 2.37–38)[46]

This claim allows Philo to maintain unbroken the connection between words and things that is characteristic of the original Hebrew texts. For Philo, the translated text preserves the revelation intact. Contrast this with the view of the Fourth Gospel: the text is corrupt, riddled with errors, to say nothing of its being read improperly, that is, literally. Only after the *Logos*-Revealer revises, restores, and reauthorizes the Scriptures—as well as reveals the manner in which they should be read—only then may it be said that they are revelatory. At the level of establishing the texts, Philo's inspired seventy translators and the Johannine *Logos* are functionally equivalent; in both cases a theory of the text is the precondition of its interpretation.

If the Fourth Gospel claims that the preexistent *Logos* was the original authorizing voice in the Scriptures and that the *Logos*-Revealer revises, restores, and reauthorizes them, then how did the Scriptures fall into the state of corruption from which they had to be rescued? To the extent that the Fourth Gospel establishes a symmetrical relationship between Scriptures and cosmos, this same question may also be formulated in the following terms: if the preexistent *Logos* was

---

[46] *Philo* (trans. F. H. Colson and G. H. Whitaker; 10 vols.; LCL; Cambridge: Harvard University Press, 1932–1962), vol. 7 (Colson's translation is slightly altered here). Contrast the parallel account in *Let. Aris.* 301–316 (followed by Josephus): there was no miraculous agreement of the translators; rather they compared their work so as to arrive at an agreed-upon text (302). Philo's claim about a divinely inspired translation was invented to serve the interests of his exegesis. See the excellent analysis of this in D. Dawson, *Allegorical Readers and Cultural Revision in Ancient Alexandria* (Berkeley: University of California Press, 1992), 83–88.

the agent responsible for the creation of the cosmos and if the *Logos*-Revealer is also the σωτὴρ τοῦ κόσμου, then how did the cosmos fall into the state of corruption from which it had to be rescued? To answer these questions, at both the cosmic and the textual levels, would require solving the following Johannine riddle: "All who came [before me] are thieves and robbers"/"Before Abraham was, I am." But now, alas, my time has run out.[47]

---

[47] This paper was presented at a panel on "Scripture in Early Judaism and Christianity" at the Annual Meeting of the Society of Biblical Literature in 1999. I have retained the oral style of the original and its necessary brevity.

8

The Festival of Weeks and the Story of Pentecost in Acts 2

James C. VanderKam

.

The writer of Luke-Acts has placed the story about the first Christian Pentecost at a prominent point in his narrative. As Jesus and his disciples stand poised at Jerusalem, that central city in the developing geography of the work, the risen Christ ascends to heaven in the first chapter, and the ascension is followed by the outpouring of the Spirit on Pentecost in the second chapter. The gift of the Spirit subsequently energizes the first travelers of the Way on their mighty mission to bring the good news first to Jerusalem, then to Judea and Samaria, and finally to the far reaches of the inhabited earth.[1]

The fact that an event so momentous as the outpouring of the Spirit on the first disciple band took place on the Festival of Pentecost leads one to wonder whether more than mere coincidence of timing might have been involved. Why was the Spirit given then rather than by Jesus himself before he departed, as John seems to depict events (John 20:19–23)? Was there something about the festival, some associations with it, that led the author of Luke-Acts to couple it with the eschatological gift of the divine Spirit? In this essay the problem will be approached by examining the biblical roots of the Festival of Weeks, which was named Pentecost in Greek sources, and the traditions that became attached to it in the Bible and especially in subsequent Jewish literature, including the Qumran texts. The relevant texts will be studied to check whether they cast any helpful light upon the interpretation of Acts 2.[2]

---

[1] See F. F. Bruce, *The Acts of the Apostles: Greek Text with Introduction and Commentary* (3d ed.; Grand Rapids: Eerdmans, 1990), 61, for a summary of "the doctrine of the Spirit" in Acts.

[2] There have been various attempts to do this, with experts coming to rather different conclusions. The most impressive studies on the subject have been G. Kretschmar, "Himmelfahrt und Pfingsten," *ZKG* 66 (1954/1955): 209–53; and J. Potin, *La fête juive de la Pentecôte: Études des textes liturgiques* (2 vols.; LD 65, 65a; Paris: Cerf, 1971). A shorter survey can be found in Str-B 2:597–620. See also R. Le Déaut, "Pentecôte et tradition juive," *Spiritus* 7 (1961): 127–44.

The Festival of Weeks in the Hebrew Bible

According to biblical lists of holidays, שבועות (šavûʿôt), or the Festival of Weeks, is one of the three times when males were required to make pilgrimage to the sanctuary; the other two are the Festival of Unleavened Bread and the Festival of Booths.[3] On these occasions the Israelite male was not "to appear before me empty-handed" (Exod 23:15; 34:20 NRSV).[4] Unlike the festivals of Unleavened Bread (celebrated in the first month, from the fifteenth through the twenty-first = 1/15–21) and Booths (observed on 7/15–21 or 22), the Festival of Weeks is never dated precisely in the Bible. Exodus 23:16 says, "You shall observe the festival of harvest [חג הקציר], of the first fruits of your labor, of what you sow in the field" (NRSV). The only hint about dating in the context comes from the fact that this harvest festival falls between the holidays of Unleavened Bread, mentioned in 23:15, and the "festival of ingathering at the end of the year" (NRSV), named in 23:16. Exodus 34:22 is the first passage, in the present order of the scriptural text, to give the festival its familiar name and to identify the harvest with which it was associated: "You shall observe the festival of weeks, the first fruits of wheat harvest" (NRSV).

Somewhat more elaborate statements about the Festival of Weeks come from Deut 16:9–12 and Lev 23:15–16, where the reader receives instructions for determining its date. Deuteronomy 16:9–10 says, "You shall count seven weeks; begin to count the seven weeks from the time the sickle is first put to the standing grain. Then you shall keep the festival of weeks for the LORD your God, contributing a freewill offering in proportion to the blessing that you have received from the LORD your God" (NRSV). Deuteronomy 16:11 adds that the entire population—male and female, slave, free, and alien—was to celebrate the holiday with joy "at the place that the LORD your God will choose as a dwelling for his name" (NRSV), that is, at the sanctuary. Leviticus 23 is the most specific and detailed pericope about such points among the biblical rosters of festivals. It legislates that "from the day after the sabbath, from the day on which you bring the sheaf of the elevation offering, you shall count off seven weeks; they shall be complete. You shall count until the day after the seventh sabbath, fifty days; then you shall present an offering of new grain to the LORD" (vv. 15–16, NRSV). Bringing "the sheaf of the elevation offering" seems to have occurred at some point not long after Passover (23:9–11, 15); by implication, the Festival of Weeks would have taken place fifty days later, that is, early in the third month. Further details about offerings, including the two loaves of bread made with leaven, appear in Lev 23:17–20 and Num 28:26–31, where the holiday is called "the day of the first fruits" (v. 26) and a Festival of Weeks. Leviticus 23:21 and Num 28:26 stipulate that an assembly was to be held on this day, and on it work was prohibited.

---

[3] For a survey on the Festival of Weeks, see J. C. VanderKam, "Weeks, Festival of," *ABD* 6:895–97.

[4] English translations of the Bible are from the NRSV.

The Torah's imprecision in dating the holiday led to disputes about when it was to be observed. Only later sources attest these debates, but perhaps they have a long history behind them. We have just seen that Leviticus 23, which is the most explicit passage for the dating of the holiday, does not name a specific date on which it was to be observed. The source of the later controversies was the statement in Lev 23:15 on when the fifty-day count to the Festival of Weeks was to begin: "from the day after the sabbath . . . you shall count off seven weeks" (NRSV). The word thought to be ambiguous here was "sabbath," and several possibilities for interpreting it presented themselves. A first and transparent option was to read it as referring to the weekly Sabbath. In this case, the Festival of Weeks would always take place on a Sunday, seven weeks and one day after the Sabbath from which the count started. The problem with this reading was that the text did not say which Sabbath after Passover was the one designated by the rule. As we will see, one Jewish tradition (in *Jubilees* and the Dead Sea Scrolls) understood Lev 23:15 as intending the first Sabbath day after the completion of the eight days of Passover and the Festival of Unleavened Bread (i.e., after 1/14–21). A second possibility was to take the word "sabbath" in the sense of a festival. This is not the most obvious meaning of the term, but it is attested in the Bible. So, for example, the Day of Atonement, which falls on the tenth day of the seventh month, whatever day of the week that may be from year to year, is termed "a sabbath of complete rest" (Lev 23:32 NRSV, see also 23:33). If the law about the Festival of Weeks is using "sabbath" in this sense, then it could refer to the first day of the Festival of Unleavened Bread (the first holiday after Passover) or the last day of the same festival (these are the two most sacred days of the seven-day celebration and are marked by special assemblies [Lev 23:7–8]). The fifty-day count would, then, begin from either 1/16 (the day after the Sabbath = festival) or 1/22.[5]

Elsewhere in the HB, the Festival of Weeks plays virtually no role. It is mentioned by name only in 2 Chr 8:13, where it figures in a list of the three annual holidays. Although the festival is not named in 15:10–15, the passage does refer to an assembly held in the third month, after the "spirit of God came upon Azariah son of Oded" (15:1) who prophesied to King Asa. On that occasion the people and the king "gathered at Jerusalem in the third month of the fifteenth year of the reign of Asa" (v. 10 NRSV). Later one reads that they entered into a covenant and sealed it with an oath (vv. 12, 14–15). The use of the term "oath" (השבועה [v. 15]) may be meant to remind the reader of the Festival of Weeks (חג השבועות) in this context of the third month.[6] In view of the fact that 3/15 was the date of the

---

[5] For a convenient summary of the debate and references to the primary texts, see R. H. Charles, *The Book of Jubilees or the Little Genesis* (London: Black, 1902), 106–7, note; M. D. Herr, "The Calendar," in *The Jewish People in the First Century* (ed. S. Safrai and M. Stern; 2 vols.; CRINT 1; vol. 1, Assen: Van Gorcum; vol. 2, Philadelphia: Fortress, 1974–1976), 2:858–60.

[6] See, e.g., S. Japhet, *I & II Chronicles: A Commentary* (OTL; Louisville: Westminster John Knox, 1993), 724–25; H. G. M. Williamson, *1 and 2 Chronicles* (NCB Commentary; Grand Rapids: Eerdmans, 1982), 270.

festival in some later traditions (see below), the reference to "fifteenth" in connection with the third month is suggestive, although it obviously refers to a regnal year, not a monthly date. It is interesting, nevertheless, that the Targum for this passage, which dates from a much later time, reads at vv. 10–11a, "They assembled *at* Jerusalem in the third month of the fifteenth year of the reign of Asa, and on that day, *at the Feast of Weeks*, they sacrificed *before* the Lord."[7]

The list of holidays in Ezek 45:18–25 omits, for reasons not entirely clear, the Festival of Weeks. The puzzling absence of one of the three pilgrimage festivals was apparently a matter of concern to the Masoretes, who introduced the term "weeks" into the text but in a peculiar way. Ezekiel 45:21 reads, "In the first month, on the fourteenth day of the month, you shall celebrate the festival of the passover and for seven days unleavened bread shall be eaten" (NRSV). That the last clause intends the Festival of Unleavened Bread is obvious, and the sequel reinforces the conclusion by also referring to a seven-day observance (v. 23). In the MT, however, the word for "seven" (שבעת) in v. 21b is vocalized as if it were the word for "weeks" (שָׁבֻעוֹת).[8] There seems to be almost no likelihood that the vocalization expresses the meaning of the consonantal text, but its presence shows something of the influence of the Festival of Weeks on the traditionists who repointed the word.

The Festival of Weeks in Later Jewish Literature

The literature written between the Testaments mentions the Festival of Weeks several times.[9] These passages demonstrate that although the festival appears not to have been especially important in the HB, it was regularly observed and even gained greater significance for some groups later in Jewish history. It figures under either the name Weeks or the Greek Pentecost (meaning "fiftieth") in the writings of Josephus, in Philo's works, and in several other texts, among them the Dead Sea Scrolls.

The Festival of Weeks in Greek Sources

Josephus provides the earliest evidence for the Pharisaic view that the term "sabbath" in Lev 23:15 referred to a holiday and that the fifty-day count began on the sixteenth of the first month (= 1/16; Josephus, *Ant.* 3.10.5–6 §§250–252).

---

[7] The translation is from J. S. McIvor, *The Targum of Chronicles* (ArBib 19; Collegeville, Minn.: Liturgical Press, 1994), 178. In this series, words that differ from the MT are italicized.

[8] W. Zimmerli (*Ezekiel 2* [Hermeneia; Philadelphia: Fortress, 1983], 481, 483–84) shows the secondary nature of the masoretic vocalization and concludes that for the author the Festival of Weeks "has faded in its significance and is not made the opportunity for a particularly full sacrifice on the part of the prince" (484).

[9] For a survey, see J. Fitzmyer, "The Ascension of Christ and Pentecost," *TS* 45 (1984), 430–32; repr. in *To Advance the Gospel: New Testament Studies* (2d ed.; Biblical Resource Series; Grand Rapids: Eerdmans, 1998), 280–82.

There he writes, "On the second day of unleavened bread, that is to say the six-teenth, our people partake of the crops which they have reaped and which have not been touched till then, and esteeming it right first to do homage to God, to whom they owe the abundance of these gifts, they offer to Him the first-fruits of the barley" (§250). This is the biblical "sheaf of the elevation offering." A few lines later he adds, "When the seventh week following this sacrifice has elapsed—these are the forty-nine days of the (so-called) 'Weeks'—on the fiftieth day, which the Hebrews call *Asartha,* the word denoting 'fiftieth,' they present to God a loaf of two *assarôns* of flour of wheat made with leaven and, as a sacrifice, two lambs" (§252).[10] In *Ant.* 13.8.4 §§251–252, besides noting that warfare is not permitted on Pentecost, he comments about an occasion in the time of John Hyrcanus, "for the festival of Pentecost had come round, following the Sabbath" (§252). Scholars have wondered whether the festival just happened to fall on a Sunday ("following the Sabbath") that year or whether it occurred on Sunday as a matter of practice, as it did for some groups (such as the authors of the Dead Sea Scrolls); there does not appear to be sufficient evidence, however, for deciding in this case.[11] In *Ant.* 14.13.4 §337 (cf. *J.W.* 1.13.3 §253) he notes that large numbers of people from the countryside went to Jerusalem for the celebration (see also *Ant.* 17.10.2 §254 [cf. *J.W.* 2.3.1 §42]; 2 Macc 12:31–32). According to *J.W.* 6.5.3 §§299–300, the priests entered the inner court of the temple during the night before the ceremonies of the holiday took place so that they would be prepared for the immense number of sacrifices that would have to be made at the altar the next day (see also Tob 2:1; Philo, *Decalogue* 160; *Spec. Laws* 2.176–87).

The Festival of Weeks in the Jubilees-Qumran Tradition

One stream in early Judaism, that from which we have received *Jubilees* and the sectarian Dead Sea Scrolls, seems to have associated more themes with the Festival of Weeks than other groups did; or at least we may say that our sources, which are more abundant for this tradition, show that the holiday was extremely important in the minds of those who found their ideological home in it. *Jubilees,* a Hebrew work written in the mid–second century B.C.E. if not before,[12] is the earliest witness to the enhanced importance of the Festival of Weeks. As the writer of the book retells the stories in Genesis and the first half of Exodus, he deals with the Festival of Weeks in a series of significant passages. A fundamental fact about the holiday in *Jubilees* is that the author connects it with the one ongoing covenant that God made and renewed several times with his people.

The first passage in which the festival and the covenant are clearly connected is *Jub.* 6:17–19, which pairs Noah's eternal covenant in Genesis 9 and the Festival of Weeks. In *Jubilees'* chronology of the flood, the earth became dry on

---

[10] St. J. Thackeray, LCL.

[11] Marcus, LCL. See Marcus's note, p. 354.

[12] See J. C. VanderKam, *Textual and Historical Studies in the Book of Jubilees* (HSM 14; Missoula, Mont.: Scholars Press, 1977), 207–85.

2/17, and on 2/27 Noah released all the animals that were on board the ark (5:31–32). He himself, however, did not emerge from the boat until 3/1, when "he left the ark and built an altar" (6:1; cf. Gen 8:19). The sacrifice that he then makes leads to the covenant between God and Noah. After the account about the covenant ends, the angel of the presence who is revealing the contents of *Jubilees* to Moses on Mount Sinai reports that

> it has been ordained and written on the heavenly tablets that they should celebrate the festival of weeks during this month—once a year—to renew the covenant each and every year. This entire festival had been celebrated in heaven from the time of creation until the lifetime of Noah. . . . Then Noah and his sons kept it . . . until Noah's death. . . . Abraham alone kept (it), and his sons Isaac and Jacob kept it until your [Moses'] lifetime. During your lifetime the Israelites had forgotten (it) until I renewed (it) for them at this mountain [Sinai].[13]

The passage underscores the importance of the Festival of Weeks in several ways. First, the laws about the holiday are inscribed on the heavenly tablets; included in the legislation is the connection between festival and covenant. Second, the Festival of Weeks, on which the covenant is renewed every year, was celebrated in heaven before it was revealed to Noah, the first human to observe it. The initial biblical reference to the holiday is, as we have seen, embedded in the stories about the laws revealed to Moses on Mount Sinai, but the writer of *Jubilees* antedates the celebration of the Festival of Weeks to the time of creation, and he makes Noah, not Moses, the first scriptural worthy to keep it. A third way in which the pericope highlights the festival is to relate it not only to Noah but also to Abraham, Isaac, Jacob, and Moses—the great heroes of the biblical story.

Jubilees 6:17–19 points the reader to the other passages in the book where the festival comes under consideration. *Jubilees* 14 retells the story about the covenant of the pieces made with Abram in Genesis 15. *Jubilees* 14:1 dates the opening events of the chapter to the first day of the third month, but the writer separates the initial appearance of the Lord to Abram from the ceremony of the animal pieces. As he tells it, two weeks elapsed between the time when the Lord ordered Abram to gather the sacrificial animals and the moment of the ritual itself. "He got all of these in the middle of the month" (*Jub.* 14:10). In *Jubilees'* solar calendar, the third month has thirty-one days, so that the middle would be the fifteenth or the sixteenth day in it.[14] The sequel follows Genesis 15 closely, but the section ends with a statement from the revealing angel: "During this night we concluded a covenant with Abram like the covenant which we concluded during this month with Noah. Abram renewed the festival and the ordinance for himself forever" (*Jub.* 14:20).

---

[13] The translations of *Jubilees* are from J. C. VanderKam, *The Book of Jubilees* (2 vols.; CSCO 510, 511, Scriptores aethiopici 87, 88; Leuven: Peeters, 1989), vol. 2.

[14] It is overwhelmingly likely, in view of the Qumran calendrical texts, that "the middle of the month" in *Jubilees* refers to the fifteenth; see esp. 44:1–5. In its calendrical system, 3/15 is a Sunday, the day of the week on which the Festival of Weeks always falls.

As we might expect, the writer also ties the eternal covenant of Genesis 17 to the Festival of Weeks: "in the third month, in the middle of the month [= 3/15]—Abram celebrated the festival of the firstfruits of the wheat harvest" (*Jub.* 15:1). He also claims that Isaac was born "in the third month; in the middle of the month, on the day that the Lord had told Abraham—on the festival of the firstfruits of the harvest" (16:13). Although, in specifying such dating, the author may appear to be arbitrarily manipulating the biblical material, there is some exegetical justification for relating these covenants with the Festival of Weeks, which falls at some point in the third month in any Jewish calendar. The two key triggers in the text of Genesis were the promise that Abraham's son would be born on the מועד ("[at this] season," Gen 17:21; 18:14; 21:2) and the prediction that the blessed event would occur "in due season" (כעת חיה [lit., "at a living time," i.e., , when things start to grow], 18:10, 14), which the author of *Jubilees* understood to be referring to a point early in the agricultural cycle.[15] In *Jubilees* Abraham dies on the Festival of Weeks (22:1), Jacob's son Judah was born on it (28:15), and Jacob and Laban concluded their treaty on 3/15 (29:7). A final reference to the Festival of Weeks occurs in the Jacob stories: Jacob observed the holiday just before descending to Egypt (44:4).

These are the explicit references to the Festival of Weeks in *Jubilees,* but the very beginning of the book shows that the entire revelation in it must be understood in light of the associations with the holiday. The prologue and *Jubilees* 1 define the setting for the appearance of God to Moses and the revelations made to him by the angel of the presence as a time when Moses was on Mount Sinai, but *Jub.* 1:1 is more explicit: "During the first year of the Israelites' exodus from Egypt, in the third month—on the sixteenth of the month—the Lord said to Moses: 'Come up to me on the mountain. I will give you the two stone tablets of the law and the commandments which I have written so that you may teach them.'" As we have seen, the date for weeks is 3/15 in *Jubilees;* hence the revelation to Moses came on the day after the festival (cf. Exod 24:4). The general time frame was fixed by the date in Exod 19:1: "On the third new moon [month] after the Israelites had gone out of the land of Egypt, on that very day, they came into the wilderness of Sinai." The implication seems to be that the date for entry into the wilderness of Sinai was the first day of the third month, and it was so understood in *Targum Pseudo-Jonathan.*[16] It is not obvious from the sequel in Exodus 19–24 how many days elapsed between Israel's arrival in the wilderness and the revelation to Moses, but *Jubilees'* view that the revelation recounted in the book came the day after the covenantal ceremony may be the same as the one found in later sources, including the commentary of the medieval scholar

---

[15] For a fuller statement of the argument, see J. C. VanderKam, "The Temple Scroll and the Book of Jubilees," in *Temple Scroll Studies: Papers Presented at the International Symposium on the Temple Scroll, Manchester, December 1987* (ed. G. J. Brooke; JSPSup 7; Sheffield, England: Sheffield Academic Press, 1989), 220.

[16] See also B. Jacob, *The Second Book of the Bible: Exodus* (Hoboken, N.J.: Ktav, 1992), 523.

Rashbam.[17] What does follow from the sequence in the prologue and *Jub.* 1:1–4, passages that are clearly based on Exod 24:12–18,[18] is that the author understood the covenantal ceremonies to have taken place on the Festival of Weeks. In other words, the Sinai covenant, too, was ratified on the very festival date on which earlier enactments of the agreement were made. For *Jubilees,* Weeks was a festival of covenant making and covenant renewal, just as 6:17 said—"to renew the covenant each and every year." It should be noted that the holiday itself is not first and foremost tied to the act of giving the Sinaitic Torah; covenant is the primary association for the holiday in *Jubilees.*[19]

This same tradition associating the Festival of Weeks with covenantal renewal is now documented in the Qumran texts.[20] There are several different kinds of references to the festival in the Qumran scrolls. For example, some of the calendrical texts mention it, and these supply the data necessary for calculating the date on which the authors observed the holiday. Thus *Calendrical Document A* (4Q320) correlates the priestly watches of 1 Chr 24:7–19 with the holidays in a 364-day calendar. That is, it mentions which priestly watch or shift would be serving during each of the festivals. Since the priestly courses were on duty for one week at a time, it is possible to determine the number of days between the holidays that are named. So, in 4Q320 frg. 4 iii, during a certain year Passover falls in the third day of Maoziah's week of service, and the waving of the elevation offering takes place on the first day in Jedaiah's week. According to the list in 1 Chronicles, one priestly watch intervenes between these two names; as a result, the wave offering, which Leviticus 23 does not date precisely but from which the fifty-day count to the Festival of Weeks begins, took place twelve days after Passover, or on 1/26. Counting, then, from 1/26 as the first day, the Festival of Weeks is dated to 3/15, as *Jubilees* (where it is called the middle of the month) implies.[21]

More important for the present purposes is the fact that in some Qumran texts the Festival of Weeks appears to be the occasion for an annual covenantal ceremony, just as in *Jubilees.* The *Rule of the Community* refers to an annual ceremony at which candidates for admission entered the group and those who were already members apparently renewed their commitment (1QS 1.16–3.12). In the ceremony as described there, the priests recite the favors that God has shown to Israel, while the Levites curse those who belong to the camp of Belial. Those entering the covenant respond with a double Amen.

---

[17] M. L. Lockshin, ed. and trans., *Rashbam's Commentary on Exodus: An Annotated Translation* (BJS 310; Atlanta: Scholars Press, 1997), 297–98.

[18] J. T. A. G. M. van Ruiten, "The Rewriting of Exodus 24:12–18 in Jubilees 1:1–4," *BN* 79 (1995): 25–29.

[19] See also Kretschmar, "Himmelfahrt und Pfingsten," 224–27; Potin, *Fête juive,* 1:123–31.

[20] For an earlier study of the topic, written before the cave 4 texts were available, see B. Noack, "The Day of Pentecost in Jubilees, Qumran, and Acts," *ASTI* 1 (1962): 73–95.

[21] For the calendrical documents, see S. Talmon, J. Ben-Dov, and U. Glessmer, *Qumran Cave 4 XVI Calendrical Texts* (DJD 21; Oxford: Clarendon, 2001).

Thus shall they do, year by year, for as long as the dominion of Belial endures. The Priests shall enter first, ranked one after another according to the perfection of their spirit; then the Levites; and thirdly, all the people one after another in their Thousands, Hundreds, Fifties, and Tens, that every Israelite may know his place in the Community of God according to the everlasting design. No man shall move down from his place nor move up from his allotted position. For according to the holy design, they shall all of them be in a Community of truth and virtuous humility, of loving-kindness and good intent one towards the other, and (they shall all of them be) sons of the everlasting Company. (1QS 2.19–25)[22]

The *Rule of the Community* does not stipulate when the covenantal ceremony was to occur, but two copies of the *Damascus Document* from cave 4— 4QD^a (4Q266) 11 16–18 = 4QD^e (4Q270) 7 ii 11–12—probably supply the missing information. "All [the inhabitants of] the camps shall congregate in the third month and curse those who turn right [or left from the] Law" (4QD^a 11 16–18).[23] If this is the occasion pictured more fully in the *Rule of the Community*,[24] the Qumran community and other groups in the wider Essene movement would have renewed the covenant on the same holiday as the one to which *Jubilees* assigns the great biblical covenants. It may be that 4QBerakhot (4Q286–290)[25] contains the blessings recited on this occasion.

The Festival of Weeks (Pentecost) in the New Testament

With the information supplied in the previous sections, we are in a position to turn to the NT evidence regarding the Festival of Weeks, or Pentecost.[26] Since all of the first followers of Jesus were Jewish, it comes as no surprise that they would celebrate a holiday mandated in the Scriptures, and we may assume that they observed it in the manner acceptable at their time. The most famous passage about the holiday is Acts 2, which is dated to the day of Pentecost (2:1), the day on

---

[22] The translation is from G. Vermes, *The Complete Dead Sea Scrolls in English* (5th ed.; New York: Allen Lane, Penguin Press, 1997). S. Metso (*The Textual Development of the Qumran Community Rule* [STDJ 21; New York: E. J. Brill, 1997]) maintains that this part of the text was not in the earliest form of the *Rule;* nevertheless, its presence in 1QS guarantees that it dates from no later than 100–75 B.C.E., the date of the manuscript. The last lines of the citation remind one of the early Christian fellowship after the miracle of Pentecost (Acts 2:42–47).

[23] The translation is from J. Baumgarten, *Qumran Cave 4, XIII: The Damascus Document (4Q266–273)* (DJD 18; Oxford: Clarendon, 1996), 77.

[24] J. T. Milik has supported the identification ("Milkî-ṣedeq et Milkî-reša^c dans les anciens écrits juifs et chrétiens," *JJS* 23 [1972]: 135–36), but Baumgarten thinks it might have preceded Pentecost (p. 78).

[25] These texts, which have been edited by B. Nitzan, have now been published in E. Eshel, J. Vanderkam, M. Brady, et al., eds., *Qumran Cave 4, VI: Poetical and Liturgical Texts, Part 1* (DJD 11; Oxford: Clarendon, 1998).

[26] For Pentecost in the NT, see Fitzmyer, "Ascension of Christ and Pentecost," 277–87.

which the miraculous gift of the Spirit was made to the followers of Jesus in Jerusalem. The purpose here is not to provide a full exegesis of Acts 2 but rather to explore how the author of that chapter may have used OT and early Jewish exegetical traditions in his literary account of the event.

Relation with Old Testament Data about the Festival of Weeks

On a superficial level, little in Acts 2 reminds one of the biblical legislation on the Festival of Weeks or of the covenantal associations with it in the *Jubilees*-Qumran tradition. For example, Acts 2 says nothing about the firstfruits of the wheat harvest, and the writer gives no indication of his view on calculating the date for the holiday. Also, there is no mention of the sacrifices that were made at the temple, nor is the joy with which the festival was to be observed brought to the attention of the reader. Furthermore, one can hardly say that Acts 2 uses the language of covenant making and covenant renewal, although there seems to be a general similarity between Pentecost as the birth of the church (the new people of God) and the covenant at Sinai as the beginning of Israel as God's chosen nation. The list of places from which the celebrants came in 2:8–11 reflects the fact that the pilgrimage festival was observed by Jews of the various diasporas. But beyond this there is little that strikes the reader as specifically related to the Festival of Weeks. What can be said therefore about influences from earlier texts and exegetical traditions on the formation of the narrative in Acts 2?

Highlights of the Account in Acts 2

There are in fact several places in which Acts 2 betrays an awareness of Jewish traditions about Pentecost. It will be useful to sketch the story and highlight a few items that can be clarified through Jewish associations with the Festival of Weeks. Developing a case for the Jewish background of Acts 2 will require the employment of some sources that are later, sometimes much later, in date than the time when Acts was written. Where possible, evidence will be adduced to show that the traditions involved in these later texts are likely to have existed at an earlier time.

First, the author states that when "the day of Pentecost had come, they were all together in one place" (2:1 NRSV). The language of the text is actually a little more expressive than the NRSV suggests. The verb translated blandly as "had come" is συμπληροῦσθαι, which suggests the notion of "fill completely" and, in time expressions, "fulfill, approach, come" (cf. Luke 9:51).[27] The entire group that was together in one place numbered about 120 people (1:15), a multiple of the suggestive twelve. The topic treated immediately before Acts 2 (1:15–26) is the selection of Matthias to fill the number of twelve apostles who were the

---

[27] BAG 787; G. Delling, "συμπληρόω," *TDNT* 6:308–9. The Greek verb is used in LXX Jer 25:12 for the seventy years until completion of the exile.

leaders of the band of 120 believers. The place where they were congregated is not named, but it is called a "house" in 2:2, a reference that has often been understood to be the temple but that is too vague to secure the point.[28]

Second, the giving of the invisible Spirit is marked by visible signs that are described briefly: "And suddenly from heaven there came a sound like the rush of a violent wind, and it filled the entire house where they were sitting. Divided tongues, as of fire, appeared among them, and a tongue rested on each of them. All of them were filled with the Holy Spirit and began to speak in other languages, as the Spirit gave them ability" (2:2–4 NRSV). That is, the images are of a heavenly sound like a powerful wind, tongues looking like fire, and speaking in other languages.

Third, after the writer depicts the reaction of those around the recipients of the Spirit and relates their varying assessments of the event, he says that Peter stood to address the audience. His apology for the group included the use of several passages from the Bible that supported his interpretation of the event. The passages that he cited are Joel 2:28–32, which he ties to the last days (Acts 2:17–21), Ps 16:8–11 (Acts 2:25–28; Ps 16:10 is repeated in Acts 2:31), Ps 132:11 (cf. 2 Sam 7:12–13 in Acts 2:30), and Ps 110:1 (Acts 2:34–35).

Fourth, the result of the event and the explanation offered for it were that the small band of 120 members was augmented with 3,000 new adherents (2:41). We learn that the entire group "devoted themselves to the apostles' teaching and fellowship, to the breaking of bread and the prayers" (v. 42 NRSV). Their fellowship was so ideal that "[a]ll who believed were together and had all things in common" (v. 44 NRSV).

Acts 2 in Its Setting

A good case can be made that Luke was indeed informed by the associations that Pentecost had attracted when he compiled his account of the beginning of the church. To see this, one must take a wider look at the chapter within the context in which the author placed it.

Acts 2 in Its New Testament Setting

The end of the Gospel of Luke already prepares the reader for what will come in Acts, the sequel to the Third Gospel. There, as Jesus speaks with his startled disciples before leaving them, he tells them that "everything written about me in the law of Moses, the prophets, and the psalms must be fulfilled" (Luke 24:44 NRSV). Jesus also informs them that what has happened and is soon to take place was recorded in the Scriptures that he expounded for them: "Thus it is written, that the Messiah is to suffer and to rise from the dead on the third day, and that repentance and forgiveness of sins is to be proclaimed in his name to all nations, beginning from Jerusalem. You are witnesses of these things. And see, I am

---

[28] See, e.g., Bruce, *Acts of the Apostles*, 114. He thinks that the phrase "where they were sitting" in v. 2 rules out identification of the place with the temple.

sending upon you what my Father promised; so stay here in the city until you
have been clothed with power from on high" (24:46–49 NRSV). The gospel ends
with Jesus' withdrawal into heaven, and it is at this point, with a fuller account of
the ascension, that Acts begins, following the summary introduction in Acts 1:1–5.

Acts 1 forms an essential part of the context for the second chapter, if for no
other reason than that it has a number of references to the Holy Spirit (Acts 1:2,
5, 8, 16). The story about Jesus' ascension in this chapter should remind the biblically literate reader of episodes from the life of Moses. For example, 1:3 refers to
the forty days between the resurrection and the ascension, a number that recalls
several time spans in Moses' career, including his two stays atop Mount Sinai.
Also, the account of the ascension, whether that in Luke 24 or that in Acts 1, contains other reminders. Luke 24:50 uses the suggestive words "he led them out"
(NRSV; ἐξήγαγεν δὲ αὐτούς), as Moses had led the people from Egypt in the exodus. We learn that the ascension took place on a mountain (Acts 1:11–12; Luke
24:50 places it at Bethany, which is on the Mount of Olives) and that a cloud hid
Jesus from the sight of the disciples who were following his upward flight (Acts
1:9, 11). His ascent had been preceded by the disciples' question, "Lord, is this the
time when you will restore the kingdom to Israel?" (v. 6 NRSV). All of these motifs
are attested in the Sinai stories. There "Moses went up to God" (Exod 19:3 NRSV;
cf. 19:20; 24:1–2). Moreover, a cloud plays a role in the Sinai stories as the Lord
comes down on the mountain in a thick cloud (Exod 19:16), and Moses is said to
have entered the cloud during his ascent (24:15–18). One wonders also whether
the disciples' question about restoring the kingdom is meant to remind the
reader of the Lord's words at Sinai: "Indeed, the whole earth is mine, but you
shall be for me a priestly kingdom and a holy nation" (19:5b–6a NRSV). And is the
command to the disciples to wait in Jerusalem (Acts 1:4; Luke 24:49) meant to recall (or perhaps serve as a contrast to) Moses' order to the elders to wait for him
and Joshua until they returned to them (Exod 24:14)? However this may be, it is
perhaps not accidental that the last part of Acts 1 is concerned with restoring the
disciple band to the number twelve with the choice of Matthias by lot, just as
the twelve tribes were a party to the covenant in Exodus 24: "He rose early in the
morning, and built an altar at the foot of the mountain, and set up twelve pillars,
corresponding to the twelve tribes of Israel" (Exod 24:4 NRSV).[29]

The result is that the reader of Luke-Acts might be expected, since Jesus'
parting words in the gospel pointed clearly to the Scriptures, to have Moses and
Mount Sinai in mind as he turned his attention to the Pentecost story in Acts 2.[30]
The chronology of Acts 1–2 could have suggested the same. Moses, according to
Jubilees, ascended Mount Sinai and renewed the covenant on 3/15, which was

---

[29] Cf. J. Fitzmyer, *The Acts of the Apostles* (AB 31; New York: Doubleday, 1998), 221,
232. As he notes, the meaning of the episode in Acts 1:21–26 is related to Acts 2: it allows
the twelve apostles to confront the twelve tribes of Israel at Pentecost.

[30] For a list of verbal parallels between Exodus 19 and 24, on the one hand, and Acts
2, on the other, see J. Dupont, "The First Christian Pentecost," in *The Salvation of the Gentiles* (Ramsey, N.J.: Paulist, 1979), 35–59.

fifty days after 1/26, but if other calculations for the timing of the Festival of Weeks were used (e.g., the Pharisaic one), the fifty-day span would run from just after the Festival of Passover to the Festival of Weeks early in the third month, when Moses ascended Sinai. That is, the fifty-day period from just after Passover to Moses' ascent is related to the fifty-day period from the crucifixion just after Passover to Jesus' gift of the Spirit (Acts 2:32–33). But it should be said that the comparable periods are not exactly parallel: one is from Passover to ascent/covenant, and the other is from Passover to Pentecost/gift of the Spirit. Here, however, an interesting point comes into play.

The close connection between Jesus' ascension (Acts 1) and the outpouring of the Spirit (Acts 2) was evident to a number of early Christian readers. There is a tradition, attested in some Eastern sources, that the ascension of Christ and Pentecost were celebrated on the same day—the fiftieth day after Easter. G. Kretschmar has compiled the evidence and offered a learned explanation of it. Sources from Syria and Palestine reflect the practice of pairing the two celebrations; one such witness is the *Teaching of Addai*. Kretschmar thinks that this kind of association probably reflects, in some sense, connections that had already been made in Judaism between the Festival of Weeks and the events of Sinai. We have seen that in *Jubilees* the two are tied together. The practice of combining the celebration of the two events on one day eventually gave way to the Lukan chronology, which separates the day of Pentecost as the time when the Spirit came.[31] For Kretschmar, the connections between the NT theology of Jesus' ascension that comes to expression in Acts 2:33–35, John 20:22–23, and Eph 4:7–12 and the early Jewish interpretation of Moses' ascent of Sinai are so strong that one can hardly deny their presence.[32]

Kretschmar and other scholars have pursued this line of evidence to show that at some point an association between the Festival of Weeks and the Sinai experience became widespread among Jewish interpreters. We have already seen that for *Jubilees* there is an intimate connection between the Festival of Weeks and the Sinai events, particularly the renewal of the covenant.[33] In this Jewish tradition, which long antedates the time when Acts 1–2 was written, we find therefore an inseparable bond between ascent, covenant renewal, and the Festival of Weeks. In Acts 1–2 we find a similarly close tie between ascent and Pentecost, when the Spirit was given. These are interesting parallels, but the similarities extend only so far; the difference lies in the theme of covenant renewal in *Jubilees* and the giving of the Spirit in Acts. Are there further parallels in Jewish texts that

---

[31] Kretschmar, "Himmelfahrt und Pfingsten," 209–12. He notes that Acts 2:32–33 connects Christ's ascent with the gift of the Spirit; see also John 20:22–23; Eph 4:7–12, where Ps 68:19 is cited in a similar context. In rabbinic exegesis, Ps 68:19 was understood with reference to Moses (note עלית in Ps 68:19 and עלה in Exod 19:3), who gave the gift of the law that he had obtained from above. Ephesians 4:7–12 takes a tradition about Moses' ascent and applies it to Christ (Kretschmar, "Himmelfahrt und Pfingsten," 216–17). Kretschmar thinks that both Ps 68:19 and Psalm 110 are behind Acts 2:33–35.

[32] Kretschmar, "Himmelfahrt und Pfingsten," 218.

[33] For Kretschmar's analysis of the *Jubilees* material, see ibid., 224–27.

could furnish a more complete case for the thesis that the writer of Acts 1–2 adapted his story of ascension and Pentecost in reliance upon Jewish understandings of the Moses–Sinaitic covenant episode?

Acts 2 in Its Jewish Setting

Using the highlights of Acts 2 that were described above (and the contents of Acts 1), it is possible to demonstrate that, in three of the four cases, parallels in midrashic traditions show the thoroughly Jewish foundation of Luke's account of Pentecost.

Συμπληροῦσθαι: As noted earlier, the verb in Acts 2:1 expresses the idea that a period of time has come to an end, has been filled up or completed. In this sense, Luke's choice of the verb may best be explained by the Hebrew word עצרת, which became a common designation for the Festival of Weeks in rabbinic sources. It means an "assembly" in this derived sense, but the verb with which it is related means "stop, halt; close," the last sense being used for time periods. It seems that עצרת was applied to the Festival of Weeks because of the holiday's connection with the Passover season: it marked the end or completion of the season that began with Passover. While the use of עצרת for the Festival of Weeks is standard in rabbinic sources,[34] we saw above that Josephus, in the late first century C.E., employed the term in referring to the holiday (*Ant.* 13.8.4 §252: "the [so-called] 'Weeks'—on the fiftieth day, which the Hebrews call *Asartha,* the word denoting 'fiftieth,' they present to God a loaf of two *assarôns* of flour of wheat made with leaven and, as a sacrifice, two lambs").[35] In other words, the term was applied to the holiday already at the time when Acts was written. Although Luke does not use a literal equivalent of עצרת and he may have attached his own added meaning to the term (as in Luke 9:51), it was a natural one for him to use in the context.[36]

Tongues as of Fire and Languages:[37] Commentators have pointed to a series of rabbinic texts that, in connection with various passages in Exodus 19–24, contain comments that remind one of features in Acts 2, such as the firelike tongues associated with the languages of the audience. Luke specifically writes about "tongues [γλῶσσαι], as of fire" (2:3), and using the same word, he says that the recipients of the Spirit spoke in other languages (v. 4, γλώσσαις). The background for this dual usage of fiery tongues and languages[38] has been traced to the

---

[34] See M. Jastrow, *A Dictionary of the Targumim, the Talmud Babli and Yerushalmi, and the Midrashic Literature* (1903; 2 vols.; repr., Brooklyn, N.Y.: P. Shalom, 1967), 1103–4. He defines it as "a festive gathering for the conclusion of a festive season, concluding feast." The Festival of Weeks is designated עצרת של פסח, i.e., the conclusion of Passover.

[35] See Potin, *Fête juive,* 1:122–23.

[36] See Fitzmyer, *Acts of the Apostles,* 237.

[37] For this section, see Potin, *Fête juive,* 1:231–59.

[38] It is perhaps worth noting that both revelations—of the divine voice at Sinai and of the Spirit in Acts 2—happened in the morning (Exod 19:16; Acts 2:15; see Potin, *Fête juive,* 1:304).

midrashic traditions that grew around Exod 19:16: "On the morning of the third day there was thunder and lightning, as well as a thick cloud on the mountain, and a blast of a trumpet so loud that all the people who were in the camp trembled" (NRSV). The key word here is קלת (translated as "thunder"), which was understood not as "thunder," which the context requires but as "voices," a standard meaning of the term. If Exod 19:16 is speaking about voices, the voices in question would seem to be God's speech.[39] The verse could also be related to Exod 20:18 ("When all the people witnessed [lit., saw] the thunder [קולת] and lightning" NRSV) and to the statements about the Lord's voice (קול) in Psalm 29, which became a lectionary psalm for the Festival of Weeks. There the voice of the Lord is mentioned and praised seven times, and one of these seven references reads, "The voice of the LORD flashes forth flames of fire" (Ps 29:7 NRSV). Conclusions drawn from such passages were that the Lord's words came in seven voices and were visible because they were accompanied by fire.[40] The Lord does, of course, appear in fiery terror at Sinai, as Exod 19:18; 24:17; Deut 4:11 indicate; moreover, Exod 20:18 refers to lightning (לפידים).

The sources for these exegetical associations date from times much later than when Luke-Acts was written, but Philo (ca. 20 B.C.E.–50 C.E.), who wrote before Luke-Acts, seems to know similar elaborations or understandings of the biblical text. In *On the Decalogue* he alludes to the voice of the Lord that the people "saw" and tries to explain what this might mean. In *Decalogue* §33 he writes that God, "giving shape and tension to the air and changing it to flaming fire, sounded forth like the breath through a trumpet an articulate voice so loud that it appeared to be equally audible to the farthest as well as the nearest." Later he says,

> Then from the midst of the fire that streamed from heaven there sounded forth to their utter amazement a voice, for the flame became articulate speech in the language familiar to the audience, and so clearly and distinctly were the words formed by it that they seemed to see rather than hear them. What I say is vouched for by the law in which it is written, "All the people saw the voice" [LXX Exod 20:18], a phrase fraught with much meaning, for it is the case that the voice of men is audible, but the voice of God truly visible. Why so? Because whatever God says is not words but deeds, which are judged by the eyes rather than the ears. (*Decalogue* §§46–47)[41]

It is interesting, in connection with Acts 2, that Philo pictures a flame as becoming articulate speech and that the language was "familiar to the audience."

Besides this explication of the voice from Sinai made visible by flames, another line of interpretation explains the קלת of Exodus 19 as languages, specifically the languages of Israel's nearest neighbors or even the languages of all the

---

[39] Luke's term ἦχος in Acts 2:2 is related to the verb ἤχει in LXX Exod 19:16 (Fitzmyer, *Acts of the Apostles,* 238).

[40] For references, see Kretschmar, "Himmelfahrt und Pfingsten," 238–39. *Mekilta, Baḥodesh* 4.3–4 says that "the Torah is fire, was given from the midst of fire, and is comparable to fire" (J. Lauterbach, *Mekilta de Rabbi Ishmael* [3 vols.; Philadelphia: Jewish Publication Society, 1949]), vol. 2.

[41] Colson, LCL.

nations on the earth.[42] The first option entailed relating the Exodus passages to other scriptural allusions to the divine appearance at Sinai:

> The nations of the world were asked to accept the Torah, and this [was done] so as not to give them grounds for saying [to God], "If we had been offered [the Torah] then of course we would have accepted it upon ourselves." So they *were* offered it and did not accept it upon themselves, for it says [with reference to the Sinai legislation], "The Lord came from Sinai and [earlier had] dawned from [Mt.] Seir [home of the Edomites] upon them, He shone forth from Mt. Paran [home of the Ishmaelites, Gen. 21:21], He proceeded from ten thousand holy ones, with the **fire of law** in His right hand to them. Yea, He favored peoples. . . ." [traditional Hebrew text of Deut. 33:1–3].[43]

The passage goes on to explain that the Edomites, Ishmaelites, and Moabites and Ammonites (as one group) rejected the Torah, which forbade transgressions with which they were intimately associated; only the Israelites accepted it (Exod 24:7) when it was offered to them. The fact that it was offered to these different nations implies that it was presented to them in their own languages.[44]

The notion that the Torah was offered to the seventy nations of the world in their seventy languages also required a combination of a number of biblical passages. Genesis 10 provides a list of the seventy nations on the earth, and Psalm 68, which has a number of references to Sinai and figures in various ancient treatments of the Sinai events, provided more information for explicating the "voices" of Exodus 19 and 20. If the קלת were understood to be languages, then the term could be related to Ps 68:12 [Eng. 11]:[45] "The Lord gives the command; great is the company of those who bore the tidings" (NRSV). R. Yohanan, who is credited in several sources with a comment on the verse, is quoted in *b. Šabb.* 88b as saying, "What is meant by the verse [Ps 68:12 is quoted]—Every single word that went forth from the Omnipotent was split up into seventy languages." The same statement is attributed to R. Yohanan in *Exod. Rab.* 28:6 in connection with the revelation at Sinai. There too Ps 68:12 is adduced.[46] Potin comments on the former saying, "R. Johanan suppose donc que Dieu s'est adressé à tous les peuples, et que tous se trouvaient présents au Sinaï."[47] In *b. Šabb.* 88b R. Yohanan's saying is followed by one from the school of R. Ishmael that brings Jer 23:29 into the discussion: "Is not my word like fire, says the Lord, and like a hammer that breaks a rock in pieces?" "The School of R. Ishmael taught: *And like a hammer that breaketh the rock in pieces:* just as a hammer is divided into many sparks, so every

---

[42] See, for some of the references, O. Betz, "The Eschatological Interpretation of the Sinai-Tradition in Qumran and in the New Testament," *RevQ* 6 (1967): 92–93.

[43] This translation from the *Mekilta de Rabbi Ishmael, Baḥodesh* 5 is that of J. L. Kugel, *The Bible As It Was* (Cambridge: Belknap Press of Harvard University Press, 1997), 411.

[44] Potin, *Fête juive,* 1:256–57, where other references are given.

[45] See Fitzmyer, *Acts of the Apostles,* 259, for a negative comment on whether Acts 2:33 alludes to Ps 68:19.

[46] Potin, *Fête juive,* 1:252–53.

[47] Ibid., 1:253.

single word that went forth from the Holy One, blessed be He, split up into seventy languages."[48]

In view of these elaborations of the Sinai story in which the divine word takes fiery form and addresses the nations of the world, it is reasonable to conclude that Luke in Acts 2 chose the symbols of fiery tongues, which enabled the apostles to speak the diverse languages of their international audience, in conscious dependence on Jewish understandings of Sinai and Pentecost/Weeks.

The Scriptural Passages Used: The scriptural passages that play a part in Acts 2 were listed above. It is striking that, in a chapter that seems to have undergone heavy influence from Jewish traditions, there is no explicit overlap between the passages cited and the ones that became the lectionary readings for the Festival of Weeks. It is possible that there were no fixed readings in the late first century C.E. or that ones other than the passages that later became standard figured in synagogue services; but the absence of agreement is striking nevertheless. Mishnah *Meg.* 3:5 reports that Deut 16:9–12 was the Torah passage for the festival. And *b. Meg.* 31a adds that Habakkuk 3 was the haftarah and that some considered Exodus 19 to be the Torah passage and Ezekiel 1 the haftarah. But *t. Meg.* 3:5 and *y. Meg.* 3:5 indicate that Exodus 19–20 was the lection. Also, the tractate *Soferim* names Psalm 29 as the psalm for the festival.[49] It appears that the only point in common between the later Jewish lectionary practice and Acts is that themes associated with Moses' ascent of a mountain and the revelation to him in Exodus 19–20 are echoed in the NT book.

The Ideal Fellowship: Another aspect of the story in Acts 2—the ideal community formed by the first Christians—may also be illumined by Jewish understandings of the events at Sinai.[50] The Bible itself gives the impetus for imagining the situation as ideal when Israel encamped at Mount Sinai and received the Torah. Upon being presented with the Lord's words by Moses, "[t]he people all answered as one: 'Everything that the LORD has spoken we will do'" (Exod 19:8 NRSV). There the people, who are to be "my treasured possession out of all the peoples" (v. 5 NRSV), consecrated themselves and washed their clothes to prepare for the Lord's appearance (vv. 10–15). At the end of the section, after the Ten Commandments and the covenantal code had been revealed to Moses, the description of the ratification ceremony includes these words: "and all the people answered with one voice, and said, 'All the words that the LORD has spoken we will do'" (24:3 NRSV; cf. v. 7, where they add that they will be obedient). Some of the sources, in commenting on the scene, indicate that Israel wore white clothes.

---

[48] The two citations from *b. Šabbat* are from H. Freedman, *Shabbath* (vols. 1 and 2 of *The Babylonian Talmud: Seder Moed;* ed. I. Epstein; London: Soncino, 1938), 2:419–20.

[49] See Potin, *Fête juive,* 1:141–42. For a more detailed treatment, see J. Mann, *The Bible as Read and Preached in the Old Synagogue* (2 vols.; Philadelphia: Jewish Publication Society, 1940–1966), 1:453–55.

[50] Betz ("Eschatological Interpretation," 93–94) relates this feature to the Qumran community's understanding of its pure and celibate character.

Philo, for example, claims that they not only abstained from intercourse (Exod 19:15) but also from all pleasures other than the ones necessary for life. After mentioning that they had washed themselves and their clothes for three days, Philo writes, "So in the whitest of raiment they stood on tiptoe with ears pricked up in obedience to the warning of Moses to prepare themselves" (*Decalogue* 45). Josephus claims that they ate more sumptuously than they normally did and that all—men, women, and children—wore splendid clothing (*Ant.* 3.5.1 §78).[51]

An especially important set of passages in this regard is found in *Pirqe R. El.* 41. There, echoing a more widespread motif, the text contrasts the strife that had characterized the Israelites' life before they arrived at Sinai and the bliss that marked their life together once they had come to the place of revelation.[52] This conclusion is drawn from Exod 19:2, where, in the phrase "Israel camped there in front of the mountain" (NRSV), the verb is in the singular (unlike elsewhere and even in the same verse), as if Israel were unified as a single entity:

> until they all came to Mount Sinai, and they all encamped opposite the mountain, like one man with one heart, as it is said, "And there Israel encamped before the mount." The Holy One, blessed be He, spake to them: Will ye receive for yourselves the Torah? Whilst the Torah had not yet been heard they said to Him: We will keep and observe all the precepts which are in the Torah, as it is said, "And they said, All that the Lord hath spoken we will do, and be obedient."[53]

The same text makes the point that both women and men received the Torah, although they were arranged at the mountain separate from one another.[54] Moreover, the meeting between Israel and God is pictured as a bride meeting her husband. When Moses awakened the people from their sleep, he said,

---

[51] For a summary of some homiletical developments of the theme, see Mann, *Bible as Read and Preached*, 1:456–59. He mentions the theme that the Torah heals all bodily ailments:

> At the giving of the Law all Jews, afflicted in their bodies as a result of the hard labor in Egypt, were healed by the ministering angels. "And *all* the people *saw* the lightnings" (Ex. 20.18), is evidence for there not being among them any blind; they said "we shall *do* and *hear*" (Ex. 24.7), ergo there were none among them of mutilated hands or being deaf; "and they stood at the bottom of the mount" (Ex. 19.17), hence there were no lame among them. Thus God renewed Israel physically, and accordingly in the initial v. of S[eder] (Ex. 19.1) there is employed the expression בחודש (instead of בירח) to denote this renewal (חדוש). (pp. 456–57)

See also *Mek. Baḥodesh* 3.37–40.

[52] There is a textual problem at this point. The Hebrew reads "smoothness," not "strife," but a confusion of two very similar words is possible. See G. Friedlander, *Pirḳê de Rabbi Eliezer* (London, 1916; repr., New York: Hermon, 1970), 320 n. 7. As he comments, the *Mekilta* and *Lev. Rab.* 9.9 support reading "strife" in this context.

[53] The translation is from Friedlander, *Pirḳê*, 321. See also *Mek. Baḥodesh* 1.108–11.

[54] This is a midrashic understanding of the parallel expressions "the house of Jacob" and "the Israelites" (lit., "the sons of Israel") in Exod 19:3. The former was taken to refer to the women, the latter to the men. See *Mek. Baḥodesh* 2.6–11.

Already the bridegroom wishes to lead the bride and to enter the bridal chamber. The hour has come for giving you the Torah, as it is said, "And Moses brought forth the people out of the camp to meet God" (Ex. xix.17). And the Holy One, blessed be He, also went forth to meet them; like a bridegroom who goes forth to meet the bride, so the Holy One, blessed be He, went forth to meet them to give them the Torah, as it is said, "O God, when thou wentest forth before thy people" (Ps. lxviii.7).[55]

The author also explains in more detail what the consecration or sanctification of the people in the wilderness entailed: "What was the sanctity of Israel in the wilderness? There were no uncircumcised people in their midst; the manna descended from heaven for them; they drank water out of the Well; clouds of glory surrounded them."[56] The great privilege enjoyed by those to whom the Torah had been revealed was expressed thus by R. Phineas:

All that generation who heard the voice of the Holy One, blessed be He, on Mount Sinai, were worthy to be like the ministering angels, so that insects had no power over them. They did not experience pollution in their lifetime, and at their death neither worm nor insect prevailed over them. Happy were they in this world and happy will they be in the world to come, and concerning them the Scripture says, "Happy is the people, that is in such a case" (Ps. cxliv.15).[57]

Some Targumim to Exod 20:18c add that the people not only responded obediently but were also at prayer (cf. Acts 1:14; 2:42).[58]

Thus Israel was an ideal society when it received the Torah, and the first Christians were an ideal society when they received the Spirit.

Conclusions

On the basis of the evidence presented above, it is possible to draw a few conclusions that are important for understanding Acts 2.

1. Although there is little in Acts 2 that reminds one of what the OT says about the Festival of Weeks, different lines of evidence indicate that, in writing his account, Luke was influenced by traditions that had grown around this festival in Jewish circles.

a. The *Jubilees*-Qumran tradition shows that already in the second century B.C.E. the Festival of Weeks was closely tied to the events at

---

[55] Friedlander, *Pirkê*, 322. See *Mek. Baḥodesh* 3.117–119.

[56] Friedlander, *Pirkê*, 323.

[57] Ibid., 327.

[58] See Potin, *Fête juive*, 1:216–17; 2:69, where the pertinent texts of the Genizah version of the Palestinian Targum and MS 110 of the Bibliothèque Nationale de Paris are given. For the entire theme of Israel as a holy nation, see 1:207–17, 305–307. The *Mekilta*, among other texts, claims that no Israelite suffered from bodily defects at that time and supplies scriptural warrant for the assertion (*Baḥodesh* 9.14–22).

Mount Sinai, especially the act of establishing the covenant between God and Israel. The Festival of Weeks was the date for making and remembering the biblical covenants and for renewing the Sinaitic covenant.

b. In Acts 1 the writer, as he relates the ascension of Jesus, uses language that reminds one of Moses and his ascent of Mount Sinai before the covenant was made and the Torah given. An early Christian tradition, attested in Palestine and Syria, by celebrating both on the same (fiftieth) day, highlighted the close connection between the ascension and the giving of the Spirit.

c. To a certain extent already in the writings of Philo and Josephus but far more extensively in later rabbinic sources, there is a series of midrashic associations with Exodus 19–20 and 24 (the theophany and covenant of Sinai) that remind one of elements in Acts 2. The manifestation of the invisible Spirit in fiery tongues that symbolized proclamation of God's mighty acts in the languages of the world reflects the widespread tradition that Israel saw the קלת ("voices") that were manifested in fiery form and addressed to the seventy nations of the world.

d. The short description of the ideal Christian fellowship in Acts 2:42–47 but also in Acts 1:14 seems to be modeled on the notion that Israel at Sinai was a harmonious nation that unanimously accepted the Torah and lacked the blemishes, social and physical, that otherwise characterize society. The Bible contains suggestions about this, and later sources expanded them considerably.

2. There are, naturally, some differences between the Sinai stories as understood in Jewish exegesis of Scripture and those in the account of Acts 1–2.

a. The most significant difference concerns what was given on the two occasions: in the case of Sinai it is the divine word, whereas in Acts 2 it is the divine Spirit. Potin thinks that these are the parallel items in the two literatures, and in particular he points to Jewish traditions in which the divine word in fiery form moves above Israel and the whole of the message (despite being broken up into ten commandments) is expressed in one utterance. In Acts 2 the Spirit in fiery form is divided and descends on each of the Twelve although it was given totally to each one.[59] Without deciding whether all of this is present in Acts 2, it is at least clear that the word and the Spirit are the comparable entities; and although they are parallel in the stories, only Acts 2 has the Spirit, a unique element in the NT story.

---

[59] Potin, *Fête juive*, 1:310. See *Mek. Baḥodesh* 4.102–104.

b. The scriptural passages that are adduced in Acts 2 are not those that became the lectionary readings in the synagogues on the Festival of Weeks. The only agreement is the fact that Acts 1–2, in evoking the Sinai stories, shows the influence of Exodus 19–20 as a lection for the day. Joel 2:28–32, which is prominent in Acts 2, never became a synagogal reading on the festival.

c. In the midrashic retellings of the Sinai stories, the one who proclaims the word is the Lord himself, and he is the one who offers the Torah to the nations; in Acts 2, the apostles (and perhaps others) proclaim the message.[60]

d. In the midrashic traditions, the Torah was offered to the nations, but they rejected it; in Acts 2, the message was offered to Jewish people who lived among the nations (they are identified as coming from many places), and many accepted it.

3. It has been a common objection that the rabbinic sources cited above are far later in date than Acts 2 and that there is no evidence that such traditions had materialized by the late first century.[61] But this objection is weaker than it may seem at first glance. The *Jubilees*-Qumran tradition shows the Sinai–Festival of Weeks connection at an early time, and Philo and Josephus already know some of the midrashic elaborations. It may not be entirely gratuitous to add that the presence of these elements in Acts 2 constitutes an argument for their early date.

There is no reason to argue that all of the elements in Acts 1–2 were conditioned by the midrashic developments of the Sinai chapters that were sketched above. Obviously, there are unique elements in the NT account, and it is possible that other OT passages, as they were later understood,[62] contributed to the shaping of Acts 1–2. But the surviving evidence shows that in Acts 1–2 Luke was heavily influenced by Jewish traditions about the Festival of Weeks.

---

[60] Potin, *Fête juive*, 1:311–12.

[61] See Str-B 2:604; E. Lohse, "πεντηκοστή," *TDNT* 6:49: "The story of Pentecost in Ac. 2 bears no relation to the Sinai tradition, nor can the Chr. Pentecost be derived directly from the Jewish" (see also n. 33).

[62] An interesting possibility is the passage about Eldad and Medad in Num 11:26–30. Some of the Targumim for this passage say that the Holy Spirit rested on them as they prophesied about Joshua's succeeding Moses. See M. McNamara, *The New Testament and the Palestinian Targum to the Pentateuch* (AnBib 27; Rome: Pontifical Biblical Institute, 1966), 235.

9

Stephen's Speech (Acts 7) in Its Exegetical Context

James L. Kugel

When it comes to NT passages that discuss or allude to passages from the HB, one principle cannot be stressed enough. Ancient Jews and Christians not only shared a common body of Scripture; they were also heir to a common body of interpretations that had accompanied that Scripture for centuries, interpretations that go back, in some cases, at least to the period of the return from Babylonian exile in the late sixth century B.C.E. Consequently, early Christian writers almost never approached a biblical text fresh; that is, they did not simply set about reading and interpreting on their own. Instead they perceived Scripture through the lens of earlier interpretation. They adopted the assumptions and methods of earlier interpreters, they focused on particular issues or problems identified by earlier interpreters, and they often (though not always) repeated or only slightly modified actual bits of interpretation that had been passed on by earlier scholars. Indeed, sometimes it appears that the writers themselves did not clearly distinguish what the biblical text itself said from what interpreters had long been saying it said.

I wish to illustrate these propositions with a few examples drawn from the well-known speech of Stephen in Acts 7. According to this chapter, Stephen, before being martyred, addresses his audience with a review of biblical history. Numerous allusions to biblical texts are thus found in these verses. Many previous scholars have identified these allusions; a few have also bothered to demonstrate the interpretive elements present in some of them. But very few have paid attention to the interpretive traditions underlying these allusions. What follows highlights some of those traditions as evidenced in earlier sources. I shall fall far short of adequately commenting even on the particulars selected, but my few illustrations may serve the interests of some more complete treatment to be undertaken in the future.

Acts 7:2–3

ὁ δὲ ἔφη· Ἄνδρες ἀδελφοὶ καὶ πατέρες, ἀκούσατε. Ὁ θεὸς τῆς δόξης ὤφθη τῷ πατρὶ ἡμῶν Ἀβραὰμ ὄντι ἐν τῇ Μεσοποταμίᾳ πρὶν ἢ κατοικῆσαι αὐτὸν ἐν Χαρρὰν καὶ εἶπεν πρὸς αὐτόν· ἔξελθε ἐκ τῆς γῆς σου καὶ [ἐκ] τῆς συγγενείας σου, καὶ δεῦρο εἰς τὴν γῆν ἣν ἄν σοι δείξω.

And Stephen said: "Brethren and fathers, hear me. The God of glory appeared to our father Abraham, when he was in Mesopotamia, before he lived in Haran, and said to him, 'Depart from your land and from your kindred and go into the land which I will show you.'" (RSV)

One unusual feature of these opening words of Stephen's speech is their insistence on the fact that God had addressed Abraham "when he was in Mesopotamia, before he lived in Haran."[1] It almost sounds as if Stephen is arguing with some other idea—which, in fact, he is.

The matter all goes back to God's words to Abraham in Gen 12:1: "And the LORD said to Abram, 'Go forth from your country and from your kindred and your father's house to the land that I will show you'" (RSV). It seems obvious that God must be addressing Abram while he is still in his "country"—namely, the city of Ur in Chaldea—and surrounded by his "kindred" there, since these are precisely what God is telling him to leave. Two verses earlier, however, the Genesis narrative had asserted, "Terah took Abram his son [and the rest of their family] and they went forth together from Ur of the Chaldeans to go into the land of Canaan; but when they came to Haran, they settled there" (11:31 RSV). If Abraham had thus already left Ur and was now in Haran, why was God telling him *now* to depart from his country and kindred? (To make matters worse, 12:4–5 refers to Abraham's departure from *Haran,* thus solidifying the impression that the words of 12:1 were indeed spoken to Abraham in Haran after his departure from Ur.)

This was precisely the sort of problem addressed by ancient interpreters of Scripture, and various solutions are evident in writings surviving from that period. One was to claim that the words "Go forth from your country..." were nonetheless spoken to Abraham in Ur and that 12:1–4 is therefore something of a flashback—as if 12:1 were really saying, "Now the Lord *had* said to Abraham [back in Ur], 'Go forth from your country...'" Such, for example, seems to be the position adopted by Philo of Alexandria, *Abraham* 62, 67:

> Under the force of an oracle which bade him leave his country and kinfolk and seek a new home, ... he [Abraham] hastened eagerly to obey, not as though he were leaving home for a strange land but rather as returning from amid strangers to

---

[1] In context, "Mesopotamia" here and in v. 4 must refer to Ur, Abraham's homeland, although other ancient texts (including that of Judith, below) seem to use "Mesopotamia" as the equivalent of Aram-Naharaim, i.e., northern Syria. Josephus (below) uses the term to indicate a broad geographic area including both Ur and Haran.

home. . . . He departed with all speed first from Chaldea, a land at that time blessed by fortune and at the height of its prosperity, and migrated to Haran.

According to this and other passages in Philo (see also *Abraham* 71; *Migration* 184–189), God spoke to Abraham in Ur and told him there to leave the land of the Chaldeans. But other interpreters held that God's words "Go forth from your country . . ." were in fact spoken to Abraham in Haran. If so, then the references to "your country" and so forth must have meant "the country in which you are now living," or perhaps, broadly speaking, the whole geographic area of Ur *and* Haran. This seems to be the position underlying a reference to Abraham's departure (though Abraham himself is not mentioned by name) found in Jdt 5:6–9, in a passage that perhaps ought to be dated to the first or second century B.C.E.:

> This people [the Jews] is descended from the Chaldeans. At one time they lived in Mesopotamia [meaning here Haran],[2] because they would not follow the gods of their fathers who were in Chaldea. For they had left the ways of their ancestors, and they worshiped the God of heaven, the God they had come to know; hence they [the Chaldeans] drove them out from the presence of their gods; and they fled to Mesopotamia, and lived there for a long time. Then their God commanded them to leave the place where they were living and go to the land of Canaan. (RSV)

Here it is not God who tells Abraham and his family to leave Ur; they are "driven out" by the people of Ur themselves because Abraham and his relatives refused to worship Ur's gods. It was only after they reached "Mesopotamia" (Haran) that God addressed them, commanding them "to leave the place where they were living and go to the land of Canaan," that is, saying the words of Gen 12:1, "Go forth from your country and your kindred and your father's house to the land that I will show you" (RSV).

There seems to be an apparent allusion to Gen 12:1 in another ancient text, the *Apocalypse of Abraham* (from the first century C.E.). The sequence of events is far from clear, but it appears that the passage, *Apoc. Ab.* 8:1–6, also presumes that God's words were spoken to Abraham in Haran:

> [God said to Abraham,] "Leave Terah your father and go forth from his house [Gen 12:1] so that you will not be killed because of the sins of your father's house." So I [Abraham] went out. And it came to pass, when I went out, that I had not even gotten as far as going beyond the doors of the courtyard when the sound of great thunder came forth and burned him and his house and everyone in the house to a distance of forty cubits.

If Terah himself is killed in this incident, then it must have taken place *after* the departure from Ur mentioned in Gen 11:31, since Terah and Abraham leave Ur together there. *Apocalypse of Abraham* 26:3 later makes it clear that Terah was indeed killed, when God asks Abraham,

> Why did your father not obey your voice and abandon the demonic worship of idols until he perished, and all his house with him?

---

[2] See the above note.

It may be that these two passages both specifically mention Terah's house because of God's words in Gen 12:1, "Go forth from your country and your kindred and your father's house" (RSV). God apparently specified leaving Terah's house, in this interpretation, because the house itself was to be destroyed.

Josephus, in his retelling of these events, also seems to favor Haran as the place where God spoke to Abraham. Thus at one point he supplies a different motive for the move from Ur to Haran, as if to say that it was not because of any divine commandment that Abraham left Ur:

> Terah hated Chaldea because of the death of Haran; they all moved to Haran in Mesopotamia, where Terah also died and was buried, after a life of 205 years. (Josephus, *Ant.* 1.6.5 §152)

But elsewhere he says,

> Because of these ideas [of Abraham], the Chaldeans and the other people of Mesopotamia rose up against him, and having resolved, in keeping with God's will and with his help, to leave his home, he settled in the land of Canaan. (*Ant.* 1.7.1 §157)

Here (and elsewhere) Josephus may be deliberately telescoping the events and places: "other people of Mesopotamia" seems designed to include Haran, in which case Abraham's "home" may be nothing less than the entire region.[3]

Jubilees 12:21 offers an extremely clever solution. Abraham travels to Haran as in Gen 11:31. He stays there for fourteen years. Then, one day, he seeks God's advice:

> "Shall I return to Ur of the Chaldeans, who are [now] earnestly requesting that I return to them? Or shall I stay here, in this place [that is, Haran]?" . . . And the word of the Lord was sent to him . . . : "Go forth from your country and your kindred and your father's house to the land which I shall show you" [Gen 12:1].

God's words in Gen 12:1 now have a new meaning: Leave "your country," that is, Ur—do not go back there. At the same time, leave "your kindred"—perhaps meaning the relatives whom Abraham had left back in Ur, or perhaps meaning Abraham's own brother Nahor and his family now living in Haran. Indeed, leave "your father's house"—that is, the very house in which your father is presently living, in Haran. Go instead to the land which I will show you.

By having Abraham thus raise the possibility of a return to Ur, the author of *Jubilees* was able to account for God's telling Abraham in Haran to leave his homeland of Ur. What God meant was: Leave it forever, do not go back there. At the same time, the Bible's mention of "your kindred and your father's house" allows the author of *Jubilees* to raise, and then reject, another possibility, that of

---

[3] In a later passage (*Ant.* 1.7.1 §154), Josephus says of Abraham, "At the age of seventy-five he left Chaldea, God having bidden him to remove to Canaan" (RSV). It seems that "Chaldea" here means Haran, since the Bible states that Abraham "was seventy-five years old when he left Haran" (Gen 12:4). Did Josephus simply make a mistake, or is greater Chaldea intended to include the city of Haran and so solve the problem?

staying in Haran. (This also makes the wording of Gen 12:1 considerably less redundant: "Go forth from your country and your kindred and from your father's
house" now refers to two quite different things.)

All this is to say that, by the time of Stephen's speech in Acts 7, the question
"Where was Abraham?" was one that had been asked and answered many times.
It is likewise clear that there was no consensus: neither Ur nor Haran had com-
pletely won the day, nor, surprisingly, the clever solution offered by *Jubilees*.
Viewed against this exegetical background, the casual phrase "before he lived in
Haran" takes on a new aspect, as if it were a *prise de position* on a much debated
issue—which, in fact, it was.

Acts 7:4–7

κακεῖθεν μετὰ τὸ ἀποθανεῖν τὸν πατέρα αὐτοῦ μετῴκισεν αὐτὸν εἰς τὴν γῆν
ταύτην εἰς ἣν ὑμεῖς νῦν κατοικεῖτε, καὶ οὐκ ἔδωκεν αὐτῷ κληρονομίαν ἐν αὐτῇ
οὐδὲ βῆμα ποδὸς καὶ ἐπηγγείλατο δοῦναι αὐτῷ εἰς κατάσχεσιν αὐτὴν καὶ τῷ
σπέρματι αὐτοῦ μετ' αὐτόν, οὐκ ὄντος αὐτῷ τέκνου. ἐλάλησεν δὲ οὕτως ὁ θεὸς
ὅτι ἔσται τὸ σπέρμα αὐτοῦ πάροικον ἐν γῇ ἀλλοτρίᾳ καὶ δουλώσουσιν αὐτὸ καὶ
κακώσουσιν ἔτη τετρακόσια· καὶ τὸ ἔθνος ᾧ ἐὰν δουλεύσουσιν κρινῶ ἐγώ, ὁ
θεὸς εἶπεν, καὶ μετὰ ταῦτα ἐξελεύσονται καὶ λατρεύσουσίν μοι ἐν τῷ τόπῳ
τούτῳ.

And after his father died, God removed him from there into this land in which you
are now living; yet he gave him no inheritance in it, not even a foot's length, but
promised to give it to him in possession and to his posterity after him, though he
had no child. And God spoke to this effect, that his posterity would be aliens in a
land belonging to others, who would enslave them and ill-treat them four hundred
years. "But I will judge the nation which they serve," said God, "and after that they
shall come out and worship me in this place." (RSV)

The timing of the death of Abraham's father was another *crux interpretum*,
since the MT and the LXX both seem to say that Abraham left his father, Terah, in
Haran and went on to Canaan alone; Terah's death apparently took place sixty
years later (see Gen 11:26, 32; 12:4). Did this mean that Abraham had abandoned
his father in his old age and allowed him to die alone? As different scholars have
shown, numerous ancient interpreters reckoned with this problem.[4] It may be
that underlying Stephen's words here is the same exculpatory tradition found in
the Samaritan Pentateuch, which holds that Terah was 145 years old at the time

---

[4] See R. H. Charles, *The Book of Jubilees; or, The Little Genesis* (1902; repr., Jerusa-
lem: Makor, 1972), 103–4; S. Brock, "Abraham and the Ravens," *JSJ* 9 (1978): 135–52;
C. Milikowsky, "Seder Olam and Jewish Chronography," *PAAJR* 52 (1985): 115–39; W.
Adler, "Jacob of Edessa and the Jewish Pseudepigrapha," in *Tracing the Threads* (ed. J.
Reeves; SBLEJL 6; Atlanta: Scholars Press, 1995), 160–64; J. Kugel, *Traditions of the Bible*
(Cambridge: Harvard University Press, 1998), 270–71.

of his death.[5] In any case, it should be clear that the phrase "after his father died" is no casual remark; it springs out of an issue that was much discussed by ancient interpreters.

Somewhat less obvious, however, is the exegetical resonance of God's telling Abraham here that God will judge the Egyptians for enslaving Israel and "after that they shall come out and worship me in this place." This whole sentence in Stephen's speech is a rewording of what God says to Abraham in Gen 15:13–14—but with an important difference:

> Know for certain that your descendants will be sojourners in a land not theirs, and that they will be slaves there and will be oppressed, for four hundred years.[6] But I will judge the nation whose slaves they will be, and afterwards they shall come out with great possessions.

In rewording these verses, Stephen omits mention of the "great possessions." Instead he substitutes a phrase borrowed from God's similar promise to Moses at the burning bush: "when you have brought forth the people out of Egypt, you shall serve God upon this mountain" (Exod 4:12 RSV).

The substitution might seem innocent enough, one designed "to make explicit what is only implied in the Genesis passage, namely, that Abraham's posterity would return to Canaan once they were released from bondage."[7] In any event, is not this act of "telescoping of distinct quotations" merely characteristic of Stephen's speech in general?[8] Yet here there seems to be another clear purpose, namely, to paper over a problem that very much bothered ancient Jewish interpreters.

The "great possessions" with which the people of Israel left Egypt appeared to many ancient interpreters to have been acquired under false pretenses—they were stolen, to put it bluntly. The Exodus narrative plainly states that the Israelites were told to "borrow" silver and gold and clothing from their Egyptian neighbors (Exod 3:21–22; 11:2), and the Egyptians did indeed "lend" these to them (12:35–36). If the Israelites then walked out of Egypt without returning them, did they not in effect steal the Egyptians' property? To this question there

---

[5] See F. F. Bruce, *The Acts of the Apostles* (3d ed.; Grand Rapids: Eerdmans, 1990), 192–93.

[6] On the exegetical problems of these "four hundred years," see P. Grelot, "Quatre cent trente ans (Ex. XII 34): Du Pentateuque au testament araméen de Lévi," in *Hommages à Dupont-Sommer* (ed. A. Caquot et M. Philonenko; Paris: Librairie de l'Amérique de l'Orient, 1971), 384–94; idem, "Quatre cent trente ans (Ex. 12:40)," in *Homenaje a Juan Prado; Miscelánea de estudios bíblicos y hebráicos* (ed. L. Alvarez Verdes and E. J. Alonso Hernández; Madrid: Instituto Montano, 1975), 559–70; J. Heinemann, *Aggadah and Its Development* (Jerusalem: Keter, 1974), 65–74; G. Larsson, "Chronology of the Pentateuch: A Comparison of the MT and the LXX," *JBL* 102 (1983): 401–9; C. Milikowsky, "Seder Olam and the Mekhilta of R. Šimᶜon b. Yoḥai on the Enslavement of Israel in Egypt," *Bar Ilan* 26/27 (1995): 221–25; Kugel, *Traditions of the Bible*, 570–74.

[7] See Paul Walaskay, *Acts* (Louisville: Westminster John Knox, 1998), 133.

[8] Bruce, *Acts*, 194.

developed an apologetic answer: the Israelites were not stealing but merely taking what was their due, the recompense for their years of involuntary servitude. This answer is reflected in a number of ancient texts:

> But ere you go I'll grant the people favor;
> one woman from another shall receive
> fine vessels, jewels of silver and of gold
> and clothing, things which one may carry off,
> so as to compensate them for their deeds.
> (Ezekiel the Tragedian, *Exagōgē* 162–166) [9]

> They asked the Egyptians for vessels and garments, vessels of silver, and vessels of gold, and vessels of bronze, in order to despoil the Egyptians in return for the bondage in which they had forced them to serve. (*Jub.* 48:18) [10]

> She [Wisdom] entered the soul of a servant of the Lord [Moses],
> and withstood dread kings with signs and wonders,
> She gave to holy men the reward for their labors. . . .
> Therefore the righteous plundered the ungodly. (Wis 10:16–17:20)

> For they took with them great spoils . . . not out of any love of lucre, nor, as their accusers would have it, out of covetousness for the property of others (whence could one get such an idea?). But, first of all, they were thus simply receiving the wages owed to them for their service all that time; and, secondly, they were taking some revenge [on the Egyptians] for having been made into slaves—and in a lesser degree and not as would be fair, for who can compare mere monetary loss to the loss of one's freedom, when, for his freedom, any thinking man is prepared to sacrifice not merely his personal property, but life itself? (Philo, *Moses* 1, 141)

> The Egyptians [once lodged a complaint against the Jews centuries after the exodus and] said: It is written in the Torah, "Let every woman ask of her neighbor jewelry of silver and gold . . ." [Exod 11:2]. Now give us back what is ours! Gebiha replied: For four hundred and thirty years Israel was enslaved in your midst, six hundred thousand people [in all]; give each of them two hundred *zuz* per year, which totals eight million six hundred thousand *mina*, and then we will return to you what is yours! *(Megillat Taʿanit)*[11]

---

[9] The specification that the items were portable seems designed not to tell us anything about the nature of the gifts per se but to supply another "proof" that the Israelites had not defrauded the Egyptians. For the Egyptians certainly knew that such valuables are easily walked off with; if they nonetheless gave them to the Israelites, it must have been in the knowledge that this was a true gift and not a loan.

[10] The "vessels of bronze" are nowhere mentioned in the biblical account. They are apparently added here because, after the Israelites have embarked on their desert wanderings, they are instructed to build a tabernacle, many of whose parts are made of bronze. The Israelites had presumably taken bronze with them from Egypt, along with the silver and gold and other fine things specifically mentioned in connection with the tabernacle.

[11] This is the reading of the Oxford MS of the text; see V. Noam, "The Scholion of *Megillat Ta'anit*—Toward an Understanding of Its Stemma," *Tarbiz* 62 (1993): 55–99; cf. Hans Lichtenstein, "Die Fastenrolle," *HUCA* 8/9 (1931/1932): 330.

Apparently, Stephen too was acutely aware of the problem raised by the Israelites' "borrowings." He could have faithfully reproduced God's words in Gen 15:14 and added an explanatory phrase à la Wisdom of Solomon above: "and afterwards they shall come out with great possessions, the just recompense for their labors." The fact that he did not may indicate that he was dissatisfied with this apologetic motif (but certainly not that he was ignorant of it, since it had been around for a very long time). But precisely because the problem of the Israelites' apparently ill-gotten gains was so well known, Stephen also did not feel himself free to cite Gen 15:14 unaltered. His solution—to conflate that verse with Exod 3:14—elegantly sidestepped the problem.

Acts 7:14–16

ἀποστείλας δὲ 'Ιωσὴφ μετεκαλέσατο 'Ιακὼβ τὸν πατέρα αὐτοῦ καὶ πᾶσαν τὴν συγγένειαν ἐν ψυχαῖς ἑβδομήκοντα πέντε. καὶ κατέβη 'Ιακὼβ εἰς Αἴγυπτον καὶ ἐτελεύτησεν αὐτὸς καὶ οἱ πατέρες ἡμῶν, καὶ μετετέθησαν εἰς Συχὲμ καὶ ἐτέθησαν ἐν τῷ μνήματι ᾧ ὠνήσατο 'Αβραὰμ τιμῆς ἀργυρίου παρὰ τῶν υἱῶν 'Εμμὼρ ἐν Συχέμ.

And Joseph sent and called to him Jacob his father and all his kindred, seventy-five souls; and Jacob went down into Egypt. And he died, himself and our fathers, and they were carried back to Shechem and laid in the tomb that Abraham had bought for a sum of silver from the sons of Hamor in Shechem. (RSV)

This passage has long made readers familiar with Hebrew Scripture wince. In saying that Jacob and "our fathers" were buried in Shechem, in a tomb that Abraham had bought from the sons of Hamor, the passage seems to conflate two traditions. On the one hand, Scripture relates that Abraham had bought a burial cave in Hebron not from the sons of Hamor but from Ephron the Hittite (Gen 23:16–20). Abraham, his wife Sarah, and some of their descendants—including, significantly, Jacob (50:13)—were buried there. On the other hand, Scripture also says that Jacob had purchased some land in Shechem from the sons of Hamor (33:19) and that Joseph was buried there (Josh 24:32). According to Stephen's account, Jacob and "our fathers" are said to be buried in the wrong place— Shechem instead of Hebron. Moreover, the purchase of the Shechem site is attributed to the wrong person—Abraham instead of Jacob.

There is little doubt that something has been mixed up here. The confusion might be mitigated somewhat by the observation that both burial sites were originally owned by Canaanites of similar-sounding origins (Ephron the *Hittite* and the sons of Hamor the *Hivite*). Moreover, if Abraham had purchased his site and had subsequently been buried there, it might seem only logical that Jacob too should have been buried in the site that he had purchased, namely, Shechem. But it is not my purpose here to indulge in apologetics. Rather I wish simply to observe that there was really no need whatsoever for Stephen to make mention of these burial arrangements at all. After all, they are a trivial element in the history of Israel. Consider the things he leaves out of his thumbnail history: the story of the binding of Isaac, Jacob's supplanting of his brother Esau, Jacob's vision of the great ladder at Bethel, his stay with Laban and marriages to Leah and Rachel, his struggle with the angel, and so forth. Given these salient omissions, why should Stephen have bothered to say a thing about where Jacob and "our fathers" were buried (especially if he was a bit foggy on the exact details)?

The answer is the same as that given regarding the previous examples. Who was buried where had been a real concern to earlier Jewish interpreters, and the author of Luke-Acts had quite naturally inherited this same concern; the removal of the patriarchs' remains for reburial in Canaan was now a "high point" of patriarchal history. The reason is simple. Although Scripture is careful to narrate the removal of Jacob's body from Egypt for burial in Canaan (Gen 50:13) and the removal of Joseph's remains to Canaan at the time of the exodus (Exod 13:19), it says nothing about any of Joseph's brothers. Reuben, Simeon, Levi, Judah, and the others all presumably died in Egypt around the time of Joseph's death. If Scripture goes to the trouble of narrating the removal of Joseph's remains (twice, in fact; see also Josh 24:32) yet says nothing of the removal of his brothers' remains or of those of any of their descendants, readers are left with the troubling implication that these distinguished Israelites were not repatriated after their death. This was particularly disturbing because it implied either that Joseph's brothers did not bother to request burial in Canaan as he had—as if they simply did not care!—or, still worse, that they had so requested but their descendants had not honored their wishes.

To avoid either of these implications, retellers of the Genesis narrative were careful to assert what Genesis had somehow failed to mention, that the other patriarchs had likewise been buried in Canaan. It is striking, for example, that the *Testaments of the Twelve Patriarchs* goes to the trouble of asserting that each of Joseph's brothers was buried in Hebron (*T. Reu* 7:1–2; *T. Sim.* 8:2; *T. Levi* 19:5; *T. Jud.* 26:4; *T. Iss.* 7:8; *T. Zeb.* 10:7; *T. Dan* 7:2; *T. Naph.* 9:1–3; *T. Gad* 8:5; *T. Ash.* 8:1–2; *T. Benj.* 12:3). Josephus, *Ant.* 2.6.8 §199, likewise relates that "His [Joseph's] brothers also died, having lived happily in Egypt; after a time their descendants carried their bodies back to Hebron and buried them there." Long before these, *Jub.* 46:9–11 had asserted,

> The Israelites brought forth the bones of Jacob's sons, all except the bones of Joseph; and they buried them in the field in the cave of the Machpelah, in the mountain. And many returned to Egypt, but a few of them were left in Mount Hebron. And Amram, your [Moses'] father, was left with them. And the king of Canaan was victorious over the king of Egypt, and he closed the gates of Egypt.

Clearly related to this same exegetical tradition are two fragments of the text known as *Visions of Amram* from Qumran:[12]

---

[12] It is not clear whether these two fragments represent two overlapping parts of a single text (so Klaus Beyer treats them in *Die aramäischen Texte vom Toten Meer* [enlarged

in this land. And I went up to[to the land of Canaan?
to bury our fathers, and I went up[to Hebron?
to a[ri]se and stay to build[
great[e]r than the sons of my uncle together[
Our very great work [   ] dead
rumor of war, panicking our [   ] to the land of E[gypt?]
quickly, and they did not b[uild the to]mbs of their fathers and [   ] left me [   ]
to build and to take for th[em fr]om the land of Canaan [
we ourselves were building. And there was wa[r between] Philistia and Egypt
     and [   ] was winning (4Q545 *Visions of Amram^c*, frg. 1, col. 2)

Qahat there, to go up and to stay and bui[ld the tombs of our father . . .
a man, and about our work it was very much until [we have buried the dead . . . and they retreat?
quickly, and they do not build the tombs of their fathers[
until we build. *Blank* And there was a war between[
And they closed the [bor]der of Egypt and it was not possible to[. . .]forty-one years, and
we could not [. . .]
between Egypt and Canaan and Philistia. *Blank* (4Q544 *Visions of Amram^b*, frg. 1, col. 1.1–7)

It is difficult to make much sense of these scattered fragments, but one thing is clear: they concern the same general theme of the removal of the bodies of Israel's ancestors from Egypt to Canaan for burial. Indeed, they seem most closely related to *Jub.* 46:9–11, cited above. And so, in the first fragment cited, Amram relates that he went up to Canaan to "bury our fathers"; apparently he was prevented from returning to Egypt because of a war among the Philistines, Egypt, and Canaan. This war is apparently the same as that mentioned in *Jubilees* between Egypt and Canaan (*Jub.* 46:9); it is mentioned as well in *T. Sim.* 8:2 and *T. Benj.* 12:3. As I have argued elsewhere, this war was essentially an exegetical creation designed to account for Joseph's otherwise inexplicable request that his body be removed for burial in Canaan not immediately (as his father Jacob had requested a short while earlier, Gen 47:29–31; 50:6–7) but only "when God remembers you" (50:24–25) at the time of the exodus. If there was a war going on (or about to take place) between Egypt and Canaan and the border between them was thus closed (or in danger of being closed), that would explain why Joseph could not request immediate reburial in Canaan; his body could be moved there only after the border was reopened, which is why he had his brothers swear that his body would be removed "when God remembers you."[13] But yesterday's ad hoc exegetical creation has a way of becoming today's quasi-biblical fact: soon everyone knew that there had indeed been such a war between Egypt and Canaan and that before it (or even during it) the bodies of some of Israel's other

---

ed.; Göttingen: Vandenhoeck & Ruprecht, 1993], 2:85–87) or two independent fragments, perhaps representing different recensions.

[13] J. Kugel, *In Potiphar's House* (San Francisco: Harper Collins, 1990), 125–55.

patriarchs had somehow been carried out of Egypt. This "fact" is what the above Qumran fragments reflect; indeed, they seem to agree with *Jub.* 46:9–10 that Amram, having gone up to Hebron, was "left at Mount Hebron" with unnamed others for a period of time—perhaps the forty-one years mentioned in the second fragment.[14]

All this is to say that, in however garbled a form, the reference in Acts 7:14–16 to the removal of Jacob and "our fathers" reflects a substantial body of already existing extrabiblical material. "Our fathers" refers specifically to Joseph's brothers, whose bodies were removed before his but sometime after the transfer of Jacob's last remains to Hebron. Indeed, it is certainly significant that the same phrase, "our fathers," occurs in the first Qumran document cited above, apparently in the same sense.

Acts 7:17–22

Καθὼς δὲ ἤγγιζεν ὁ χρόνος τῆς ἐπαγγελίας ἧς ὡμολόγησεν ὁ θεὸς τῷ Ἀβραάμ, ηὔξησεν ὁ λαὸς καὶ ἐπληθύνθη ἐν Αἰγύπτῳ ἄχρι οὗ ἀνέστη βασιλεὺς ἕτερος [ἐπ Αἴγυπτον] ὃς οὐκ ᾔδει τὸν Ἰωσήφ. οὗτος κατασοφισάμενος τὸ γένος ἡμῶν ἐκάκωσεν τοὺς πατέρας [ἡμῶν] τοῦ ποιεῖν τὰ βρέφη ἔκθετα αὐτῶν εἰς τὸ μὴ ζῳογονεῖσθαι. Ἐν ᾧ καιρῷ ἐγεννήθη Μωϋσῆς καὶ ἦν ἀστεῖος τῷ θεῷ· ὃς ἀνετράφη μῆνας τρεῖς ἐν τῷ οἴκῳ τοῦ πατρός, ἐκτεθέντος δὲ αὐτοῦ ἀνείλατο αὐτὸν ἡ θυγάτηρ Φαραὼ καὶ ἀνεθρέψατο αὐτὸν ἑαυτῇ εἰς υἱόν. καὶ ἐπαιδεύθη Μωϋσῆς [ἐν] πάσῃ σοφίᾳ Αἰγυπτίων, ἦν δὲ δυνατὸς ἐν λόγοις καὶ ἔργοις αὐτοῦ.

But as the time of the promise drew near, which God had granted to Abraham, the people grew and multiplied in Egypt till there arose over Egypt another king who had not known Joseph. He dealt craftily with our race and forced our fathers to expose their infants, that they might not be kept alive. At this time Moses was born, and was beautiful before God. And he was brought up for three months in his father's house; and when he was exposed, Pharaoh's daughter adopted him and brought him up as her own son. And Moses was instructed in all the wisdom of the Egyptians, and he was mighty in his words and deeds. (RSV)

Two points about this passage have long been noticed. The description of Moses as "beautiful before God" does not precisely match the language of the LXX, which says only that Moses' mother saw that he was "beautiful" (ἀστεῖος). Moreover, the assertion that Moses was "instructed in all the wisdom of the Egyptians" does not seem to derive from anything stated in the HB, although it might perhaps be inferred from the fact that Moses was brought up in the royal court. Previous commentators have also drawn attention to parallel statements found in Philo (*Moses* 1.9; 1.20–24) and Josephus (*Ant.* 2.9.7 §232; 2.9.6

---

[14] J. T. Milik, "4Q: Visions de 'Amram et une citation d'Origène," *RB* 79 (1972): 76–97.

§§229–230). But to my knowledge, the reason behind these assertions in Acts and other sources has not been sufficiently explained.

The plain assertion of Exod 2:2 that Moses' mother "conceived and bore a son; and she saw that he was good [טוב], and she hid him for three months" must have raised questions in the minds of ancient interpreters. Certainly the implication that if he had not been "good" she would not have bothered hiding him away was repugnant to most readers. Especially was this true of readers of the LXX, since ἀστεῖος, the translation of טוב there, often suggests specifically physical beauty, and the assertion that Moses' mother *saw* that he was ἀστεῖος, in any case, seemed to indicate that physical beauty, rather than "urbanity," "grace," or "charm," was what she found in her newborn son.[15] Moreover, what could be the significance of her finding that he was good? Is not nearly every newborn good in the eyes of his or her mother? To these questions various answers were developed.[16] The one reflected in Acts 7 not only elaborates the significance of "good" in the Exodus passage—Moses was "good before God," that is, it was not merely his mother who found him good but God also (and presumably, therefore, the goodness in question was not of the external kind)—but also suggests that there was some connection between his mother's perception of this goodness and her hiding him. For if indeed she had seen that the child was "good before [or 'to'] God," then the implication was that God had somehow communicated this finding to her. This theme—that God had revealed to Moses' family his choice of Moses as the future savior of Israel—is indeed explicit in several ancient works— for example, in the following passages:[17]

> [God tells Amram, Moses' future father,] "This child, whose birth has filled the Egyptians with such dread that they have condemned to destruction all the off-spring of the Israelites, will indeed be yours. He shall escape those who are watching to destroy him, and, reared in unusual manner, he shall deliver the Hebrew race from their bondage in Egypt." (Josephus, *Ant.* 2.9.3 §§215–216)

> [Miriam is told by God,] "Go and say to your parents, 'Behold, he who will be born from you will be cast forth into the water; likewise through him will the water be dried up.' And I will work signs through him and save my people, and he will exercise leadership always." (*L.A.B.* 9:9–10)

> "And she saw that he was good" [Exod 2.2] . . . R. Nehemiah said, [Moses' mother saw prophetically] that he was worthy of the office of prophet . . . (*b. Soṭah* 12a)

---

[15] On this word, see "ἀστεῖος," LSJ and BAGD. It seems that the LXX translators had originally been led to the word ἀστεῖος rather than καλός (a closer rendering of טוב) precisely because of the larger context: if Moses' mother had seen his goodness, then he must have been ἀστεῖος. But in so translating, they unwittingly raised other questions.

[16] Kugel, *Traditions of the Bible*, 527.

[17] See further ibid., 611. The origins of this motif may, as I suggested there, be connected with the description of Miriam as a "prophetess" in Exod 15:20. But midrash engenders midrash: it seems altogether likely that, knowing the motif of Miriam's prophetic foreknowledge of Moses' mission, the author of Luke-Acts (or his source) therefore sought to explain Moses' mother's seeing that he was good as meaning good before God (and not merely ἀστεῖος).

In short, the phrase "good before God" in Acts 7:20 is not merely an elaboration of Exod 2.2; it reflects an attempt to understand what this verse's assertion could mean in the light of other ancient traditions. The child was not handsome or well behaved but had been determined to be "good" by God; that is, God had preordained him to survive the persecution of the Egyptians and lead the Israelites out of slavery and had communicated his choice to Moses' mother. It was this that she saw.

As for Moses' education "in all the wisdom of the Egyptians," the key to the exegetical significance of this phrase lies in the words that immediately follow it, "and he was mighty in his words and deeds." For the Bible's assertion that Moses was "heavy of speech and heavy of tongue" (Exod 4:10) might lead ordinary readers to suppose that he was simply uneducated. Such an implication would have been especially difficult for readers in the orbit of Graeco-Roman culture, where instruction in eloquence was an important and basic part of any person's development. So it was that ancient retellers of the exodus narrative went out of their way to say what the book of Exodus had somehow omitted, that Moses had indeed been well educated and so was "mighty in his words and deeds." The implication, then, was that if he was nonetheless "heavy of speech and heavy of tongue," this phrase must refer not to a defect in his education but to some physical infirmity. The tradition of Moses' education is found, in addition to the sources mentioned, in Ezekiel the Tragedian, *Exagōgē* 36–38, and *Jub.* 47.9, as well as, by implication, in Artapanus (cited in Eusebius, *Praep. ev.* 9.27.24), Eupolemus (cited in Eusebius, *Praep. ev.* 9.26.1), and later sources.[18]

Much more could be said about the exegetical background of this speech; indeed, a thorough treatment of the subject could, without exaggeration, fill a book. The angel who "spoke to him [Moses] at Mount Sinai" (Acts 7:38 RSV), "law as delivered by angels" (7.53 RSV), and a great many other of Stephen's exempla might likewise be shown to reflect other well-known exegetical motifs.[19] I hope, however, that for the various incidental details presented in this essay, the essential part of its theme has not been lost. The OT in the NT is an old topic and certainly one worthy of further exploration. But it is important to realize that NT authors did not just read the HB and pass on their considered reflections. They approached that Bible through an established tradition; with a little spadework, we can restore the tradition(s) through which they viewed the biblical text, and our understanding will be thereby greatly enhanced.

---

[18] Kugel, *Traditions of the Bible,* 509–10, 530–31.
[19] See ibid., 584–85, 670–71, 735–36.

10

Hagar between Genesis and Galatians: The Stony Road to Freedom

Brigitte Kahl

Counterreading a Text of Terror

"But what does scripture say: Drive out the slave woman and her son, because the son of the slave woman shall not inherit with the son of the free woman" (Gal 4:30; Gen 21:10).[1] If we look back at the Occidental history of biblical interpretation, Paul's verdict on Hagar—pronounced by Sarah in Genesis, converted into the voice of Scripture in Galatians—evokes images of horror. Christian superiority transfers the "other" into a position of the inferior, dispossessed, expelled, exterminated—the other race, the other class, the other sex, the other religion. Hagar became the synagogue with the broken tablets and the blinded eyes, faced by a triumphant *ecclesia,* at the entrance of many medieval cathedrals in Europe. She could stand for the abused black slave woman, the welfare mother, and the resident alien without legal protection as much as for the Muslim, the pagan, and all the other "others" deprived of their legitimate share in God, in humanity, in justice.[2]

---

[1] This article is based on a paper presented at the panel on Hagar in the Biblical Theology Consultation at the annual meeting of the Society of Biblical Literature, Nashville, November 2000. It preserves its provisional flavor as a discussion paper meant to stimulate debate by outlining some challenging questions and strategies for rereading the Genesis and Galatian Hagar. All of the issues raised will be treated more comprehensively in a forthcoming study on Paul's dealing with "one" and "other" in Galatians. I am indebted to the participants of the panel for helping me clarify some of these ideas, among whom I may mention Carol Bakhos, Daniel Boyarin, Alan Cooper, Tom Dozeman, Richard Hays, Joel Marcus, Troy A. Miller, and Delores Williams. The English translations are essentially NRSV with my own modifications.

[2] Hagar as a symbol of the oppressed has caught considerable attention, especially in the feminist discussion on biblical theology, since Phyllis Trible's influential essay, "Hagar: The Desolation of Rejection," in *Texts of Terror: Literary-Feminist Readings of Biblical Narratives* (Philadelphia: Fortress, 1984), 28. Also in 1984, an important article of Elsa Tamez that deals with Hagar from a third-world perspective appeared in Spanish: "The Woman Who Complicated the History of Salvation," in *New Eyes for Reading: Biblical and Theological Reflections by Women from the Third World* (ed. J. S. Pobee and B. von

Explored here is whether this reading of the Genesis and the Galatian Hagar might be not primarily the reading of Paul or the Scripture he quotes but that of a dominant Christianity that was unable or unwilling to understand what was written in a nondominant context of resistance and survival struggles. The argument will be based on a few observations about (1) the three Hagar texts in Genesis 16, 21 and Galatians 4 in their literary contexts, (2) the puzzling intertextuality between the Genesis and the Galatian Hagar, and (3) possible sociopolitical connotations of Hagar's slavery in a pre-70 context.

Our Freedom—Their Slavery: Does Paul (Re-)inscribe Hierarchical Dichotomies and Imperial Oneness (Gal 3:28–5:13)?

"Drive out the slave woman . . . for we, brothers, are not children of the slave woman but of the free woman" (Gal 4:30–31). At the end of 4:21–31, "we" (= "free") are clearly put into a dominant position over "them" (= "slaves"). Does this mean that Paul's theology operates within the semantic and social system of hierarchical dichotomies firmly established since Aristotle, thus perpetuating the system of slavery, as Sheila Briggs and Elisabeth Schüssler Fiorenza have argued?[3] Or to take up the argument of Daniel Boyarin, does Hagar in this most exclusionary text stand for difference as such—Jewishness as physically, genealogically, ethnically, and historically marked otherness that contradicted the Pauline vision of universal oneness? Then indeed Paul's driving out of Hagar would have paved the way for the "coercive universalism" that has marked the history of the Christian West, with all its damaging consequences.[4]

I would like to start with a short textual reflection. The terms "freedom" and "slavery" in Galatians almost exclusively and massively occur only in one section that runs from 3:28 to 5:13. If we take the literary coherence and integrity of the letter seriously, 4:21–31 cannot be read independently of this whole passage. It starts with the well-known key statement about slave and free no longer existing but being "one" in Christ (3:28). Therefore "you" are entitled to inherit according to the promise (3:29). Even the free ones (as minors) and all of "us" together have been slaves to the "elements of the kosmos" (4:1–3) and the law (4:5)—but now "you" and "we" are all together crying "abba" as (free) sons (4:6). Remember, then, "you" are no more slave; "you" are son, "you" are an heir (4:7).

Wartenberg-Potter; Geneva: World Council of Churches, 1986), 5–17. From within the African-American context, Delores Williams became another prominent voice in the current Hagar debate; cf. *Sisters in the Wilderness: The Challenge of Womanist God-Talk* (Maryknoll, N.Y.: Orbis, 1993).

[3] S. Briggs, "Galatians," in *Searching the Scriptures* (ed. E. Schüssler Fiorenza; 2 vols.; New York: Crossroad, 1993–1994), 2:224; idem, *Rhetoric and Ethic: The Politics of Biblical Studies* (Minneapolis: Fortress, 1999), 164.

[4] D. Boyarin, *A Radical Jew: Paul and the Politics of Identity* (Berkeley: University of California Press, 1994), 32–36; cf. E. Castelli, *Imitating Paul: A Discourse of Power* (Louisville: Westminster John Knox, 1991), 124ff.

After a warning that "you" should not go back into slavery (4:9), the topic is taken up ten verses later. At the opening of the Sarah-Hagar allegory, Paul appears as a troubled mother trying to rebirth her children into their true messianic identity and the "form of Christ" (μορφωθῇ Χριστός)—children not of Hagar but of the free woman, and therefore legitimate, exclusive heirs (4:19–31).

Paul, it seems, indeed operates on a dichotomy of slave and free. This dichotomy, however, appears as a rather fluid, nonstatic, and nonhierarchical one. That "our freedom" is not a status of dominance becomes very obvious at the end of the whole free-slave section in 5:13. Paul declares that freedom and not going back under the yoke of slavery (4:31–5:12) in fact mean nothing else than mutual slave service: "For you were called to freedom . . . but through love be slaves to one another" (5:13). Thus two climactic statements about slave and free frame the whole 3:28–5:13 section: free and slave becoming "one" in Christ, and free exercising their freedom as mutual slave service.

All we can say at this point is that the overall context of Hagar's expulsion in 4:30 deals with liberation. Former slaves and freeborn (who once were slaves as well) are called into freedom. On the other hand, the text, to a certain extent, blurs the established polarities in the very moment of using them. The slave-free passage 3:28–5:13 builds upon the dichotomy of slave and free, but it also subverts it. We are no more slave but free—to be slaves to each other. A highly dialectic pattern of turning a hierarchical structure upside-down emerges. If one takes 3:28 and 5:13 as "headline" and "conclusion" of the slave-free section, its logic could be summarized as something like this: Slavery becomes freedom by exercising freedom as slave service to one another—this is how free and slave are turned into "one."

This does not yet solve the puzzle of Paul driving out the slave woman. But it indicates that the term "freedom," for Paul, is something much more sophisticated and dialectic than simply a hierarchical binary opposition to slavery—and that his concept of oneness does not necessarily have imperial connotations. In a weird way, it seems to integrate and equalize the inferiority of the "other" instead of suppressing it.

Slave Woman and Free Woman: Who Is Who in Gal 4:21–31?

With this slightly confusing result of our first contextual reading in mind, we need to have a look at the allegory itself. Who actually is Hagar, the driven-out slave, and who is Sarah, the free woman, in Galatians 4? The text clearly takes up the Genesis configuration (Genesis 16 and 21) of Abraham, Sarah, Hagar, Ishmael, and Isaac. All of them are there, even if Sarah and Ishmael are not mentioned by name. But in both texts, freedom, barrenness, and "metabiological birth" by divine intervention and promise are attached to Sarah. Slavery, ordinary biological fertility, and birth "according to the flesh" are linked to Hagar (Gen 16:1–4; Gal 4:23). In Genesis, as in Galatians, Hagar and her son are or should be expelled "out," and Sarah stays "in" (Gen 21:10; Gal 4:30).

On the other hand, if the "allegorical" Hagar and Sarah of Galatians, in some very basic ways, are identical to their Genesis counterparts, they are also their complete reversal and transformation. First of all, very obviously, Hagar, who represents Egypt/the nations/the "other" in Genesis (16:1), is taking over two key categories of Jewish identity in Galatians: Mount Sinai (law) and Jerusalem (Gal 4:24–25). She thus becomes at least partly the Genesis Sarah, that is, Israel/"us." On the other hand, the Galatian Sarah is, with half of her identity, reaching out to the nations, the uncircumcised Gentiles in Galatia ("you"), that is, the Genesis Hagar. "You"/Gentiles (Genesis Hagar) and "we"/Jews (Genesis Sarah) now together have the Galatian Sarah as "our" mother, the "Jerusalem above" (Gal 4:26). That means that the Galatian Hagar and Sarah partly keep, partly exchange their Genesis identities—in other words, the allegorical Hagar is a hybrid of both the Genesis Hagar and the Genesis Sarah, and so also is the allegorical Sarah.

Not only are the identities of Sarah and Hagar confused and merged; the power dynamics of their story are completely transformed. Leaving out all other elements, Paul condenses the Genesis narrative into the conflict of the two sons and into the very moment when Ishmael appears in a position of power and dominance that throughout the Genesis text was primarily occupied by Sarah. Changing the Hebrew root צחק and the LXX παίζοντα of Gen 21:9 into the clearly negative and violent ἐδίωκεν, Paul lets Hagar's son in Gal 4:29 appear as the "persecutor" of Isaac, the "son of the free." Whereas the Genesis Sarah just "sees" that "the son of Hagar, the Egyptian, whom she bore to Abraham was joking"(Gen 21:9), Paul's Ishmael actively threatens the child born "according to the Spirit." This newly inserted element of persecution makes the demand "to drive out the slave woman and her son" sound much more justifiable in Gal 4:30 than it sounded in Gen 21:10, where Sarah imposes the same harsh punishment on Ishmael and his mother for merely "joking."[5]

Paul further emphasizes in two ways the violence and power he ascribes to Ishmael-Hagar. First, by aligning Hagar and her children under the rubric of "Sinai" and "Jerusalem now" (Gal 4:25), Paul links them to the two most powerful Jewish institutions of his time: the law and a temple still undestroyed. Second, the term "persecution" clearly relates them to the "opponents" with whom Paul is struggling throughout Galatians and who are somehow identified with Jerusalem and the law, even if the exact nature of this relationship is not quite clear.[6] The

---

[5] Paul here appears embedded in the Jewish history of interpretation of Gen 21:9 that tried to fill in the obvious lacunae of the text. Already in the LXX Isaac was added as a target of Ishmael's "joking." In *Jub.* 17:4, on the other hand, Isaac is not included in the scene; rather it is Ishmael who makes Sarah jealous by merely "playing and dancing and Abraham enjoying very greatly." Closer to Paul is Josephus, who, in his retelling of the story (*Ant.* 1.6.1 §215), interprets Sarah's reaction as fear that Ishmael could become a threat to Isaac after Abraham's death. Nevertheless, the term "persecution" as a condensation of the whole Hagar-Sarah story in Galatians seems to be Paul's own invention, as it links Ishmael-Hagar to the Galatian opponents and "troublemakers" (see following note).

[6] The term "persecute" (διώκω) is used for the law-based pre-Damascus Paul himself in Gal 1:13–14, 23, and then two more times to describe the activity of a third party

Galatian Hagar, like the Genesis one, is a slave with her children and to be expelled, but she is also the Genesis Sarah, as she represents circumcision and fights against Paul's uncircumcised "sons" (cf. 4:19) from a dominant position, that is, in the name of Sinai/law and Jerusalem/Israel "now."

If the allegorical Hagar thus in fact is the Genesis Hagar and Sarah together, frozen in violence before the background of the dominant power system(s)—what could this mean? I think that Paul's Hagar, narratively reduced to the single feature persecution, represents the Genesis Hagar *and* Sarah in the very moment and also the eternal drama of their and their sons' fighting each other. Allegory, as Daniel Boyarin has put it, is "speaking of the other" and revealing the "inner meaning of the outward sign."[7] But contrary to Boyarin, I see the "structure of reality" signified by the signifier Hagar in Galatians not (yet) as Judaism and difference, which are opposed to Sarah, signifying (a not yet existing) "universal Christianity." Rather, Hagar stands allegorically for the hostile dichotomy that naturally and inevitably turns first and second son, second and first wife, Jews and Gentiles, "in" and "out" into enemies—the very structure of the Pythagorean opposites that since ever and forever divide the world into the hierarchical polarities of "us" versus "them." Hagar, for Paul, represents "one-against-other."[8]

---

that the "opponents" want to escape by "forcing" circumcision (6:12; 5:11; cf. 2:3). The ambiguous role of Jerusalem is explained in Galatians 2: In Paul's retrospective account, Jerusalem is essentially the place where his controversial "gospel of the foreskin," after much struggle and power gaming, finally had been accepted, putting it at equal terms with Peter's "gospel of the circumcision" (2:1–10). But soon afterwards this consensus was betrayed by Jerusalem authorities associated with James, causing the famous Antioch split of table community with Gentiles. At that point Paul was completely isolated (2:13). So wherever within the Jewish (messianic or nonmessianic) "power" structures, negatively marked by Jerusalem/law/Hagar, we have to locate Paul's "opponents" in Galatians, and whatever relationship to the overarching Roman power structures this implied, Paul argues from a position of utmost weakness. After his defeat at Antioch, Scripture seems to be the only ally left (cf. 3:8, 22) that "speaks" in favor of his "gospel of the foreskin" (4:21–22, 30). The whole rhetorical dynamics of Galatians in general (and of the retelling of the Abraham-Sarah-Hagar story in particular) was turned upside down when the historical Paul was converted into the canonical Paul and the "gospel of circumcision" was banned, thus making "foreskin" the marker of an exclusive and dominant Christianity instead of having foreskin and circumcision coexist within an inclusive Judaism.

[7] Boyarin, *Radical Jew*, 35.

[8] The use of the term συστοιχέω ("align under the rubric of," "correspond to") in 4:25 suggests that Paul thinks within the framework of the Pythagorean opposites, which structure the world into hierarchical dichotomies; cf. J. Louis Martyn, *Galatians* (AB 33A; New York: Doubleday, 1997), 100–101, 393–406. As quoted by Aristotle in *Metaph.* 986a, they are arranged in parallel columns of "one" (e.g., right, male, straight, light, good) and the corresponding inferior "other" (left, female, curved, dark, bad). In contrast to Boyarin (*Radical Jew*, 31, 35), I believe that Paul not only uses this pattern but also fundamentally subverts it; cf. B. Kahl, "No Longer Male: Masculinity Struggles behind Gal 3:28?" *JSNT* 79 (2000): 44.

"One against Other": The Galatian Hagar Pattern in Genesis

We should have another and closer look at the Genesis stories now. At first sight, Paul seems to turn them upside down and steal the Jewish genealogical identity by taking away Sarah as Israel's legitimate ancestress, replacing her by Hagar as "other."[9] But if Paul's Hagar, at a closer look, is not just "other" but both "one" and "other"—more precisely, "one against other"—does this mean that the Galatian Hagar is a purely Pauline invention without scriptural base? Undoubtedly, Paul's polemical reinterpretation and reapplication of the Sarah-Hagar conflict contains a strong element of innovation. This does not preclude, however, a formative influence of the Genesis material. I would like to explore the following hypothesis: Paul's Hagar, far from marking the apostle's departure from Scripture and Judaism, is in fact shaped by a highly dialectical and rebellious identity pattern that is firmly rooted in the narrative deep structures of Genesis itself.

From Abraham onwards, all throughout Genesis Israel's promised descendancy is complicated in one way or another by two problems: female infertility and the fact that none of the firstborn sons gets his lawful status but is replaced by his younger brother. This motif of the barren mother and the second brother (and the resulting conflicts between first and second brothers/mothers) in Genesis is a well-known literary phenomenon that has received widely divergent explanations.[10] I see it as a key for decoding the complex Genesis-Galatians intertextuality in order to understand how Galatians—which, in its essential theological argument in chapters 3 and 4, is a rereading of Genesis—deals with oneness and difference, in and out, us and them.[11]

The pattern becomes most obvious at the end of Genesis, when Jacob/Israel, in the blessing ceremony of his two grandsons, to the great bewilderment of their father, Joseph, crosses his hands and gives the right to the wrong one on his

---

[9] Briggs, "Galatians," 2:225.

[10] See, e.g., F. Greenspahn, *When Brothers Dwell Together: The Preeminence of Younger Siblings in the Hebrew Bible* (New York: Oxford University Press, 1993); R. Syrén, *The Forsaken Firstborn: A Study of a Recurrent Motif in the Patriarchal Narratives* (JSOTSup 133; Sheffield, England: Sheffield Academic Press, 1993).

[11] R. B. Hays, *Echoes of Scripture in the Letters of Paul* (New Haven: Yale University Press, 1989), has developed an understanding of biblical intertextuality that reaches far beyond the traditional emphasis on passages that Paul (or any other author) explicitly or even consciously quotes; see also the debate on this book in C. A. Evans and J. A. Sanders, eds., *Paul and the Scriptures of Israel* (JSNTSup 83; Sheffield, England: Sheffield Academic Press, 1993), 42–96. Following and further elaborating this approach, R. E. Ciampa, in a comprehensive textual and intertextual analysis of Galatians 1–2, has shown that exodus themes shape these two chapters in a much more complex, subtle, and powerful way than a "myopic" focus on direct, isolated quotations and quotation techniques would reveal; cf. *The Presence and Function of Scripture in Galatians 1 and 2* (WUNT, 2. Reihe, 102; Tübingen: Mohr Siebeck, 1998), esp. 1–7. In a similar manner, I would see the dynamic, multilayered interaction of Galatians 3–4 with Genesis patterns in terms of mutual (re)interpretation as a decisive hermeneutical key—even if I would put a stronger emphasis on the role of the historical context in deciphering this literary intertextuality.

left, making the second son the first and the first the second (Gen 48:12–14). At this point in the Genesis narrative its actors should be used to the stubborn insistence of their story on the first always being transferred to the position of the inferior "others," whereas the "others" become the "ones"—ever since Abel/Seth and Cain in the postparadise story (cf. 4:25–26; 5:3).[12] Israel, the "firstborn of God" (Exod 4:22), is made out of second-born sons. It is also made out of barren mothers. Its divine descent is explained in terms of unlikelihood: (pro)creation out of social otherness and biological nothingness. It is exactly these two elements of a divine birth and divine (pro)creation that are signified by the barren mother–second brother motif in Genesis and activated by Paul in Galatians. Social and ethnic otherness/nothingness and how it relates to "us" as the one people of the one God is the issue at stake when Paul retells Genesis as a story of motherhood "according to the promise" against "motherhood according to the flesh."[13]

In Genesis 16 and 21 Ishmael in the most intense way embodies the "firstborn dilemma" and the deadly conflict between dominant and dominated, in and out underlying it. He is the son of Hagar brought into life for no other reason than to be Abraham's firstborn son—and the firstborn son of the barren mistress Sarah, who can "take" and "give" (16:3), exploit and expropriate the body and fertility of her slave Hagar in whichever way she wants. But Ishmael is also the son of Hagar's resistance. The slave woman wants to keep her son as her own and refuses to accept Sarah's superiority once she has "seen" that her pregnancy weakens Sarah's position (16:4). Within the system of slavery and patriarchy, this leaves only two ways for Hagar: either to replace Sarah as mistress and Abraham's wife or (after this has failed) to run away from slavery into the nowhere land of the desert.

Within the same system of slavery and patriarchy, Sarah's choice of possible responses to Hagar's resistance is likewise very limited—even for a mistress and especially if her barrenness threatens her position. She can try either to keep Hagar down and out (16:5–6) or to get rid of her and her child, which was meant to stabilize Sarah's position but now has turned out to be a dreadful danger (21:10). This whole dilemma is not about moral judgments; it is more about structural traps in which both Sarah and Hagar are imprisoned, even if Sarah has the more pleasant place. This is why it does not matter so much whether Ishmael in Genesis 21 really "persecuted" and abused his younger brother Isaac. According to the law (Deut 21:15–17), Ishmael is Abraham's firstborn son, his main heir by her, Sarah's, own arrangement—and Isaac is inferior though being the son of the "loved" and freeborn wife. Whatever the children playing there in front of Sarah did, their play is not allowed to be "innocent." As the pregnant Hagar had "seen" her advantage over

---

[12] See B. Kahl, "And She Called His Name Seth . . . (Gen 4:25): The Birth of Critical Knowledge and the Unread End of Eve's Story," *USQR* 53 (1999): 19–28.

[13] Galatians 4:21–31 with its focus on motherhood is the climax of the whole Genesis section of Galatians, which starts in 3:6–29 with Abraham and a dismantling of physical fatherhood; cf. Kahl, "No Longer Male," 41–44. The theme of oneness is present in 3:16 ("one sperm"), 3:20 ("God is one"), 3:28 ("one in Christ"), and 5:14 (the "one" commandment of love as fulfillment of the whole Torah).

Sarah in Gen 16:4, Sarah now in 21:9 "sees" behind the scene the structural violence and deadly competition that inescapably turn the "one" into the enemy of the
"other." And she thinks she can solve the problem by another abusive act toward
Hagar: "Drive out that slave woman with her son" (21:10). It is this hopelessness of
an irreconcilable struggle between dominant "ones" and dominated "others" that
Paul attaches allegorically to "the" slave woman in Gal 4:30—that is, slavery in general—and wants to be driven out in Galatians.[14]

"One-an(d)-Other": The Allegorical Sarah and the Genesis Pattern of Reconciliation

What about the allegorical Sarah? If our reading of the allegorical Hagar is correct, then the allegorical Sarah must be her counterpart. What would be the opposite of the despair, blood, and tears linked to Hagar? It is hope amidst
hopelessness for both the Genesis Sarah and Hagar, for Ishmael and Isaac likewise. It is messianic peace ending the cosmic warfare between "one" and "other,"
Sarah/Israel and Hagar/Egypt-Arabia. Interestingly, for Paul it is "scripture," not
Sarah as in Genesis, that pleads for Hagar to be driven out (Gal 4:30). But does
Scripture, does Genesis, have indeed some sort of vision how the enslaving
struggle between the two women and their sons might be ended, how Hagar's
otherness could be justified, integrated, reconciled in a nonimperial and non-
coercive way to Sarah's oneness? Or does it just declare Sarah to be the chosen
one—chosen at the expense of the Hagarites and Ishmaelites, who are rightfully
excluded, expelled, expropriated, exterminated?

There is something fundamental in Genesis that links the "divine (pro)cre-
ation" out of the nothingness/otherness of barren mothers and second sons to
Paul's "new (pro)creation," which raises life out of death and turns the deadly divisions of humanity—Jews versus Greeks, slaves versus free, male versus female
(cf. Gal 3:28)—into kinship and peace (6:14–16). Let's have a look at Genesis
first. Through long and painful transformations between in and out, high and
low, all the significant brothers in Genesis finally more or less dramatically reconcile: Jacob and Esau, Joseph and his brothers, even Ishmael and Isaac—when they
bury Abraham together, when Isaac dwells at Hagar's well, when Ishmaelites
"save" Joseph out of the pit (Gen 33:10; 45:5; 25:9–11; 37:25–27). The fighting
women in Genesis, however, do not reconcile. Or perhaps Leah and Rachel finally
do in strange way (30:15)—but not Sarah and Hagar. They die unreconciled.
Nevertheless, the text in Genesis 16 contains a profound double-sidedness and
dialectic that resists any clear-cut pro-Sarah interpretation. If it is a "text of
terror," it is also a text of transformation, liberation, and survival.

---

[14] That Paul changes "that" slave woman (in both the Hebrew and the Greek text of
Gen 21:10) into "the" slave woman, i.e., replaces the concrete by an abstract, could support my thesis that he wants to deal not just with his "opponents" but with the issue of Israel's slavery under the Roman yoke in a much more general way (see below).

It is true that the angel in the wilderness sends Hagar, the mistreated runaway slave and surrogate mother, back into submission to her mistress (16:9). But the old law and order is totally subverted from within: (1) Hagar, the never asked, never speaking maid of Abraham and Sarah in vv. 1–3, is addressed by the divine messenger and speaks for the first time (v. 8). (2) Her son will not be Sarah's son but her own, free and wild, growing into a countless multitude (vv. 10–12)—a promise very close to that which Abraham receives in the chapter before (15:5). The angel of the Lord declares the surrogate's mother's right to her child and denies Sarah's expectation to "build" (cf. 16:2) her genealogy on him. (3) Hagar will thus become the ancestress of a great twelve-tribe nation, like Abraham (cf. 25:12–18). (4) Like only very few outstanding characters in the Bible, Hagar's unborn child is named by God: "You shall call his name Ishmael, for the Lord has heard your misery" (16:11). Although she is sent back into slavery, Hagar gets the promise of liberation. In the name of her son, the deprived and depreciated maid receives justice—as Israel later will be "heard" in the misery of the Egyptian house of slavery. The divine intervention reverses all the relationships and expectations set up by Sarah in the first part of the narrative. Now it is Hagar's misery that counts, Hagar who is addressed by God and speaks, and Hagar's child who will be born. (5) This change of perspectives reaches its climax when Hagar finally spells out the name of God as she has experienced it: "You are a God who sees me" (16:13). Now the woman, foreigner, slave, surrogate mother does something that nowhere in the Bible anybody else does: she gives God a name. Even Moses at the burning bush had to ask for God's name and identity (Exod 3:13); Hagar "knows" it. She becomes an outstanding prophetess who, long before Moses and the exodus events, proclaims that Abraham's and Sarah's God is a God who takes care of oppressed slaves in a foreign country—something that Abraham and Sarah themselves at this point do not seem to be aware of. But their story all too soon will become Hagar's story when Israel will be deprived of her sons and oppressed by foreign masters, escaping into the freedom of the desert and encountering God there. [15]

---

[15] The theologically outstanding elements of a pro-Hagar reading in Genesis 16 have been listed by Phyllis Trible, "Hagar": Hagar is the first person in Scripture to be visited by a divine messenger, the only person to dare name the Deity, the first woman to hear an annunciation, and the only one to receive a divine promise of descendants. Trible also shows the numerous textual parallels between the Hagar and exodus texts, pointing out that Hagar's story foreshadows the story of Israel from exodus to exile. But for Trible, this foreshadowing is "through contrast" as Hagar experiences "exodus without liberation, revelation without salvation, wilderness without covenant, wanderings without land, promise without fulfillment, and unmerited exile without return" (28). God's interaction with Hagar stays basically on the side of the oppressors, because he first sends her back into slavery (Gen 16:9) and later agrees to her expulsion in order to protect Abraham's and Sarah's inheritance (21:10–12). Trible's analysis has yielded very important insights, yet it fails to explain the function of 16:10–14 in the overall narrative weaving of the Hagar texts and Genesis as a whole. The fundamental dialectics of a pro-Hagar *and* a pro-Sarah reading within one and the same text is replaced by an either-or interpretation.

The text of Genesis 16 and its ongoing retelling throughout the exodus story refuse any simplistic us-versus-them logic. It profoundly wrestles with the conflict of "ones" against "others," constantly reverting and mirroring "ones" and/as "others." The Egyptian's slavery and liberation in and from Israel foreshadows Israel's slavery and liberation in and from Egypt.[16] This means that the merging of Sarah and Hagar we discovered in Galatians is already in a certain way underlying the narrative structure of Genesis-Exodus. It perhaps has its deepest theological roots in the "other" image of the "one" God of Israel, whose oneness is radically different from the imperial oneness of Babel (Gen 11:1–6). This "other" God who is "one" can be the God of Sarah without being a God against Hagar. He can stay with Hagar even if Sarah is against her—as he stays the God of Sarah even if Hagar is fighting her, a God whose "seeing" of Hagar changes the "evil eye" with which Hagar and Sarah (have to) look at each other,[17] because this God's oneness means justification and salvation, not suppression of otherness— or, to use Paul's terms, blessing for the nations rather than curse (Gal 3:13–14), inclusive justification, faith, and grace, not exclusive "works of the Law" (Gal 2:11–21). If Paul's allegorical Sarah in Galatians is the final reconciliation of the unreconciled Genesis Sarah and Hagar (the allegorical Hagar), this is a reframing of Genesis that is profoundly shaped by the inner dynamics of the Genesis narrative itself.[18]

This brings us back to Galatians. The "promise" that defines Sarah's motherhood in Gal 4:23 is explained all throughout the preceding chapter as the blessing waiting for the Gentiles since Abraham (Gen 12:3; Gal 3:8, 14, 16, 21, 29). In the overall context of Galatians, "Sarah"—that is, the Genesis Hagar and Sarah finally finding each other—represents Jews and Gentiles eating together at Antioch (Gal 2:12), Gentiles sending money to the poor in Jerusalem (2:10), and the "right hand of community" extended by the Jerusalem "gospel of circumcision"

---

[16] An even more immediate linkage between Hagar and Israel is made in Genesis 22. The Aqedah of Isaac in many ways textually mirrors the story of Hagar-Ishmael in Genesis 21. The elements of this striking parallelism also have been listed by Trible ("Hagar," 27 n. 71) who, however, does not draw any theological conclusions. Regarding the narrative strategy and the intertextual phenomenon of "inverted" Genesis stories, see also Y. Zakovitch, "Through the Looking Glass: Reflections/Inversions of Genesis Stories in the Bible," *BibInt* 1 (1993): 139–52.

[17] Cf. the emphasis on "seeing" and "eyes"/"vision" in Gen 16:4, 5, 6, 13, 14 and Gen 21:9, 16, 19 and Paul's allusion to the "evil eye"(ἐβάσκανεν) and misperceptions of the cross in Gal 3:1.

[18] There are earlier scriptural echoes of Hagar and Sarah reconciling, however, most notably in the Ruth-Naomi narrative, which is later mirrored by Luke in his messianic-birth story around Elizabeth and Mary and their two sons: both mothers and sons have given up fighting each other (Luke 1:41–44). Another echo of Hagar related to the "birth" of a border-transgressing messianic community occurs in John 4; cf. B. Kahl, "Die Frau am Väterbrunnen—von der Kirchenmutterschaft Hagars: Versuch einer synchronen Lektüre von Johannes 4 und Genesis 16," in *Für Gerechtigkeit streiten: Theologie im Alltag einer bedrohten Welt* (ed. D. Sölle; Gütersloh: Christian Kaiser/Gütersloher Verlagshaus, 1994), 53–58.

toward the Gentile "gospel of the foreskin" (2:9). All throughout Galatians, Sarah stands for an oneness that no longer excludes but embraces otherness by bearing one another's burdens (6:2) and exercising freedom as slave service to "one-an-other" (5:13). Sarah, the "Jerusalem above" as "our mother"(4:26), represents the metropolis of a new worldwide reality of reconciliation and peace between Israel and the nations, "ones" and "others." She also redefines Israel as the new and inclusive category of humanity and being humane. This is what Paul sees as the apocalyptic rebirth of creation (4:19; 6:15). It is inaugurated by the crucified, resurrected Messiah. But its "seed" (cf. 3:16) has been present since Genesis.

"Drive Out the Slave": Jerusalem's Slavery and Freedom from a Pre-70 C.E. Perspective

If our interpretation of the allegorical Hagar is correct, then Paul's claim to drive out and disinherit the slave would not mean driving out the socially weak, the black, the foreigner, the woman, the single mother, the abused slave, the Jew, the Muslim, the "other." The "flesh" Hagar stands for is neither the Platonic "body" signifying Jewish difference, Israel, circumcision, and genealogy in particular,[19] nor inferiority/slave woman in general. It is, on the contrary, the cosmic structure and fight of the oppositional "two columns" that is dominated by "sin" and needs to be exorcised. "Drive out the slave" means the whole hierarchical division of humanity into superior and inferior, excluded and included, which shapes the present world order *(kosmos)*. This is what Paul sees embodied in the "Law" and those who want to impose it on the Galatians.

Could we try to hear this for one moment in a slightly less abstract, less purely theological way? Jerusalem in slavery and/or Jerusalem free—a pre-70 C.E. Jew or Gentile would probably have had great difficulties not to hear the political overtones in this question. Paul's presentation of the Hagar texts is not dealing with scriptural intertextuality in a sociohistorical vacuum but within the concrete contextuality of his time. In other words, the Sarah-Hagar allegory in the literary context of Galatians interacts with its contemporary Roman and Greek contexts as intensely as it interacts with the Genesis texts. When Paul wrote to the Galatians, somewhere in the fifties of the first century, the slavery of Jerusalem "now" was not primarily a theological construct but a political reality—the omnipresent colonial reality of the Roman Empire.[20]

We might illustrate this by using Flavius Josephus, Paul's younger first-century contemporary, as another "intertext." In the famous speech Josephus assigns to

---

[19] *Pace* Boyarin, *Radical Jew*, 31.

[20] For a recent paradigm shift toward taking the political context of Paul's theology and his anti-imperial message more seriously, see the essays in R. E. Horsley, ed., *Paul and Empire: Religion and Power in Roman Imperial Society* (Harrisburg, Pa.: Trinity Press International, 1997); and idem, ed., *Paul and Politics: Ekklesia, Israel, Imperium, Interpretation* (Harrisburg, Pa.: Trinity Press International, 2000).

King Agrippa II (28–94 C.E.) at the moment before the outbreak of the Jewish war (*J.W.* 2.16.3–5 §§342–404), the whole problem of Jewish and Gentile existence in the Roman Empire is organized around the two key words of "slavery" versus "freedom." Outlining the political, military, and economic anatomy of the Pax Romana in a strikingly realistic way, Agrippa tries to make clear that there is no chance for the Jews or any other of the colonialized nations to become free:

> Look at the Athenians, the men who, to maintain the liberty [ἐλευθερία] of Greece, once consigned their city to the flames; the men before whose pursuit the haughty Xerxes, who navigated the land and trod the sea . . . fled like a fugitive slave. . . . Those men today are the servants [δουλεύουσιν] of the Romans and the city that was the queen of Greece is governed by orders from Italy. (*J.W.* 2.16.4 §368)

> Myriads of other nations, swelling with greater pride in the assertion of their liberty, have yielded. And will you alone disdain to serve those to whom the universe is subject? (*J.W.* 2.16.4 §361)

For the literary Agrippa, the answer to this rhetorical question, repeated in numerous variations, is clear: universal submission and slavery to the Romans has to be accepted by every nation under the sun, including the Jews. Even God is supposedly on their side now—Rome is too strong to be resisted (*J.W.* 2.16.4 §390). Being submissive to the law and power of the Roman world order is the only way to guarantee the precious privilege of an at least limited freedom to obey the Jewish law (cf. *J.W.* 2.16.4 §393).

If we look at Hagar again from this angle, Paul's answer to the question of global enslavement (cf. Gal 4:3, 8–9) sounds notably different. There is nothing about accepting slavery, nothing about universal power handed over to Caesar by God. The slavery of the allegorical Hagar's children is mentioned twice in vv. 21–31. Hagar/Sinai/law allegorically "bears" children "for slavery" and also corresponds to the "Jerusalem now—for she is in slavery with her children" (vv. 24–25). On the opposite side is the "other" Jerusalem above (v. 26), the metropolis of freedom. "Drive out the slave woman and her son" (v. 30) in this context very much means, "Drive out slavery—the slavery of 'Jerusalem now.'"[21] From this perspective, the Sarah-Hagar allegory would become part of a "coded" political discourse on liberation from the yoke of Roman colonialism, instead of confirming slavery as a social institution.[22]

---

[21] Cf. n. 14 above.

[22] On coded language in the NT in general, see the interesting study by N. A. Beck, *Anti-Roman Cryptograms in the New Testament: Symbolic Messages of Hope and Liberation* (New York: Peter Lang, 1997). Cf. J. C. Scott, *Domination and the Arts of Resistance: Hidden Transcripts* (New Haven: Yale University Press, 1990). If liberation is at the core of Paul's slave-free section in Gal 3:28–5:13 and his rereading of Genesis, this would be very much in line with Ciampa's illuminating demonstration of exodus themes shaping Galatians 1 and 2 (cf. n. 11 above). See also S. C. Keesmaat, *Paul and His Story: (Re)interpreting the Exodus Tradition* (JSNTSup 181; Sheffield, England: Sheffield Academic Press, 1999).

Paul probably would have shared the fictive Agrippa's concern regarding the disastrous outcome of a violent Jewish uprising against the Romans even if he never saw what Agrippa's ghostwriter, Josephus, actually had seen: how Jerusalem and the temple were buried in blood and ashes by Titus in 70 C.E. after four years of a suicidal anti-Roman struggle for freedom. On the other hand, Paul would also have agreed to some of the basic theological and political assumptions of the rebellious crowds Josephus has appear before Agrippa II: that the complicity and compromise of Roman and Jewish law as it was embodied in the whole system of temple rule and client kingship ("Jerusalem") were shameful. Nevertheless, Paul draws consequences radically different from both: not, like Agrippa, to proclaim the divinely ordained world rule of the (Roman) law in order to safeguard the limited space for an independent Jewish law. Nor, like the groups aiming at violent resistance, did he turn the (Jewish) law one more time against the "others," Romans and Greeks, for example, by enforcing circumcision as a boundary marker between us and them, insisting on ritual purity against all elements of foreignness and otherness.[23] Rather Paul advocates a nonviolent subversion of the Roman law and a messianic-apocalyptic reinterpretation of the Jewish law by having Jews and Gentiles, circumcised and uncircumcised, eat together at one table and serve each other in one universal community. For him, this is how the worldwide kingdom of God replaces Caesar's empire, how "we" as citizens of the Jerusalem above can become free despite the present Jerusalem's slavery: together with, not against, the "others." The basis of this universal community and peace is not Caesar's law or military power but a kind of inclusive Judaism from below that rests on the power of resurrection. Operating from the underground of the Roman world order, the crucified Messiah replaces the emperor in his function as mediator and peacemaker between the defeated nations.[24]

"Drive out the slave woman and her son" in this context would mean a dialectical call to freedom as service to one another (Gal 5:13) for addressees who found themselves as Gentiles in the same situation of universal Roman enslavement as the Jews, a call to "lawlessness" by transgressing boundaries drawn by both Roman and Jewish law. The world order rests on these boundaries toward the neighbor and (br)other, the law of divide and rule. Sin, as the universally destroying and enslaving power (cf. 3:22), makes use of these boundaries and their hierarchical "law," setting up Jews against Gentiles, Gentiles against Jews, forever—the same sin and the same hierarchical polarities as have been operating in

---

[23] Josephus (*J.W.* 2.17.2–3 §§409–412) reports that after the failure of Agrippa's peace effort and the king's angry withdrawal, the rebellion started in the Jerusalem temple with a refusal of gifts from non-Jews, thus ending the daily sacrifices on behalf of the Roman emperor and the Roman nation. It is interesting that in the following debate the terminology of "foreign/other" (ἀλλόφυλος; ἀλλότριος) plays an important role.

[24] On the strikingly parallel and thereby conflicting structures of Paul's messianic peace concept and the Roman peace concept (*pax gentium*), see, e.g., the comprehensive background studies in E. Faust, *Pax Christi und Pax Caesaris: Religionsgeschichtliche, traditionsgeschichtliche und sozialgeschichtliche Studien zum Epheserbrief* (Göttingen: Vandenhoeck & Ruprecht, 1993).

the murderous conflicts between Cain and Abel, Ishmael and Isaac, and all the other fighting brothers and their mothers since the first steps of humanity out of Eden. Therefore the messianic reconciliation of "one" and "other" on a world-wide scale for Paul is both transgression and fulfillment of the law. It embodies "love and slave service" toward the (br)other as the "one" core commandment of God and "Law of Christ" (5:13–14; 6:2); it also embodies the one essential feature in the genetic structure of Israel as the "one" chosen and firstborn nation of God generated out of second-born and barren "others."

No wonder that Paul almost certainly was executed by Nero a few years after he wrote Galatians.[25] No wonder that both Jews and Gentiles, in their mutual hostility, which ignited the great Jewish rebellion shortly afterwards (see, e.g., Josephus, *J.W.* 2.14.4 §§285–296), found his message annoying, foolish, and scandalous (cf. 1 Cor 1:23). No wonder that all he said polemically against a still strong Jerusalem sounded totally different after Jerusalem was no longer Jerusalem "now" but had been defeated and destroyed. No wonder, finally, that, within the imperial hermeneutics of a Constantinian Christianity, Paul's massive polemic against Hagar as a self-destructive and enslaving concept of liberation was (mis)used to turn Sarah against Hagar again. Hagar understood in terms of slavery/Egypt/Rome, and the eternal logic of "one-against-other" had made Paul's violent anti-Hagar rhetoric more than plausible. Ironically, this rhetorical violence later helped to substantiate exactly the hierarchical and polarizing reading pattern Paul himself had been fiercely fighting against: Sarah again became the dominant "one" standing against an inferior Hagar as "other."

The two women and their sons are still fighting.

---

[25] Cf. D. Georgi, "God Turned Upside Down," in *Paul and Empire: Religion and Power in Roman Imperial Society* (ed. R. E. Horsley; Harrisburg, Pa.: Trinity Press International, 1997), 157.

11

The Culpability of Eve: From Genesis to Timothy

Gary A. Anderson

The LORD God commanded the man, "You may freely eat of every tree of the garden; but of the tree of the knowledge of good and evil you shall not eat, for in the day that you eat of it you shall die. . . ." [Eve is created.] [The serpent] said to the woman, "Did God say, 'You shall not eat from any tree in the garden?'" The woman said to the serpent, "We may eat of the fruit of the trees in the garden; but God said, 'You shall not eat of the fruit of the tree that is in the middle of the garden, nor shall you touch it, or you shall die.'" . . . [The woman] took of its fruit and ate; and she also gave some to her husband, who was with her, and he ate. (Gen 2:16–17; 3:1–3, 6 NRSV)

I desire, then, that in every place the men should pray, lifting up holy hands without anger or argument; also that the women should dress themselves modestly and decently in suitable clothing, not with their hair braided, or with gold, pearls, or expensive clothes, but with good works, as is proper for women who profess reverence for God. Let a woman learn in silence with full submission. I permit no woman to teach or to have authority over a man; she is to keep silent. For Adam was formed first, then Eve; and Adam was not deceived, but the woman was deceived and became a transgressor. Yet she will be saved through childbearing, provided they continue in faith and love and holiness, with modesty. (1 Tim 2:8–15 NRSV)

If one were to peruse the collection of writings that makes up our present NT canon, one would find it difficult to name a text more bothersome to many present-day readers than 1 Tim 2:8–15. In this text women are asked to subordinate themselves to men and not presume to exercise leadership roles over them. The grounding for these prescriptions is ostensibly biblical: "For Adam was created first and only then Eve. And Adam was not deceived, but rather the woman having succumbed to deception fell into sin." At one level, the arguments Paul (or, as others would have it, someone writing in Paul's name) makes in support of his argument appear self-evidently biblical. No one could deny that the Genesis narratives document the creation of Adam before Eve (Gen 2:18–23), nor could

one deny the fact that Eve was deceived. This is the very word she uses to describe
her transgression when she addresses her Creator: "The snake deceived me and
I ate" (3:13). Yet why does the author claim that Adam was not deceived? In putting forward this negative proposition, one could conjecture that Adam was, in
fact, innocent of any wrongdoing. Nowhere in Genesis 2–3 is Adam explicitly exonerated for his role in the fall. The question we must pose is how the story of
the fall as recorded in Genesis could yield such an asymmetrical understanding
of guilt.

There are several options for construing responsibility for the fall. Adam
and Eve could be equally culpable, or culpability could fall more heavily on one
than the other. Clearly, there are conditions external to the text of Genesis that
have some bearing on the matter. To bring to mind the most obvious, we need
only mention our text from 1 Timothy. Because this text has an interest in limit-
ing the leadership roles of woman, one could argue that its interpretation of the
fall is really an act of legerdemain: having already determined in advance the inferior status of woman, Paul simply read this back into the account of Genesis.[1]
Similar arguments have been made about the positive role of Eve in certain gnos-
tic retellings of the fall. In these materials the high estimation of women as leaders would correlate positively with the positive portrayal of Eve.[2] But such
functionalist arguments can also badly flounder. As Jaroslav Pelikan has recently
reminded us, Eve's role in the fall can frequently be portrayed negatively in order
that the person of Mary (the true *mulier fortis*) can shine with even stronger efful-
gence.[3] No broadside against the feminine gender this. But those who would
argue that Eve's role in the fall is determined solely by catechetical norms about
gender disappoint for another reason. They fail to consider what textual elements
in the Bible itself occasioned the exegetical portraits of Eve. In the brief space of
this essay, we cannot consider all the exegetical options exploited by early biblical
interpreters. Instead we will consider two representative options: one that portrays Eve positively; the other, negatively.

The Nature of the Command and Warning about the Tree

The complications with our biblical story begin with the very giving of the command. According to our narrative, the command is not given to Adam and Eve
together but to Adam alone (Gen 2:15–17):

---

[1] For a review of modern scholarship on this problem, see J. Roloff, *Der erste Brief
an Timotheus* (EKKNT 15; Neukirchen-Vluyn: Neukirchener Verlag, 1988).

[2] This thesis has been advanced in boldest terms in E. Pagels, *Adam, Eve, and the
Serpent* (New York: Random House, 1988), 57–77.

[3] See J. Pelikan, *Mary through the Centuries* (New Haven: Yale University Press,
1996). In particular, consult ch. 3, "The Second Eve," 39–54. The reference to the *mulier
fortis* comes from Prov 31:10.

The LORD God took the man and put him in the garden of Eden to till it and keep it. And the LORD God commanded the man, "You may freely eat of every tree of the garden; but of the tree of the knowledge of good and evil you shall not eat, for in the day that you eat of it you shall die." [וּמֵעֵץ הַדַּעַת טוֹב וָרָע לֹא תֹאכַל מִמֶּנּוּ כִּי בְּיוֹם אֲכָלְךָ מִמֶּנּוּ מוֹת תָּמוּת:]

Eve had not yet been created and therefore had no opportunity to hear it. One may object and say that it is a very easy matter to presume that Adam, at some point not made explicit by our storyteller, had informed Eve about the tree and its danger. This would seem rather obvious from Eve's citation of the command when she converses with the snake (Gen 3:2–3):

The woman said to the serpent, "We may eat of the fruit of the trees in the garden; but God said, 'You shall not eat of the fruit of the tree that is in the middle of the garden, nor shall you touch it, or you shall die.'" [לֹא תֹאכְלוּ מִמֶּנּוּ וְלֹא תִגְּעוּ בּוֹ פֶּן־תְּמֻתוּן:]

Surely, the reader will conclude, Adam taught this command to Eve. Scripture need not disclose every detail. But if we presume this, our problems have not ended. For when Eve iterates the command in the presence of the snake, she does not repeat the original command in a literal fashion. She makes what appears to be a slight addition to what God had declared. "We may eat of the fruit of the trees in the garden," Eve declares, but regarding the tree in the middle, "you shall not eat . . . nor shall you touch it [וְלֹא תִגְּעוּ בּוֹ]." By the small addition "nor shall you touch it," Eve claims that the command is twofold: the tree is not to be eaten from or even touched.[4]

The LXX presents the reader with a slightly different set of data. Evidently aware of the potential difficulties of the Hebrew original, the LXX translators put the command to Adam in the grammatical plural. Thus, instead of reading,

"But of the tree of the knowledge of good and evil, thou shalt not eat of it: for on the day that thou eatest thereof, thou shalt surely die,"

the translators put the command this way:

ἀπὸ δὲ τοῦ ξύλου τοῦ γινώσκειν καλὸν καὶ πονηρόν οὐ φάγεσθε ἀπ' αὐτοῦ, ᾗ δ' ἂν ἡμέρᾳ φάγητε ἀπ' αὐτοῦ θανάτῳ ἀποθανεῖσθε.

---

[4] It is worth noting that this interdiction against touching or drawing near knows its closest parallels in biblical texts concerned with the dangers of encroaching on *sancta*. In the Pentateuch these injunctions are closely associated with Mount Sinai and the tent of meeting that was established there (cf. Exod 19:12, 13 [JE] and 29:3; 30:29 [P]). It is perhaps for this reason that many early interpreters took this command as an indication that the garden of Eden was laid out like a temple with concentric bands of holiness guarding its central zone. For a consideration of how Eden functioned as a "temple" in early exegesis, see G. A. Anderson, "Celibacy or Consummation in the Garden: Reflections on Early Jewish and Christian Interpretations of the Garden of Eden," *HTR* 82 (1989): 121–48.

"But of the tree of knowledge of good and evil you [pl.] shall not eat of it: for on the day that you [pl.] eat thereof, you [pl.] shall die."

By framing the command this way, the translators leave no room for ambiguity about those who are addressed. Yet another question is raised. How was Adam to understand this plural address when he was still alone? One solution would be that God was intimating to Adam what was about to take place. Another way around this problem would be to assume that the versification of the story does not coincide with the actual progression of events. In this manner of exegesis, we would assume that though the command about the tree is narrated before Eve's creation, it actually took place afterwards.[5] Such an understanding is found in early Christian iconography, where frequently God is depicted as issuing his command about the tree to both Adam and Eve.[6]

The Jewish rabbis of the first few centuries C.E. took the evidence in a different direction.[7] They chose to highlight the asymmetry between Eve's version of the command and that of God as evidence that something had been lost in the transmission. Adam—reasoned these rabbinic readers—being suspicious of Eve's moral virtuosity, decided to hedge the original command with an additional codicil. Not only should we refrain from eating of this tree; we must not even draw near to it lest we die! This precautionary measure taken by Adam proved to be the undoing of both him and Eve. For when the snake approached Eve and learned that she was mistaken about the dangers that attended the tree, he saw the perfect avenue for his deception. Drawing near to the tree, he grabbed hold of its limbs and shook them vigorously. When it became evident to Eve that this act of disobedience brought no untoward consequences upon the snake, she reasoned that the other part of the command must be false as well. And so she ate. In this

---

[5] This redivision of order in Scripture is very common among early interpreters and frequently misunderstood by modern readers. Though these redivisions of Scripture's chronology can be quite fanciful and even highly contrived, they need not be understood this way in all situations. Like many of the observations of these early exegetes, they often reflect deep knowledge about biblical poetics. On this literary problem and how it was perceived by medieval Jewish readers, see the masterful treatment of Y. Elman, " 'It Is No Empty Thing': Nahmanides and the Search for Omnisignificance," *Torah u-madda Journal* 5 (1994): 1–83. For a consideration of the problem of narrative chronology from a modern critical perspective, see S. Talmon, "The Presentation of Synchroneity and Simultaneity in Biblical Narrative," in *Studies in Hebrew Narrative Art throughout the Ages* (ed. J. Heinemann and S. Werses; Scripta Hierosolymitana 27; Jerusalem: Magnes, 1978), 9–26; repr. in *Literary Studies in the Hebrew Bible* (Jerusalem: Magnes, 1993), 112–33.

[6] This is true of nearly every iconographic cycle up to the late Middle Ages. It has not been the subject of a serious art-historical examination. For one example of this, compare the Genesis cycle found in the *Hortus deliciarum* (Rosalie Green et al., *Herrad of Hohenbourg: Hortus deliciarum* [2 vols.; London: University of London Press, 1979]).

[7] The tradition we will discuss comes from *ʾAbot de Rabbi Nathan*. It can be found in both the A and the B versions. Excellent English translations for both exist in J. Goldin, *The Fathers according to Rabbi Nathan* (YJS 10; New Haven: Yale University Press, 1955); and A. J. Saldarini, *The Fathers according to Rabbi Nathan Version B: A Translation and Commentary* (SJLA 11; Leiden: Brill, 1975).

midrashic understanding, Adam is the one at fault, for it was his improper instruction of Eve that occasioned her transgression.[8]

When we pursue the question of culpability from the perspective of what was known about the command, we end up with one of two scenarios: either Adam and Eve are both equally culpable on the grounds that they both heard it plainly and distinctly, or Eve is to be exonerated because her knowledge of the command was faulty due to Adam's zealous attempt to improve on the initial interdiction.

The *Life of Adam and Eve*

There is another question to be asked concerning the culpability for the fall. Was the sin knowingly committed or not? Biblical law knows of two categories of violating a command—with full intention or by mistake. Not surprisingly, sins committed without full intention are treated far less severely than brazen acts of disobedience. And so our question: what did Adam and Eve think they were doing when they ate of the fruit?

If one wished to clear Adam of responsibility for the fall, one could not do it on the grounds used to clear Eve. The Bible provides no evidence that there was any miscommunication of the command to Adam. He heard the command directly from God. If one was to make a case for Adam's relative innocence, the only way to do it would be on the grounds of how self-aware he was when he ate. Did he know that the fruit he was eating was the fruit interdicted by God? Or was he somehow tricked into it? Some sort of trickery seems to be implied in the apocryphal story the *Life of Adam and Eve*.[9]

---

[8] This midrash, delightful in its own right, only works if we presume that the snake knows the command in advance, for only then can we explain how he could perceive Eve's misapprehension of it. A good question to ask, then, is whether the creator of the midrash has made up this detail—always an option in midrash—or whether some tiny troublesome detail in our biblical text has suggested this idea to him. It would seem that the latter possibility is more likely. In Gen 3:4 the snake declares to the woman, "You shall certainly not die!" Although the English is clear, the Hebrew is not. In biblical Hebrew one normally forms an asseverative clause by directly appending the infinitival form to the finite verb: *môt tāmût,* "[by] death you shall die." In order to negate this type of clause, the negative particle is placed between the infinitive and the finite verb: *môt lo' tāmût,* "[by] death you won't die." Quite anomalously, this text negates the verbal asseveration by putting the negative particle in front of the infinitive *(lo' môt tāmût).* Is the snake simply a poor speaker of Hebrew? Perhaps. But a more intriguing strategy of interpretation is to presume that the snake knows the exact verbal form of the command given by God and has chosen to negate these precise words. We could paraphrase the snake's words this way: God said, "You shall surely die"; I say, "It is not the case that 'you shall surely die.'" This grammatical anomaly of the snake would have suggested to an early interpreter that the snake knew the original form of the warning that God had declared to Adam *(môt tāmût),* and has negated this very warning in the form of a quotation.

[9] Texts that are most fully discussed appear in the appendix. For a full version of this text, see G. A. Anderson and M. E. Stone, *A Synopsis of the Books of Adam and Eve* (SBLEJL 5; Atlanta: Scholars Press, 1994).

Apocryphal narratives are difficult because they cloak all their exegetical decisions in the form of a new rewritten narrative. On the surface, we might judge such a tale as a complete work of fiction and see little evidence of exegesis. But if we attend carefully to the subtle details of such a story, we can often discover an enormous body of exegetical lore lurking below the surface. The rewritten biblical story becomes a storehouse of information about how early Jews (and Christians) read their Bibles.

The *Life of Adam and Eve* was no doubt written in Greek and has been dated by some scholars to the later Second Temple period. It is almost certain that the work existed by the fourth century C.E.[10] The account of the fall in the *Life of Adam and Eve* is retrospective in outlook. As the story begins, we join Adam and Eve outside the garden. We are treated, over the course of this narrative, to a long and elaborate story about the postlapsarian life and times of Adam and Eve, something that the Bible takes virtually no interest in. As to those fateful moments Adam and Eve spent in paradise, we learn about them only by way of narrative flashbacks.

A striking feature of the story is the ignorance of Adam about the circumstances in which he finds himself once he had been expelled from the garden (see Appendix 1, pp. 246–48). The first thing he discovers is that the angelic food they once were able to enjoy is no longer available. All that lies before them is the herbage of the earth, a food source more proper to animals than to humans (*L.A.E.* 2:1–3:1; 4:1–5:3). As they take full cognizance of this fact, they decide to embark on a forty-day fast while submerged in water, in the hope of securing a better food supply (6:1). Adam manages to endure the terms of this fast whereas Eve succumbs to the temptations of the devil a second time and prematurely interrupts her fast (9:1–5). Eve, forlorn over her second failure, decides to absent herself from Adam, give up the opportunity of finding suitable food, and go into exile in the direction of the setting sun to die (18:1). As grim as this moment may appear, things grow worse when she begins to go into labor while separated from Adam (19:1). Fearing that the pain will be so great as to end her life, she cries in desperation to Adam for help (19:2). Adam hears her cry but, before going off to meet her, receives seeds sent by the angel Michael (20:1). When Adam arrives, he prays on Eve's behalf, and her pains are ameliorated, so that she does not die but safely delivers the child she has been carrying.

This curious narrative, which is nowhere to be found in the Bible itself, is constructed on the punishments meted out to Adam and Eve in Gen 3:16–19.

---

[10] We will treat the Armenian/Georgian version of the story. This version goes back to a Greek original that is very different from the Greek *Apocalypse of Moses* and represents an independent line of textual transmission. For arguments regarding the priority of the Armenian/Georgian witness over the parallel traditions found in the Greek and Latin, see M. Stone, *A History of the Literature of Adam and Eve* (SBLEJL 3; Atlanta: Scholars Press, 1992); and G. A. Anderson, "The Penitence Narrative in the *Life of Adam and Eve*," *HUCA* 63 (1993): 1–38. For an argument for the priority of the Greek, see M. de Jonge and J. Tromp, *The Life of Adam and Eve and Related Literature* (Guides to Apocrypha and Pseudepigrapha 4; Sheffield, England: Sheffield Academic Press, 1997), 28–44.

These punishments touch on the pains of childbearing that will plague Eve and the difficulties that will attend Adam when he begins to farm the land.[11] What is striking about the punishments in the *Life* is both how and when they occur in the narrative. They are discovered by surprise after the expulsion! How could Adam and Eve be surprised by these punishments? According to the Bible, this roster of punishments was recited to Adam and Eve before they left Eden.

We can only appreciate the surprise of Adam and Eve at the beginning of the *Life of Adam and Eve* by attending to another surprise that Adam discloses about the fall as he lies dying on his deathbed later in the tale.[12] As Adam reviews the circumstances of their life in the garden before the children, he comes to the moment when God discovered the violation of his command (see Appendix 2, pp. 248–50). When God discovered their sin, God waxed wroth and declared, "Because you have forsaken my commandment . . . I will bring upon your body 70 afflictions. You will be racked with pains from the top of your head, eyes, and ears, to the bottom of your feet, and in every single member of your body." This narrative detail is very hard to square with our biblical story. Not only does the author of the *Life of Adam and Eve* ignore the punishments that the Bible says God spoke about before expulsion; he puts in their place a punishment that has no biblical referent.

Or is there a biblical ground for this detail? A careful inspection of how Genesis 3 was read by early Jewish and Christian interpreters is revealing. The author of this apocryphal narrative has hardly trotted out his own freely composed story; rather he has put in narrative form a well-known piece of exegesis about the fall, one that was extremely popular in both Jewish and Christian sources.[13]

---

[11] On the exegetical sources of these literary motifs, see Anderson, "Penitence Narrative."

[12] On this problem, see G. A. Anderson, "The Garments of Skin in Apocryphal Narrative and Biblical Commentary," in J. Kugel, ed., *Studies in Ancient Midrash* (Cambridge, Mass.: Harvard, 2001), 101–44.

[13] The topic and the associated bibliography are vast. The following sources have been consulted and used: S. Brock, "Clothing Metaphors as a Means of Theological Expression in Syriac Tradition," in *Typus, Symbol, Allegorie bei den östlichen Vätern und ihren Parallelen im Mittelalter: Internationales Kolloquium, Eichstätt, 1981* (ed. M. Schmidt and C. F. Geyer; Regensburg: Friedrich Pustet, 1982), 11–37; J. Daniélou, "Les tuniques de peau chez Grégroire de Nysse," in *Glaube, Geist, Geschichte* (ed. G. Müller and W. Zeller; Leiden: Brill, 1967), 355–67; M. Harl, "La prise de conscience de la 'nudité' d'Adam: Une interprétation de Gen 3,7 chez les pères grecs," *St Patr* 7 (1966): 486–95; A. Kowalski, "Rivesti di gloria: Adamo ed Eva nel commento di sant'Efrem a Gen 2,25: Ricerca sulle fonti dell'esegesi siriaca," *CNS* 3 (1982): 41–60; S. Lambden, "From Fig Leaves to Fingernails: Some Notes on the Garments of Adam and Eve in the Hebrew Bible and Select Early Post-biblical Jewish Writings," in *A Walk in the Garden: Biblical, Iconographical, and Literary Images of Eden* (ed. P. Morris and D. Sawyer; JSOTSup 136; Sheffield, England: JSOT Press, 1992), 74–90; B. Murdoch, "The Garments of Paradise," *Euphorion* 61 (1967): 375–82; M. Simonetti, "Alcune osservazioni sull'interpretazione origeniana di Genesi 2,7 e 3,21," *Aev* 36 (1962): 370–81; E. Peterson, "Theologie des Kleides," *Benediktinische Monatsschrift* 16 (1934): 347–56; J. Z. Smith, "The Garments of Shame," *HR* 5 (1965/1966): 217–38.

Early readers of the Bible were puzzled, as moderns also have been, by the very curious text of Gen 3:20–21. In these verses the biblical writer interrupts his tale about God's listing of the punishments of Adam and Eve (vv. 16–19) and their subsequent banishment from the garden (vv. 22–24) with a brief interlude about the naming of Eve and the clothing of the couple with garments of skin. These verses puzzle because they so dramatically alter the tone and force of what seems a rather clear and climactic literary figure: the listing of sentences and then banishment. One way to solve this puzzle was to assume that these verses were narrated in improper chronological order. The clothing of Adam and Eve with skins took place immediately after their sin. But there is another problem: what is the sense of the phrase "garments of skin"? One possible meaning is that God clothed Adam and Eve with animals skins before their expulsion. The problem with this view is that the Bible is quite explicit that the slaying of animals for human use is not supposed to begin until after the flood (9:1–6). A more popular way to understand the verse was to construe the "garments of skin" as an idiom for the putting on of human or, better, "mortal" flesh.[14] If we combine these two pieces of ancient exegesis, we arrive at a narrative scenario that was very common among early biblical interpreters: Adam and Eve lost their immortal nature immediately upon transgressing the command and put on mortal human flesh.

Frequently this moment of investiture, when Adam and Eve lose their immortal garments and put on perishable ones, is also marked by an immediate departure from Eden. Because the purity of Eden cannot abide mortal, perishable flesh, Adam and Eve are instantly expelled once they are so clothed. If we return to the *Life of Adam and Eve* with these pieces of early exegesis in hand, all of a sudden a story that appeared so unbiblical looks biblical through and through. The punishment concerning mortal flesh is hardly nonbiblical; it reflects a repositioning of the story of "donning human flesh" (3:21) to a point immediately after transgression (v. 7). This, in turn, occasions the necessity of a prompt dismissal of Adam and Eve from Eden. Finding themselves, quite by surprise, upon the earth, Adam and Eve begin to discover the punishments that accompany mortal life (vv. 15–19). The discovery of these punishments outside Eden is demanded by the exegetical decision to move the clothing scene up to the moment just after transgression.

But there is one small flaw in our reconstruction of how this portion of the *Life of Adam and Eve* came to be. Adam and Eve are not equally surprised by their expulsion from Eden. When they discover themselves outside Eden, they first

---

[14] Although this might strike one as a rather unusual translation, it is paralleled elsewhere in the Bible. Consider how Job describes his own physical origins: "You clothed me with skin and flesh" (Job 10:11 NRSV). In the famous text about the resurrection, Ezekiel describes the refashioning of the human form as an act of "stretching" skin over flesh and bones (Ezek 37:6, 8). Indeed, this idiom was such a commonplace that it became a free construction in halakhic argument. In *b. Nid.* 25a, a debate about the origins of human life, Rabbi Yehoshua b. Hanina cites Gen 3:21 and then glosses it as follows: "This text teaches us that the Holy One blessed be He does not make skin for a man unless he has been [bodily] formed." To be clothed in skin is to become human.

construct a hut to live in and mourn there for seven days over their lamentable condition. After this first period of mourning, Eve turns to Adam and says, "My lord, I am hungry. Arise, seek food so that we may live and know that God is going to come and bring us to the Garden" (*L.A.E.* 2:2). Adam makes a careful inspection of the area around them and discovers no food fit for human consumption. Eve, despondent at this discovery, cries out, "I am dying of this hunger. It would be better if I were dead, my lord; perhaps (then) they would bring you into the Garden for because of me God is angry" (3:2a). The certainty of Eve's exclamation is countered by a more doubtful response from Adam. "Great wrath has come upon us," Adam answers, "[but] I know not whether because of you or because of me" (3:2b). Eve, shedding all uncertainty about the matter, demands a rasher course of action. "Kill me if you wish," she declares "so that the wrath and anger may abate from before you—for this has come about because of me—and they will bring you into the Garden" (3:2c). Adam, taken aback by this proposal, refuses this proposal on the grounds that God would bring even greater punishments upon them should he attempt such an evil on his own flesh and blood (3:3).

The striking feature about this entire cycle is that Eve is not only sure that the fault for their expulsion is hers ("for this has come about because of me"); she seems also adamant about the solution to it ("Kill me . . . for this has come about because of me and they will bring you into the Garden"). Adam denies Eve's proposal not because she is wrong—about this Adam is completely in the dark ("I know not whether [this wrath is] because of you or because of me")—but because he believes killing to be wrong. This ignorance of Adam is not due to a greater obtuseness on his part. Later in the narrative, when Eve suggests a harsher penitential discipline (5:3), Adam must reprimand her again for her rash proposal and suggest a more prudent path of repentance (6:1a). The ignorance of Adam appears to be rooted in the nature of the expulsion itself; Eve knows something that Adam does not.

Much later in our narrative, when Adam has gathered his children around his deathbed, we learn the cause of his ignorance immediately following their expulsion. "When God made us," Adam says as he begins to rehearse the story to his children, "he gave us a command not to eat of that tree" (32[7]:1). It is worth noting that there is no sense, in this version of the story, that Adam heard the command first and then relayed it to Eve. Adam's version of the story conforms closely with what we saw in the Greek Bible; the command was addressed to the two of them.

Satan finds his opportunity to approach Eve when the angels who are appointed to guard her ascend to heaven to worship God. This is a striking datum, for many who follow the biblical story in English translation will wonder how it could be that Adam and Eve were separated during the moment of transgression. The biblical text seems to say quite clearly that Eve gave some of the fruit to Adam, "who was with her, and he ate." To be "with her" certainly implies that Adam is immediately beside her. This common interpretation of this verse is confirmed by the hundreds of iconographic images of the fall that show Adam and

Eve together beside the tree as they eat the fruit. If Adam was with Eve at the moment of the transgression, how could he be ignorant? Our problem is one of translation. The original Hebrew could also be rendered, "she also gave some of the fruit to her husband and he ate along with her [וַתִּתֵּן גַּם־לְאִישָׁהּ עִמָּהּ וַיֹּאכַל]." In this translation, the emphasis is on the fact that both ate, not on physical proximity at the time of eating. The text does not explicitly say that Adam was beside the tree as Eve consumed the fruit. Because of this ambiguity, a rather large stream of interpreters preferred to understand the transgression as a two-part process. First Eve ate while standing beside the tree, talking with the snake; then, at a later time in an undisclosed place, Eve fed the fruit to Adam. The presumption of a physical separation is an important point to the author of the *Life of Adam and Eve*. It allows him to exculpate Adam from any acquaintance with wrongdoing. "Eve caused me," Adam explains, "who did not know, to eat it" (*L.A.E.* 32[7]:3a = 33:3) Immediately thereafter God announces the punishment: God will bring seventy afflictions upon their bodies in due consequence of this act, and then they were sent forth to the earth (34[8]:2). Through this retrospective rehearsal of the fall, we can now understand the ignorance of Adam and the knowledge of Eve at the beginning of the story. Eve ate the fruit with full cognizance of what she was doing. For her, the expulsion was no surprise. Adam was fed the fruit surreptitiously and found himself suddenly outside Eden for no apparent reason.

The innocence of Adam over against the guilt of Eve is mapped out in the *Life of Adam and Eve* one more time in the subsequent history of their life and times outside Eden. Falling into great distress over their inability to find food capable of sustaining human life, they decide to embark on a severe act of penance, hoping to move their Creator to have pity and provide some form of sustenance. Adam, taking on the role of God from Genesis 2, commands Eve to enter the Tigris River, put a rock under her feet, and stand up to her neck in its water for thirty-four days (*L.A.E.* 6:1b). This reference to waters that reach to the neck certainly derives from the penitential psalms (cf. Ps 69:2) and connotes a potentially life-threatening situation. Eve stands at risk of death. Adam, for his part, will go to the Jordan River and reside there forty days (6:2). He makes no mention of a rock, and the waters do not reach his neck. Indeed, the waters hardly touch his person.

Just one day beyond the halfway mark of her penance, Satan appears in the form of a cherub before Eve and declares that the time of mourning has ended prematurely. "Come forth from the water and rest," he says, "for God has hearkened to your penitence" (9:2). Eve succumbs to this second temptation, and comes out from the Tigris. Her physical condition after enduring the turbulent waters of this river for eighteen days is not good. The writer observes that "her flesh was withered like rotten vegetables because of the coldness of the water. All the form of her beauty had been destroyed" (10:1). Undeterred by her wretched state, she returns to Adam, only to learn from him that she has fallen yet a second time. Now thoroughly shamed and despondent, Eve declares, "You [Adam] are innocent of the first sin and of this second one. Only me alone did Satan overcome, as a result of God's word and yours. . . . Behold, I shall go to the west and I shall be there and my food (will be) grass until I die; for henceforth I am unworthy of the foods of life" (18:1).

Especially noteworthy is the manner in which Eve's second fall is patterned on the first. From her Creator she receives a command not to eat from a tree, a command that she then violates at the instigation of Satan; from her spouse she receives a command to abide in the Tigris thirty days, a command she also disobeys at the temptation of Satan. As a result of the first sin, she and Adam are given mortal bodies; as a result of the second sin, Eve finds that "the form of her beauty had been destroyed." Adam, in contrast, is innocent of both transgressions. Although he, along with Eve, bears the marks of the first transgression within his body, he escapes from his sojourn in the Jordan River unscarred. The forty days he spends in that river takes no toll on his body. Why? Because Adam prays that the animals be gathered round about him and form a wall blocking the flow of the waters so that Adam will not be pummeled by the relentless current of the river (8:1–3).

The *Life of Adam and Eve* and 1 Timothy

What is the relationship of the story about Eve in the apocryphal *Life of Adam and Eve* to the portrayal in 1 Timothy? There are three basic approaches to this complicated problem.

First, one could consider the *Life of Adam and Eve* a possible source for 1 Timothy. Much will depend on how we date this pseudepigraphal text. Because 1 Timothy was written sometime in the second half of the first century C.E., an argument for the influence of the *Life of Adam and Eve* on Timothy will be made much easier if we presume that it was circulating in the first century.[15] Until very recently, most of the scholars who have worked on the *Life of Adam and Eve* have agreed that the text should be dated to the Second Temple period.[16] This would mean that the document and its traditions predate the rise of the Christian church.

---

[15] We have touched on the presentation of Eve in only one section of our text. The full text of the *Life of Adam and Eve* contains two traditions regarding who was culpable for the fall. In the sections we have assessed (chs. 1–14), told from the perspective of either Adam or the narrator, Eve is more culpable. In a later portion of the tale, when Eve tells the story on her own (chs. 15–30), the culpability is shared. On the presentation of Eve's innocence in this second tale of the fall, see the fine study of J. R. Levison, "The Exoneration of Eve in the Apocalypse of Moses 15–30," *JSJ* 20 (1989): 135–50.

We should not leave the problem of these two different traditions about the guilt of Eve without considering the unique reading of the Armenian corresponding to Greek 21:1–6 (see appendix 3). The Armenian writer has left out the entire description of Adam's willing consumption of the fruit. The result is a narrative that does not contradict the position of the earlier narration (Armenian 32[7]3a, "Eve caused me, who did not know, to eat it"). The reading of the Armenian is clearly secondary here, representing an attempt to harmonize the two independent versions.

[16] Those who ascribe the work to a Jewish author and date it to the first century C.E. include D. Bertrand, *La vie grecque d'Adam et Eve* (Paris: Maisonneuve, 1987), 29; A. Denis, *Introduction aux pseudépigraphes grecs d'Ancien Testament* (SVTP 1; Leiden:

During the past recent decade or so, however, this consensus has begun to unravel. Beginning with the seminal essay of Robert Kraft, "The Pseudepigrapha in Christianity," a growing area of concern has been the transmission history of the pseudepigrapha themselves.[17] Kraft has argued that if these texts were copied and expanded by Christians, then we must begin with the hypothesis that they are Christian in origin and only consider the question of Jewish authorship if forced by the data (either internal or external criteria) themselves. Kraft's arguments have been seconded by the work of Marinus de Jonge and Johannes Tromp in the Netherlands and Michael Stone and David Satran in Israel.[18] If we presume that the *Life of Adam and Eve* was written by Christians—and there are clear hints of Christian authorship within the text—then we would have to date the document to the second century at the earliest. And so our second methodological option: we must consider the possibility that 1 Timothy had some influence on the *Life of Adam and Eve,* rather than the reverse.

Third, we could attribute the *Life of Adam and Eve* to Christian hands but argue that some of the traditions utilized by the author were very ancient and most likely Jewish. There is considerable evidence that Christian writers of the first few centuries C.E. borrowed and adapted Jewish sources for various exegetical purposes. That a Christian writer of the *Life of Adam and Eve* would have chosen to do so should occasion no surprise.[19]

The possibility that 1 Timothy had some influence on the *Life of Adam and Eve* is worth pausing over. Contrary to what one may think, the meaning and influence of this scriptural text in the life of the early church did not tend toward a unilateral blaming of Eve. Here we need to be cognizant of a striking feature found in later Christian reflection on this Pauline text. According to Augustine and all those who followed in his wake, the text of 1 Timothy did not pin the blame for the fall on Eve but rather on Adam. How was this interpretation reached? Augustine noted that 1 Timothy was very difficult to square with Rom 5:12–21.[20] The former put the blame solely on Eve; the latter, solely on Adam. Both could not be true. Augustine then reasoned that 1 Timothy must not be telling us about culpability for the fall, but about what Adam and Eve thought they

---

Brill, 1970), 6; O. Eissfeldt, *Old Testament: An Introduction* (Oxford: Blackwell, 1965), 637; C. Torrey, *The Apocryphal Literature* (New Haven: Yale University Press, 1945), 133; and L. Wells, "The Books of Adam and Eve," *APOT* 2:126. In the secondary literature on Paul, the *Life of Adam and Eve* is frequently quoted as a contemporary Jewish source.

[17] Robert Kraft, "The Pseudepigrapha in Christianity," in *Tracing the Threads: Studies in the Vitality of Jewish Pseudepigrapha* (ed. J. Reeves; SBLEJL 6; Atlanta: Scholars Press, 1995), 55–86. The essay was first delivered as a paper in 1975.

[18] Jonge and Tromp, *Life of Adam and Eve,* 65–79; Stone, *History of the Literature,* 53–58; D. Satran, *Biblical Prophets in Byzantine Palestine: Reassessing the Lives of the Prophets* (SVTP 11; Leiden: Brill, 1995), 2–33.

[19] See esp. Anderson, "Penitence Narrative."

[20] See esp. Anderson, "Is Eve the Problem?" in *Theological Exegesis: Essays in Honor of Brevard S. Childs* (ed. C. R. Seitz and K. Greene-McCreight; Grand Rapids, Mich.: Eerdmans, 1999), 96–103.

were doing when they sinned. "Adam was not deceived" meant that Adam was not in any way fooled by the false promises of the serpent; when he sinned, he did so with full intention of violating a divine command. On the other hand, the fact that "Eve was deceived" conveyed for Augustine that Eve was fooled by the serpent into thinking that the command was apt. The result was that both were guilty for the fall, but Adam's guilt was greater still.

How might this be relevant? It is striking to note that we have three versions of the *Life of Adam and Eve* that tell of the penance of Adam and Eve. The Armenian and Georgian versions, our earliest witnesses, present Eve as guilty and damnable whereas Adam is innocent and altogether exonerated. The Latin text alters this earlier version at nearly every turn to make the culpability appear equal. Not only is all reference to the fact of Adam's eating unawares deleted; the theme of Adam's ignorance about the transgression after the expulsion is also absent. Moreover, Adam declares that the sin is his own doing, a feature not found in the Armenian or Georgian. Why would the Latin version show such resolve to make Adam an equal partner in the fall? It would be impossible to prove that the Latin version was dependent on the profoundly influential reading of St. Augustine, but the homologous relation between the two is striking.

At all events, the *Life of Adam and Eve* provides us with valuable evidence about the early interpretation of the story of Adam and Eve. Although most readers of the Bible would not conclude from Genesis 3 that Adam was innocent, one must concede that his personal culpability is not made clear in the story of the transgression itself. In order to assess blame for the fall, one must determine exegetically the level of culpability for the transgression. According to Jewish legal tradition, one could sin either with full cognizance of the misdeed or inadvertently. To sin knowingly was, of course, the more serious breach of responsibility. One line of Jewish tradition exonerated Eve by making a case for her inadvertence. By claiming that Adam had misled her about the nature of the command ("don't eat and don't touch"), it lessened Eve's own responsibility considerably.

Yet not all believed that Eve's addition of the codicil "don't touch" to the command constituted an improvisation on God's word. Nearly all Christian and not a few Jewish exegetes considered the command of God to include both parts.[21] For some reason, these interpreters must argue, our biblical author only

---

[21] The only Christian commentator I know of who claims that Eve has added to God's original commandment is Ambrose. In *On Paradise* (trans. J. J. Savage; FC 42; New York: Fathers of the Church, 1961), he reflects firsthand knowledge of a tradition we know from Jewish sources (pp. 335–37):

> But the woman's reply will indicate that there was nothing questionable in the command of God: "Of the fruit of all the trees in the garden we may eat, but of the fruit of the tree in the middle of the garden, God said, 'You shall not eat of it neither shall you touch it, lest you die.'" There was nothing inexact about the command itself. The error lay in the report of the command. The scriptural passage under discussion is self-explanatory. We realize that we ought not to make any addition to a command even by way of instruction. Any addition or qualification of a command is in the nature of a falsification. . . .

gave us the first part in Gen 2:16–17, while saving the fuller version of the command for the moment when Eve encountered the snake (3:2–3). If the command included both parts, then the exoneration of Eve becomes more difficult. It is not by accident that the *Life of Adam and Eve* has understood the command as bipartite and originally heard by Adam and Eve. Eve is a fully responsible moral agent when she meets the snake. According to the *Life of Adam and Eve,* Eve ate the fruit first while physically separated from Adam. She later fed Adam the forbidden fruit while he was completely unaware of what he was doing. This tradition, or one very similar to it, must have been in the mind of the author of 1 Timothy when he ascribed the fall to the person of Eve alone.

Appendix 1. *Life of Adam and Eve* 1:1–3:3

According to the Armenian and Georgian versions, which both go back to an earlier Greek original, Eve is the cause of the fall, not Adam. In this section, Adam shows complete ignorance of the grounds for the fall—he evidently ate the fruit completely unawares. Eve, on the other hand, knows exactly what has happened. Italics are added to indicate where this theme is evident. Note that the Latin version is not happy with this detail and has omitted it in certain places. The Latin preserves a very rough narrative at 3:2 that could be explained by its conscious decision to drop 3:2b from its account.

Latin	Armenian	Georgian
1:1 When Adam and Eve were expelled from paradise they made for themselves a tent and spent seven days mourning and lamenting in great sadness.	1:1 It came to pass, when Adam went forth from the Garden with his wife, outside, to the east of the Garden, they made themselves a hut to live in and went inside. . . .	1:1 It came to pass, when Adam went out from the Garden with his wife Eve, they went out at the eastern part of the Garden. And Adam made a hut to live in. . . .
2:1 But after seven days they began to be hungry and sought food to eat and did not find any.	2:1 Then, after seven days, they grew hungry and looked for food.	2:1 And after seven days, they were hungry and looked for something to eat.

And many believe that this was Adam's fault—not the woman's. They reason that Adam, in his desire to make her more cautious, had said to the woman that God had given the additional instruction: "Neither shall you touch it." . . . It seems to me, however, that the initial violation and deceit was due to the woman. . . . Hence Paul says: "Adam was not deceived, but the woman was deceived and was in sin." (1 Tim 2:14)

Ambrose follows the lead of the rabbis in declaring that Eve added to the command, but he denies that the fault for this was the instruction of Adam. He clearly knows that those who propound this tradition make exactly that deduction. But for Ambrose, the text from 1 Timothy rules out any exoneration of Eve on these grounds.

2:2 Then Eve said to Adam: "My lord, I am hungry. Go, seek for us something to eat. Perhaps the Lord God will look upon us and have mercy on us and will call us back to the place where we were previously."

3:1 And Adam arose and walked for seven days over all that land but did not find food such as they had in paradise.

3:2 Eve said to Adam: "My lord, would that I might die. Perhaps then the Lord God would bring you back into the Garden, for it was because of me that the Lord God grew angry with you.

Do you wish to kill me, that I might die? Perhaps the Lord God will bring you back into the Garden, *since on account of my action you were expelled from there."*

2:2 Eve said to Adam. "My lord, I am hungry. Arise, seek food so that we may live and know that God is going to come and bring us to the Garden, to our place."

3:1 They arose and went about upon the earth, and they did not find food like the food by which they had been nourished in [the Garden].

3:2a Eve said to Adam, "I am dying of this hunger. It would be better if I were dead, my lord; perhaps (then) they would bring [you] into the Garden, for because of me God is angry."

3:2b Adam said, "Great wrath has come upon us, *I know not whether because of you or because of me."*

3:2c Eve said, to h[im], "Kill me if you wish, so that the wrath and anger may abate from before you—*for this has come about because of me*—and they will bring you into the Garden."

2:2 Eve told Adam: "Adam, my lord, arise and (go) search for food for me that we may eat, until we find out—who knows—(perhaps) the Lord will accept us and take us back to the same place in the Garden."

3:1 And Adam arose after seven days and went about upon the face of the earth and he did not find any food like that which they used to eat in the Garden. Adam replied to Eve and told her, "We are going to die a death."

3:2a Eve told Adam, "Oh, if only I were dead, then God would have accepted you in the Garden!"

3:2b Adam replied to Eve and said to her, "Because of us a great anger lies upon all creatures. *(However) I do not know this: whether it is because of me or because of you."*

3:2c Eve replied to Adam, "My lord, if you think it wise, kill me so that I will be exterminated from the sight of God and his angels, so that God's anger against you may cease, *which came about because of me*: and he will bring you back into the Garden."

| 3:3 Adam responded: "Don't say such things, Eve, lest the Lord God bring upon us some other curse. How could it be that I should raise my hand against my own flesh?" | 3:3 Adam said to her. "Eve, do not (even) mention this matter; lest God bring upon us even greater evils and we become contemptible. How, indeed, can I do you any evil, for you are my body?" | 3:3 Adam replied and told her, "No, no! Do not mention this matter, lest God send another judgment upon us because of (this) killing. How could I raise my hand and cause my own flesh to suffer?" |

Appendix 2. *Life of Adam and Eve* 32(8):1–34(8):2

In this section Adam tells the story of how the sin came about. He declares, in both the Armenian and the Georgian versions, that he did not know what he was doing when he ate the fruit. Eve must have given it to him unawares. The Latin has removed this detail.

Latin	Armenian	Georgian
	32(7):2 "Satan deceived us at the hour when [the] angels [who] were guardians of the tree ascended to worship God. Then, Satan caused Eve to eat that fruit;	32(7):2 "And the serpent deceived your mother and caused her to eat of it, because of which, now, we are going to die. When it was the hour for the guardian angels [to ascend] to worship God, the enemy deceived her and she ate of it
	32(7):3a Eve gave [it] to me to eat *when I did not know.*	32(7):3a and she deceived me, my children, *for I did not know.*
32:2 "God, however, gave part of the Garden to me, and part to your mother: to me he gave the tree of the eastern and northern part which is against the north, and to your mother he gave the southern and western part.	32(7):3b For, my son Seth, God divided the Garden between me and your mother Eve, that we might watch it. To me he gave the eastern portion and the [northern], and to your mother, the western and the [southern].	32(7):3b And God had divided the [Garden] between us—myself and your mother Eve—so that we might guard it. As for me, he had given me the eastern and northern portion; to your mother Eve he had entrusted the southern and the western portion.

33:1 The Lord God gave us two angels to watch over us.

33:1 We had twelve angels who went around with each of us, because of the guarding of the Garden, until the time of the light.

33:1 And there were twelve angels with each of us to guard us until the time of the dawn,

33:2 The hour came for the angels to ascend to the sight of God for worship. At once, the Devil, our adversary, found the place while the angels were absent. And the Devil deceived your mother so that she ate from the unlawful and forbidden tree.

33:2 Since every day they would go forth [to worship the Lord], at the time when they went to the heavens, at that time Satan deceived your mother and caused her to eat of the fruit. Satan knew that I was not with her, nor the angels, at that time he caused her to eat.

33:2 but each day, they ascended (there). And at the moment of their ascent, the serpent deceived your mother and caused her to eat of the tree, for he had seen that I was not with her any more than the angels.

33:3 Then she ate it and gave it to me to eat.

33:3 [Afterwards, also, she gave (it) to me.]

33:3 She also made me eat of it *and I did not understand.*

34:1 Immediately, the Lord God grew angry with us and said to me:
34:2 'Because you have forsaken my mandate and have not kept my word which I entrusted to you, I will bring upon your body seventy afflictions. You will be racked with pains from the top of your head, eyes, and ears, to the toe-nails on your feet, and in every single member.' This he counted as punishment fitting in suffering [to the seriousness of our transgression] concerning the trees (of suffering for the transgression of the fruit of the tree?). The Lord sent all these ills upon me and all our generations."

34(8):1 I knew then, when I ate the fruit, that God was angry with us.
34(8):2 God said, 'Because you transgressed my commandment, I shall bring seventy afflictions [upon] your body, pain of the eyes and ringing of the ears and all the joints.' It will be reckoned for me (?) among the afflictions of sickness which are preserved in the treasuries, so that God might send them in the last times."

34(8):1 When we had eaten, God became angry with us
34(8):2 and he told us, 'You have, therefore, scorned my commandment; I too will scorn you.' And he sent seventy evils upon us, to our eyes, and to our ears, and as far as our feet, plagues and portents laid up in (his) treasuries. This God did to me to cause me to die a death."

Appendix 3. *Life of Adam and Eve* [44]21:1–[44]21:5

This section presents us with quite a different tradition from the two texts printed above. Here Adam eats willingly, and both he and Eve are cast out of the garden after being punished. In the two texts above, however, Adam eats unknowingly, Adam and Eve are evicted from the garden immediately, and they subsequently discover the penalties imposed by God after they begin their lives outside the garden. Most likely we have two different exegetical traditions combined by the author. This section is not extant in the Latin.

Greek	Armenian	Georgian
21:1 "And I cried out in that very hour, 'Adam, Adam, where are you? Rise up, come to me and I will show you a great mystery.'	[44](21):1 "I cried out to Adam in a loud voice, 'Arise, come to me and I will show you this way.'	
21:2a But when your father came,	[44](21):2 Then Adam came to me with his great glory,	[44](21):2a "Then your father Adam came.
		[44](21):2b He had thought thus: that a beast had entered the Garden and he said to me, 'What are you shouting for and why do you have this fig-leaf on yourself?'
21:2b I spoke to him words of transgression which have brought us down from our great glory.		[44](21):2c I replied to him and I told him, 'Don't you wish me to tell you something or do you wish me to? Until today we were like animals.
21:3 For, when he came, I opened my mouth and the devil was speaking, and I began to exhort him and said, 'Come hither, my lord Adam, hearken to me and eat of the fruit of the tree of which God told us not to eat of it, and you shall be as a God.'		[44](21):3 When I understood [that of which] the Lord had said to us, "Do not eat of this" and when I saw its splendor, I took of it and ate of it and I learned good and evil. Now, eat also of it and you will become like God.'

21:4a And your father answered and said, 'I fear lest God be angry with me.'

21:4b And I said to him, 'Fear not, for as soon as you have eaten you shall know good and evil.'

21:5 And speedily I persuaded him, and he ate and his eyes were opened and he too knew his nakedness."

[44](21):5 and I gave him to eat of the fruit, and I made him like me. Subsequently, he, too, came (and) took a fig-leaf and covered his nakedness."

[44](21):4a Adam replied to me and told me, 'I fear lest God be angry with me and tell me, "You did not keep my commandment which I gave to you!"'

[44](21):4b But I told the father, 'This blame shall be on me. If he asks you, say thus: "This woman whom you have given me said she is to blame for that; [she told me]: See the flavor of this glory!"'

[44](21):5 Then I gave [him of it and he ate of it and became like me, and he also took a leaf of the fig tree and covered his nakedness with it.]"

12

From Prophecy to Testament: An Epilogue

James A. Sanders

My teacher, Samuel Sandmel, whose work centered on Hellenistic Judaism, especially Philo and the NT, often said that Judaism is Torah and Torah is Judaism and until one understood the double equation, one could not comprehend any form of Judaism. No other body of literature served its culture in the same life-sustaining way. By "Torah" he understood the broad meaning of Scripture and the tradition that flowed from it, oral and written. Torah *sensu lato* was the wellspring from which Judaism issued and by which it lived. Tradition harbors many an expression to illustrate the point, such as Torah being the *sefer hayyim,* the book of life for Judaism, or *hasefer shekol bo,* the book with everything in it. The pretension was not that Torah precluded the need for other disciplines of study; it did not. But Torah gave Judaism its ongoing life in ever-changing contexts, and Judaism, by its reverence for it, continually kept Torah a living and vibrant gift. And once Scripture was understood to be verbally, indeed literally inspired (by the beginning of the second century C.E.), all one needed to do was find the hermeneutic technique *(middah)* by which to find the "torah" or guidance sought.

But it was not only the rabbinic form of Judaism to which Sandmel referred. He meant all forms of Judaism of the so-called postbiblical period, no matter how hellenized. Indeed, he was among the first to show that some biblical literature derived in some measure from earlier traditions.[1] The process of actualization and resignification of nascent "Scripture" (oral and written) started early on. One sees many references in the Prophets and, in the Ketuvim, to early traditions that are included in the Bible.[2] In fact, there is hardly any biblical literature, even the earliest, that was not in some measure based on yet earlier tradition, Israelite or non-Israelite, whether to resignify it or to refute it. This was the

---

[1] S. Sandmel, "The Haggadah within Scripture," *JBL* 80 (1961): 105–22. See J. A. Sanders, *Torah and Canon* (Philadelphia: Fortress, 1972), 1–30; and M. Fishbane, "Revelation and Tradition: Aspects of Inner-biblical Exegesis," *JBL* 99 (1980): 343–61.

[2] J. A. Sanders, *Canon and Community* (Philadelphia: Fortress, 1984), 46–60.

nascent canonical process, for the very concept of "canon" is in the adaptability of that literature, which over time was accumulated because of a repetition/recitation process, to the ever-changing community life of those who found their identity in it.[3] What scholars call "secondary" or "spurious" passages in biblical literature is actually the rich evidence that later communities found earlier biblical literature relevant to their lives enough to gloss it to their needs and thus continue the canonical process.

"Drashing" Scripture is in the very nature of Judaism. Searching Torah for guidance in ever-changing situations was the work of Judaism. "You search the Scriptures because you think that in them you find eternal life" (John 5:39; cf. Sir 45:5) would have made sense to Jesus' interlocutors. Torah is made up of both halakah and haggadah.[4] Torah meant "instruction" in various forms. The belief was that God continued to teach through Torah, often in surprising ways. Torah for a Jew could never mean "law" in a narrow sense.[5] Eventually it came to mean what had been received as the literary vessel, oral and written, through which God continued to speak to his people. Jewish communities, we now know, had different forms of Scripture in pre-rabbinic Judaism. But the concept of "canon" as the durable and adaptable process by which to discern the mind and will of God started at the inception of Scripture and is what persisted, by one hermeneutic or another, no matter how textually stable a particular canon became.

The essays in this volume all attest to Scripture's textual fluidity in early Judaism. Accurate copying, citing, or translating was not a basic concern in the period before the fall of Jerusalem to Rome for the First Testament, or before the conversion of Constantine for the Second.[6] The passage referenced had to be stable enough to be recognized by those addressed, but the focus in the earlier period was on the community addressed and not on the text as such.

---

[3] J. A. Sanders, "Adaptable for Life: The Nature and Function of Canon," in *Magnalia Dei—The Mighty Acts of God: Essays on the Bible and Archaeology in Memory of G. E. Wright* (ed. F. M. Cross et al.; New York: Doubleday, 1976), 531–60; D. Harman Akenson, *Surpassing Wonder: The Invention of the Bible and the Talmuds* (New York: Harcourt Brace, 1998); J. A. Sanders, "The Issue of Closure in the Canonical Process," in *The Canon Debate* (ed. L. McDonald and J. A. Sanders; Peabody, Mass.: Hendrickson, 2002), 252–63. See also the whole thrust of C. A. Evans and S. Talmon, eds., *The Quest for Context and Meaning: Studies in Biblical Intertextuality in Honor of James A. Sanders* (BIS 28; New York: Brill, 1997). Function precedes form in human experience just as praxis precedes theory.

[4] A. J. Heschel, "A Time for Renewal," *Midstream* 18, no. 5 (1972): 46–51; and J. A. Sanders, "Torah and Christ," *Int* 29 (1975): 372–90.

[5] See C. H. Dodd, *The Bible and the Greeks* (London: Hodder & Stoughton, 1935), 25–41, on the relation of Torah and *nomos*. But see the corrective on the ancient meanings of *nomos* in Laurent Monsengwo Pasingya, *La notion de nomos dans le Pentateuque grec* (AnBib 52; Rome: Biblical Institute Press, 1973).

[6] E. C. Colwell, *New or Old? The Christian Struggle with Change and Tradition* (Philadelphia: Westminster, 1970), 1–21. Also see L. M. McDonald, *The Formation of the Christian Biblical Canon: Revised and Expanded Edition* (Peabody, Mass.: Hendrickson, 1995), 250–57.

Understanding Scripture's relevance to ever-changing contexts was the focus. Not until the beginnings of the proto-Masoretic period after the defeat of Judah by Rome was verbal accuracy a focused concern.[7] The focus then shifted from the community to the text itself, which soon led to closed canons.[8]

Torah, nonetheless, remained a living thing for Jews of all stripes and conditions, whether they developed a body of halakah, like rabbinic Judaism, or insisted on continuing to exegete Scripture to develop rules and codes, like those at Qumran or the Sadducees. Torah in its basic but broad sense replaced the oracles and prophets of the preexilic period whenever a guidance or instruction was sought. Drashing Torah became the center and heart of Judaism.[9] And during the early Jewish period, before stabilization, it was acceptable, in translating it and in quoting it, even in a scribe's copying it, to modify the text to make it understandable and relevant to the community's needs being addressed. It is largely for this reason that ascertaining the text-critical value of citations and allusions in the literature of early Judaism, including the NT, is so difficult. Although some certainly were true variants, most variants in pre-Masoretic texts and versions were testimony not to different *Vorlagen* of Scripture but to the conviction that Torah was, by one means or another, malleable and adaptable to the ongoing life of the community.[10]

The main constraint on adapting a passage in the pre-Masoretic period was that of being sure the community would recognize the adapted citation, lest it lose the authority sought in the exercise. Passages that were similar could be meshed and mingled to achieve the desired result. And there are numerous doublets and triplets and interweavings of texts in the received text itself and in the massive "new" literature of the early Jewish period. Scripture had authority and value in more than one context and in more than one form. But this had gone on earlier in the preexilic literature with oral and even written traditions; it was not new.[11] Just because Israel's traditions attained written status did not change the conviction that, if they were shared by numerous scattered communities and repeated/recited in them, they were still relevant and adaptable.

Another common thread in these studies is recognition of the relevance of Scripture to claims on it. Many early Jewish communities, notably the Qumran

---

[7] J. A. Sanders, "Text and Canon: Concepts and Method," *JBL* 98 (1979): 5–29. And see idem, "Text and Canon: Old Testament and New," in *Mélanges Dominique Barthélemy* (ed. P. Casetti et al.; Fribourg: Editions Universitaires, 1981), 373–94.

[8] See Sanders, "Issue of Closure."

[9] What to us appears like ancient proof-texting may actually have been the searching of Scripture for the terms in which to report the new based on the old. If what needed to be said was worthy, it had to be related in the highest terms possible, namely, Torah terms.

[10] See my tribute to the lifework of Dominique Barthélemy (who died February 10, 2002) in textual criticism, in *TIC Talk: Newsletter of the United Bible Societies Translation Information Clearinghouse* 51 (2002): 1–3; and *The Folio: Bulletin of the Ancient Biblical Manuscript Center* 19, no. 1 (Spring 2002): 1, 7–8.

[11] Sanders, *Torah and Canon*, 1–30.

community and the early Christians but others as well, fully believed that Scripture spoke directly to their day. There was little to no concern for "original" or historical meanings of passages; on the contrary, if it was Torah (i.e., functionally canonical), by its very nature it spoke directly to the end time, and many Jewish communities in the pre-rabbinic period believed they lived in the end time. As Karl Elliger showed already in 1953, the hermeneutic of Scripture at Qumran could be simply stated: (a) Scripture spoke to the end time; (b) the Qumran community was convinced they were living in the end time; hence (c) Scripture spoke directly to their situation.[12]

The same hermeneutic dominates the NT. Few, if any, Jews of the period were interested in what Isaiah or David originally meant; Scripture, or "functional canon," did not belong to the past but to the ongoing and ever-changing present. Critical scholarship since the Enlightenment focuses on "original" meanings in "original" historical contexts; not so Jews or Christians in antiquity. The more that circumstances and sociopolitical contexts changed, the more Scripture was relevant, especially to the meaning or end of human history, if the hermeneutic applied rendered it so. The fact that this hermeneutic is also that of current "conservative" Christians and Zionist Jews helps to understand the ancients perhaps, but not Scripture itself.

The title of the present collection is interesting in this regard, *From Prophecy to Testament*. Critical scholarship has clearly shown that prophecy in the First Testament had little to do with long-term prediction, but the Qumran and early Christian hermeneuts, on the contrary, believed it did. How did the term "prophet," therefore, which basically meant a spokesperson for God in specific situations of the past, come to mean "Bible prophecy" in the popular sense used by so-called conservative Christian groups today?

I suggest it came about because of the eschatological hermeneutic just noted. The Hebrew Bible and the Protestant First Testament have the same basic Hebrew text (because of Jerome and Luther) but very different structures or literary forms.[13] The one is tripartite (TaNaK = Torah, Nevi'im [Prophets], Ketuvim), and the other quadripartite (Pentateuch, Historical Books, Wisdom/Poetic Books, Prophets). All Christian First Testaments have the prophetic corpus last, whereas in the Tanak the Prophets always follow the Pentateuch or Torah *(sensu stricto)*. There are other differences as well, but clearly the reason Christians put the Prophets last in the four-part First Testament of their new double-Testament Bible was that they believed that the prophets foretold Christ.[14] It was a common Christian conviction, just as belief that the church superseded Judaism as God's true Israel was common to all forms of early Christianity (whether Judaizers, Hellenizers, Petrine, or Pauline).

---

[12] K. Elliger, *Studien zum Habakuk-Kommentar vom Toten Meer* (Tübingen: Mohr [Siebeck], 1953).

[13] See J. A. Sanders, "Hermeneutics of Text Criticism," in *Textus* 18 (1995): 1–26.

[14] J. A. Sanders, "'Spinning' the Bible," *BRev* 14, no. 3 (1998): 22–29, 44–45.

The debates between Jews and Christians in the first centuries C.E. centered on this question. The reason Origen drew up his Hexapla (ca. 240 C.E.), providing literate Christians Hebrew texts of the First Testament as well as the various Greek translations up to his time, though they were text-critically very valuable, was basically to provide Christians with texts for the debate, even how to pronounce Hebrew in Greek transliteration. It was not because Origen was pro-Jewish or the like. On the contrary, Jerome later, after the triumph of the church under Constantine, likewise wanted Christians to have a Latin translation from the Hebrew in order to refute the rabbis or, by that time, to show how wrong they were. Just so Luther, a millennium later, provided a translation into the German vernacular of his day to support both the Protestant rebellion against Rome and the continuing Christian claim to be God's true Israel, with deep consequent bias against Jews. The Christian puzzlement over why most Jews did not accept the Christian supersessionist claim has until recently been called "obduracy" or "hardness of heart."

In what sense, then, can modern critical scholarship speak of the New Testament as fulfillment of the Old? Certainly not simply in a supersessionist sense, lest it revert to precritical thinking. Jesus' statement that he had come not to abolish Torah but to fulfill it (Matt 5:19) offers a way of understanding all Scripture as prophecy, and not just the prophetic corpus. By the time of Christ, many Jews had begun to think of all the great personages of the Bible as prophets. In the Dead Sea Scrolls, David was viewed as a prophet, even Abraham. In what sense, then, can critical scholarship understand all Torah as prophetic? If it is the nature of a canon to be continually relevant and adaptable to the life of the community that finds its identity in it, then the community needs to believe that it is, in some sense, being true to that identity, worthy of its relevance, and part of its fulfillment of it. Belief in the ongoing relevance of Scripture was understood as its potential for continual fulfillment, and not just a single fulfillment. This was the case for Jews and Christians alike. Luke-Acts, the first history of Christianity, makes it clear that Scripture continued to be "fulfilled" (Acts) well after the Christ event (Gospel).

The difference is in the role of critical scholarship in the quest. Those who believe that modern critical scholarship was and is "a gift of God in due season" use it as a constraint on adapting Scripture to say whatever anyone might think it should say to believing communities today (from the most conservative to the most liberal).[15] This means that Scripture must first be critically read, as the constraining factor in the discernment of its abiding truth, and then faithfully (i.e., rendering it relevant to a community's needs). The discipline by which to trace the *Nachleben* of Scripture through early Jewish literature into the Christian and rabbinic periods is comparative midrash—the comparative study of each instance the same passage or figure was "drashed" or "fulfilled" in each

---

[15] See R. D. Weis and D. M. Carr, eds., *A Gift of God in Due Season: Essays on Scripture and Community in Honor of James A. Sanders* (JSNTSup 225; Sheffield, England: Sheffield Academic Press, 1996).

sociopolitical context in which it was claimed to happen.[16] Many citations/adaptations of Scripture throughout early Judaism were to show that Scripture had been fulfilled in one sense or another. Only by doing comparative midrashic study of the *Nachleben* of Scripture can the full impact of Torah/Scripture be discerned in the life of early Judaism and Christianity.

Although Isaiah did not foretell Christ in a precritical sense, Scripture as a whole, nonetheless, can be viewed as going somewhere, having a thrust, moving in broad, often divergent directions. These may include what both Christian and Jewish traditions see Scripture to be and, indeed, some Muslims see the Qur'an to be. If some emphasize what God has done and can yet do whereas others denigrate theological speculation but emphasize living a life of Torah (as various Jewish groups interpret this) or a life based on the Qur'an (as each Muslim group may interpret this), are they really in exclusivist conflict? Do they not rather need to hear each other, if indeed both Torah and gospel include both faith in, and faithfulness to, the same God?

There is, in this view, a thrust to the multiform canonical process, that history of various early Jewish communities' application and reapplication of Scripture to ever-changing sociopolitical contexts (oral or written).[17] And this thrust is the monotheizing process the Bible describes in its pilgrimage from inception in the ancient Near East to final formations in the Greco-Roman period. The monotheizing process was not steady or always on track but can be traced in and through the cultural givens in which it was expressed. This was true not only for surviving rabbinic Judaism but also for the early churches, all of which held two tenets in common: monotheism and supersessionism. Rabbinic Judaism's claim

---

[16] Comparative midrash as a discipline is well explained and worked out in M. Callaway, *Sing, O Barren One: A Study in Comparative Midrash* (SBLDS 91; Atlanta: Scholars Press, 1986). An earlier example is J. A. Sanders, "From Isaiah 61 to Luke 4," in *Christianity, Judaism, and Other Greco-Roman Cults: Studies for Morton Smith at Sixty* (ed. J. Neusner; 4 vols.; SJLA 12; Leiden: Brill, 1975), 1:75–106. See also C. A. Evans, *To See and Not Perceive: Isaiah 6.9–10 in Early Jewish and Christian Interpretation* (JSOTSup 64; Sheffield, England: JSOT Press, 1989). A conclusion reached from working in comparative midrash for forty years is that no two understandings of a Scripture passage are ever quite the same.

For a sampling of technical studies that explore this interpretive diversity, see C. A. Evans and J. A. Sanders, eds., *Paul and the Scriptures of Israel* (JSNTSup 83; SSEJC 1; Sheffield, England: JSOT Press, 1993); C. A. Evans and J. H. Charlesworth, eds., *The Pseudepigrapha and Early Biblical Interpretation* (JSPSup 14; SSEJC 2; Sheffield, England: JSOT Press, 1993); C. A. Evans and W. R. Stegner, eds., *The Gospels and the Scriptures of Israel* (JSNTSup 104; SSEJC 3; Sheffield, England: Sheffield Academic Press, 1994); C. A. Evans and J. A. Sanders, eds., *Early Christian Interpretation of the Scriptures of Israel: Investigations and Proposals* (JSNTSup 148; SSEJC 5; Sheffield, England: Sheffield Academic Press, 1997); and idem, eds., *The Function of Scripture in Early Jewish and Christian Tradition* (JSNTSup 154; SSEJC 6; Sheffield, England: Sheffield Academic Press, 1998).

[17] D. Carr, "Canonization in the Context of Community: An Outline of the Formation of the Tanak and the Christian Bible," in *A Gift of God in Due Season: Essays on Scripture and Community in Honor of James A. Sanders* (ed. R. D. Weis and D. M. Carr; JSNTSup 225; Sheffield, England: Sheffield Academic Press, 1996), 22–64.

to be the only true heir to all the varieties of early Judaism was and is also basically supersessionist.

The ultimate fulfillment of Torah as prophecy will surely be human recognition that God is truly One, the ultimate Integrity, both ontological and ethical, of reality. The One God of all cannot be limited to any one perception of God, whether Jewish, Christian, Muslim, Buddhist, or any other.[18] This is probably the greatest hurdle most Christians have to face. Not only does popular Christianity think the Trinity includes three distinct gods; it is basically idolatrous in its making of Jesus a personal deity. Popular Christianity also makes of "the Devil" a rival deity. Popular Christianity, which is basically sectarian—that is, it tends to be exclusivist in its claims for its particular understanding of salvation—flirts with both polytheism and idolatry.

But we are not primarily obliged here to wrestle with the problem of popular religion. Our first obligation as scholars is to see if we can appropriately understand the canonical thrust of the Bible in critical terms. To do so, however, we cannot limit ourselves to working in an academic box, scoring schools of thought against each other in a quest for "the meaning of the text" while packing footnotes to do so. We must, as scholars and critical tradents, be responsible, within our own limited sociopolitical settings and peculiar individual identities, for trying to understand the past in our limited contemporary terms—critically and responsibly. This is ultimately why we do what we do, no matter how well we think of ourselves.

The essays here collected attest to the critical need to understand the life-giving role of Torah, and of the ensuing canons of Scripture, in the lives of all early Jews and Christians, of whatever cultural expression. They show how Scripture was and is adaptable for life.

---

[18] J. C. Hough Jr., "Ways of Knowing God," *BRev* 18, no. 3 (2002): 16–19, 43–44.

Index of Modern Authors

Index of Ancient Sources